Medical Terminology Success

By Lewis Morris

Copyright © Network4Learning, Inc. 2018.

www.insiderswords.com/MedTerminology

ISBN-13: 978-1728802787

Table of Contents

Introduction	5
Crossword Puzzles	28
Multiple Choice	59
Matching	100
Word Search	100

What is "Insider Language"?

Recent research has confirmed what we have known for decades: The strongest students and leaders in industry have a mastered an Insider Language in their subject and field. This Insider language is made up of the technical terms and vocabulary necessary to communicate effectively in classes or the workplace. For those who master it, learning is easier, faster, and much more enjoyable.

Most students who are surveyed report that the greatest challenge to any course of study is learning the vocabulary. When we examine typical college courses, we discover that there is, on average, 250 Insider Terms a student must learn over the course of a semester. Further, most exams rely heavily on this set of words for assessment purposes. The structure of multiple choice exams lends itself perfectly to the testing of this Insider Language. Students who can differentiate between Insider Language terms can handle challenging exam questions with ease and confidence.

From recent research on learning and vocabulary we have learned:

- Your knowledge of any subject is contained in the content-specific words you know. The more of these terms that you know, the easier it is to understand and recall important information; the easier it will be to communicate your ideas to peers, professors, supervisors, and co-workers. The stronger your content-area vocabulary is, the higher your scores will be on your exams and written assignments.

- Students who develop a strong Insider Language perform better on tests, learn faster, retain more information, and express greater satisfaction in learning.

- Familiarizing yourself with subject-area vocabulary before formal study (pre-learning) is the most effective way to learn this language and reap the most benefit.

- The vocabulary on standardized exams come directly from the stated objectives of the test-makers. This means that the vocabulary found on standardized exams is predictable. Our books focus on this vocabulary.

- Most multiple-choice exams are glorified vocabulary quizzes. Think about the format of a multiple-choice question. The question stem is a definition of a term and the choices (known as distractors) are 4 or 5 similar words. Your task is to differentiate between the meanings of those terms and choose the correct word.

- It takes a person several exposures to a new word to be able to use it with confidence in conversation or in writing. You need to process these words several different ways to make them part of your long-term memory.

The goals of this book are:
- To give you an "Insider Language" for your subject.
- Pre-teach the most important words before you set out on a traditional course of review or study.
- Teach you the most important words in your subject area.
- Teach you strategies for learning subject-area words on your own.
- Boost your confidence in your ability to master this language and support you in your study.
- Reduce the stress of studying and provide you with fun activities that work.

How it works:

The secret to mastering Insider Language is through repetition and exposure. We have eleven steps for you to follow:

1. Read the word and definition in the glossary out loud. "See it, Say it"
2. Identify the part of speech the word belongs to such as noun, verb, adverb, or adjective. This will help you group the word and identify similar words.
3. Place the word in context by using it in a sentence. Write this sentence down and read it aloud.
4. Use "Chunking" to group the words. Make a diagram or word cloud using these groups.
5. Make connections to the words by creating analogies.
6. Create mnemonics that help you recognize patterns and orders of words by substituting the words for more memorable items or actions.
7. Examine the morphology of the word, that is, identify the root, prefix, and suffix that make up the word. Identify similar and related words.
8. Complete word games and puzzles such as crosswords and word searches.
9. Complete matching questions that require you to differentiate between related words.
10. Complete Multiple-choice questions containing the words.
11. Create a visual metaphor or "memory cartoon" to make a mental picture of the word and related processes.

By completing this word study process, you will be exposed to the terminology in various ways that will activate your memory and create a lasting understanding of this language.

The strategies in this book are designed to make you an independent expert at learning insider language. These strategies include:

- Verbalizing the word by reading it and its definition aloud ("See It, Say It"). This allows you to make visual, auditory, and speech connections with its meaning.

- Identifying the type of word (Noun, verb, adverb, and adjective). Making this distinction helps you understand how to visualize the word. It helps you "chunk" the words into groups, and gives you clues on how to use the word.

- Place the word in context by using it in a sentence. Write this sentence down and read it aloud. This will give you an example of how the word is used.

- "Chunking". By breaking down the word list into groups of closely related words, you will learn them better and be able to remember them faster. Once you have group the terms, you can then make word clouds using a free online service. These word clouds provide visual cues to remembering the words and their meanings.

- Analogies. By creating analogies for essential words, you will be making connections that you can see on paper. These connections can trigger your memory and activate your ability to use the word in your writing as you begin to use them. Many of these analogies also use visual cues. In a sense, you can make a mental picture from the analogy.

- Mnemonics. A device such as a pattern of letters, ideas, or associations that assists in remembering something. A mnemonic is especially useful for remembering the order of a set of words or the order of a process.

- Morphology. The study of word roots, prefixes, and suffixes. By examining the structure of the words, you will gain insight into other words that are closely related, and learn how to best use the word.

- Visual metaphors. This is the most sophisticated and entertaining strategy for learning vocabulary. Create a "memory cartoon" using one or more of the vocabulary terms. This activity triggers the visual part of your memory and makes fast, permanent, imprints of the word on your memory. By combining the terms in your visual metaphor, you can "chunk" the entire set of vocabulary terms into several visual metaphors and benefit from the brain's tendency to group these terms.

The activities in this book are designed to imprint the words and their meanings in your memory in different ways. By completing each activity, you will gain the necessary exposures to the word to make it a permanent part of your vocabulary. Each activity uses a different part of your memory. The result is that you will be comfortable using these words and be able to tell the difference between closely related words. The activities include:

A. Crossword Puzzles and Word Searches- These are proven to increase test scores and improve comprehension. Students frequently report that they are fun and engaging, while requiring them to analyze the structure and meaning of the words.

B. Matching- This activity is effective because it forces you to differentiate between many closely related terms.

C. Multiple Choice- This classic question format lends itself to vocabulary study perfectly. Most exams are in this format because they are simple to make, easy to score, and are a reliable type of assessment. (Perfect for the Vocabulary Master!) One strategy to use with multiple choice questions that enhance their effectiveness is to cover the answer choices while you read the question. After reading the question, see if you can answer it before looking at the choices. Then look at the choices to see if you match one of them.

Conducting a thorough "word study" of your insider language will take time and effort, but the rewards will be well worth it. By following this guide and completing the exercises thoughtfully, you will become a stronger, more effective, and satisfied student. Best of luck on your mastery of this Insider Language!

Insider Language Strategies

"See It, Say It!" Reading your Insider Language set aloud

"IT IS BETTER TO FAIL IN ORIGINALITY THAN TO SUCCEED IN IMITATION."
–HERMAN MELVILLE

Reading aloud is the foundation for the development of an Insider Language. It is the single most important thing you can do for vocabulary acquisition. Done correctly, it engages the visual, auditory, and speech centers of the brain and hastens its storage in your long-term memory.

Reading aloud demonstrates the relationship between the printed word and its meaning.

You can read aloud on a higher level than you can initially understand, so reading aloud makes complex ideas more accessible and exposes you to vocabulary and patterns that are not part of your typical speech. Reading aloud helps you understand the complicated text better and makes more challenging text easier to grasp and understand. Reading aloud helps you to develop the "habits of mind" the strongest students use.

Reading aloud will make connections to concepts in the reading that requires you to relate the new vocabulary to things you already know. Go to the glossary at the end of this book and for each word complete the five steps outlined below:

1. Read the word and its definition aloud. Focus on the sound of the word and how it looks on the paper.
2. Read the word aloud again try to say three or four similar words; this will help you build connections to closely related words.
3. Read the word aloud a third time. Try to make a connection to something you have read or heard.
4. Visualize the concept described in the term. Paint a mental picture of the word in use.
5. Try to think of the opposite of the word. Discovering a close antonym will help you place this word in context.

Create a sentence using the word in its proper context

"OPPORTUNITIES DON'T HAPPEN. YOU CREATE THEM." –CHRIS GROSSER

Context means the circumstances that form the setting for an event, statement, or idea, and which it can be fully understood and assessed. Synonyms for context include conditions, factors, situation, background, and setting.
Place the word in context by using it in a sentence. Write this sentence down and read it aloud. By creating sentences, you are practicing using the word correctly. If you strive to make these sentences interesting and creative, they will become more memorable and effective in activating your long-term memory.

Identify the Parts of Speech
"SUCCESS IS NOT FINAL; FAILURE IS NOT FATAL: IT IS THE COURAGE TO CONTINUE THAT COUNTS." –WINSTON S. CHURCHILL

Read through each term in the glossary and make a note of what part of speech each term is. Studying and identifying parts of speech shows us how the words relate to each other. It also helps you create a visualization of each term. Below are brief descriptions of the parts of speech for you to use as a guide.

VERB: A word denoting action, occurrence, or existence. Examples: walk, hop, whisper, sweat, dribbles, feels, sleeps, drink, smile, are, is, was, has.

NOUN: A word that names a person, place, thing, idea, animal, quality, or action. Nouns are the subject of the sentence. Examples: dog, Tom, Florida, CD, pasta, hate, tiger.

ADJECTIVE: A word that modifies, qualifies, or describes nouns and pronouns. Generally, adjectives appear immediately before the words they modify. Examples: smart girl, gifted teacher, old car, red door.

ADVERB: A word that modifies verbs, adjectives and other adverbs. An "ly" ending almost always changes an adjective to an adverb. Examples: ran swiftly, worked slowly, and drifted aimlessly. Many adverbs do not end in "ly." However, all adverbs identify when, where, how, how far, how much, etc. Examples: run hot, lived hard, moved right, study smart.

Chunking

"YOUR POSITIVE ACTION COMBINED WITH POSITIVE THINKING RESULTS IN SUCCESS." SHIV KHERA

Chunking is when you take a set of words and break it down into groups based on a common relationship. Research has shown that our brains learn by chunking information. By grouping your terms, you will be able to recall large sets of these words easily. To help make your chunking go easily use an online word cloud generator to make a set of word clouds representing your chunks.

1. Study the glossary and decide how you want to chunk the set of words. You can group by part of speech, topic, letter of the alphabet, word length, etc. Try to find an easy way to group each term.
2. Once you have your different groups, visit www.wordclouds.com to create a custom word cloud for each group. Print each one of these clouds and post it in a prominent place to serve as constant visual aids for your learning.

Analogies

"CHOOSE THE POSITIVE. YOU HAVE CHOICE, YOU ARE MASTER OF YOUR ATTITUDE, CHOOSE THE POSITIVE, THE CONSTRUCTIVE. OPTIMISM IS A FAITH THAT LEADS TO SUCCESS."– BRUCE LEE

An analogy is a comparison in which an idea or a thing is compared to another thing that is quite different from it. Analogies aim at explaining an idea by comparing it to something that is familiar. Metaphors and similes are tools used to create analogies.

Analogies are useful for learning vocabulary because they require you to analyze a word (or words), and then transfer that analysis to another word. This transfer reinforces the understanding of all the words.

As you analyze the relationships between the analogies you are creating, you will begin to understand the complex relationships between the seemingly unrelated words.

_A_ is to _B_ as _C_ is to _D_

This can be written using colons in place of the terms "is to" and "as."

A:B::C:D

The two items on the left (items A & B) describe a relationship and are separated by a single colon. The two items on the right (items C & D) are shown on the right and are also separated by a colon. Together, both sides are then separated by two colons in the middle, as shown here: Tall: Short :: Skinny: Fat. The relationship used in this analogy is the antonym.

How to create an analogy

Start with the basic formula for an analogy:

____ : ____ :: ____ : ____

Next, we will examine a simple synonym analogy:

automobile : car :: box : crate

The key to figuring out a set of word analogies is determining the relationship between the paired set of words.

Here is a list of the most common types of Analogies and examples

Synonym	Scream : Yell :: Push : Shove
Antonym	Rich : Poor :: Empty : Full
Cause is to Effect	Prosperity : Happiness :: Success : Joy
A Part is to its Whole	Toe : Foot :: Piece : Set
An Object to its Function	Car : Travel :: Read : Learn
A Item is to its Category	Tabby : House Cat :: Doberman : Dog
Word is a symptom of the other	Pain : Fracture :: Wheezing : Allergy
An object and it's description	Glass : Brittle :: Lead : Dense
The word is lacking the second word	Amputee : Limb :: Deaf : Hearing
The first word Hinders the second word	Shackles : Movement :: Stagger : Walk
The first word helps the action of the second	Knife : Bread :: Screwdriver : Screw
This word is made up of the second word	Sweater : Wool :: Jeans : Denim
A word and it's definition	Cede: Break Away :: Abolish : To get rid of

Using words from the glossary, make a set of analogies using each one. As a bonus, use more than one glossary term in a single analogy.

_____ : _____ :: _____ : _____

Name the relationship between the words in your analogy: _____

_____ : _____ :: _____ : _____

Name the relationship between the words in your analogy: _____

_____ : _____ :: _____ : _____

Name the relationship between the words in your analogy: _____

Mnemonics

"IT ISN'T THE MOUNTAINS AHEAD TO CLIMB THAT WEAR YOU OUT; IT'S THE PEBBLE IN YOUR SHOE."   –MUHAMMAD ALI

A mnemonic is a learning technique that helps you retain and remember information. Mnemonics are one of the best learning methods for remembering lists or processes in order. Mnemonics make the material more meaningful by adding associations and creating patterns. Interestingly, mnemonics may work better when they utilize absurd, startling, or shocking examples and references. Mnemonics help organize the information so that you can easily retrieve it later. By giving you associations and cues, mnemonics allow you to form a mental structure ordering a list or process to help you remember it better. This mental structure allows you to create a structure of association between items that may not appear to have any relationship. Mnemonics typically use references that are easy to visualize and thus easier to remember. Through visualization of vivid images and references, the information is much easier to imprint into long-term memory. The power of making mnemonics lies in converting dull, inert and uninspiring information into something vibrant and memorable.

How to make simple and effective mnemonics
Some of the best mnemonics help us remember simple rules or lists in order.

Step 1. Take a list of terms you are trying to remember in order. For example, we will use the scientific method:

observation, question, hypothesis, methods, results, and conclusion.

Next, we will replace each word on the list with a new word that starts with the same letter. These new words will together form a vivid sentence that is easy to remember:

Objectionable Queens Haunted Macho Rednecks Creatively.

As silly as the above sentence seems, it is easy to remember, and now we can call on this sentence to remind us of the order of the scientific method.

Visit http://www.mnemonicgenerator.com/ and try typing in a list of words. It is fun to see the mnemonics that it makes and shows how easy it is to make great mnemonics to help your studying.

Using vivid words in your mnemonics allows you to see the sentence you are making. Words that are gross, scary, or name interesting animals are helpful. Profanity is also useful because the shock value can trigger memory. The following are lists of vivid words to use in your mnemonics:

Gross words
Moist, Gurgle, Phlegm, Fetus, Curd, Smear, Squirt, Chunky, Orifice, Maggots, Viscous, Queasy, Bulbous, Pustule, Putrid, Fester, Secrete, Munch, Vomit, Ooze, Dripping, Roaches, Mucus, Stink, Stank, Stunk, Slurp, Pus, Lick, Salty, Tongue, Fart, Flatulence, Hemorrhoid.

Interesting Animals
Aardvark, Baboon, Chicken, Chinchilla, Duck, Dragonfly, Emu, Electric Eel, Frog, Flamingo, Gecko, Hedgehog, Hyena, Iguana, Jackal, Jaguar, Leopard, Lynx, Minnow, Manatee, Mongoose, Neanderthal, Newt, Octopus, Oyster, Pelican, Penguin, Platypus, Quail, Racoon, Rattlesnake, Rhinoceros, Scorpion, Seahorse, Toucan, Turkey, Vulture, Weasel, Woodpecker, Yak, Zebra.

Superhero Words
Diabolical, Activate, Boom, Clutch, Dastardly, Dynamic, Dynamite, Shazam, Kaboom, Zip, Zap, Zoom, Zany, Crushing, Smashing, Exploding, Ripping, Tearing.

Scary Words
Apparition, Bat, Chill, Demon, Eerie, Fangs, Genie, Hell, Lantern, Macabre, Nightmare, Owl, Ogre, Phantasm, Repulsive, Scarecrow, Tarantula, Undead, Vampire, Wraith, Zombie.

There are several types of mnemonics that can help your memory.

1. Images
Visual mnemonics are a type of mnemonic that works by associating an image with characters or objects whose name sounds like the item that must be memorized. This is one of the easiest ways to create effective mnemonics. An example would be to use the shape of numbers to help memorize a long list of them. Numbers can be memorized by their shapes, so that: 0 -looks like an egg; 1 -a pencil, or a candle; 2 -a snake; 3 -an ear; 4 -a sailboat; 5 -a key; 6 -a comet; 7 -a knee; 8 -a snowman; 9 -a comma.

Another type of visual mnemonic is the word-length mnemonic in which the number of letters in each word corresponds to a digit. This simple mnemonic gives pi to seven decimal places:

3.141582 becomes "How I wish I could calculate pi."

Of course, you could use this type of mnemonic to create a longer sentence showing the digits of an important number. Some people have used this type of mnemonic to memorize thousands of digits.

Using the hands is also an important tool for creating visual objects. Making the hands into specific shapes can help us remember the pattern of things or the order of a list of things.

2. Rhyming
Rhyming mnemonics are quick ways to make things memorable. A classic example is a mnemonic for the number of days in each month:
"30 days hath September, April, June, and November.
All the rest have 31
Except February, my dear son.
It has 28, and that is fine
But in Leap Year it has 29."

Another example of a rhyming mnemonic is a common spelling rule:
"I before e except after c
or when sounding like a
in neighbor and weigh."

Use **rhymer.com** to get large lists of rhyming words.

3. Homonym
A homonym is one of a group of words that share the same pronunciation but have different meanings, whether spelled the same or not.

Try saying what you're attempting to remember out loud or very quickly, and see if anything leaps out. If you know other languages, using similar-sounding words from those can be effective.

You could also browse this list of homonyms
at http://www.cooper.com/alan/homonym_list.html.

4. Onomatopoeia
An Onomatopeia is a word that phonetically imitates, resembles or suggests the source of the sound that it describes. Are there any noises made by the thing you're trying to memorize? Is it often associated with some other sound? Failing that, just make up a noise that seems to fit.

Achoo, ahem, baa, bam, bark, beep, beep beep, belch, bleat, boo, boo hoo, boom, burp, buzz, chirp, click clack, crash, croak, crunch, cuckoo, dash, drip, ding dong, eek, fizz, flit, flutter, gasp, grrr, ha ha, hee hee, hiccup, hiss, hissing, honk, icky, itchy, jiggly, jangle, knock knock, lush, la la la, mash, meow, moan, murmur, neigh, oink, ouch, plop, pow, quack, quick, rapping, rattle, ribbit, roar, rumble, rustle, scratch, sizzle, skittering, snap crackle pop, splash, splish splash, spurt, swish, swoosh, tap, tapping, tick tock, tinkle, tweet, ugh, vroom, wham, whinny, whip, whooping, woof.

5. Acronyms

An acronym is a word or name formed as an abbreviation from the initial components of a word, such as NATO, which stands for North Atlantic Treaty Organization. If you're trying to memorize something involving letters, this is often a good bet. A lot of famous mnemonics are acronyms, such as ROYGBIV which stands for the order of colors in the light spectrum (Red, Orange, Yellow, Green, Blue, Indigo, and Violet).
A great acronym generator to try is: www.all-acronyms.com.

A different spin on an acronym is a backronym. A **backronym** is a specially constructed phrase that is supposed to be the source of a word that is an acronym. A backronym is constructed by creating a new phrase to fit an already existing word, name, or acronym.

The word is a combination of *backward* and *acronym*, and has been defined as a "reverse acronym." For example, the United States Department of Justice assigns to their Amber Alert program the meaning "**A**merica's **M**issing: **B**roadcast **E**mergency **R**esponse." The process can go either way to make good mnemonics.

Visit: https://arthurdick.com/projects/backronym/ to try out a simple backronym generator.

6. Anagrams

An anagram is a direct word switch or word play, the result of rearranging the letters of a word or phrase to produce a new word or phrase, using all the original letters exactly once; for example, the word anagram can be rearranged into nag-a-ram.

Try re-arranging letters or components and see if anything memorable emerges. Visit http://www.nameacronym.net/ to use a simple anagram generator.

One particularly memorable form of anagram is the spoonerism, where you swap the initial syllables or letters of words to make new phrases. These are usually humorous, and this makes them easier to remember. Here are some examples:

"Is it kisstomary to cuss the bride?" (as opposed to "customary to kiss")
"The Lord is a shoving leopard." (instead of "a loving shepherd")
"A blushing crow." ("crushing blow")
"A well-boiled icicle" ("well-oiled bicycle")
"You were fighting a liar in the quadrangle." ("lighting a fire")
"Is the bean dizzy?" (as opposed to "is the dean busy?")

7. Stories

Make up quick stories or incidents involving the material you want to memorize. For larger chunks of information, the stories can get more elaborate. Structured stories are particularly good for remembering lists or other sequenced information. Have a look at https://en.wikipedia.org/wiki/Method_of_loci for a more advanced memory sequencing technique.

Visual Metaphors

"LIMITS, LIKE FEAR, IS OFTEN AN ILLUSION." –MICHAEL JORDAN

What is a Metaphor?

A metaphor is a figure of speech that refers to one thing by mentioning another thing. Metaphors provide clarity and identify hidden similarities between two seemingly unrelated ideas. A visual metaphor is an image that creates a link between different ideas.

Visual metaphors help us use our understanding of the world to learn new concepts, skills, and ideas. Visual metaphors help us relate new material to what we already know. Visual metaphors must be clear and simple enough to spark a connection and understanding. Visual metaphors should use familiar things to help you be less fearful of new, complex, or challenging topics. Metaphors trigger a sense of familiarity so that you are more accepting of the new idea. Metaphors work best when you associate a familiar, easy to understand idea with a challenging, obscure, or abstract concept.

How to make a visual metaphor

1. Brainstorm using the words of the concept. Use different fonts, colors, or shapes to represent parts of the concept.

2. Merge these images together

3. Show the process using arrows, accents, etc.

4. Think about the story line your metaphor projects.

Examples of visual metaphors:

A skeleton used to show a framework of something.

A cloud showing an outline.

A bodybuilder whose muscles represent supporting ideas and details.

A sandwich where the meat, tomato, and lettuce represent supporting ideas.

A recipe card to show a process.

Your metaphor should be accurate. It should be complex enough to convey meaning, but simple and clear enough to be easily understood.

Morphology
"SCIENCE IS THE CAPTAIN, AND PRACTICE THE SOLDIERS." LEONARDO DA VINCI

Morphology is the study of the origin, roots, suffixes, and prefixes of the words. Understanding the meaning of prefixes, suffixes, and roots make it easier to decode the meaning of new vocabulary. Having the ability to decode using morphology increases text comprehension when initially reading as well.

The capability of identifying meaningful parts of words (morphemes), including prefixes, suffixes, and roots can be helpful. Identifying morphemes improves decoding accuracy and fluency. Reading speed improves when you can decode larger chunks of text quickly. When you can recognize morphemes in words, you will be better able to make sense of new words in context. Below are charts containing the most common prefixes, suffixes, and root words. Use them to help you decode your vocabulary terms.

Prefixes

Prefix	Meaning	Example words	and meanings
a, ab, abs	away from	absent abdicate	not to be present, to give up an office or throne.
ad, a, ac, af, ag, an, ar, at, as	to, toward	Advance advantage	To move forward To have the upper hand
anti	against	Antidote antisocial antibiotic	To repair poisoning refers to someone who's not social
bi, bis	two	bicycle binary biweekly	two-wheeled cycle two number system every two weeks
circum, cir	around	circumnavigate circle	Travel around the world a figure that goes all around
com, con, co, col	with, together	Complete Complement	To finish To go along with
de	away from, down, the opposite of	depart detour	to go away from to go out of your way
dis, dif, di	apart	dislike dishonest distant	not to like not honest away
En-, em-	Cause to	Entrance	the way in.
epi	upon, on top of	epitaph epilogue epidemic	writing upon a tombstone speech at the end, on top of the rest
equ, equi	equal	equalize equitable	to make equal fair, equal
ex, e, ef	out, from	exit eject exhale	to go out to throw out to breathe out
Fore-	Before	Forewarned	To have prior warning

Prefix	Meaning	Example Words and Meanings	
in, il, ir, im, en	in, into	Infield Imbibe	The inner playing field to take part in
in, il, ig, ir, im	not	inactive ignorant irreversible irritate	not active not knowing not reversible to put into discomfort
inter	between, among	international interact	among nations to mix with
mal, male	bad, ill, wrong	malpractice malfunction	bad practice fail to function, bad function
Mid	Middle	Amidships	In the middle of a ship
mis	wrong, badly	misnomer	The wrong name
mono	one, alone, single	monocle	one lensed glasses
non	not, the reverse of	nonprofit	not making a profit
ob	in front, against, in front of, in the way of	Obsolete	No longer needed
omni	everywhere, all	omnipresent omnipotent	always present, everywhere all powerful
Over	On top	Overdose	Take too much medication
Pre	Before	Preview	Happens before a show.
per	through	Permeable pervasive	to pass through, all encompassing
poly	many	Polygamy polygon	many spouses figure with many sides
post	after	postpone postmortem	to do after after death
pre	before, earlier than	Predict Preview	To know before To view before release
pro	forward, going ahead of, supporting	proceed pro-war promote	to go forward supporting the war to raise or move forward
re	again, back	retell recall reverse	to tell again to call back to go back
se	apart	secede seclude	to withdraw, become apart to stay apart from others
Semi	Half	Semipermeable	Half-permeable

Prefix	Meaning	Example Words and Meanings	
Sub	under, less than	Submarine	under water
super	over, above, greater	superstar superimpose	a start greater than her stars to put over something else
trans	across	transcontinental transverse	across the continent to lie or go across
un, uni	one	unidirectional unanimous unilateral	having one direction sharing one view having one side
un	not	uninterested unhelpful unethical	not interested not helpful not ethical

Roots

Root	Meaning	Example words & meanings	
act, ag	to do, to act	Agent Activity	One who acts as a representative Action
Aqua	Water	Aquamarine	The color of water
Aud	To hear	Auditorium	A place to hear music
apert	open	Aperture	An opening
bas	low	Basement Basement	Something that is low, at the bottom A room that is low
Bio	Living thing	Biological	Living matter
cap, capt, cip, cept, ceive	to take, to hold, to seize	Captive Receive Capable Recipient	One who is held To take Able to take hold of things One who takes hold or receives
ced, cede, ceed, cess	to go, to give in	Precede Access Proceed	To go before Means of going to To go forward
Cogn	Know	Cognitive	Ability to think
cred, credit	to believe	Credible Incredible Credit	Believable Not believable Belief, trust
curr, curs, cours	to run	Current Precursory Recourse	Now in progress, running Running (going) before To run for aid
Cycle	Circle	Lifecycle	The circle of life
dic, dict	to say	Dictionary Indict	A book explaining words (sayings)

Root	Meaning	Examples	and meanings
duc, duct	to lead	Induce Conduct Aqueduct	To lead to action To lead or guide Pipe that leads water somewhere
equ	equal, even	Equality Equanimity	Equal in social, political rights Evenness of mind, tranquility
fac, fact, fic, fect, fy	to make, to do	Facile Fiction Factory Affect	Easy to do Something that is made up Place that makes things To make a change in
fer, ferr	to carry, bring	Defer Referral	To carry away Bring a source for help/information
Gen	Birth	Generate	To create something
graph	write	Monograph Graphite	A writing on a particular subject A form of carbon used for writing
Loc	Place	Location	A place
Mater	Mother	Maternity	Expecting birth
Mem	Recall	Memory	The recall experiences
mit, mis	to send	Admit Missile	To send in Something sent through the air
Nat	Born	Native	Born in a place
par	equal	Parity Disparate	Equality No equal, not alike
Ped	Foot	Podiatrist	Foot doctor
Photo	Light	Photograph	A picture
plic	to fold, to bend, to turn	Complicate Implicate	To fold (mix) together To fold in, to involve
pon, pos, posit, pose	to place	Component Transpose Compose Deposit	A part placed together with others A place across To put many parts into place To place for safekeeping
scrib, script	to write	Describe Transcript Subscription	To write about or tell about A written copy A written signature or document
sequ, secu	to follow	Sequence	In following order

Root	Meaning	Examples and Meanings	
Sign	Mark	Signal	to alert somebody
spec, spect, spic	to appear, to look, to see	Specimen Aspect	An example to look at One way to see something
sta, stat, sist, stit, sisto	to stand, or make stand Stable, steady	Constant Status Stable Desist	Standing with Social standing Steady (standing) To stand away from
Struct	To build	Construction	To build a thing
tact	to touch	Contact Tactile	To touch together To be able to be touched
ten, tent, tain	to hold	Tenable Retentive Maintain	Able to be held, holding Holding To keep or hold up
tend, tens, tent	to stretch	Extend Tension	To stretch or draw out Stretched
Therm	Temperature	Thermometer	Detects temperature
tract	to draw	Attract Contract	To draw together An agreement drawn up
ven, vent	to come	Convene Advent	To come together A coming
Vis	See	Invisible	Cannot be seen
ver, vert, vers	to turn	Avert Revert Reverse	To turn away To turn back To turn around

Crossword Puzzles

1. Using the Across and Down clues, write the correct words in the numbered grid below.

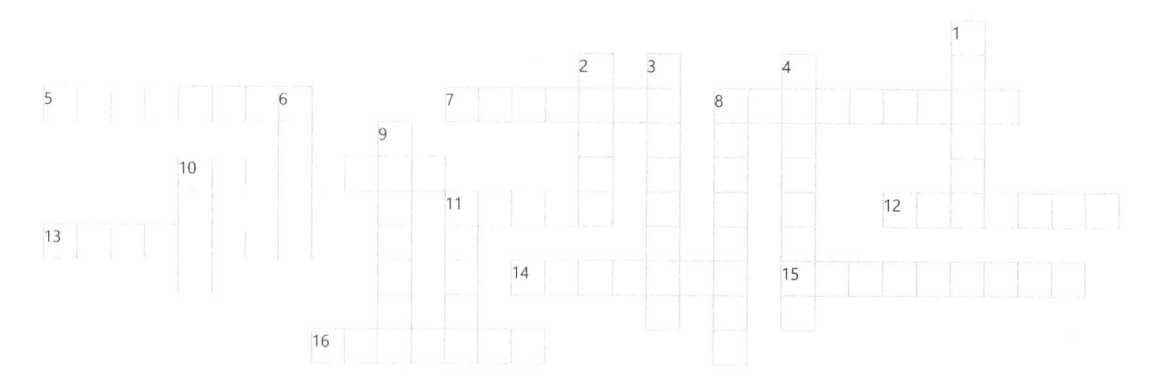

ACROSS

5. An instrument that holds an opening of the body open so that an examination can be performed, or a sample can be taken
7. A coiled organ in the inner ear that plays a large role in hearing by picking up sound vibrations and transmitting them as electrical signals
8. A tiny blood vessel that connects the smallest arteries to the smallest veins and allows exchange of oxygen and other materials between blood cells and body tissue cells
10. The main form that glucose, the body's energy source, takes when it is stored
11. An involuntary muscle contraction
12. A hormone made in the pancreas that plays an important role in the absorption of glucose (the body's main source of energy) into muscle cells
13. An organism that is dependent on another organism for nourishment
14. The feeling that one or one's surroundings are spinning
15. A disease of the joints characterized by inflammation, pain, stiffness, and redness
16. The long, flat bone located at the center of the chest

DOWN

5. An instrument that holds an opening of the body open so that an examination can be performed, or a sample can be taken
7. A coiled organ in the inner ear that plays a large role in hearing by picking up sound vibrations and transmitting them as electrical signals
8. A tiny blood vessel that connects the smallest arteries to the smallest veins and allows exchange of oxygen and other materials between blood cells and body tissue cells
10. The main form that glucose, the body's energy source, takes when it is stored
11. An involuntary muscle contraction
12. A hormone made in the pancreas that plays an important role in the absorption of glucose (the body's main source of energy) into muscle cells
13. An organism that is dependent on another organism for nourishment
14. The feeling that one or one's surroundings are spinning
15. A disease of the joints characterized by inflammation, pain, stiffness, and redness
16. The long, flat bone located at the center of the chest

A. Capillary	B. Sternum	C. Spasm	D. Insulin
E. Gout	F. Ilium	G. Vertigo	H. Cochlea
I. Dermis	J. Semen	K. Clubfoot	L. Narcosis
M. Speculum	N. Fungus	O. Arthritis	P. Optician
Q. Glycogen	R. Mucus	S. Seizure	

2. Using the Across and Down clues, write the correct words in the numbered grid below.

ACROSS

1. Any single, functioning form of life
4. The term used to refer to an unborn child from 8 weeks after fertilization to birth
8. A drug that neutralizes stomach acids
10. A nerve cell that responds to a stimulus and produces a nerve impulse
11. A small, parasitic worm that can live in the intestines of a human and may cause diarrhea, abdominal pain, and anemia
13. Another term for measles
15. Feeling the need to vomit
16. A preparation of weakened microorganisms given to create resistance to a certain disease
18. A chemical, originating in a cell, that regulates reactions in the body
19. A surgical technique in which the flow of blood or another body fluid is redirected around a blockage
20. Pertaining to blood vessels
21. Dangerously decreased acidity of the blood, which can be caused by high altitudes, hyperventilation, and excessive vomiting
22. The hollow female reproductive organ in which a fertilized egg is implanted, and a fetus develops

DOWN

1. Any single, functioning form of life
4. The term used to refer to an unborn child from 8 weeks after fertilization to birth
8. A drug that neutralizes stomach acids
10. A nerve cell that responds to a stimulus and produces a nerve impulse
11. A small, parasitic worm that can live in the intestines of a human and may cause diarrhea, abdominal pain, and anemia
13. Another term for measles
15. Feeling the need to vomit
16. A preparation of weakened microorganisms given to create resistance to a certain disease
18. A chemical, originating in a cell, that regulates reactions in the body
19. A surgical technique in which the flow of blood or another body fluid is redirected around a blockage
20. Pertaining to blood vessels
21. Dangerously decreased acidity of the blood, which can be caused by high altitudes, hyperventilation, and excessive vomiting
22. The hollow female reproductive organ in which a fertilized egg is implanted, and a fetus develops

A. Receptor	B. Vaccine	C. Bile duct
F. Radon	G. Sperm	H. Alkalosis
K. Vascular	L. Cast	M. Rubeola
P. Antacid	Q. Suture	R. Uterus
U. Immunity	V. Fetus	W. Organism
D. Liver	E. Nausea	
I. Whipworm	J. Fracture	
N. Lungs	O. Lateral	
S. Bypass	T. Enzyme	

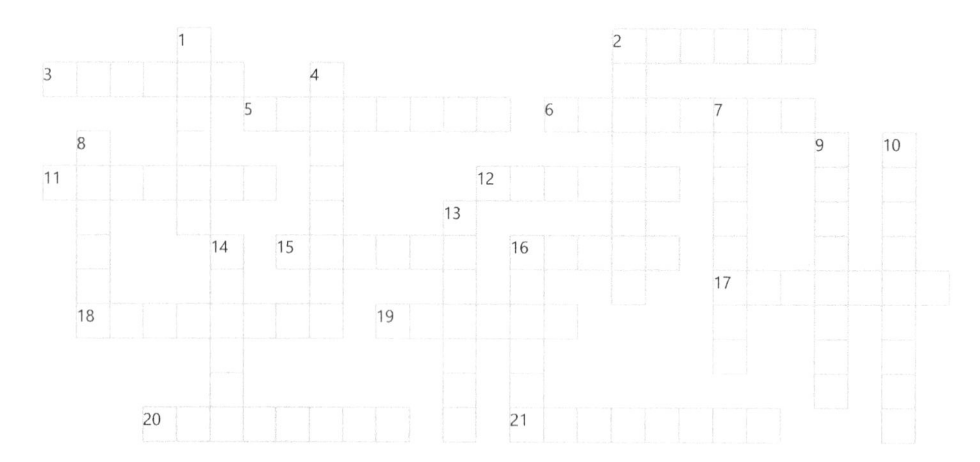

3. Using the Across and Down clues, write the correct words in the numbered grid below.

ACROSS

2. Mucus and other material produced by the lining of the respiratory tract
3. A term used to describe something situated on or near the midline of the body or a body structure
5. A drug (or other chemical) induced drowsiness or stupor
6. Small spots that float across the field of vision, caused by debris floating in the gel-like substance that fills the eye
11. The pigment that gives skin, hair, and eyes their coloring
12. A condition in which the blood does not contain enough hemoglobin, the compound that carries oxygen from the lungs to other parts of the body
15. Damage to part of the brain because of a lack of blood supply or the rupturing of a blood vessel
16. A sample of cells spread across a glass slide to be examined through a microscope
17. Any substance that causes a fever
18. Inflammation of a nerve, often characterized by pain, numbness, or tingling
19. A surgical stitch that helps close an incision or wound so that it can heal properly
20. Affecting the whole body
21. Urination or a sleep- disturbing need to urinate during the night

DOWN

2. Mucus and other material produced by the lining of the respiratory tract
3. A term used to describe something situated on or near the midline of the body or a body structure
5. A drug (or other chemical) induced drowsiness or stupor
6. Small spots that float across the field of vision, caused by debris floating in the gel-like substance that fills the eye
11. The pigment that gives skin, hair, and eyes their coloring
12. A condition in which the blood does not contain enough hemoglobin, the compound that carries oxygen from the lungs to other parts of the body
15. Damage to part of the brain because of a lack of blood supply or the rupturing of a blood vessel
16. A sample of cells spread across a glass slide to be examined through a microscope
17. Any substance that causes a fever
18. Inflammation of a nerve, often characterized by pain, numbness, or tingling
19. A surgical stitch that helps close an incision or wound so that it can heal properly
20. Affecting the whole body
21. Urination or a sleep- disturbing need to urinate during the night

A. Proximal
B. Orchitis
C. Medial
D. Neuritis
E. Bacterium
F. Systemic
G. Pepsin
H. Pathogen
I. Floaters
J. Epilepsy
K. Pyrogen
L. Nocturia
M. Melanin
N. Strain
O. Anemia
P. Coitus
Q. Vertigo
R. Narcosis
S. Phlegm
T. Suture
U. Vagina
V. Stroke
W. Smear

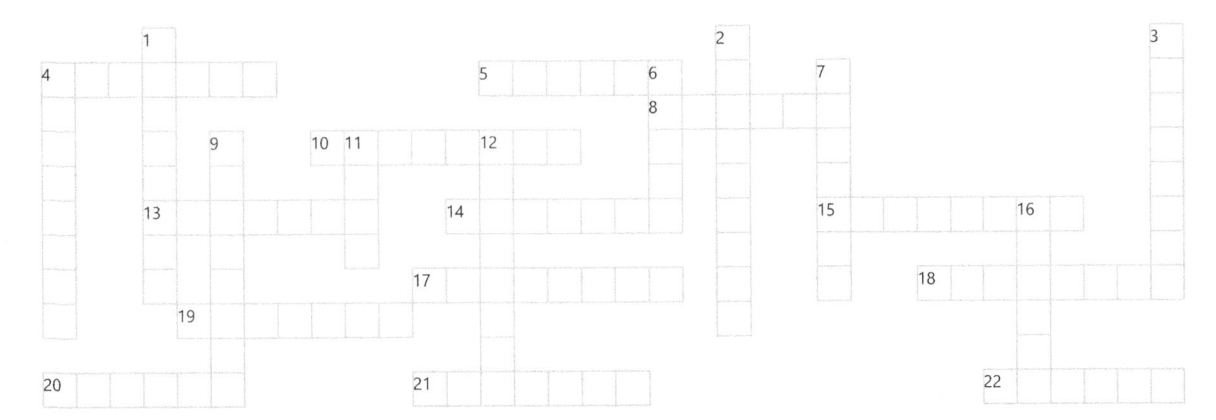

4. Using the Across and Down clues, write the correct words in the numbered grid below.

ACROSS

4. A noncancerous tumor of connective tissue
5. A surgical technique in which the flow of blood or another body fluid is redirected around a blockage
8. The roof of the mouth
10. Inflammation of a testicle, which can be caused by infection with the mumps virus
13. The process by which most cells divide to reproduce
14. A plentiful mineral in the body and the basic component of teeth and bones
15. Inflammation of the lining of the lungs and chest cavity usually caused by a lung infection
17. A bluish discoloration of the skin caused by low levels of oxygen in the blood
18. Any one of the 33 bones that make up the spine
19. A skin disorder that is characterized by patches of red skin on the nose and cheeks and acne- like bumps
20. A raised, firm, thick scar that forms because of a defect in the natural healing process
21. Difficulty breathing
22. Strong connective tissue cords that attach muscle to bone or muscle to muscle

DOWN

4. A noncancerous tumor of connective tissue
5. A surgical technique in which the flow of blood or another body fluid is redirected around a blockage
8. The roof of the mouth
10. Inflammation of a testicle, which can be caused by infection with the mumps virus
13. The process by which most cells divide to reproduce
14. A plentiful mineral in the body and the basic component of teeth and bones
15. Inflammation of the lining of the lungs and chest cavity usually caused by a lung infection
17. A bluish discoloration of the skin caused by low levels of oxygen in the blood
18. Any one of the 33 bones that make up the spine
19. A skin disorder that is characterized by patches of red skin on the nose and cheeks and acne- like bumps
20. A raised, firm, thick scar that forms because of a defect in the natural healing process
21. Difficulty breathing
22. Strong connective tissue cords that attach muscle to bone or muscle to muscle

A. Tendon
B. Bilateral
C. Calcium
D. Retinoid
E. Palate
F. Dyspnea
G. Trachoma
H. Keloid
I. Proximal
J. Relapse
K. Spasm
L. Thalamus
M. Vertebra
N. Rosacea
O. Pleurisy
P. Rash
Q. Foreskin
R. Mitosis
S. Suture
T. Orchitis
U. Fibroma
V. Cyanosis
W. Bypass

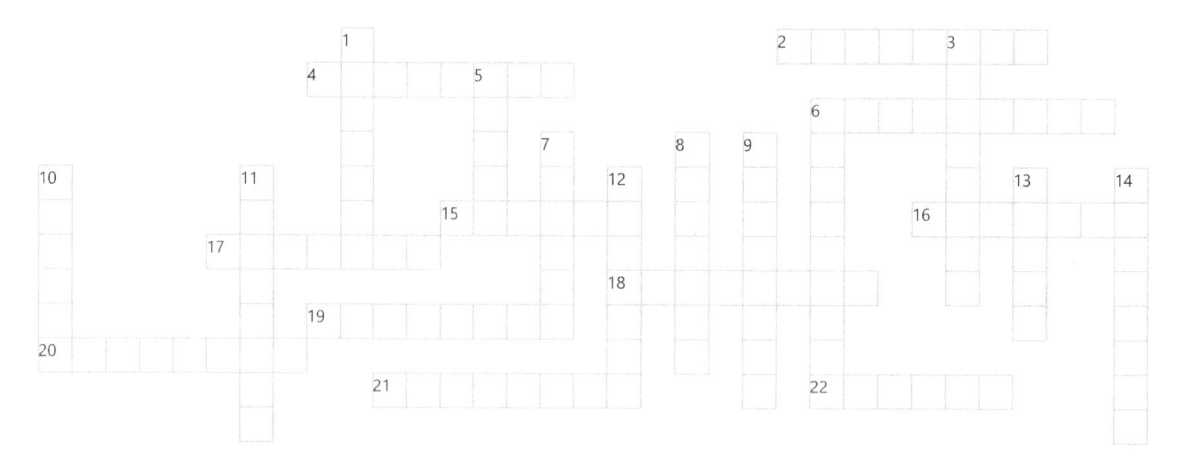

5. Using the Across and Down clues, write the correct words in the numbered grid below.

ACROSS

2. A tiny pouchlike cavity in a structure of the body, such as a hair follicle
4. The medical term for the death of tissue cells
6. Inflammation of the walls of an artery that causes the passageway to become narrower
15. "in the living body"; a biological process that occurs inside of the body
16. The center part of an organ or body structure
17. Another term for smallpox
18. Baldness or loss of hair, mainly on the head, either in defined patches or completely
19. The three membranes that surround and protect the spinal cord and brain
20. The surgical removal of diseased tissue
21. A deficiency of the vitamin niacin; causes dermatitis, diarrhea, and mental disorders
22. A mineral that plays a role in the body's water balance, heart rhythm, nerve impulses, and muscle contraction

DOWN

2. A tiny pouchlike cavity in a structure of the body, such as a hair follicle
4. The medical term for the death of tissue cells
6. Inflammation of the walls of an artery that causes the passageway to become narrower
15. "in the living body"; a biological process that occurs inside of the body
16. The center part of an organ or body structure
17. Another term for smallpox
18. Baldness or loss of hair, mainly on the head, either in defined patches or completely
19. The three membranes that surround and protect the spinal cord and brain
20. The surgical removal of diseased tissue
21. A deficiency of the vitamin niacin; causes dermatitis, diarrhea, and mental disorders
22. A mineral that plays a role in the body's water balance, heart rhythm, nerve impulses, and muscle contraction

A. Arteritis	B. Excision	C. Sodium	D. Thymoma	E. Trachoma	F. Medulla
G. Meninges	H. Follicle	I. Alopecia	J. In vivo	K. Plague	L. Semen
M. Tumor	N. Coitus	O. Variola	P. Rosacea	Q. Carotene	R. Familial
S. Leukemia	T. Vertigo	U. Necrosis	V. Pellagra	W. Arthritis	

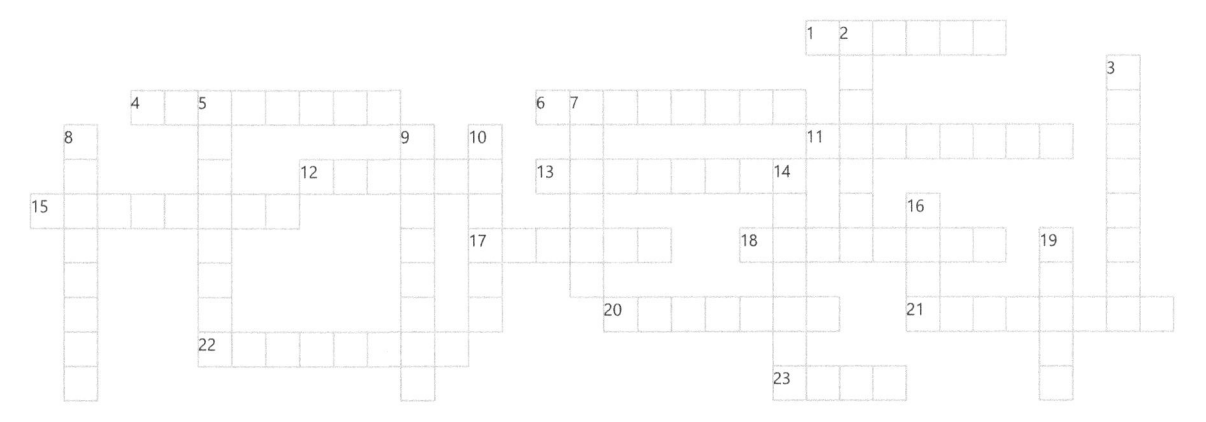

6. Using the Across and Down clues, write the correct words in the numbered grid below.

ACROSS

1. A high-pitched sound produced during breathing because of narrowing of the airways
4. An excessively large dose of a drug, which can lead to coma and death
6. The lack of sensation in a part of the body because of interruption of nerve impulses
11. Death of a tissue because of a lack of blood supply
12. The cell that results when an egg is fertilized by a sperm
13. A gradual decline in mental ability usually caused by a brain disease, such as Alzheimer's disease
15. The largest part of the brain and the site of most of its activity, including sensory and motor functions
17. The muscular passage connecting the uterus with the outside genitals
18. A bone break
20. The sugar found in dairy products
21. Inflammation of the lining of the lungs and chest cavity usually caused by a lung infection
22. Urination or a sleep-disturbing need to urinate during the night
23. A "warning" signal that comes before a migraine headache or an epileptic seizure, which might include emotions or sensations of movement or discomfort

DOWN

1. A high-pitched sound produced during breathing because of narrowing of the airways
4. An excessively large dose of a drug, which can lead to coma and death
6. The lack of sensation in a part of the body because of interruption of nerve impulses
11. Death of a tissue because of a lack of blood supply
12. The cell that results when an egg is fertilized by a sperm
13. A gradual decline in mental ability usually caused by a brain disease, such as Alzheimer's disease
15. The largest part of the brain and the site of most of its activity, including sensory and motor functions
17. The muscular passage connecting the uterus with the outside genitals
18. A bone break
20. The sugar found in dairy products
21. Inflammation of the lining of the lungs and chest cavity usually caused by a lung infection
22. Urination or a sleep-disturbing need to urinate during the night
23. A "warning" signal that comes before a migraine headache or an epileptic seizure, which might include emotions or sensations of movement or discomfort

A. Wheeze
B. Cervix
C. Speculum
D. Numbness
E. Nerve
F. Pleurisy
G. Pulp
H. Hepatic
I. Aura
J. Zygote
K. Cerebrum
L. Estrogen
M. Uremia
N. Nocturia
O. Polyuria
P. Overdose
Q. Atresia
R. Dementia
S. Osteitis
T. Fracture
U. Vagina
V. Gangrene
W. Lactose

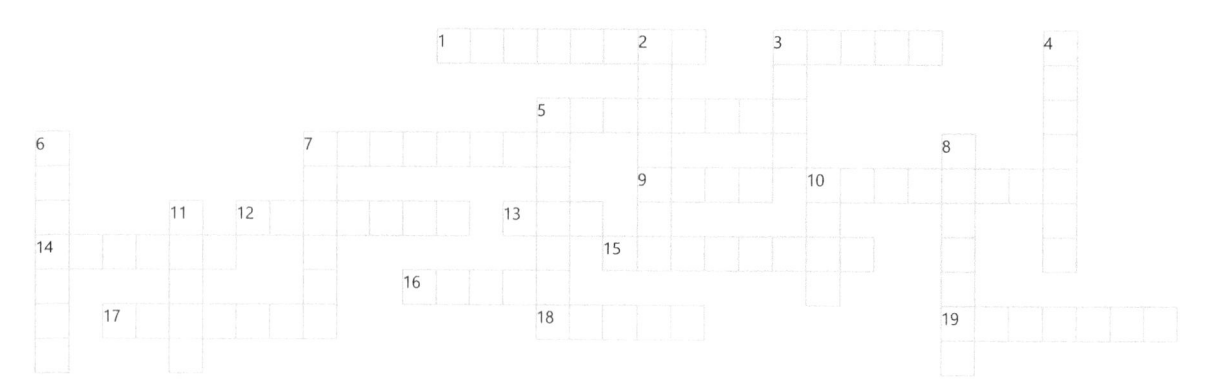

7. Using the Across and Down clues, write the correct words in the numbered grid below.

ACROSS

1. An abnormal swelling of the wall of an artery, caused by a weakening in the vessel wall
3. The expansion and contraction of a blood vessel due to the blood pumped through it
5. An oral contraceptive containing only the synthetic hormone progesterone (birth control pills contain estrogen and progesterone)
7. A group of symptoms that indicate a certain disorder when they occur together
9. A structure consisting of the colored area of the eye and the middle layer of the eye that contains blood vessels
10. Any single, functioning form of life
12. A disorder in which a person eats large amounts of food then forces vomiting or uses laxatives to prevent weight gain (called binging and purging)
13. A thick, yellowish or greenish fluid that contains dead white blood cells, tissues, and bacteria; occurs at the site of a bacterial infection
14. A small, round organ making up the neck of the uterus and separating it from the vagina
15. An element needed by the body only in very small amounts that helps maintain tissue elasticity
16. Another term for feces
17. A painless sore that has a thick, rubbery base and a defined edge
18. Describes a condition or illness that begins suddenly and is usually short- lasting
19. A childhood disease in which bones lack calcium and are deformed because of vitamin d deficiency

DOWN

1. An abnormal swelling of the wall of an artery, caused by a weakening in the vessel wall
3. The expansion and contraction of a blood vessel due to the blood pumped through it
5. An oral contraceptive containing only the synthetic hormone progesterone (birth control pills contain estrogen and progesterone)
7. A group of symptoms that indicate a certain disorder when they occur together
9. A structure consisting of the colored area of the eye and the middle layer of the eye that contains blood vessels
10. Any single, functioning form of life
12. A disorder in which a person eats large amounts of food then forces vomiting or uses laxatives to prevent weight gain (called binging and purging)
13. A thick, yellowish or greenish fluid that contains dead white blood cells, tissues, and bacteria; occurs at the site of a bacterial infection
14. A small, round organ making up the neck of the uterus and separating it from the vagina
15. An element needed by the body only in very small amounts that helps maintain tissue elasticity
16. Another term for feces
17. A painless sore that has a thick, rubbery base and a defined edge
18. Describes a condition or illness that begins suddenly and is usually short- lasting
19. A childhood disease in which bones lack calcium and are deformed because of vitamin d deficiency

A. Organism B. Saline C. Acute D. Rickets E. Uvea F. Aneurysm
G. Toxemia H. Bulimia I. Pulse J. Selenium K. Medulla L. Seizure
M. In vitro N. Vaccine O. Ovum P. Pus Q. Syndrome R. Viral
S. Stool T. Chancre U. Minipill V. Cervix W. Pulp

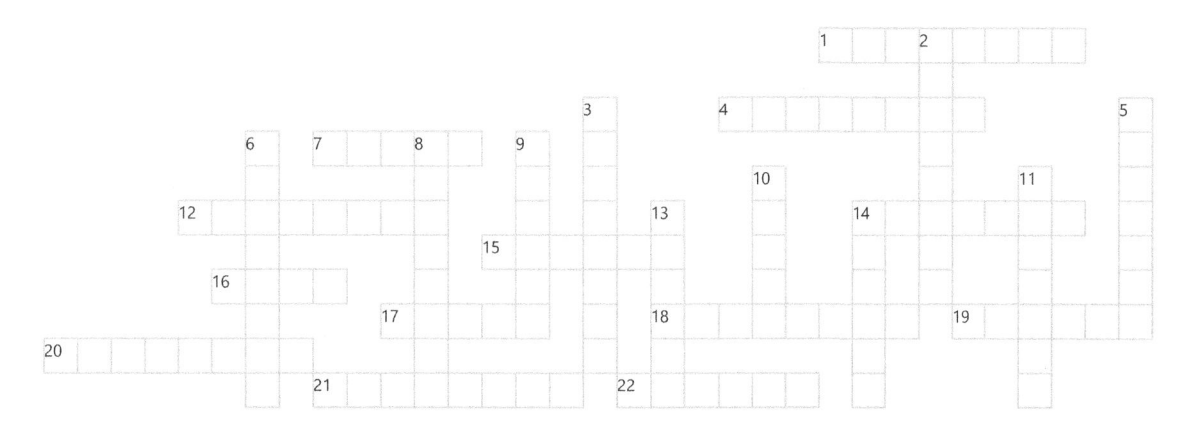

8. Using the Across and Down clues, write the correct words in the numbered grid below.

ACROSS

1. A parasite- caused or infectious disease in animals that can be transferred to humans
4. A deficiency of the vitamin niacin; causes dermatitis, diarrhea, and mental disorders
7. Two organs in the chest that take in oxygen from the air and release carbon dioxide
12. Urination or a sleep- disturbing need to urinate during the night
14. A sometimes fatal disease affecting the brain and spinal cord
15. One of two organs that are part of the urinary tract
16. A desire to eat materials that are not food
17. Intestine
18. Determination of the amount of oxygen in the blood by measuring the amount of light transmitted through an area of skin
19. The liquid part of the blood, containing substances such as nutrients, salts, and proteins
20. A sexually transmitted disease
21. A disorder in which a person becomes overly suspicious and emotionally sensitive
22. The hard deposit formed on teeth when mineral salts in saliva combine with plaque

DOWN

1. A parasite- caused or infectious disease in animals that can be transferred to humans
4. A deficiency of the vitamin niacin; causes dermatitis, diarrhea, and mental disorders
7. Two organs in the chest that take in oxygen from the air and release carbon dioxide
12. Urination or a sleep- disturbing need to urinate during the night
14. A sometimes fatal disease affecting the brain and spinal cord
15. One of two organs that are part of the urinary tract
16. A desire to eat materials that are not food
17. Intestine
18. Determination of the amount of oxygen in the blood by measuring the amount of light transmitted through an area of skin
19. The liquid part of the blood, containing substances such as nutrients, salts, and proteins
20. A sexually transmitted disease
21. A disorder in which a person becomes overly suspicious and emotionally sensitive
22. The hard deposit formed on teeth when mineral salts in saliva combine with plaque

A. Plasma	B. Myxoma	C. Lumbago	D. Thrill	E. Sebum
F. Lungs	G. Nocturia	H. Narcotic	I. Tartar	J. Bowel
K. Pellagra	L. Thorax	M. Tetanus	N. Pica	O. Kidney
P. Zoonosis	Q. Paranoia	R. Oximetry	S. Sarcoma	T. Syphilis
U. Orchitis	V. Glaucoma	W. Meconium		

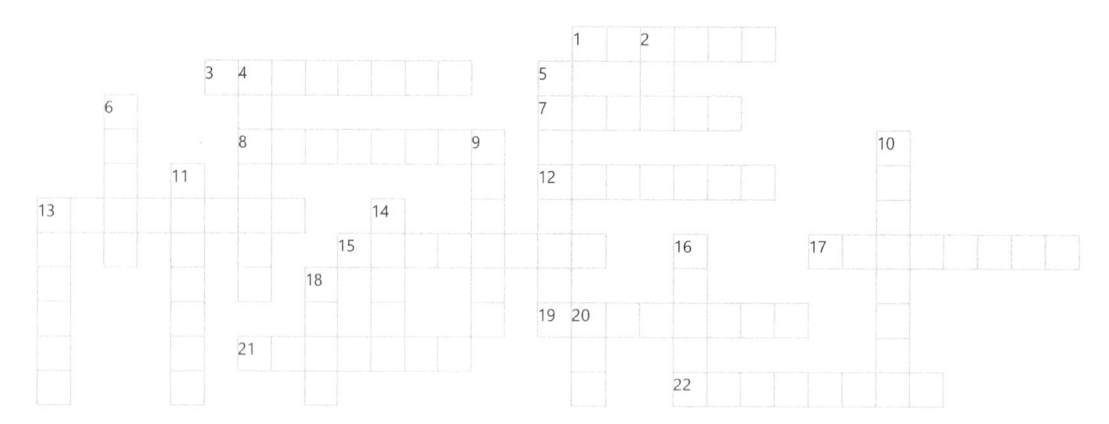

9. Using the Across and Down clues, write the correct words in the numbered grid below.

ACROSS

1. A candidiasis infection
3. A drug that increases the amount of water in the urine, removing excess water from the body
7. Involuntary contraction of genital muscles experienced at the peak of sexual excitement
8. A condition in which people are born with insufficient amounts of the pigment melanin, which is responsible for hair, skin, and eye color
12. Excess fluid in the abdominal cavity, which leads to swelling
13. Affecting the whole body
15. A hormone produced by the thyroid gland that helps regulate energy production in the body
17. An extremely rare condition in which the body ages prematurely
19. A term used to describe a disease that is rare then suddenly affects more people than usually expected
21. An additional dose of a vaccine taken after the first dose to maintain or renew the first one
22. A word describing any condition that is not present at birth, but develops some time during life

DOWN

1. A candidiasis infection
3. A drug that increases the amount of water in the urine, removing excess water from the body
7. Involuntary contraction of genital muscles experienced at the peak of sexual excitement
8. A condition in which people are born with insufficient amounts of the pigment melanin, which is responsible for hair, skin, and eye color
12. Excess fluid in the abdominal cavity, which leads to swelling
13. Affecting the whole body
15. A hormone produced by the thyroid gland that helps regulate energy production in the body
17. An extremely rare condition in which the body ages prematurely
19. A term used to describe a disease that is rare then suddenly affects more people than usually expected
21. An additional dose of a vaccine taken after the first dose to maintain or renew the first one
22. A word describing any condition that is not present at birth, but develops some time during life

A. Imaging   B. Booster   C. Shunt   D. Ascites   E. Dopamine   F. Diuretic
G. RNA   H. Systemic I. Fluoride J. Orgasm   K. Bursa   L. Pus
M. Albinism N. Progeria O. Thyroxin P. Edema   Q. Epidemic   R. Thrush
S. Myxoma   T. Acquired U. Splint   V. Meiosis W. Iron

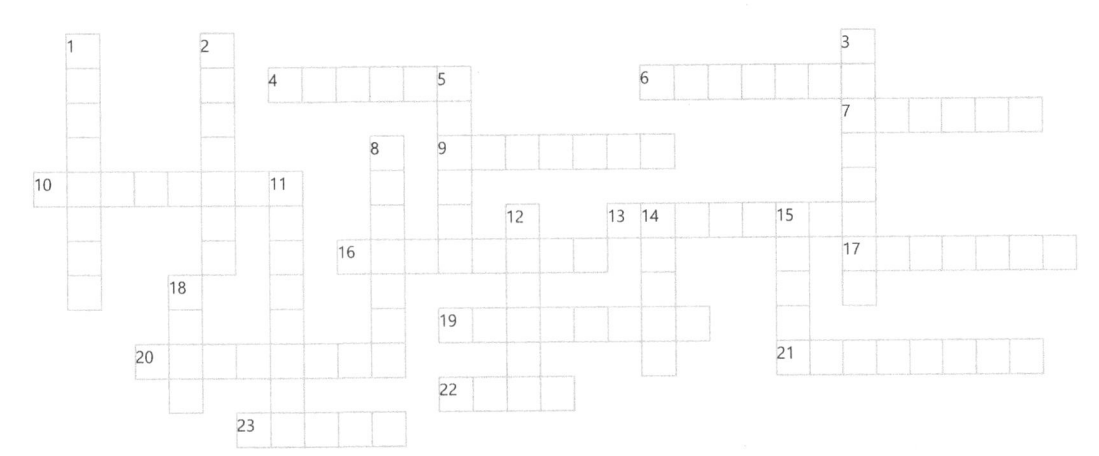

10. Using the Across and Down clues, write the correct words in the numbered grid below.

ACROSS

4. Enlargement of the thyroid gland, which produces a swelling on the neck
6. The shrinkage or near disappearance of a tissue or organ
7. A serious infectious disease transmitted to humans through bites of rodent fleas
9. A sometimes fatal disease affecting the brain and spinal cord
10. Infestation by a small, round, blood-sucking parasite
13. The inward curvature of the spine at the lower back, which is normal to a certain degree
16. A skin tumor composed of cells called melanocytes
17. An organ, tissue, or device surgically inserted and left in the body
19. Tightness of the foreskin, which prevents it from being moved back over the head of the penis
20. Baldness or loss of hair, mainly on the head, either in defined patches or completely
21. Narrowing of a body passageway
22. A waste product of the metabolism of proteins that is formed by the liver and secreted by the kidneys
23. The term used to refer to an unborn child from 8 weeks after fertilization to birth

DOWN

4. Enlargement of the thyroid gland, which produces a swelling on the neck
6. The shrinkage or near disappearance of a tissue or organ
7. A serious infectious disease transmitted to humans through bites of rodent fleas
9. A sometimes fatal disease affecting the brain and spinal cord
10. Infestation by a small, round, blood-sucking parasite
13. The inward curvature of the spine at the lower back, which is normal to a certain degree
16. A skin tumor composed of cells called melanocytes
17. An organ, tissue, or device surgically inserted and left in the body
19. Tightness of the foreskin, which prevents it from being moved back over the head of the penis
20. Baldness or loss of hair, mainly on the head, either in defined patches or completely
21. Narrowing of a body passageway
22. A waste product of the metabolism of proteins that is formed by the liver and secreted by the kidneys
23. The term used to refer to an unborn child from 8 weeks after fertilization to birth

A. Alopecia
B. Androgen
C. Melanoma
D. Mucocele
E. Plague
F. Optic
G. Sinus
H. Iodine
I. Retina
J. Urea
K. Hookworm
L. Bile
M. Stenosis
N. Fetus
O. Kyphosis
P. Atrophy
Q. Goiter
R. Lordosis
S. Phimosis
T. Anatomy
U. Viremia
V. Implant
W. Tetanus

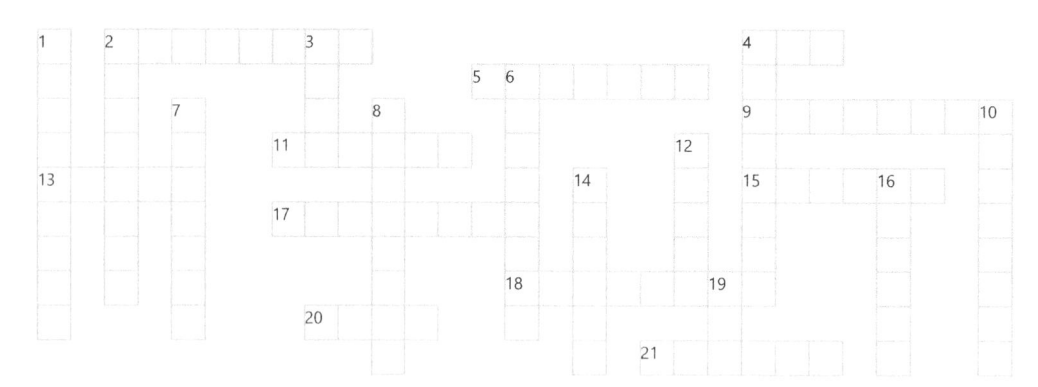

11. Using the Across and Down clues, write the correct words in the numbered grid below.

ACROSS

2. The medical term for itching
4. An involuntary, repetitive movement such as a twitch
5. Controlled analgesia- a system for administering pain-killing drugs in which the amount of drug delivered is controlled by the patient
9. An addictive substance that blunts the senses
11. Abnormally pale skin
13. Healthy tissue that is used to replace diseased or defective tissue
15. "in place"; often describes a cancer that has not spread
17. The main form that glucose, the body's energy source, takes when it is stored
18. A nerve infection caused by the chickenpox virus, causing areas of painful rash covered with blisters
20. A form of phototherapy that combines the use of psoralens and ultraviolet light to treat skin disorders
21. Involuntary contraction of genital muscles experienced at the peak of sexual excitement

DOWN

2. The medical term for itching
4. An involuntary, repetitive movement such as a twitch
5. Controlled analgesia- a system for administering pain-killing drugs in which the amount of drug delivered is controlled by the patient
9. An addictive substance that blunts the senses
11. Abnormally pale skin
13. Healthy tissue that is used to replace diseased or defective tissue
15. "in place"; often describes a cancer that has not spread
17. The main form that glucose, the body's energy source, takes when it is stored
18. A nerve infection caused by the chickenpox virus, causing areas of painful rash covered with blisters
20. A form of phototherapy that combines the use of psoralens and ultraviolet light to treat skin disorders
21. Involuntary contraction of genital muscles experienced at the peak of sexual excitement

A. Bowel	B. Glycogen	C. Albinism	D. Prolapse	E. Patient	F. Bunion
G. ECG	H. Orgasm	I. Tinnitus	J. PUVA	K. Fitness	L. Shingles
M. Tic	N. Uvea	O. Cyanosis	P. Elective	Q. Pallor	R. Narcotic
S. Typhus	T. Pruritus	U. Analgesic	V. Graft	W. In situ	

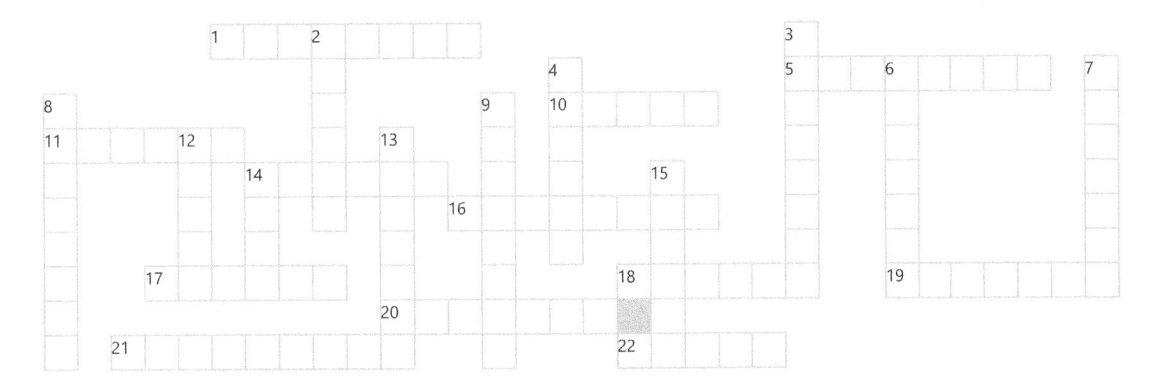

12. Using the Across and Down clues, write the correct words in the numbered grid below.

ACROSS

1. A hormone produced in the pituitary gland that causes contraction of the uterus during childbirth and stimulation of milk flow during breast-feeding.
5. Any single, functioning form of life
10. The expansion and contraction of a blood vessel due to the blood pumped through it
11. A noncancerous tumor of fatty tissue
14. The group of bones in the lower part of the trunk that support the upper body and protect the abdominal organs
16. A nerve cell that responds to a stimulus and produces a nerve impulse
17. The roof of the mouth
18. A hard, fluid-filled pad along the inside joint of the big toe
19. A negative reaction to a substance that in most people causes no reaction
20. A hormone made in the pancreas that plays an important role in the absorption of glucose (the body's main source of energy) into muscle cells
21. Inflammation of the walls of an artery that causes the passageway to become narrower
22. The bone located between the hip and the knee

DOWN

1. A hormone produced in the pituitary gland that causes contraction of the uterus during childbirth and stimulation of milk flow during breast-feeding.
5. Any single, functioning form of life
10. The expansion and contraction of a blood vessel due to the blood pumped through it
11. A noncancerous tumor of fatty tissue
14. The group of bones in the lower part of the trunk that support the upper body and protect the abdominal organs
16. A nerve cell that responds to a stimulus and produces a nerve impulse
17. The roof of the mouth
18. A hard, fluid-filled pad along the inside joint of the big toe
19. A negative reaction to a substance that in most people causes no reaction
20. A hormone made in the pancreas that plays an important role in the absorption of glucose (the body's main source of energy) into muscle cells
21. Inflammation of the walls of an artery that causes the passageway to become narrower
22. The bone located between the hip and the knee

A. Organism	B. Pulse	C. Pelvis	D. Nodule
E. Bone spur	F. Lipoma	G. Allergy	H. Mania
I. Atrophy	J. Insulin	K. Spleen	L. Bunion
M. Foreskin	N. Glaucoma	O. Thrill	P. Femur
Q. Arteritis	R. Receptor	S. Palate	T. Oxytocin
U. PUVA	V. Angioma	W. Mitosis	

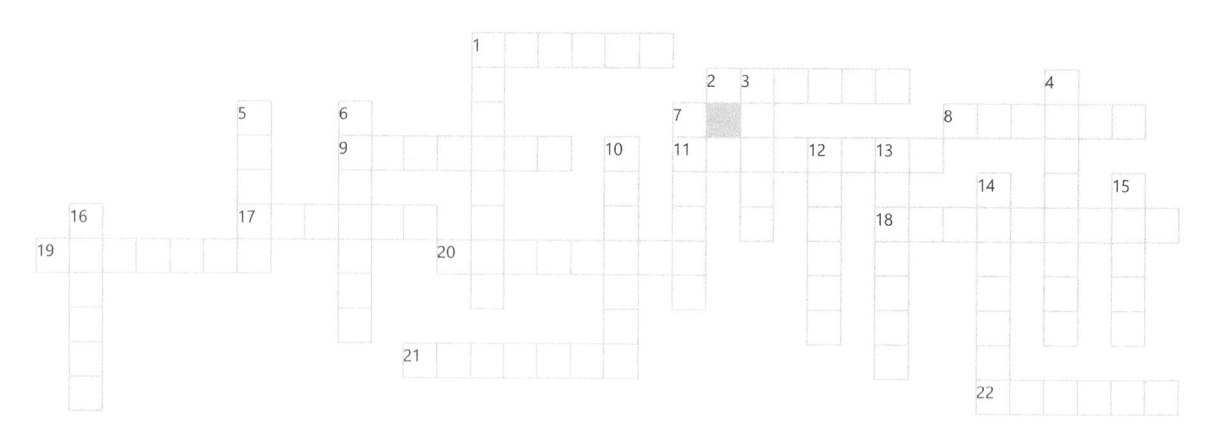

13. Using the Across and Down clues, write the correct words in the numbered grid below.

ACROSS

1. Mucus and other material produced by the lining of the respiratory tract
2. An organism that is dependent on another organism for nourishment
8. A brain tumor arising from cells that support nerve cells
9. A coiled organ in the inner ear that plays a large role in hearing by picking up sound vibrations and transmitting them as electrical signals
11. The surgical removal of diseased tissue
17. A noncancerous tumor made of mucous material and fibrous connective tissue
18. Inflammation of the walls of an artery that causes the passageway to become narrower
19. Another term for smallpox
20. Urination or a sleep-disturbing need to urinate during the night
21. The tube by which urine is released from the bladder
22. A surgical stitch that helps close an incision or wound so that it can heal properly

DOWN

1. Mucus and other material produced by the lining of the respiratory tract
2. An organism that is dependent on another organism for nourishment
8. A brain tumor arising from cells that support nerve cells
9. A coiled organ in the inner ear that plays a large role in hearing by picking up sound vibrations and transmitting them as electrical signals
11. The surgical removal of diseased tissue
17. A noncancerous tumor made of mucous material and fibrous connective tissue
18. Inflammation of the walls of an artery that causes the passageway to become narrower
19. Another term for smallpox
20. Urination or a sleep-disturbing need to urinate during the night
21. The tube by which urine is released from the bladder
22. A surgical stitch that helps close an incision or wound so that it can heal properly

A. Ulcer
B. Myxoma
C. Ovaries
D. Smallpox
E. Excision
F. Glioma
G. Cochlea
H. Medial
I. Edema
J. Nocturia
K. Suture
L. Measles
M. Fungus
N. Follicle
O. Cilia
P. Patent
Q. Arteritis
R. Fibroma
S. Sputum
T. Scrotum
U. Variola
V. Sacrum
W. Urethra

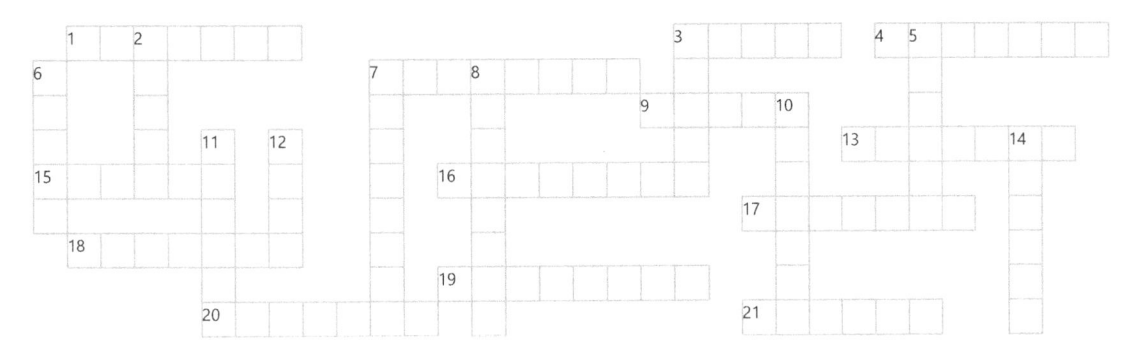

14. Using the Across and Down clues, write the correct words in the numbered grid below.

ACROSS

1. An accumulation of pus in a body tissue, usually caused by a bacterial infection
3. The bone located between the hip and the knee
4. The common name for the visual defect resulting from untreated strabismus, in which the eyes are not correctly aligned
7. Any bacteria that is rod- shaped
9. A surgically formed opening on a body surface
13. A device used to introduce a powdered or misted drug into the lungs through the mouth, usually to treat respiratory disorders such as asthma
15. An organ located in the upper left abdomen behind the ribs that removes and destroys old red blood cells and helps fight infection
16. Inflammation of a bursa due to excessive pressure or friction, or from injury
17. A spasm of the jaw muscles that prevents the mouth from opening, such as that caused by tetanus
18. A disorder in which a person eats large amounts of food then forces vomiting or uses laxatives to prevent weight gain (called binging and purging)
19. An abnormal growth of bone out of another bone, often located on the heel and usually painful
20. The structure of bodies
21. The cell that results when an egg is fertilized by a sperm

DOWN

1. An accumulation of pus in a body tissue, usually caused by a bacterial infection
3. The bone located between the hip and the knee
4. The common name for the visual defect resulting from untreated strabismus, in which the eyes are not correctly aligned
7. Any bacteria that is rod- shaped
9. A surgically formed opening on a body surface
13. A device used to introduce a powdered or misted drug into the lungs through the mouth, usually to treat respiratory disorders such as asthma
15. An organ located in the upper left abdomen behind the ribs that removes and destroys old red blood cells and helps fight infection
16. Inflammation of a bursa due to excessive pressure or friction, or from injury
17. A spasm of the jaw muscles that prevents the mouth from opening, such as that caused by tetanus
18. A disorder in which a person eats large amounts of food then forces vomiting or uses laxatives to prevent weight gain (called binging and purging)
19. An abnormal growth of bone out of another bone, often located on the heel and usually painful
20. The structure of bodies
21. The cell that results when an egg is fertilized by a sperm

A. Atrophy	B. Bursitis	C. Bone spur	D. Infusion	E. Sprue	F. Spasm
G. PUVA	H. Zygote	I. Anatomy	J. Asthma	K. Lockjaw	L. Stoma
M. Eczema	N. Spleen	O. Inhaler	P. Fetus	Q. Bulimia	R. Abscess
S. Femur	T. Bacillus	U. Botulism	V. Lazy eye	W. Anemia	

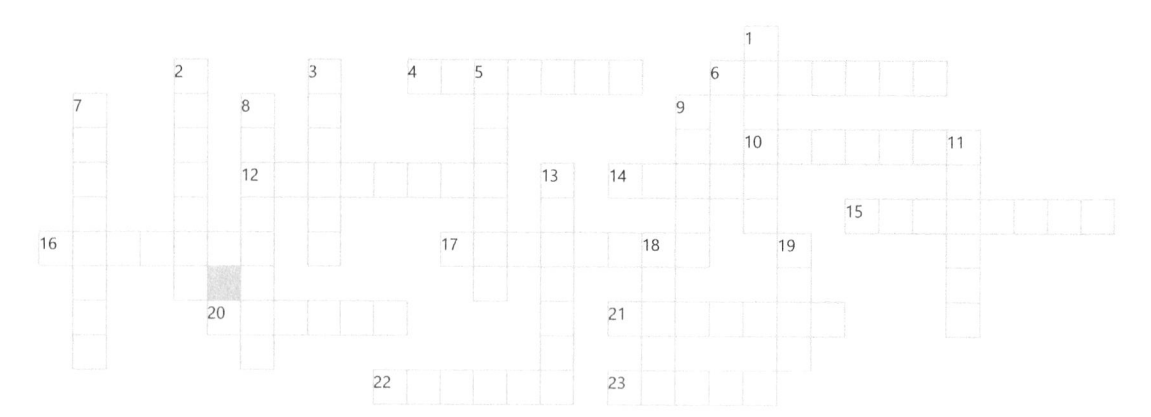

15. Using the Across and Down clues, write the correct words in the numbered grid below.

ACROSS

4. A small blister containing pus
6. An abscess on the end of a finger or a toe that is caused by the herpes simplex virus or a bacterial infection
10. The tube by which urine is released from the bladder
12. A discharge from an inflamed ear
14. The common term for urticaria, an itchy, inflamed rash that results from an allergic reaction
15. The surgical removal of diseased tissue
16. A condition in which one eye turns outward
17. Complex substances that are necessary in small amounts to maintain health and ensure proper development and functioning of the body
20. A mental disorder characterized by an inability to relate to other people and extreme withdrawal
21. An unaware clenching or grinding of the teeth, usually during sleep
22. An automatic, involuntary response of the nervous system to a stimulus
23. Fluid released during ejaculation that contains sperm along with fluids produced by the prostate gland and the seminal vesicles

DOWN

4. A small blister containing pus
6. An abscess on the end of a finger or a toe that is caused by the herpes simplex virus or a bacterial infection
10. The tube by which urine is released from the bladder
12. A discharge from an inflamed ear
14. The common term for urticaria, an itchy, inflamed rash that results from an allergic reaction
15. The surgical removal of diseased tissue
16. A condition in which one eye turns outward
17. Complex substances that are necessary in small amounts to maintain health and ensure proper development and functioning of the body
20. A mental disorder characterized by an inability to relate to other people and extreme withdrawal
21. An unaware clenching or grinding of the teeth, usually during sleep
22. An automatic, involuntary response of the nervous system to a stimulus
23. Fluid released during ejaculation that contains sperm along with fluids produced by the prostate gland and the seminal vesicles

A. Otorrhea
B. Hives
C. Reflex
D. Walleye
E. Somatic
F. Pustule
G. Semen
H. Autism
I. Pharynx
J. Cast
K. Nerve
L. Migraine
M. Thrush
N. Duodenum
O. Excision
P. Bruxism
Q. Pyrogen
R. Nevus
S. Urethra
T. Glioma
U. Whitlow
V. Vitamins
W. Axilla

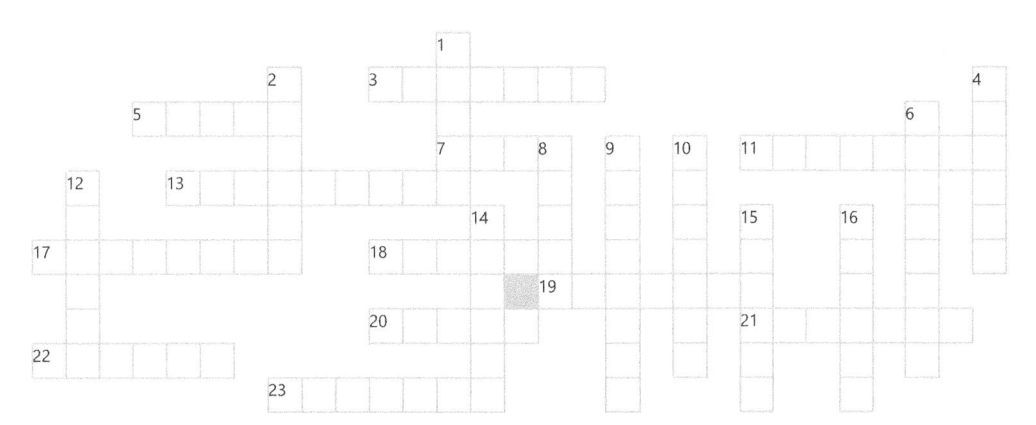

16. Using the Across and Down clues, write the correct words in the numbered grid below.

ACROSS

3. The throat
5. A sample of cells spread across a glass slide to be examined through a microscope
7. The colored part of the eye
11. A tumor composed of cells not normally found in the part of the body when the tumor occurred
13. Microorganisms that cause several human infections and can be transmitted sexually
17. Death of a tissue because of a lack of blood supply
18. A vibration felt when the hand is placed flat on the chest
19. On one side
20. A mental disorder characterized by extreme excitement, happiness, overactivity, and agitation
21. The medical term for an earache
22. An automatic, involuntary response of the nervous system to a stimulus
23. Inflammation of the uvea

DOWN

3. The throat
5. A sample of cells spread across a glass slide to be examined through a microscope
7. The colored part of the eye
11. A tumor composed of cells not normally found in the part of the body when the tumor occurred
13. Microorganisms that cause several human infections and can be transmitted sexually
17. Death of a tissue because of a lack of blood supply
18. A vibration felt when the hand is placed flat on the chest
19. On one side
20. A mental disorder characterized by extreme excitement, happiness, overactivity, and agitation
21. The medical term for an earache
22. An automatic, involuntary response of the nervous system to a stimulus
23. Inflammation of the uvea

A. Thrill
B. Skull
C. Malaria
D. Abortion
E. Iris
F. Ocular
G. Chlamydia
H. Reflex
I. Mania
J. Teratoma
K. Triage
L. Lipids
M. Keloid
N. Otalgia
O. Plasma
P. Gangrene
Q. Labia
R. Pharynx
S. Plague
T. Lateral
U. Uveitis
V. Smear
W. Zoonosis

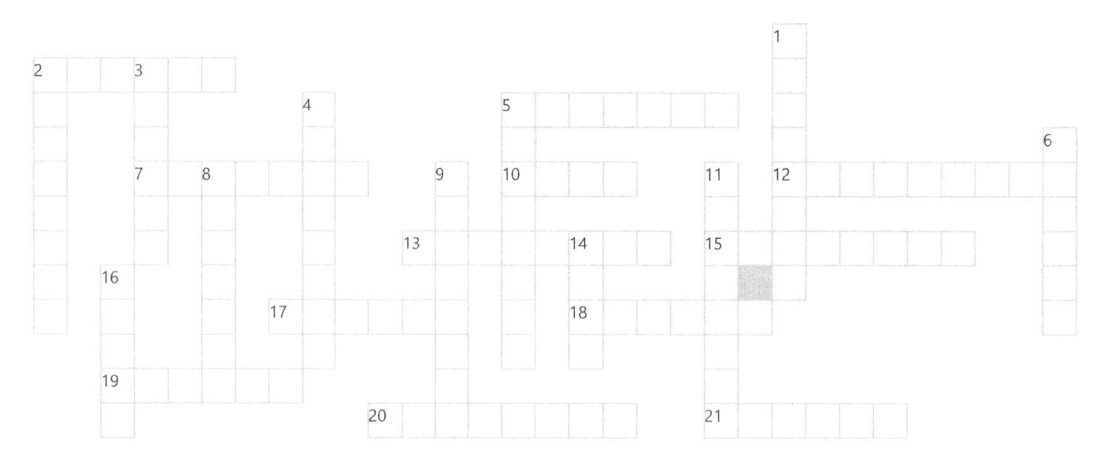

17. Using the Across and Down clues, write the correct words in the numbered grid below.

ACROSS

2. Describes something related to the eyes
5. A noncancerous tumor of the uterus made up of smooth muscle and connective tissue
7. The technique of creating pictures of structures inside of the body using x-rays, ultrasound waves, or magnetic fields
10. A structure consisting of the colored area of the eye and the middle layer of the eye that contains blood vessels
12. Microorganisms that cause several human infections and can be transmitted sexually
13. A hormone (such as testosterone) that causes development of male characteristics and sex organs
15. Any substance capable of causing a disease
17. A thickened area of skin due to consistent pressure or friction, or the area around a bone break where new bone is formed
18. Another term for a nerve cell
19. An egg cell that has not developed completely
20. An orange pigment present in colored plants such as carrots that is converted by the body to the essential nutrient vitamin a
21. A mineral that plays a role in the body's water balance, heart rhythm, nerve impulses, and muscle contraction

DOWN

2. Describes something related to the eyes
5. A noncancerous tumor of the uterus made up of smooth muscle and connective tissue
7. The technique of creating pictures of structures inside of the body using x-rays, ultrasound waves, or magnetic fields
10. A structure consisting of the colored area of the eye and the middle layer of the eye that contains blood vessels
12. Microorganisms that cause several human infections and can be transmitted sexually
13. A hormone (such as testosterone) that causes development of male characteristics and sex organs
15. Any substance capable of causing a disease
17. A thickened area of skin due to consistent pressure or friction, or the area around a bone break where new bone is formed
18. Another term for a nerve cell
19. An egg cell that has not developed completely
20. An orange pigment present in colored plants such as carrots that is converted by the body to the essential nutrient vitamin a
21. A mineral that plays a role in the body's water balance, heart rhythm, nerve impulses, and muscle contraction

A. Pathogen	B. Toxicity	C. Sodium
G. Lesion	H. Androgen	I. Kyphosis
M. Carotene	N. Ocular	O. Gene
S. Fibroid	T. Oocyte	U. Chlamydia
D. Imaging	E. Fluoride	F. Callus
J. Bone spur	K. Pancreas	L. Autopsy
P. Uvea	Q. Optician	R. Tartar
V. Labor	W. Neuron	

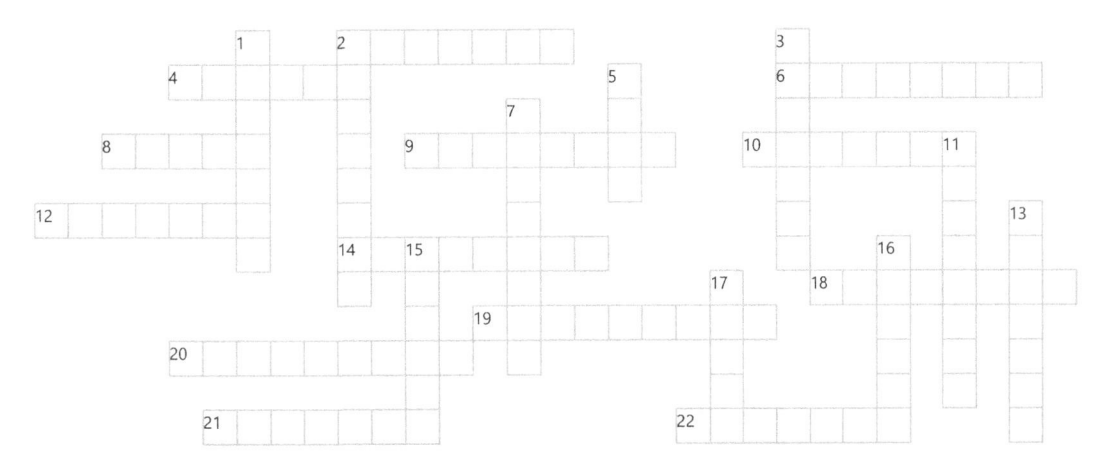

18. Using the Across and Down clues, write the correct words in the numbered grid below.

ACROSS

2. The complete or partial failure of any organ or tissue to grow
4. The inner skin layer
6. A hormone (such as testosterone) that causes development of male characteristics and sex organs
8. An artificially constructed or an abnormal passage connecting two usually separate structures in the body
9. A sac or body cavity that is swollen because of the production of mucus by the cells in its lining
10. A childhood disease in which bones lack calcium and are deformed because of vitamin d deficiency
12. An organ located in the pelvis whose function is to collect and store urine until it is expelled
14. The introduction of a substance, such as a drug or nutrient, into the bloodstream or a body cavity
18. The failure either to produce or to ejaculate sperm
19. Dangerously decreased acidity of the blood, which can be caused by high altitudes, hyperventilation, and excessive vomiting
20. A connective tissue (softer than bone) that is part of the skeletal system, including the joints
21. Enlarged or twisted blood or lymph vessels
22. A thin, oval-shaped membrane that separates the inner ear from the outer ear and is responsible for transmitting sound waves

DOWN

2. The complete or partial failure of any organ or tissue to grow
4. The inner skin layer
6. A hormone (such as testosterone) that causes development of male characteristics and sex organs
8. An artificially constructed or an abnormal passage connecting two usually separate structures in the body
9. A sac or body cavity that is swollen because of the production of mucus by the cells in its lining
10. A childhood disease in which bones lack calcium and are deformed because of vitamin d deficiency
12. An organ located in the pelvis whose function is to collect and store urine until it is expelled
14. The introduction of a substance, such as a drug or nutrient, into the bloodstream or a body cavity
18. The failure either to produce or to ejaculate sperm
19. Dangerously decreased acidity of the blood, which can be caused by high altitudes, hyperventilation, and excessive vomiting
20. A connective tissue (softer than bone) that is part of the skeletal system, including the joints
21. Enlarged or twisted blood or lymph vessels
22. A thin, oval-shaped membrane that separates the inner ear from the outer ear and is responsible for transmitting sound waves

A. Urethra
B. Aplasia
C. Sputum
D. Shunt
E. Cartilage
F. Fungus
G. Mucocele
H. Syndrome
I. Cilia
J. Trisomy
K. Androgen
L. Alkalosis
M. Bladder
N. Follicle
O. Asphyxia
P. Mole
Q. Rickets
R. Infusion
S. Aspermia
T. Eardrum
U. Varices
V. Dermis
W. Patient

19. Using the Across and Down clues, write the correct words in the numbered grid below.

ACROSS

4. A cancer that occurs on the surface or lining of an organ
7. A chemical produced by a gland or tissue that is released into the bloodstream
10. A skin infection caused by a fungus that spreads out in an even circle, characterized by ring- like, scaly patches of red skin
11. An accumulation of pus in a body tissue, usually caused by a bacterial infection
12. Infection and inflammation of a gland, especially a lymph node
13. The triangular bone located at the bottom of the spine that is connected to the tailbone
16. A slippery fluid produced by mucous membranes that lubricates and protects the internal surfaces of the body
18. The medical term for lockjaw
19. A change in the genetic information within a cell
20. The practice, maintenance, and study of health
21. A term used to describe a disease that is rare then suddenly affects more people than usually expected

DOWN

4. A cancer that occurs on the surface or lining of an organ
7. A chemical produced by a gland or tissue that is released into the bloodstream
10. A skin infection caused by a fungus that spreads out in an even circle, characterized by ring- like, scaly patches of red skin
11. An accumulation of pus in a body tissue, usually caused by a bacterial infection
12. Infection and inflammation of a gland, especially a lymph node
13. The triangular bone located at the bottom of the spine that is connected to the tailbone
16. A slippery fluid produced by mucous membranes that lubricates and protects the internal surfaces of the body
18. The medical term for lockjaw
19. A change in the genetic information within a cell
20. The practice, maintenance, and study of health
21. A term used to describe a disease that is rare then suddenly affects more people than usually expected

A. Narcotic
B. Clubfoot
C. Mania
D. Epidemic
E. Pandemic
F. Uvea
G. Oximetry
H. Hookworm
I. Mutation
J. Mucus
K. Trismus
L. Hygiene
M. Dextrose
N. Mites
O. Carcinoma
P. Adenitis
Q. Sacrum
R. Hormone
S. Stool
T. Abscess
U. Ringworm
V. Paresis
W. Hiccup

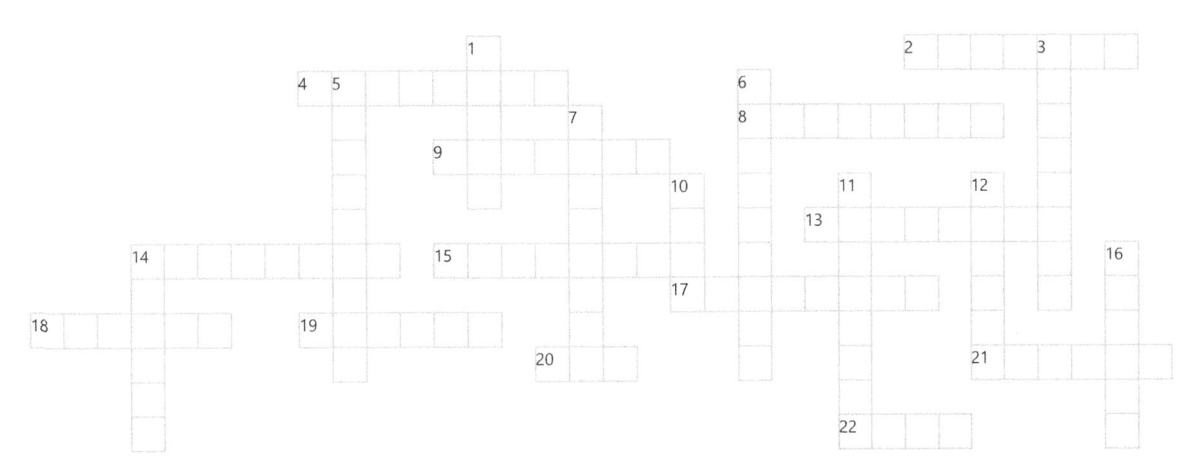

20. Using the Across and Down clues, write the correct words in the numbered grid below.

ACROSS

2. The medical term for the kneecap
4. Yellowing of the skin and whites of the eyes because of the presence of excess bilirubin in the blood; usually a sign of a disorder of the liver
8. The failure either to produce or to ejaculate sperm
9. The period during which sexual development occurs
13. An orange pigment present in colored plants such as carrots that is converted by the body to the essential nutrient vitamin a
14. Infection and inflammation of a gland, especially a lymph node
15. The medical term for the death of tissue cells
17. The use of tension to hold a body part in place or to correct or prevent an alignment problem
18. Mucus and other material produced by the lining of the respiratory tract
19. Involuntary sudden contraction of the diaphragm along with the closing of the vocal cords, producing a "hiccup" sound
20. An electrocardiogram, which is a record of the electrical impulses that trigger the heartbeat; used to diagnose heart disorders
21. The area of the retina that allows fine details to be observed at the center of vision
22. A pus- filled abscess in the follicle of an eyelash

DOWN

2. The medical term for the kneecap
4. Yellowing of the skin and whites of the eyes because of the presence of excess bilirubin in the blood; usually a sign of a disorder of the liver
8. The failure either to produce or to ejaculate sperm
9. The period during which sexual development occurs
13. An orange pigment present in colored plants such as carrots that is converted by the body to the essential nutrient vitamin a
14. Infection and inflammation of a gland, especially a lymph node
15. The medical term for the death of tissue cells
17. The use of tension to hold a body part in place or to correct or prevent an alignment problem
18. Mucus and other material produced by the lining of the respiratory tract
19. Involuntary sudden contraction of the diaphragm along with the closing of the vocal cords, producing a "hiccup" sound
20. An electrocardiogram, which is a record of the electrical impulses that trigger the heartbeat; used to diagnose heart disorders
21. The area of the retina that allows fine details to be observed at the center of vision
22. A pus- filled abscess in the follicle of an eyelash

A. Arthritis
B. Rectum
C. Capillary
D. Sputum
E. Jaundice
F. Aspermia
G. Adenitis
H. Hiccup
I. Patella
J. Cyst
K. Carotene
L. Stye
M. Macula
N. Bacillus
O. ECG
P. Ligament
Q. Asthma
R. Puberty
S. Necrosis
T. Traction
U. Orthotic
V. Axilla
W. Virus

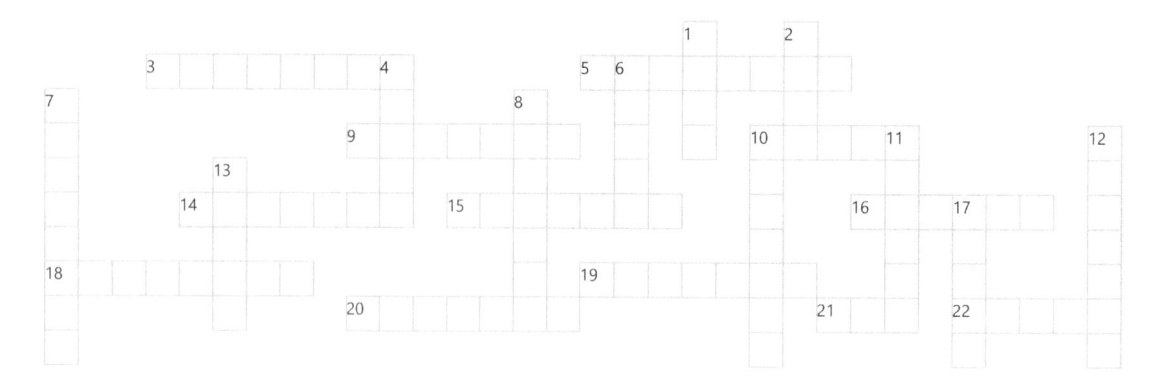

21. Using the Across and Down clues, write the correct words in the numbered grid below.

ACROSS

3. A hormone produced by the thyroid gland that helps regulate energy production in the body
5. The failure either to produce or to ejaculate sperm
9. The tube running from the larynx (the voice box) down the neck and into the upper part of the chest
10. The term used to refer to an unborn child from 8 weeks after fertilization to birth
14. Inflammation of the membrane that covers the white of the eyes and lines the eyelids
15. Difficulty breathing
16. The liquid part of the blood, containing substances such as nutrients, salts, and proteins
18. A nerve infection caused by the chickenpox virus, causing areas of painful rash covered with blisters
19. Anything that can increase the rate of abnormal change in cells, which can lead to cancer
20. The throat
21. Ribonucleic acid, which helps to decode and process the information contained in DNA
22. An exact copy of a gene, cell, or organism

DOWN

3. A hormone produced by the thyroid gland that helps regulate energy production in the body
5. The failure either to produce or to ejaculate sperm
9. The tube running from the larynx (the voice box) down the neck and into the upper part of the chest
10. The term used to refer to an unborn child from 8 weeks after fertilization to birth
14. Inflammation of the membrane that covers the white of the eyes and lines the eyelids
15. Difficulty breathing
16. The liquid part of the blood, containing substances such as nutrients, salts, and proteins
18. A nerve infection caused by the chickenpox virus, causing areas of painful rash covered with blisters
19. Anything that can increase the rate of abnormal change in cells, which can lead to cancer
20. The throat
21. Ribonucleic acid, which helps to decode and process the information contained in DNA
22. An exact copy of a gene, cell, or organism

A. Shingles   B. Trachea   C. Aspermia   D. Pharynx   E. RNA   F. Fibrosis
G. Fetus   H. Thyroxin   I. Shock   J. Nerve   K. Villi L. Gene
M. Sclera   N. Plasma   O. Forceps   P. Mutagen   Q. Sprue R. Scabies
S. Pinkeye   T. Bile   U. Version   V. Clone   W. Dyspnea

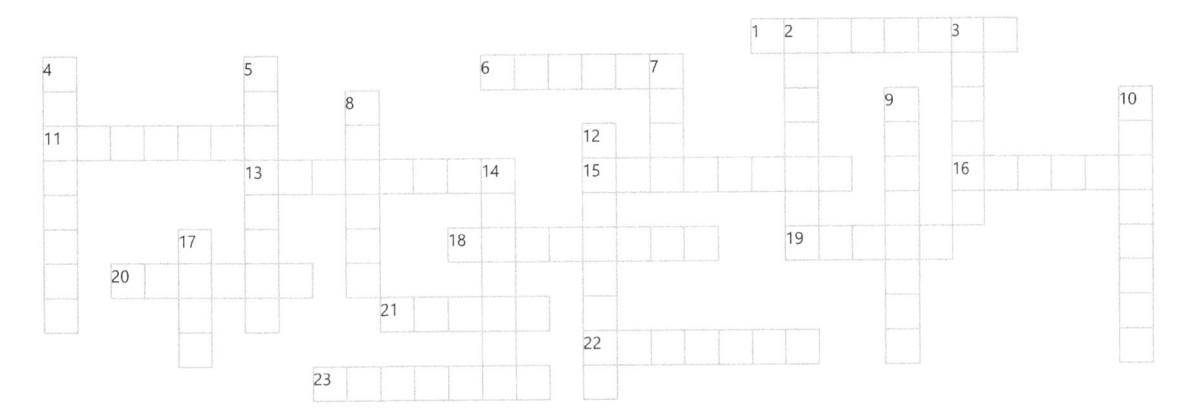

22. Using the Across and Down clues, write the correct words in the numbered grid below.

ACROSS

1. A long gland located behind the stomach that produces enzymes that help to break down food and hormones (insulin and glucagon) that help to regulate glucose levels in the blood
6. The hollow female reproductive organ in which a fertilized egg is implanted, and a fetus develops
11. Dull, aching pain in the lower back
13. A disease in which eye damage is caused by an increase in the pressure of the fluid within the eye
15. An abnormal swelling of the wall of an artery, caused by a weakening in the vessel wall
16. An element for the formation of thyroid hormones
18. The displacement of an organ from its normal position to a new one
19. A possibly life-threatening condition in which breathing stops, for either a short or long period of time
20. The drooping of the upper eyelid
21. A tunnel-like passage
22. The medical term for lockjaw
23. A sugar that is the main source of energy for the body

DOWN

1. A long gland located behind the stomach that produces enzymes that help to break down food and hormones (insulin and glucagon) that help to regulate glucose levels in the blood
6. The hollow female reproductive organ in which a fertilized egg is implanted, and a fetus develops
11. Dull, aching pain in the lower back
13. A disease in which eye damage is caused by an increase in the pressure of the fluid within the eye
15. An abnormal swelling of the wall of an artery, caused by a weakening in the vessel wall
16. An element for the formation of thyroid hormones
18. The displacement of an organ from its normal position to a new one
19. A possibly life-threatening condition in which breathing stops, for either a short or long period of time
20. The drooping of the upper eyelid
21. A tunnel-like passage
22. The medical term for lockjaw
23. A sugar that is the main source of energy for the body

A. Glaucoma
B. Pancreas
C. Progeria
D. Node
E. Overdose
F. Duodenum
G. Uterus
H. Aneurysm
I. Apnea
J. Silicone
K. Canal
L. Anemia
M. Airways
N. Trismus
O. Prolapse
P. Sputum
Q. Stye
R. Iodine
S. Ptosis
T. Lumbago
U. Parasite
V. Atresia
W. Glucose

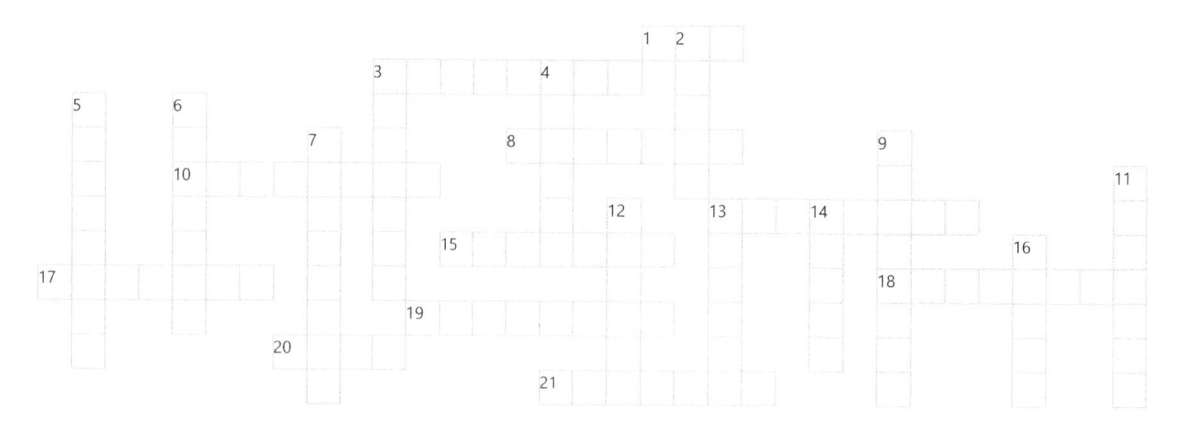

23. Using the Across and Down clues, write the correct words in the numbered grid below.

ACROSS

1. An involuntary, repetitive movement such as a twitch
3. A protein made by white blood cells that reacts with a specific foreign protein as part of the immune response
8. The sac containing the testicles
10. The failure either to produce or to ejaculate sperm
13. A long gland located behind the stomach that produces enzymes that help to break down food and hormones (insulin and glucagon) that help to regulate glucose levels in the blood
15. A substance that is a necessary part of a healthy diet (such as potassium, calcium, sodium, phosphorus, and magnesium)
17. Inflammation of the membrane that covers the white of the eyes and lines the eyelids
18. Another name for the sugar glucose
19. A disorder in which a person becomes overly suspicious and emotionally sensitive
20. A contagious, harmless growth caused by a virus that occurs on the skin or a mucous membrane
21. An accumulation of pus in a body tissue, usually caused by a bacterial infection

DOWN

1. An involuntary, repetitive movement such as a twitch
3. A protein made by white blood cells that reacts with a specific foreign protein as part of the immune response
8. The sac containing the testicles
10. The failure either to produce or to ejaculate sperm
13. A long gland located behind the stomach that produces enzymes that help to break down food and hormones (insulin and glucagon) that help to regulate glucose levels in the blood
15. A substance that is a necessary part of a healthy diet (such as potassium, calcium, sodium, phosphorus, and magnesium)
17. Inflammation of the membrane that covers the white of the eyes and lines the eyelids
18. Another name for the sugar glucose
19. A disorder in which a person becomes overly suspicious and emotionally sensitive
20. A contagious, harmless growth caused by a virus that occurs on the skin or a mucous membrane
21. An accumulation of pus in a body tissue, usually caused by a bacterial infection

A. Cilia	B. Paranoia	C. Pinkeye	D. Angioma
E. Pelvis	F. Radius	G. Familial	H. Ovaries
I. Pancreas	J. Graft	K. Oocyte	L. Proximal
M. Mineral	N. Aspermia	O. Overdose	P. Antibody
Q. Abscess	R. Scrotum	S. Tic	T. Wart
U. Pyrexia	V. Dextrose	W. Ilium	

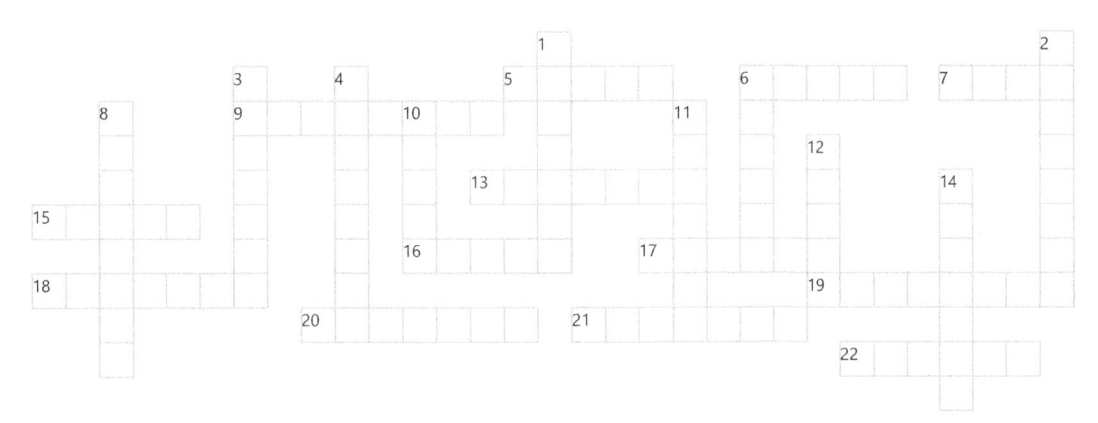

24. Using the Across and Down clues, write the correct words in the numbered grid below.

ACROSS

5. Abnormal crackling or bubbling sounds heard in the lungs during breathing
6. The bone located between the hip and the knee
7. A yellow-green liquid produced in the liver whose function is to remove waste from the liver and break down fats as food is digested
9. An excessively large dose of a drug, which can lead to coma and death
13. The complete or partial failure of any organ or tissue to grow
15. A tunnel-like passage
16. Abnormal buildup of fluid in the body, which may cause visible swelling
17. The infection of a wound or tissue with bacteria, causing the spread of the bacteria into the bloodstream
18. A small blister containing pus
19. The medical term for wetting the bed
20. An organ located in the pelvis whose function is to collect and store urine until it is expelled
21. The process by which most cells divide to reproduce
22. A membrane lining the inside of the back of the eye that contains light-sensitive nerve cells that convert focused light into nerve impulses, making vision possible

DOWN

5. Abnormal crackling or bubbling sounds heard in the lungs during breathing
6. The bone located between the hip and the knee
7. A yellow-green liquid produced in the liver whose function is to remove waste from the liver and break down fats as food is digested
9. An excessively large dose of a drug, which can lead to coma and death
13. The complete or partial failure of any organ or tissue to grow
15. A tunnel-like passage
16. Abnormal buildup of fluid in the body, which may cause visible swelling
17. The infection of a wound or tissue with bacteria, causing the spread of the bacteria into the bloodstream
18. A small blister containing pus
19. The medical term for wetting the bed
20. An organ located in the pelvis whose function is to collect and store urine until it is expelled
21. The process by which most cells divide to reproduce
22. A membrane lining the inside of the back of the eye that contains light-sensitive nerve cells that convert focused light into nerve impulses, making vision possible

A. Ozone	B. Sepsis	C. Aplasia	D. Pulse
E. Meninges	F. Proximal	G. Fungus	H. Maxilla
I. Bile	J. Bladder	K. Rales	L. Femur
M. Pyrexia	N. Cyanosis	O. Placebo	P. Pustule
Q. Retina	R. Hospice	S. Overdose	T. Edema
U. Mitosis	V. Canal	W. Enuresis	

25. Using the Across and Down clues, write the correct words in the numbered grid below.

ACROSS

3. A raised, firm, thick scar that forms because of a defect in the natural healing process
5. A tear or break in an organ or tissue
8. A painful, persistent erection without sexual arousal, requiring emergency treatment
14. The triangular bone located at the bottom of the spine that is connected to the tailbone
17. The presence of bacterial toxins in the blood
18. Another term for a tumor
19. A chemically inactive substance given in place of a drug to test how much of a drug's effectiveness can be attributed to a patient's expectations that the drug will have a positive effect
20. Inflammation of the heart
21. An orange pigment present in colored plants such as carrots that is converted by the body to the essential nutrient vitamin a
22. Medical term for the armpit

DOWN

3. A raised, firm, thick scar that forms because of a defect in the natural healing process
5. A tear or break in an organ or tissue
8. A painful, persistent erection without sexual arousal, requiring emergency treatment
14. The triangular bone located at the bottom of the spine that is connected to the tailbone
17. The presence of bacterial toxins in the blood
18. Another term for a tumor
19. A chemically inactive substance given in place of a drug to test how much of a drug's effectiveness can be attributed to a patient's expectations that the drug will have a positive effect
20. Inflammation of the heart
21. An orange pigment present in colored plants such as carrots that is converted by the body to the essential nutrient vitamin a
22. Medical term for the armpit

A. Neoplasm B. Cecum C. Carditis D. Trauma E. Pleurisy F. Pandemic
G. Macula H. Rupture I. Stye J. Priapism K. Insulin L. Estrogen
M. Smallpox N. Toxemia O. Sacrum P. Croup Q. Placebo R. Trisomy
S. Carotene T. Paranoia U. Axilla V. Iris W. Keloid

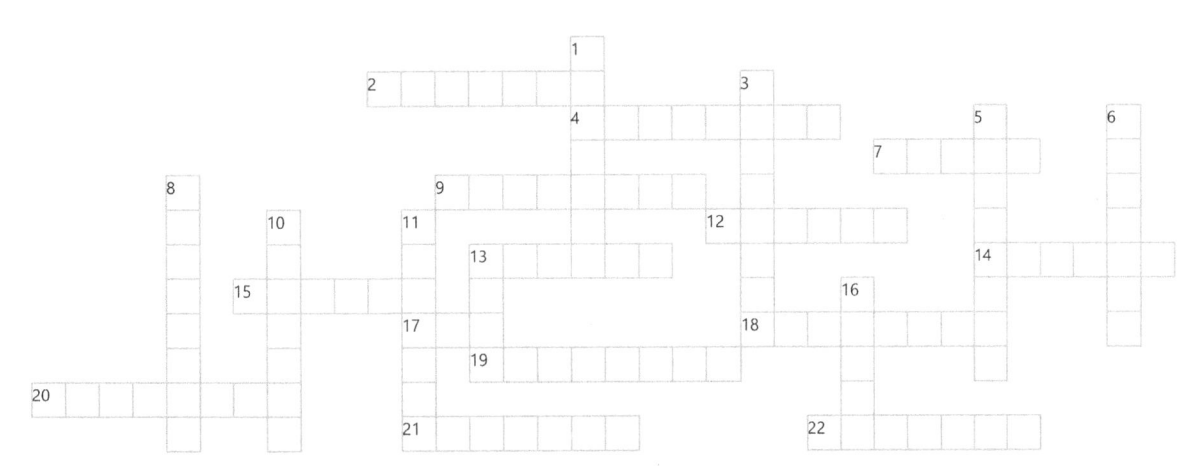

26. Using the Across and Down clues, write the correct words in the numbered grid below.

ACROSS

2. A chemical produced by a gland or tissue that is released into the bloodstream
4. A sexually transmitted disease
7. A possibly life-threatening condition in which breathing stops, for either a short or long period of time
9. A person who specializes in the making and adjustment of eyeglasses and contact lenses
12. The medical term for the voice box, the organ in the throat that produces voice and prevents food from entering the airway
13. Not obstructed; open
14. An infectious viral disease primarily affecting animals
15. A serious infectious disease transmitted to humans through bites of rodent fleas
17. An involuntary, repetitive movement such as a twitch
18. Inflammation of a nerve, often characterized by pain, numbness, or tingling
19. An abnormal swelling of the wall of an artery, caused by a weakening in the vessel wall
20. Inflammation of the breast, which is usually caused by a bacterial infection
21. The structure of bodies
22. The medical term for an earache

DOWN

2. A chemical produced by a gland or tissue that is released into the bloodstream
4. A sexually transmitted disease
7. A possibly life-threatening condition in which breathing stops, for either a short or long period of time
9. A person who specializes in the making and adjustment of eyeglasses and contact lenses
12. The medical term for the voice box, the organ in the throat that produces voice and prevents food from entering the airway
13. Not obstructed; open
14. An infectious viral disease primarily affecting animals
15. A serious infectious disease transmitted to humans through bites of rodent fleas
17. An involuntary, repetitive movement such as a twitch
18. Inflammation of a nerve, often characterized by pain, numbness, or tingling
19. An abnormal swelling of the wall of an artery, caused by a weakening in the vessel wall
20. Inflammation of the breast, which is usually caused by a bacterial infection
21. The structure of bodies
22. The medical term for an earache

A. Urethra
B. Anatomy
C. Neuritis
D. Tic
E. Aneurysm
F. Rabies
G. Hormone
H. Glucagon
I. Patent
J. Mastitis
K. Larynx
L. Plague
M. Syphilis
N. Lazy eye
O. Osteitis
P. Otalgia
Q. Apnea
R. Vesicle
S. Relapse
T. Dextrose
U. Pica
V. Optician
W. Orbit

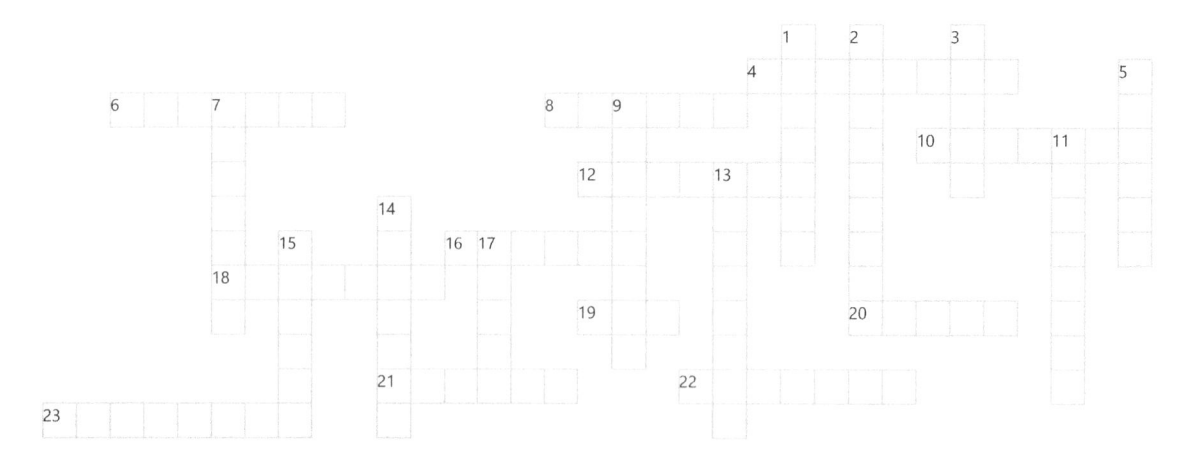

27. Using the Across and Down clues, write the correct words in the numbered grid below.

ACROSS

4. Any substance capable of causing a disease
6. Inflammation of the large intestine (the colon), which usually leads to abdominal pain, fever, and diarrhea with blood and mucus
8. An element for the formation of thyroid hormones
10. A childhood disease in which bones lack calcium and are deformed because of vitamin d deficiency
12. A chemical produced by a gland or tissue that is released into the bloodstream
16. An area of buildup of fat deposits in an artery, causing narrowing of the artery and possibly heart disease
18. A term used to describe a newborn infant from birth to 1 month of age
19. A thick, yellowish or greenish fluid that contains dead white blood cells, tissues, and bacteria; occurs at the site of a bacterial infection
20. Describes a condition or illness that begins suddenly and is usually short- lasting
21. The triangular bone located at the bottom of the spine that is connected to the tailbone
22. The process by which most cells divide to reproduce
23. A tiny pouchlike cavity in a structure of the body, such as a hair follicle

DOWN

4. Any substance capable of causing a disease
6. Inflammation of the large intestine (the colon), which usually leads to abdominal pain, fever, and diarrhea with blood and mucus
8. An element for the formation of thyroid hormones
10. A childhood disease in which bones lack calcium and are deformed because of vitamin d deficiency
12. A chemical produced by a gland or tissue that is released into the bloodstream
16. An area of buildup of fat deposits in an artery, causing narrowing of the artery and possibly heart disease
18. A term used to describe a newborn infant from birth to 1 month of age
19. A thick, yellowish or greenish fluid that contains dead white blood cells, tissues, and bacteria; occurs at the site of a bacterial infection
20. Describes a condition or illness that begins suddenly and is usually short- lasting
21. The triangular bone located at the bottom of the spine that is connected to the tailbone
22. The process by which most cells divide to reproduce
23. A tiny pouchlike cavity in a structure of the body, such as a hair follicle

A. Labor
B. Oocyte
C. Pathogen
D. Pus
E. Iodine
F. Duodenum
G. Mitosis
H. In situ
I. Chlamydia
J. Embolism
K. Implant
L. Colitis
M. Osteitis
N. Follicle
O. Sacrum
P. Rickets
Q. Walleye
R. Neonate
S. Acute
T. Autopsy
U. Hormone
V. Renin
W. Plaque

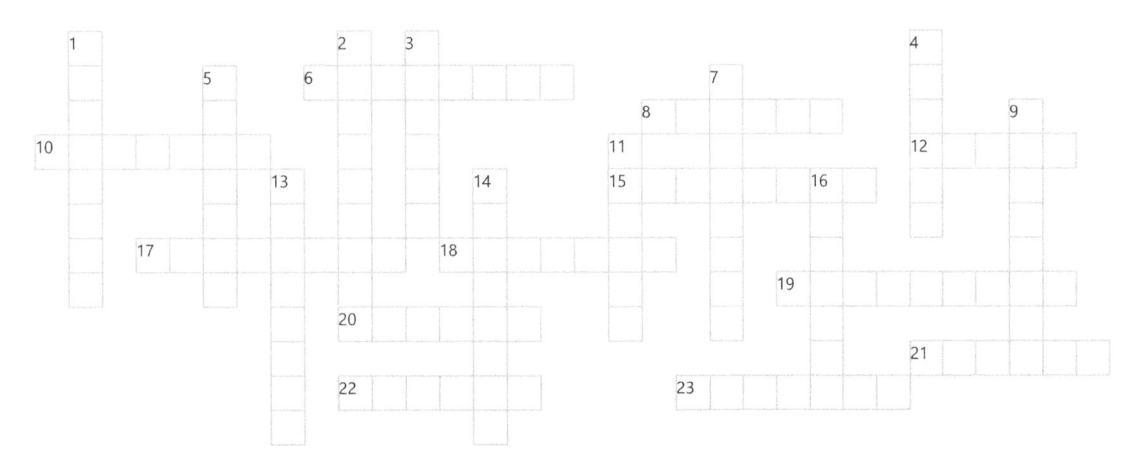

28. Using the Across and Down clues, write the correct words in the numbered grid below.

ACROSS

6. Inflammation of a testicle, which can be caused by infection with the mumps virus
8. The roof of the mouth
10. The complete or partial failure of any organ or tissue to grow
12. A possibly life-threatening condition in which breathing stops, for either a short or long period of time
15. A long gland located behind the stomach that produces enzymes that help to break down food and hormones (insulin and glucagon) that help to regulate glucose levels in the blood
17. Organisms that lives on or in other organisms, from which it obtains nutrients
18. A skin disorder that is characterized by patches of red skin on the nose and cheeks and acne- like bumps
19. Any area of discolored skin that is present when a baby is born
20. The tearing or stretching of the ligaments in a joint, characterized by pain, swelling, and an inability to move the joint
21. Abnormally high levels of waste products such as urea in the blood
22. The chest
23. Any disease caused by a fungus

DOWN

6. Inflammation of a testicle, which can be caused by infection with the mumps virus
8. The roof of the mouth
10. The complete or partial failure of any organ or tissue to grow
12. A possibly life-threatening condition in which breathing stops, for either a short or long period of time
15. A long gland located behind the stomach that produces enzymes that help to break down food and hormones (insulin and glucagon) that help to regulate glucose levels in the blood
17. Organisms that lives on or in other organisms, from which it obtains nutrients
18. A skin disorder that is characterized by patches of red skin on the nose and cheeks and acne- like bumps
19. Any area of discolored skin that is present when a baby is born
20. The tearing or stretching of the ligaments in a joint, characterized by pain, swelling, and an inability to move the joint
21. Abnormally high levels of waste products such as urea in the blood
22. The chest
23. Any disease caused by a fungus

A. Birthmark	B. Mycosis	C. Parasite	D. Arthritis	E. Glycogen	F. Seizure
G. Gavage	H. Rosacea	I. Apnea	J. Aplasia	K. Sprain	L. Cerebrum
M. Insomnia	N. Spleen	O. Palate	P. Uremia	Q. Proximal	R. Orchitis
S. Thorax	T. Neoplasm	U. Pancreas	V. Thrush	W. Ascites	

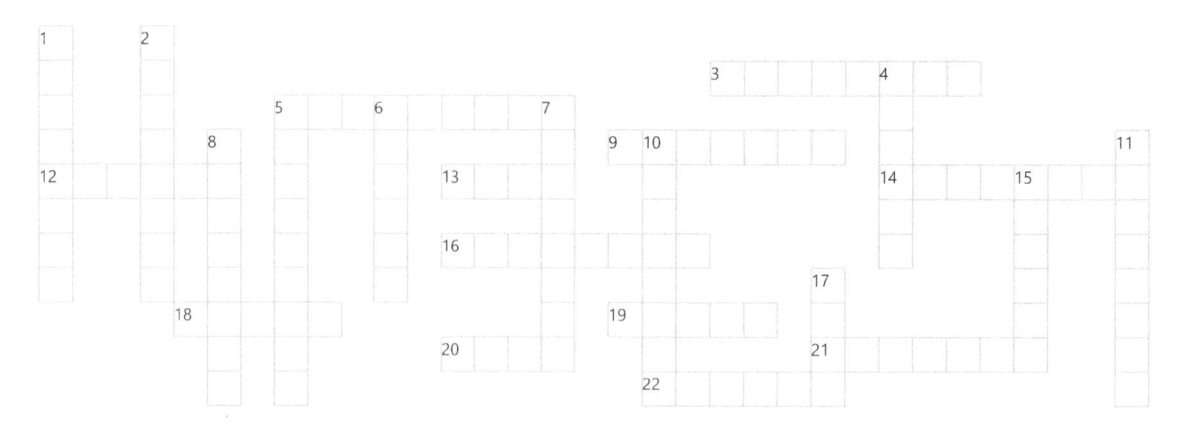

29. Using the Across and Down clues, write the correct words in the numbered grid below.

ACROSS

3. An abnormal growth of bone out of another bone, often located on the heel and usually painful
5. A tiny, single-celled microorganism, commonly known as a germ
9. A preparation of weakened microorganisms given to create resistance to a certain disease
12. Describes something related to the eyes
13. A lump filled with either fluid or soft material, occurring in any organ or tissue
14. Pain along the sciatic nerve, which runs down the length of the leg to the foot
16. Urination or a sleep-disturbing need to urinate during the night
18. A sample of cells spread across a glass slide to be examined through a microscope
19. The thicker of the two long bones in the lower leg
20. A mineral necessary for the formation of important biological substances such as hemoglobin, myoglobin, and certain enzymes
21. Inflammation of the large intestine (the colon), which usually leads to abdominal pain, fever, and diarrhea with blood and mucus
22. A noncancerous tumor made of mucous material and fibrous connective tissue

DOWN

3. An abnormal growth of bone out of another bone, often located on the heel and usually painful
5. A tiny, single-celled microorganism, commonly known as a germ
9. A preparation of weakened microorganisms given to create resistance to a certain disease
12. Describes something related to the eyes
13. A lump filled with either fluid or soft material, occurring in any organ or tissue
14. Pain along the sciatic nerve, which runs down the length of the leg to the foot
16. Urination or a sleep-disturbing need to urinate during the night
18. A sample of cells spread across a glass slide to be examined through a microscope
19. The thicker of the two long bones in the lower leg
20. A mineral necessary for the formation of important biological substances such as hemoglobin, myoglobin, and certain enzymes
21. Inflammation of the large intestine (the colon), which usually leads to abdominal pain, fever, and diarrhea with blood and mucus
22. A noncancerous tumor made of mucous material and fibrous connective tissue

A. Albinism	B. Vaccine	C. Ptosis	D. Typhus	E. Ocular	F. Iron
G. Smallpox	H. Myxoma	I. Steroids	J. Colitis	K. Nocturia	L. Thorax
M. Narcotic	N. Birthmark	O. Smear	P. Pica	Q. Proximal	R. Sciatica
S. Bacterium	T. Mutation	U. Cyst	V. Tibia	W. Bone spur	

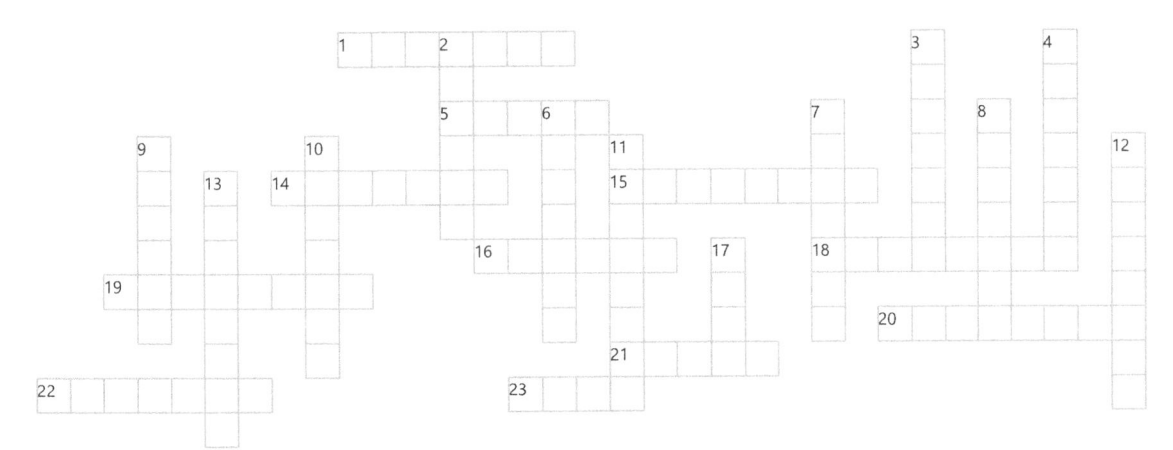

30. Using the Across and Down clues, write the correct words in the numbered grid below.

ACROSS

1. A chemically inactive substance given in place of a drug to test how much of a drug's effectiveness can be attributed to a patient's expectations that the drug will have a positive effect
5. Waves of pain in the abdomen that increase in strength, disappear, and return
14. Inflammation of the membrane that covers the white of the eyes and lines the eyelids
15. A hormone (such as testosterone) that causes development of male characteristics and sex organs
16. Not obstructed; open
18. A cancerous tumor of the liver
19. The external genitals, usually referring to the female
20. Complex substances that are necessary in small amounts to maintain health and ensure proper development and functioning of the body
21. A tunnel-like passage
22. The process of passage of the solvent portion of a lesser-concentrated solution through a semipermeable membrane into a higher-concentrated solution until the two solutions are equal in concentration
23. The basic unit of DNA, which is responsible for passing genetic information

DOWN

2. Four fused bones that form a triangular shape at the base of the spine (also known as the tailbone)
3. A noncancerous tumor of connective tissue
4. A noncancerous bone tumor
6. "in glass"; a biological test or process that is carried out in a laboratory
7. The tube by which urine is released from the bladder
8. A noncancerous tumor occurring in nerve tissue
9. The triangular bone located at the bottom of the spine that is connected to the tailbone
10. An abnormal passageway from one organ to another or from an organ to the body surface
11. Yellowing of the skin and whites of the eyes because of the presence of excess bilirubin in the blood; usually a sign of a disorder of the liver
12. A procedure to treat kidney failure in which artificial means are used to filter waste, maintain acid-base balance, and remove excess fluid from the body
13. A short, tube-like structure that branches off the large intestine
17. A "warning" signal that comes before a migraine headache or an epileptic seizure, which might include emotions or sensations of movement or discomfort

A. Hepatoma
B. Colic
C. Fistula
D. Osmosis
E. Appendix
F. Sacrum
G. Fibroma
H. Pinkeye
I. Dialysis
J. Coccyx
K. Patent
L. Osteoma
M. Neuroma
N. Androgen
O. Canal
P. Aura
Q. Jaundice
R. Vitamins
S. Urethra
T. Gene
U. Placebo
V. In vitro
W. Pudendum

31. Using the Across and Down clues, write the correct words in the numbered grid below.

ACROSS

1. A small, round organ making up the neck of the uterus and separating it from the vagina
3. A blood clot in a blood vessel
5. A plentiful mineral in the body and the basic component of teeth and bones
7. Infection and inflammation of a gland, especially a lymph node
13. An organ formed in the uterus during pregnancy that links the blood of the mother to the blood of the fetus
14. The expansion and contraction of a blood vessel due to the blood pumped through it
15. The return of a disease or symptom after it had disappeared
17. Deoxyribonucleic acid; responsible for passing genetic information in nearly all organisms
18. A bacterial infection of the small intestine that causes severe watery diarrhea, dehydration, and possibly death
19. The examination of a body following death, possibly to determine the cause of death or for research
20. The bones that form the framework of the head and enclose and protect the brain and other sensory organs
21. The failure either to produce or to ejaculate sperm

DOWN

2. A bronchodilator drug that is used to treat asthma
4. Sudden uncontrolled waves of electrical activity in the brain, causing involuntary movement or loss of consciousness
5. A coiled organ in the inner ear that plays a large role in hearing by picking up sound vibrations and transmitting them as electrical signals
6. A discharge from an inflamed ear
8. The first part of the small intestine, immediately following the stomach
9. A painful, persistent erection without sexual arousal, requiring emergency treatment
10. The medical term for the kneecap
11. A yellow-green liquid produced in the liver whose function is to remove waste from the liver and break down fats as food is digested
12. The loose skin that covers the head of the penis
14. Loss of sensation or ability to move
16. A surgical stitch that helps close an incision or wound so that it can heal properly

A. Aspermia
B. Skull
C. Cochlea
D. Relapse
E. Calcium
F. Palsy
G. Seizure
H. Bile
I. Autopsy
J. Placenta
K. DNA
L. Thrombus
M. Patella
N. Cholera
O. Pulse
P. Foreskin
Q. Suture
R. Priapism
S. Xanthine
T. Cervix
U. Otorrhea
V. Adenitis
W. Duodenum

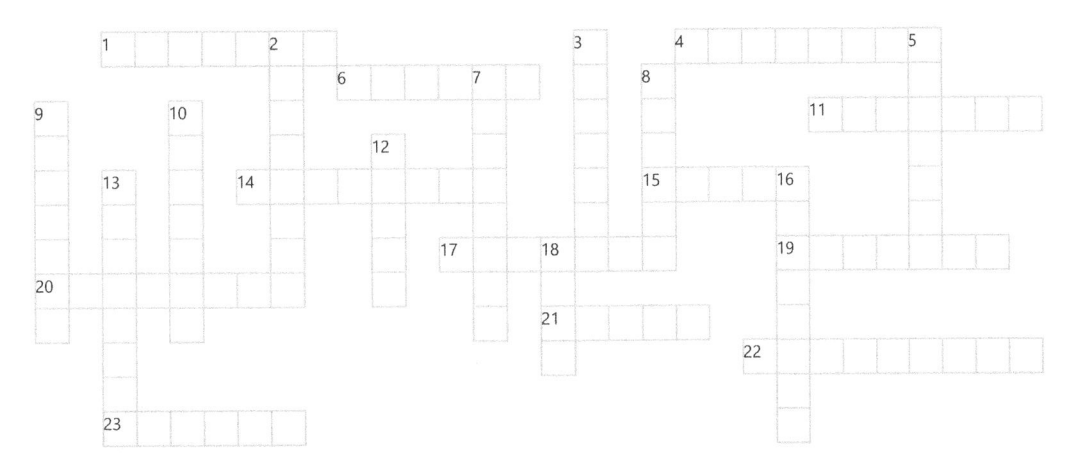

32. Using the Across and Down clues, write the correct words in the numbered grid below.

ACROSS

1. Another term for a microorganism, especially one that causes disease
4. A device used to correct or control deformed bones, muscles, or joints
6. Describes something related to the eyes
11. A tough protein found in skin, nails, and hair
14. A mineral that helps protect teeth against decay
15. The clear, watery fluid that separates from clotted blood
17. Instruments resembling tweezers that are used to handle objects or tissue during surgery
19. The center or most important point of an object
20. Infection and inflammation of a gland, especially a lymph node
21. The bones that form the framework of the head and enclose and protect the brain and other sensory organs
22. Any area of discolored skin that is present when a baby is born
23. Damage to part of the brain because of a lack of blood supply or the rupturing of a blood vessel

DOWN

2. Any bacteria that is rod-shaped
3. The common name for the visual defect resulting from untreated strabismus, in which the eyes are not correctly aligned
5. A painless sore that has a thick, rubbery base and a defined edge
7. Fatty deposits on the inner walls of blood vessels, which can cause narrowing and decrease blood flow
8. The drooping of the upper eyelid
9. A spasm of the jaw muscles that prevents the mouth from opening, such as that caused by tetanus
10. The type of cell division that occurs only in the ovaries and testicles, producing cells with half the genes of the original cell
12. Healthy tissue that is used to replace diseased or defective tissue
13. Inflammation of bone
16. An oral contraceptive containing only the synthetic hormone progesterone (birth control pills contain estrogen and progesterone)
18. A lump filled with either fluid or soft material, occurring in any organ or tissue

A. Skull
B. Minipill
C. Nucleus
D. Ptosis
E. Cyst
F. Stroke
G. Serum
H. Bacillus
I. Meiosis
J. Chancre
K. Adenitis
L. Fluoride
M. Keratin
N. Lockjaw
O. Osteitis
P. Graft
Q. Lazy eye
R. Ocular
S. Orthotic
T. Birthmark
U. Forceps
V. Microbe
W. Atheroma

33. Using the Across and Down clues, write the correct words in the numbered grid below.

ACROSS

1. A tumor composed of cells not normally found in the part of the body when the tumor occurred
8. The complete set of an organism's genes
9. The smallest known disease-causing microorganism
15. Pain along the sciatic nerve, which runs down the length of the leg to the foot
16. Inflammation of the mucous membrane lining the nose
17. Measures taken to reduce the risk of acquiring a sexually transmitted disease, such as the use of a condom
18. A drug that relieves pain, such as aspirin or acetaminophen
19. A "warning" signal that comes before a migraine headache or an epileptic seizure, which might include emotions or sensations of movement or discomfort
20. A mineral that helps protect teeth against decay
21. A long gland located behind the stomach that produces enzymes that help to break down food and hormones (insulin and glucagon) that help to regulate glucose levels in the blood
22. The basic unit of DNA, which is responsible for passing genetic information

DOWN

1. A tumor of the thymus gland
2. An organ formed in the uterus during pregnancy that links the blood of the mother to the blood of the fetus
3. A severe headache, usually accompanied by vision problems and
4. A tiny pouchlike cavity in a structure of the body, such as a hair follicle
5. A candidiasis infection
6. Infestation by a small, round, blood-sucking parasite
7. Another term for a nerve cell
10. The external genitals, usually referring to the female
11. An abnormal passageway from one organ to another or from an organ to the body surface
12. A nerve infection caused by the chickenpox virus, causing areas of painful rash covered with blisters
13. A protein made by white blood cells that reacts with a specific foreign protein as part of the immune response
14. A condition in which patches of skin on the body lose their color

A. Shingles
B. Fluoride
C. Virus
D. Antibody
E. Sciatica
F. Fistula
G. Aura
H. Rhinitis
I. Hookworm
J. Placenta
K. Gene
L. Follicle
M. Vitiligo
N. Analgesic
O. Pancreas
P. Pudendum
Q. Genome
R. Neuron
S. Thymoma
T. Safe sex
U. Migraine
V. Teratoma
W. Thrush

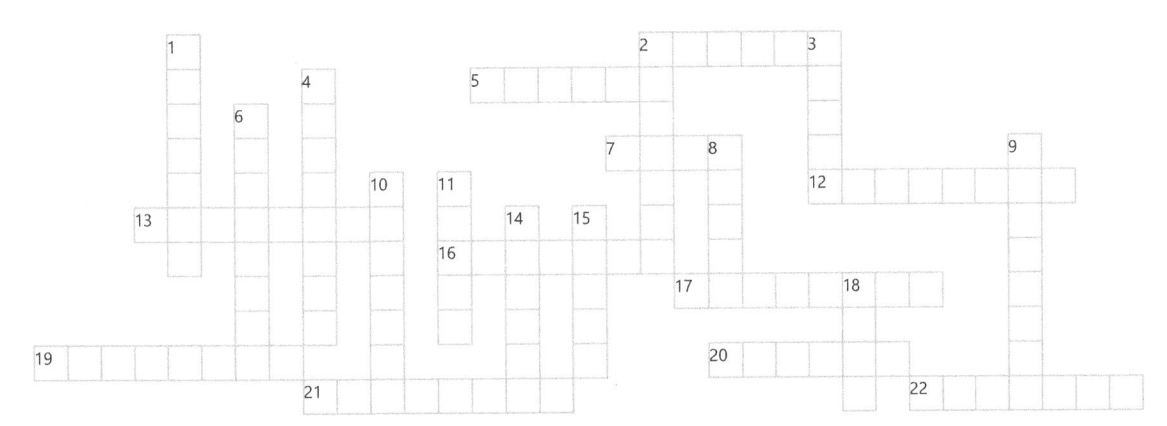

34. Using the Across and Down clues, write the correct words in the numbered grid below.

ACROSS

2. The infection of a wound or tissue with bacteria, causing the spread of the bacteria into the bloodstream
5. A condition in which the blood does not contain enough hemoglobin, the compound that carries oxygen from the lungs to other parts of the body
7. The tiny structures that make up all the tissues of the body and carry out all its functions
12. The beginning of menstruation
13. A type of testicular cancer that is made up of only a single type of cell
16. The throat
17. Any substance capable of causing a disease
19. A sudden attack or worsening of a disease's symptoms
20. A thickened area of skin due to consistent pressure or friction, or the area around a bone break where new bone is formed
21. An excessively large dose of a drug, which can lead to coma and death
22. An illness caused by a viral infection, causing a characteristic rash and a fever

DOWN

1. Any substance that causes a fever
2. Measures taken to reduce the risk of acquiring a sexually transmitted disease, such as the use of a condom
3. The oily, lubricating substance that is secreted by glands in the skin
4. The main form that glucose, the body's energy source, takes when it is stored
6. Any bacteria that is rod- shaped
8. The two pairs of skinfolds that protect the opening of the vagina
9. Tightness of the foreskin, which prevents it from being moved back over the head of the penis
10. A condition in which one eye turns outward
11. The opening at the center of the iris in the eye that constricts (contracts) and dilates (widens) in response to light
14. One of the two long bones of the forearm located on the thumb side of the arm
15. A thin fold of membrane partly closing the opening of the vagina
18. A disorder marked by high levels of uric acid in the blood

A. Sepsis
B. Pupil
C. Paroxysm
D. Callus
E. Bacillus
F. Seminoma
G. Pathogen
H. Anemia
I. Pharynx
J. Pyrogen
K. Overdose
L. Measles
M. Menarche
N. Safe sex
O. Phimosis
P. Walleye
Q. Sebum
R. Glycogen
S. Gout
T. Cell
U. Labia
V. Hymen
W. Radius

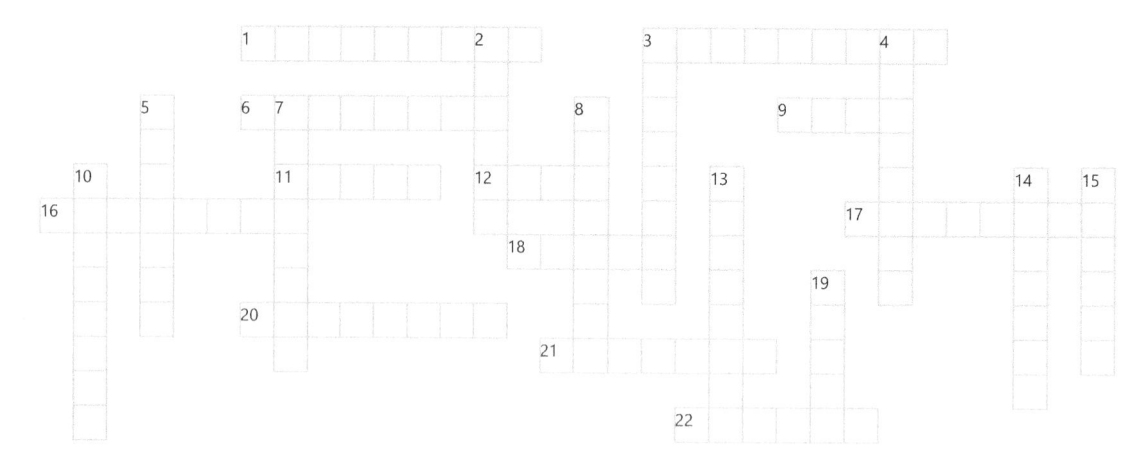

35. Using the Across and Down clues, write the correct words in the numbered grid below.

ACROSS

1. A cancer that occurs on the surface or lining of an organ
3. Dependence on a substance (such as alcohol or other drugs) or an activity, to the point that stopping is very difficult and causes severe physical and mental reactions
6. A highly contagious skin infection caused by bacteria, usually occurring around the nose and mouth
9. A brown to dark-brown spot on the skin that can be flat or raised
11. A milky fluid containing white blood cells, proteins, and fats
12. A mineral necessary for the formation of important biological substances such as hemoglobin, myoglobin, and certain enzymes
16. A bronchodilator drug that is used to treat asthma
17. The excessive production of urine
18. A structure that allows fluid flow in only one direction
20. A small female organ located near the opening of the vagina that swells when sexually aroused
21. A hormone made in the pancreas that plays an important role in the absorption of glucose (the body's main source of energy) into muscle cells
22. A term used to describe something situated on or near the midline of the body or a body structure

DOWN

2. The medical term for nearsightedness
3. A hormone (such as testosterone) that causes development of male characteristics and sex organs
4. An excessively large dose of a drug, which can lead to coma and death
5. A tear or break in an organ or tissue
7. The smallest unit of a substance that possesses its characteristics
8. A fluid-filled cyst attached to a tendon sheath or joint
10. A parasitic worm that lives in the intestines
13. A mineral that helps protect teeth against decay
14. A disease that began in the affected location
15. The medical term for the voice box, the organ in the throat that produces voice and prevents food from entering the airway
19. The outer, visible portion of the female genitals

A. Xanthine	B. Addiction	C. Valve
F. Lymph	G. Insulin	H. Iron
K. Polyuria	L. Myopia	M. Molecule
P. Ganglion	Q. Carcinoma	R. Mole
U. Vulva	V. Primary	W. Tapeworm
D. Androgen	E. Larynx
I. Impetigo	J. Rupture
N. Overdose	O. Fluoride
S. Medial	T. Clitoris

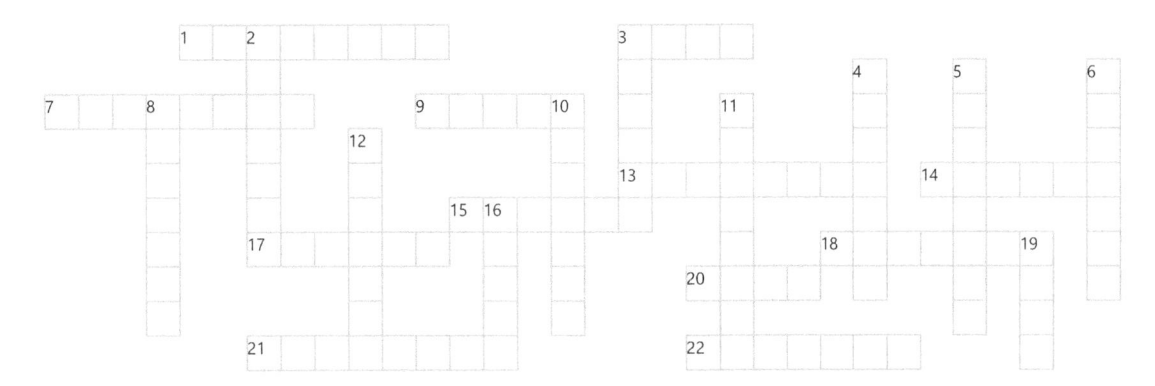

36. Using the Across and Down clues, write the correct words in the numbered grid below.

ACROSS

1. Inflammation of a nerve, often characterized by pain, numbness, or tingling
3. The colored part of the eye
7. The three membranes that surround and protect the spinal cord and brain
9. A fluid-filled sac that cushions and reduces friction in certain parts of the body
13. A group of drugs that widen blood vessels
14. The drooping of the upper eyelid
15. The roof of the mouth
17. An organ located in the upper left abdomen behind the ribs that removes and destroys old red blood cells and helps fight infection
18. A noncancerous tumor occurring in nerve tissue
20. A thickened callus on the foot that is caused by an improperly fitting shoe
21. A chemical that transmits messages in the brain and plays a role in movement
22. A condition in which one eye turns outward

DOWN

2. Inflammation of the uvea
3. An element for the formation of thyroid hormones
4. An additional dose of a vaccine taken after the first dose to maintain or renew the first one
5. Another name for the sugar glucose
6. The presence in the cells of three copies of a certain chromosome instead of the normal two copies
8. The technique of creating pictures of structures inside of the body using x-rays, ultrasound waves, or magnetic fields
10. The complete or partial failure of any organ or tissue to grow
11. A tumor composed of cells not normally found in the part of the body when the tumor occurred
12. The medical term for the kneecap
16. Describes a condition or illness that begins suddenly and is usually short-lasting
19. A skin condition characterized by inflamed, pus-filled areas that occur on the skin's surface, most commonly occurring during adolescence

A. Ptosis	B. Iris	C. Bursa	D. Uveitis	E. Acne	F. Walleye
G. Palate	H. Acute	I. Imaging	J. Neuritis	K. Nitrates	L. Booster
M. Iodine	N. Dopamine	O. Spleen	P. Patella	Q. Neuroma	R. Dextrose
S. Trisomy	T. Meninges	U. Teratoma	V. Aplasia	W. Corn	

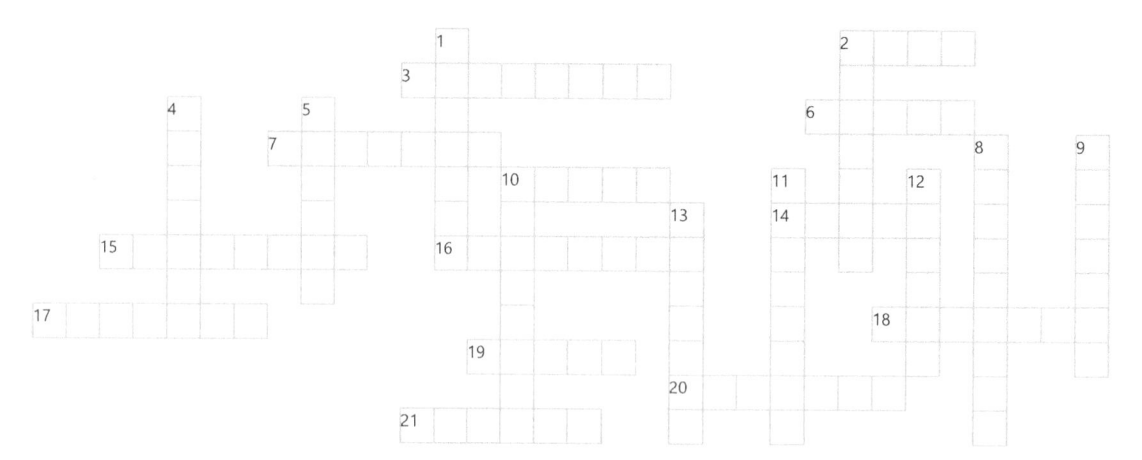

37. Using the Across and Down clues, write the correct words in the numbered grid below.

ACROSS

2. A form of phototherapy that combines the use of psoralens and ultraviolet light to treat skin disorders
3. Inflammation of the heart
6. A cavity within bone or a channel that contains blood
7. Describes a disease that is always present in a certain population of people
10. A viral infection that causes inflammation of salivary glands
14. A digestive disorder in which nutrients cannot be properly absorbed from food, causing weakness and loss of weight
15. Inflammation of the mucous membrane lining the nose
16. Baldness or loss of hair, mainly on the head, either in defined patches or completely
17. A disorder in which a person eats large amounts of food then forces vomiting or uses laxatives to prevent weight gain (called binging and purging)
18. A chemical produced by a gland or tissue that is released into the bloodstream
19. Another term for feces
20. "in glass"; a biological test or process that is carried out in a laboratory
21. The medical term for the voice box, the organ in the throat that produces voice and prevents food from entering the airway

DOWN

1. Another term for smallpox
2. A disease that began in the affected location
4. A plentiful mineral in the body and the basic component of teeth and bones
5. A condition in which the blood does not contain enough hemoglobin, the compound that carries oxygen from the lungs to other parts of the body
8. Any area of discolored skin that is present when a baby is born
9. Anything that can increase the rate of abnormal change in cells, which can lead to cancer
10. A muscle disease, usually one that results in the deterioration of muscle
11. The failure either to produce or to ejaculate sperm
12. Strong connective tissue cords that attach muscle to bone or muscle to muscle
13. A unit that is used to measure the energy content in food

A. Calorie
B. Alopecia
C. PUVA
D. Hormone
E. Bulimia
F. Endemic
G. Tendon
H. Mumps
I. Sinus
J. Carditis
K. Stool
L. Mutagen
M. Primary
N. Anemia
O. Sprue
P. Larynx
Q. Calcium
R. Myopathy
S. In vitro
T. Aspermia
U. Variola
V. Rhinitis
W. Birthmark

38. Using the Across and Down clues, write the correct words in the numbered grid below.

ACROSS
2. Abnormal formation of connective or scar tissue
4. The external male reproductive organ, which passes urine and semen out of the body
7. A parasitic disease spread by mosquitos that causes chills and fever
9. A thin, oval-shaped membrane that separates the inner ear from the outer ear and is responsible for transmitting sound waves
11. A high-pitched sound produced during breathing because of narrowing of the airways
14. Pertaining to blood vessels
16. An illness caused by a viral infection, causing a characteristic rash and a fever
17. A small lump of tissue that is usually abnormal
19. Urination or a sleep-disturbing need to urinate during the night
20. The loose skin that covers the head of the penis
21. A mineral that plays a role in the body's water balance, heart rhythm, nerve impulses, and muscle contraction
22. A structure in the brain that relays and processes incoming sensory information from the eyes and ears and from pressure and pain receptors

DOWN
1. A tiny, single-celled microorganism, commonly known as a germ
3. A discharge from an inflamed ear
4. Partial paralysis
5. A raised, firm, thick scar that forms because of a defect in the natural healing process
6. The expansion and contraction of a blood vessel due to the blood pumped through it
8. The two upper chambers of the heart
10. The thick, greasy substance that covers the skin of a newborn baby
12. A parasitic flatworm that can infest humans
13. A brain tumor arising from cells that support nerve cells
15. A device used to hold tissues in place, such as to support a skin graft
18. The two pairs of skinfolds that protect the opening of the vagina

A. Stent   B. Nodule   C. Eardrum   D. Vascular   E. Bacterium   F. Sodium
G. Foreskin H. Pulse   I. Vernix   J. Fibrosis   K. Keloid   L. Paresis
M. Thalamus N. Labia   O. Glioma   P. Atria   Q. Otorrhea   R. Penis
S. Malaria T. Fluke   U. Measles   V. Wheeze   W. Nocturia

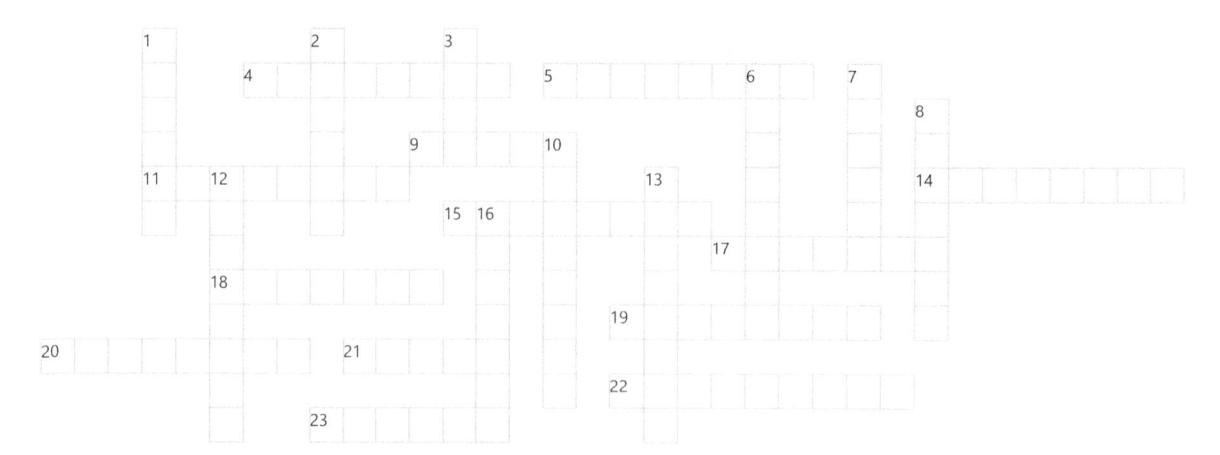

39. Using the Across and Down clues, write the correct words in the numbered grid below.

ACROSS

4. A hormone produced in the pituitary gland that causes contraction of the uterus during childbirth and stimulation of milk flow during breast-feeding.
5. An oral contraceptive containing only the synthetic hormone progesterone (birth control pills contain estrogen and progesterone)
9. A colorless, odorless, tasteless radioactive gas that is produced by materials in soil, rocks, and building materials; suspected of causing cancer
11. Determination of the amount of oxygen in the blood by measuring the amount of light transmitted through an area of skin
14. An element needed by the body only in very small amounts that helps maintain tissue elasticity
15. A hormone produced by the pancreas that converts stored carbohydrates (glycogen) into glucose, the body's energy source
17. A small skin blister, or any sac in the body, that contains fluid
18. The passageways that air moves through while traveling in and out of the lungs during breathing
19. A change in the genetic information within a cell
20. A person who specializes in the making and adjustment of eyeglasses and contact lenses
21. A parasitic flatworm that can infest humans
22. Any area of discolored skin that is present when a baby is born
23. The complete set of an organism's genes

DOWN

1. Another term for a nerve cell
2. The cell that results when an egg is fertilized by a sperm
3. A desire to eat materials that are not food
6. A tough, elastic band of tissue that connects bones and supports organs
7. A drug that causes the pupil to constrict
8. An accumulation of pus in a body tissue, usually caused by a bacterial infection
10. The medical term for the death of tissue cells
12. Describes something that spreads throughout body tissues, such as a tumor or microorganism
13. The excessive production of urine
16. The common name for the visual defect resulting from untreated strabismus, in which the eyes are not correctly aligned

A. Airways B. Oxytocin C. Ligament D. Genome E. Radon F. Vesicle
G. Birthmark H. Optician I. Lazy eye J. Polyuria K. Neuron L. Abscess
M. Necrosis N. Selenium O. Zygote P. Glucagon Q. Pica R. Mutation
S. Fluke T. Oximetry U. Minipill V. Invasive W. Miotic

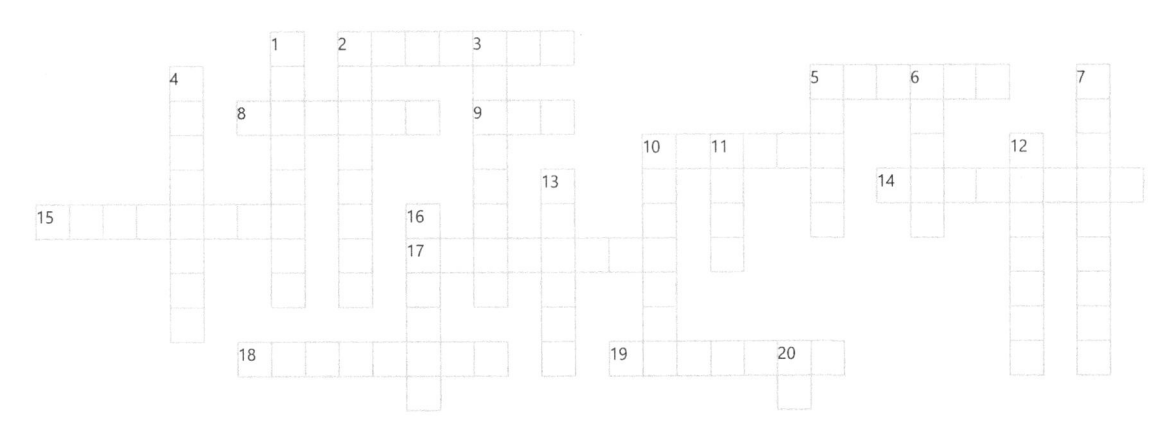

40. Using the Across and Down clues, write the correct words in the numbered grid below.

ACROSS

2. A condition in which one eye turns outward
5. Mucus and other material produced by the lining of the respiratory tract
8. A group of fats stored in the body and used for energy
9. An involuntary, repetitive movement such as a twitch
10. A serious infectious disease transmitted to humans through bites of rodent fleas
14. A group of bone marrow cancers in which white blood cells divide uncontrollably, affecting the production of normal white blood cells, red blood cells, and platelets
15. Inflammation of a testicle, which can be caused by infection with the mumps virus
17. Describes a treatment or procedure that is not urgent and can be arranged at the patient's convenience
18. Inflammation of the lining of the lungs and chest cavity usually caused by a lung infection
19. A reduced level of oxygen in tissues

DOWN

1. A condition marked by abnormally high acid levels in the blood, associated with some forms of diabetes, lung disease, and severe kidney disease
2. A small, parasitic worm that can live in the intestines of a human and may cause diarrhea, abdominal pain, and anemia
3. A group of hormones (produced mainly in the ovaries) that are necessary for female sexual development and reproductive functioning
4. The medical term for the collarbone
5. A device used to hold tissues in place, such as to support a skin graft
6. A group of common infections occurring on the skin, hair, and nails that are caused by a fungus
7. A graph showing a person's hearing ability, determined from a set of tests examining hearing acuity of different sound frequencies
10. The period during which sexual development occurs
11. A "warning" signal that comes before a migraine headache or an epileptic seizure, which might include emotions or sensations of movement or discomfort
12. A shift in the position of the fetus inside of the uterus, either occurring naturally or as performed by a doctor to facilitate delivery
13. A large blood vessel that carries blood from the heart to tissues and organs in the body
16. The infection of a wound or tissue with bacteria, causing the spread of the bacteria into the bloodstream
20. Intelligence quotient; a measure of a person's intelligence as determined by specific tests

A. Audiogram
B. Puberty
C. Sepsis
D. Leukemia
E. Hypoxia
F. Acidosis
G. Orchitis
H. Whipworm
I. Clavicle
J. Aura
K. Tic
L. Elective
M. Lipids
N. Version
O. Plague
P. Tinea
Q. Sputum
R. Pleurisy
S. Stent
T. Estrogen
U. Walleye
V. IQ
W. Artery

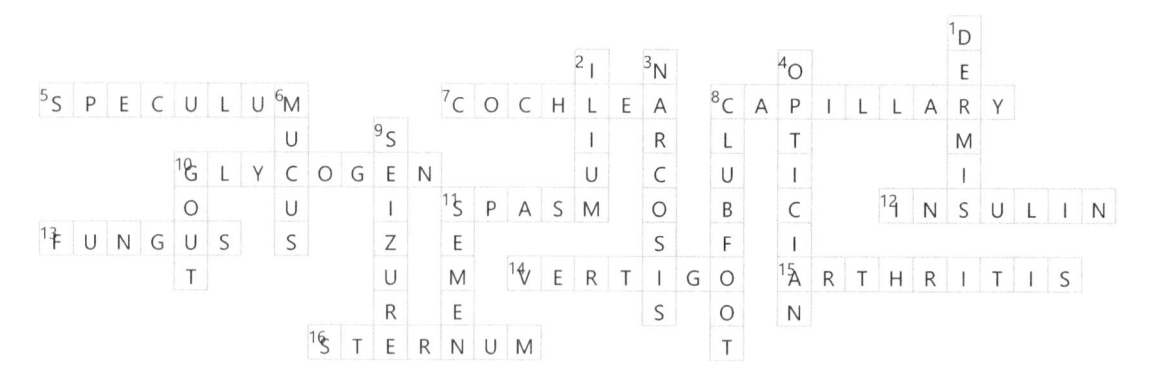

1. Using the Across and Down clues, write the correct words in the numbered grid below.

```
                                    ¹D
                                     E
 ⁵S P E C U L U ⁶M      ⁷C O C H L E A  ⁸C A P I L L A R Y
               U   ⁹S        I    R   L            M
            ¹⁰G L Y C O G E N    U    C   U            I
               O   U      ¹¹S P A S M    C   ¹²I N S U L I N
 ¹³F U N G U S S   Z E            S    F    I
               T   U M  ¹⁴V E R T I G O  ¹⁵A R T H R I T I S
                   R E            S    O    N
                  ¹⁶S T E R N U M        T
```

ACROSS

5. An instrument that holds an opening of the body open so that an examination can be performed, or a sample can be taken
7. A coiled organ in the inner ear that plays a large role in hearing by picking up sound vibrations and transmitting them as electrical signals
8. A tiny blood vessel that connects the smallest arteries to the smallest veins and allows exchange of oxygen and other materials between blood cells and body tissue cells
10. The main form that glucose, the body's energy source, takes when it is stored
11. An involuntary muscle contraction
12. A hormone made in the pancreas that plays an important role in the absorption of glucose (the body's main source of energy) into muscle cells
13. An organism that is dependent on another organism for nourishment
14. The feeling that one or one's surroundings are spinning
15. A disease of the joints characterized by inflammation, pain, stiffness, and redness
16. The long, flat bone located at the center of the chest

DOWN

5. An instrument that holds an opening of the body open so that an examination can be performed, or a sample can be taken
7. A coiled organ in the inner ear that plays a large role in hearing by picking up sound vibrations and transmitting them as electrical signals
8. A tiny blood vessel that connects the smallest arteries to the smallest veins and allows exchange of oxygen and other materials between blood cells and body tissue cells
10. The main form that glucose, the body's energy source, takes when it is stored
11. An involuntary muscle contraction
12. A hormone made in the pancreas that plays an important role in the absorption of glucose (the body's main source of energy) into muscle cells
13. An organism that is dependent on another organism for nourishment
14. The feeling that one or one's surroundings are spinning
15. A disease of the joints characterized by inflammation, pain, stiffness, and redness
16. The long, flat bone located at the center of the chest

A. Capillary   B. Sternum   C. Spasm   D. Insulin   E. Gout   F. Ilium
G. Vertigo   H. Cochlea   I. Dermis   J. Semen   K. Clubfoot   L. Narcosis
M. Speculum   N. Fungus   O. Arthritis   P. Optician   Q. Glycogen   R. Mucus
S. Seizure

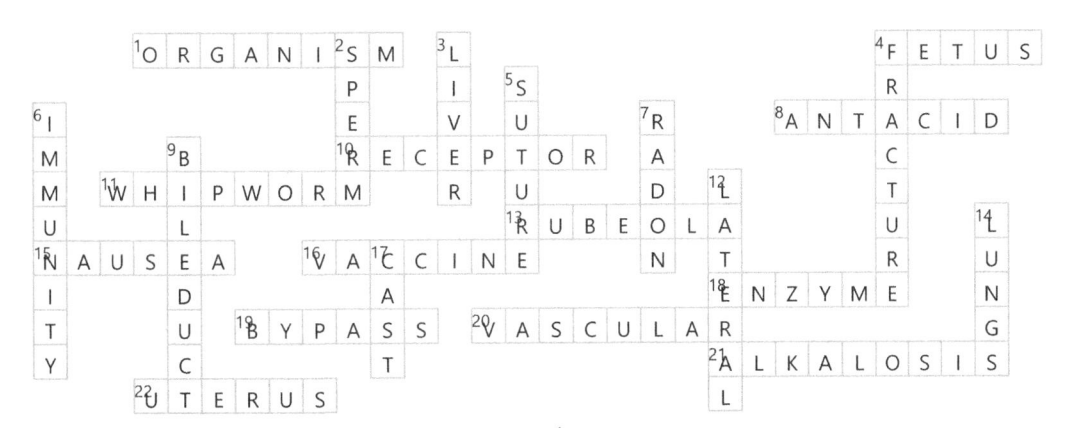

2. Using the Across and Down clues, write the correct words in the numbered grid below.

```
 ¹O R G A N I ²S M      ³L                                    ⁴F E T U S
               P         I      ⁵S                             R
 ⁶I            E         V      U         ⁷R      ⁸A N T A C I D
  M      ⁹B    ¹⁰R E C E P T O R          A                    C
  M    ¹¹W H I P W O R M         R        D   ¹²L              T
  U      L                      ¹³R U B E O L A                U   ¹⁴L
 ¹⁵N A U S E A        ¹⁶V A ¹⁷C I N E      N   T               R    U
  I      D               A                    ¹⁸E N Z Y M E         N
  T      U    ¹⁹B Y P A S S    ²⁰V A S C U L A R                    G
  Y      C               T               ²¹A L K A L O S I S
         ²²U T E R U S                    L
```

ACROSS
1. Any single, functioning form of life
4. The term used to refer to an unborn child from 8 weeks after fertilization to birth
8. A drug that neutralizes stomach acids
10. A nerve cell that responds to a stimulus and produces a nerve impulse
11. A small, parasitic worm that can live in the intestines of a human and may cause diarrhea, abdominal pain, and anemia
13. Another term for measles
15. Feeling the need to vomit
16. A preparation of weakened microorganisms given to create resistance to a certain disease
18. A chemical, originating in a cell, that regulates reactions in the body
19. A surgical technique in which the flow of blood or another body fluid is redirected around a blockage
20. Pertaining to blood vessels
21. Dangerously decreased acidity of the blood, which can be caused by high altitudes, hyperventilation, and excessive vomiting
22. The hollow female reproductive organ in which a fertilized egg is implanted, and a fetus develops

DOWN
1. Any single, functioning form of life
4. The term used to refer to an unborn child from 8 weeks after fertilization to birth
8. A drug that neutralizes stomach acids
10. A nerve cell that responds to a stimulus and produces a nerve impulse
11. A small, parasitic worm that can live in the intestines of a human and may cause diarrhea, abdominal pain, and anemia
13. Another term for measles
15. Feeling the need to vomit
16. A preparation of weakened microorganisms given to create resistance to a certain disease
18. A chemical, originating in a cell, that regulates reactions in the body
19. A surgical technique in which the flow of blood or another body fluid is redirected around a blockage
20. Pertaining to blood vessels
21. Dangerously decreased acidity of the blood, which can be caused by high altitudes, hyperventilation, and excessive vomiting
22. The hollow female reproductive organ in which a fertilized egg is implanted, and a fetus develops

A. Receptor   B. Vaccine   C. Bile duct   D. Liver   E. Nausea
F. Radon   G. Sperm   H. Alkalosis   I. Whipworm   J. Fracture
K. Vascular   L. Cast   M. Rubeola   N. Lungs   O. Lateral
P. Antacid   Q. Suture   R. Uterus   S. Bypass   T. Enzyme
U. Immunity   V. Fetus   W. Organism

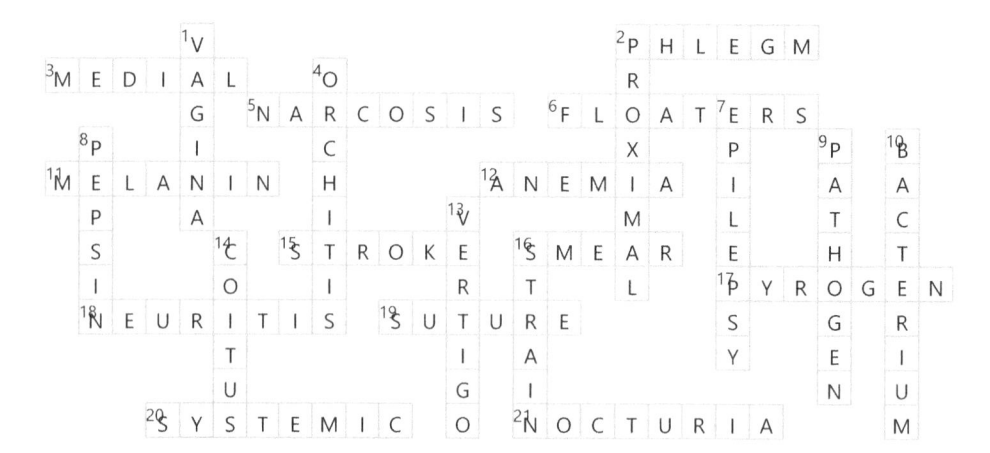

3. Using the Across and Down clues, write the correct words in the numbered grid below.

```
                    ¹V                          ²P H L E G M
³M E D I A L        ⁴O              R
          G   ⁵N A R C O S I S   ⁶F L O A T ⁷E R S
    ⁸P    I       C               X         P   ⁹P   ¹⁰B
¹¹M E L A N I N   H   ¹²A N E M I A         I   A    A
    P     A       I       M                 E   T    C
    S        ¹⁴C ¹⁵S T R O K E ¹⁶S M E A R  L   H    T
    I         O   I       R     T          ¹⁷P Y R O G E N
¹⁸N E U R I T I S ¹⁹S U T U R E             S   G    R
          T       I       A                  Y   E    I
          U       G       I                      N    U
         ²⁰S Y S T E M I C ²¹N O C T U R I A     M
```

ACROSS

2. Mucus and other material produced by the lining of the respiratory tract
3. A term used to describe something situated on or near the midline of the body or a body structure
5. A drug (or other chemical) induced drowsiness or stupor
6. Small spots that float across the field of vision, caused by debris floating in the gel-like substance that fills the eye
11. The pigment that gives skin, hair, and eyes their coloring
12. A condition in which the blood does not contain enough hemoglobin, the compound that carries oxygen from the lungs to other parts of the body
15. Damage to part of the brain because of a lack of blood supply or the rupturing of a blood vessel
16. A sample of cells spread across a glass slide to be examined through a microscope
17. Any substance that causes a fever
18. Inflammation of a nerve, often characterized by pain, numbness, or tingling
19. A surgical stitch that helps close an incision or wound so that it can heal properly
20. Affecting the whole body
21. Urination or a sleep- disturbing need to urinate during the night

DOWN

2. Mucus and other material produced by the lining of the respiratory tract
3. A term used to describe something situated on or near the midline of the body or a body structure
5. A drug (or other chemical) induced drowsiness or stupor
6. Small spots that float across the field of vision, caused by debris floating in the gel-like substance that fills the eye
11. The pigment that gives skin, hair, and eyes their coloring
12. A condition in which the blood does not contain enough hemoglobin, the compound that carries oxygen from the lungs to other parts of the body
15. Damage to part of the brain because of a lack of blood supply or the rupturing of a blood vessel
16. A sample of cells spread across a glass slide to be examined through a microscope
17. Any substance that causes a fever
18. Inflammation of a nerve, often characterized by pain, numbness, or tingling
19. A surgical stitch that helps close an incision or wound so that it can heal properly
20. Affecting the whole body
21. Urination or a sleep- disturbing need to urinate during the night

A. Proximal	B. Orchitis	C. Medial	D. Neuritis	E. Bacterium	F. Systemic
G. Pepsin	H. Pathogen	I. Floaters	J. Epilepsy	K. Pyrogen	L. Nocturia
M. Melanin	N. Strain	O. Anemia	P. Coitus	Q. Vertigo	R. Narcosis
S. Phlegm	T. Suture	U. Vagina	V. Stroke	W. Smear	

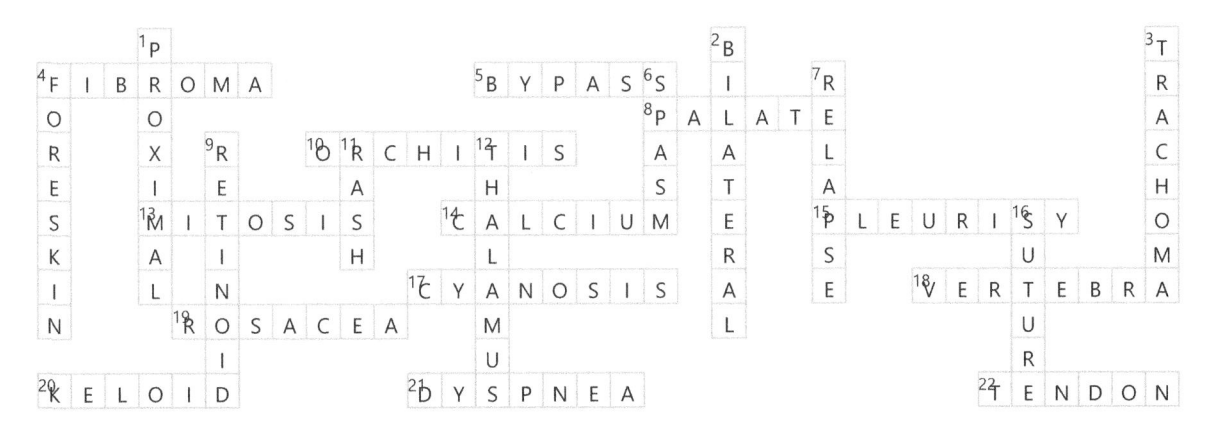

4. Using the Across and Down clues, write the correct words in the numbered grid below.

```
         ¹P                              ²B              ³T
⁴F I B R O M A          ⁵B Y P A S ⁶S    I      ⁷R       R
O        O                       ⁸P A L  A T E           A
R        X   ⁹R   ¹⁰O ¹¹R C H I ¹²T S    A      L        C
E        I   E       A           H       S      A        H
S       ¹³M  I T O S I S   ¹⁴C A L C I U M E   ¹⁵P L E U R I ¹⁶S Y
K        A   I       H           L       R      S        U    O
I        L   N         ¹⁷C Y A N O S I S A     ¹⁸V E R T E B R A
N          ¹⁹R O S A C E A       M       L      E        U    M
           I                     U                       R
²⁰K E L O I D          ²¹D Y S P N E A                  ²²T E N D O N
```

ACROSS

4. A noncancerous tumor of connective tissue
5. A surgical technique in which the flow of blood or another body fluid is redirected around a blockage
8. The roof of the mouth
10. Inflammation of a testicle, which can be caused by infection with the mumps virus
13. The process by which most cells divide to reproduce
14. A plentiful mineral in the body and the basic component of teeth and bones
15. Inflammation of the lining of the lungs and chest cavity usually caused by a lung infection
17. A bluish discoloration of the skin caused by low levels of oxygen in the blood
18. Any one of the 33 bones that make up the spine
19. A skin disorder that is characterized by patches of red skin on the nose and cheeks and acne- like bumps
20. A raised, firm, thick scar that forms because of a defect in the natural healing process
21. Difficulty breathing
22. Strong connective tissue cords that attach muscle to bone or muscle to muscle

DOWN

4. A noncancerous tumor of connective tissue
5. A surgical technique in which the flow of blood or another body fluid is redirected around a blockage
8. The roof of the mouth
10. Inflammation of a testicle, which can be caused by infection with the mumps virus
13. The process by which most cells divide to reproduce
14. A plentiful mineral in the body and the basic component of teeth and bones
15. Inflammation of the lining of the lungs and chest cavity usually caused by a lung infection
17. A bluish discoloration of the skin caused by low levels of oxygen in the blood
18. Any one of the 33 bones that make up the spine
19. A skin disorder that is characterized by patches of red skin on the nose and cheeks and acne- like bumps
20. A raised, firm, thick scar that forms because of a defect in the natural healing process
21. Difficulty breathing
22. Strong connective tissue cords that attach muscle to bone or muscle to muscle

A. Tendon	B. Bilateral	C. Calcium	D. Retinoid	E. Palate	F. Dyspnea
G. Trachoma	H. Keloid	I. Proximal	J. Relapse	K. Spasm	L. Thalamus
M. Vertebra	N. Rosacea	O. Pleurisy	P. Rash	Q. Foreskin	R. Mitosis
S. Suture	T. Orchitis	U. Fibroma	V. Cyanosis	W. Bypass	

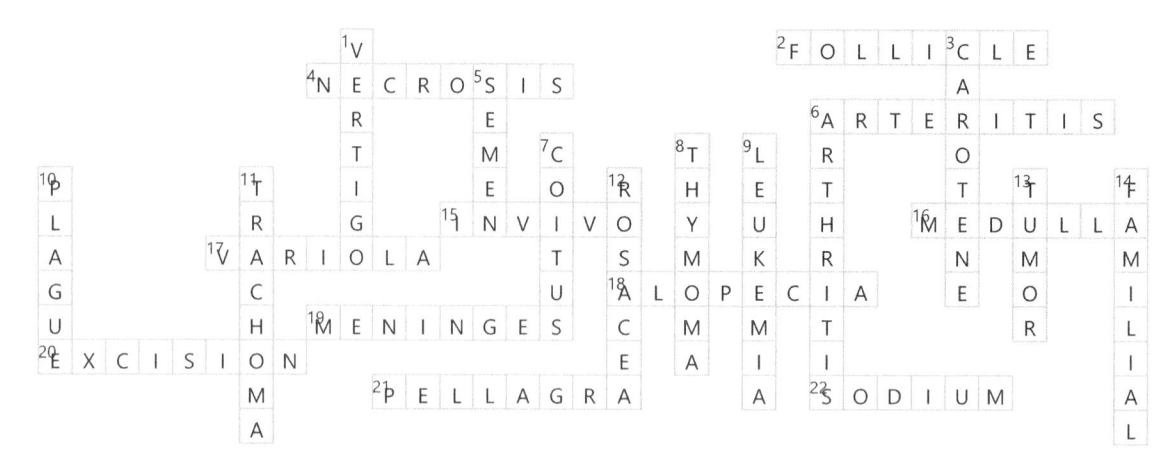

5. Using the Across and Down clues, write the correct words in the numbered grid below.

```
                    ¹V                              ²F O L L I ³C L E
              ⁴N E C R O ⁵S I S                            A
                    R       E                        ⁶A R T E R I T I S
                    T       M       ⁷C         ⁸T  ⁹L       O
     ¹⁰P         ¹¹T       E        O         H   E        T    ¹³T      ¹⁴F
       L          R         G    ¹⁵I N V I V O    Y   U       H    ¹⁶M E D U L L A
       A       ¹⁷V A R I O L A        T        S   M   K     R       N       M
       G          C                    U    ¹⁸A L O P E C I A        E       M
       U          H    ¹⁹M E N I N G E S       C   M   M   T         R       I
     ²⁰E X C I S I O N                  E        A   I   I                   L
                    M       ²¹P E L L A G R A            A    ²²S O D I U M  I
                    A                                                         A
                                                                              L
```

ACROSS

2. A tiny pouchlike cavity in a structure of the body, such as a hair follicle
4. The medical term for the death of tissue cells
6. Inflammation of the walls of an artery that causes the passageway to become narrower
15. "in the living body"; a biological process that occurs inside of the body
16. The center part of an organ or body structure
17. Another term for smallpox
18. Baldness or loss of hair, mainly on the head, either in defined patches or completely
19. The three membranes that surround and protect the spinal cord and brain
20. The surgical removal of diseased tissue
21. A deficiency of the vitamin niacin; causes dermatitis, diarrhea, and mental disorders
22. A mineral that plays a role in the body's water balance, heart rhythm, nerve impulses, and muscle contraction

DOWN

2. A tiny pouchlike cavity in a structure of the body, such as a hair follicle
4. The medical term for the death of tissue cells
6. Inflammation of the walls of an artery that causes the passageway to become narrower
15. "in the living body"; a biological process that occurs inside of the body
16. The center part of an organ or body structure
17. Another term for smallpox
18. Baldness or loss of hair, mainly on the head, either in defined patches or completely
19. The three membranes that surround and protect the spinal cord and brain
20. The surgical removal of diseased tissue
21. A deficiency of the vitamin niacin; causes dermatitis, diarrhea, and mental disorders
22. A mineral that plays a role in the body's water balance, heart rhythm, nerve impulses, and muscle contraction

A. Arteritis	B. Excision	C. Sodium	D. Thymoma	E. Trachoma	F. Medulla
G. Meninges	H. Follicle	I. Alopecia	J. In vivo	K. Plague	L. Semen
M. Tumor	N. Coitus	O. Variola	P. Rosacea	Q. Carotene	R. Familial
S. Leukemia	T. Vertigo	U. Necrosis	V. Pellagra	W. Arthritis	

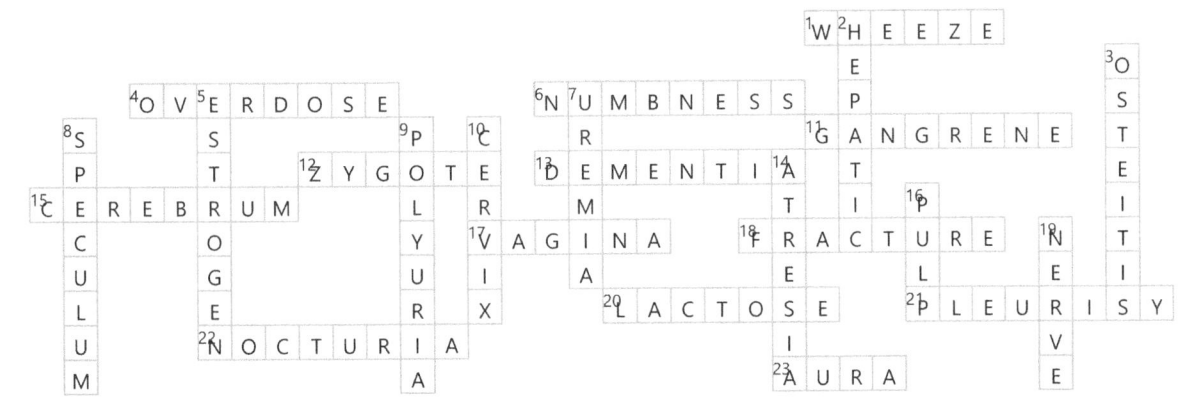

6. Using the Across and Down clues, write the correct words in the numbered grid below.

```
                                              ¹W ²H  E  E  Z  E
                                                 E                    ³O
         ⁴O  V  ⁵E  R  D  O  S  E       ⁶N ⁷U  M  B  N  E  S  S    P     S
    ⁸S           S                  ⁹P    ¹⁰C    R                ¹¹G  A  N  G  R  E  N  E    T
    P           T         ¹²Z  Y  G  O  T  E    ¹³D  E  M  E  N  T  I  ¹⁴A    T                E
¹⁵C  E  R  E  B  R  U  M          L           R        M              T    I    ¹⁶P           I
    C           O                  Y    ¹⁷V  A  G  I  N  A    ¹⁸F  R  A  C  T  U  R  E    ¹⁹N    T
    U           G                  U           I        A              E        L        E    I
    L           E                  R           X        ²⁰L  A  C  T  O  S  E    ²¹P  L  E  U  R  I  S  Y
    U         ²²N  O  C  T  U  R  I  A                                 I                V
    M                              A                    ²³A  U  R  A                    E
```

ACROSS

1. A high-pitched sound produced during breathing because of narrowing of the airways
4. An excessively large dose of a drug, which can lead to coma and death
6. The lack of sensation in a part of the body because of interruption of nerve impulses
11. Death of a tissue because of a lack of blood supply
12. The cell that results when an egg is fertilized by a sperm
13. A gradual decline in mental ability usually caused by a brain disease, such as Alzheimer's disease
15. The largest part of the brain and the site of most of its activity, including sensory and motor functions
17. The muscular passage connecting the uterus with the outside genitals
18. A bone break
20. The sugar found in dairy products
21. Inflammation of the lining of the lungs and chest cavity usually caused by a lung infection
22. Urination or a sleep-disturbing need to urinate during the night
23. A "warning" signal that comes before a migraine headache or an epileptic seizure, which might include emotions or sensations of movement or discomfort

DOWN

1. A high-pitched sound produced during breathing because of narrowing of the airways
4. An excessively large dose of a drug, which can lead to coma and death
6. The lack of sensation in a part of the body because of interruption of nerve impulses
11. Death of a tissue because of a lack of blood supply
12. The cell that results when an egg is fertilized by a sperm
13. A gradual decline in mental ability usually caused by a brain disease, such as Alzheimer's disease
15. The largest part of the brain and the site of most of its activity, including sensory and motor functions
17. The muscular passage connecting the uterus with the outside genitals
18. A bone break
20. The sugar found in dairy products
21. Inflammation of the lining of the lungs and chest cavity usually caused by a lung infection
22. Urination or a sleep-disturbing need to urinate during the night
23. A "warning" signal that comes before a migraine headache or an epileptic seizure, which might include emotions or sensations of movement or discomfort

A. Wheeze
B. Cervix
C. Speculum
D. Numbness
E. Nerve
F. Pleurisy
G. Pulp
H. Hepatic
I. Aura
J. Zygote
K. Cerebrum
L. Estrogen
M. Uremia
N. Nocturia
O. Polyuria
P. Overdose
Q. Atresia
R. Dementia
S. Osteitis
T. Fracture
U. Vagina
V. Gangrene
W. Lactose

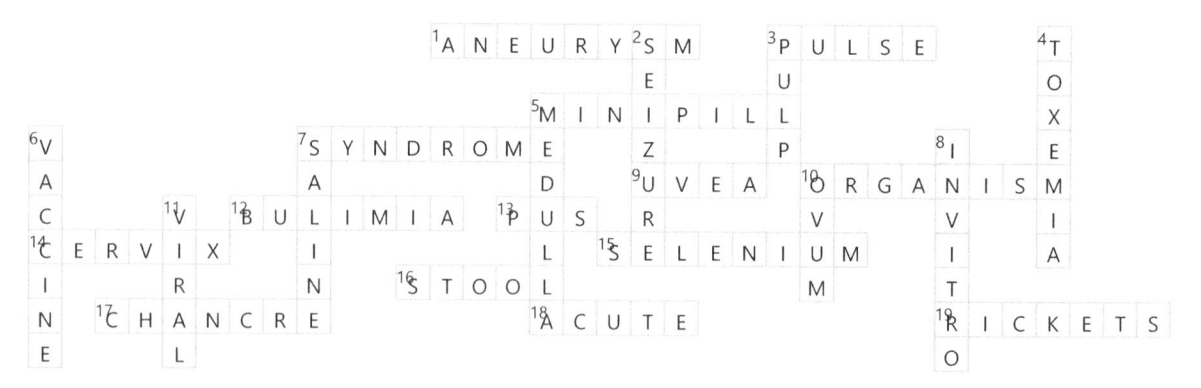

7. Using the Across and Down clues, write the correct words in the numbered grid below.

```
        ¹A N E U R Y ²S M        ³P U L S E           ⁴T
                    E              U                   O
                 ⁵M I N I P I L L                      X
⁶V           ⁷S Y N D R O M E      Z              ⁸I   E
 A            A                    D    ⁹U V E A ¹⁰O R G A N I S M
 C      ¹¹V ¹²B U L I M I A ¹³P U S                    V         I
¹⁴C E R V I X      I              L   ¹⁵S E L E N I U M          A
 I          R      N            ¹⁶S T O O L        M   I
 N     ¹⁷C H A N C R E         ¹⁸A C U T E        ¹⁹R I C K E T S
 E          L                                          O
```

ACROSS

1. An abnormal swelling of the wall of an artery, caused by a weakening in the vessel wall
3. The expansion and contraction of a blood vessel due to the blood pumped through it
5. An oral contraceptive containing only the synthetic hormone progesterone (birth control pills contain estrogen and progesterone)
7. A group of symptoms that indicate a certain disorder when they occur together
9. A structure consisting of the colored area of the eye and the middle layer of the eye that contains blood vessels
10. Any single, functioning form of life
12. A disorder in which a person eats large amounts of food then forces vomiting or uses laxatives to prevent weight gain (called binging and purging)
13. A thick, yellowish or greenish fluid that contains dead white blood cells, tissues, and bacteria; occurs at the site of a bacterial infection
14. A small, round organ making up the neck of the uterus and separating it from the vagina
15. An element needed by the body only in very small amounts that helps maintain tissue elasticity
16. Another term for feces
17. A painless sore that has a thick, rubbery base and a defined edge
18. Describes a condition or illness that begins suddenly and is usually short-lasting
19. A childhood disease in which bones lack calcium and are deformed because of vitamin d deficiency

DOWN

1. An abnormal swelling of the wall of an artery, caused by a weakening in the vessel wall
3. The expansion and contraction of a blood vessel due to the blood pumped through it
5. An oral contraceptive containing only the synthetic hormone progesterone (birth control pills contain estrogen and progesterone)
7. A group of symptoms that indicate a certain disorder when they occur together
9. A structure consisting of the colored area of the eye and the middle layer of the eye that contains blood vessels
10. Any single, functioning form of life
12. A disorder in which a person eats large amounts of food then forces vomiting or uses laxatives to prevent weight gain (called binging and purging)
13. A thick, yellowish or greenish fluid that contains dead white blood cells, tissues, and bacteria; occurs at the site of a bacterial infection
14. A small, round organ making up the neck of the uterus and separating it from the vagina
15. An element needed by the body only in very small amounts that helps maintain tissue elasticity
16. Another term for feces
17. A painless sore that has a thick, rubbery base and a defined edge
18. Describes a condition or illness that begins suddenly and is usually short-lasting
19. A childhood disease in which bones lack calcium and are deformed because of vitamin d deficiency

A. Organism   B. Saline   C. Acute   D. Rickets   E. Uvea   F. Aneurysm
G. Toxemia   H. Bulimia   I. Pulse   J. Selenium   K. Medulla   L. Seizure
M. In vitro   N. Vaccine   O. Ovum   P. Pus   Q. Syndrome   R. Viral
S. Stool   T. Chancre   U. Minipill   V. Cervix   W. Pulp

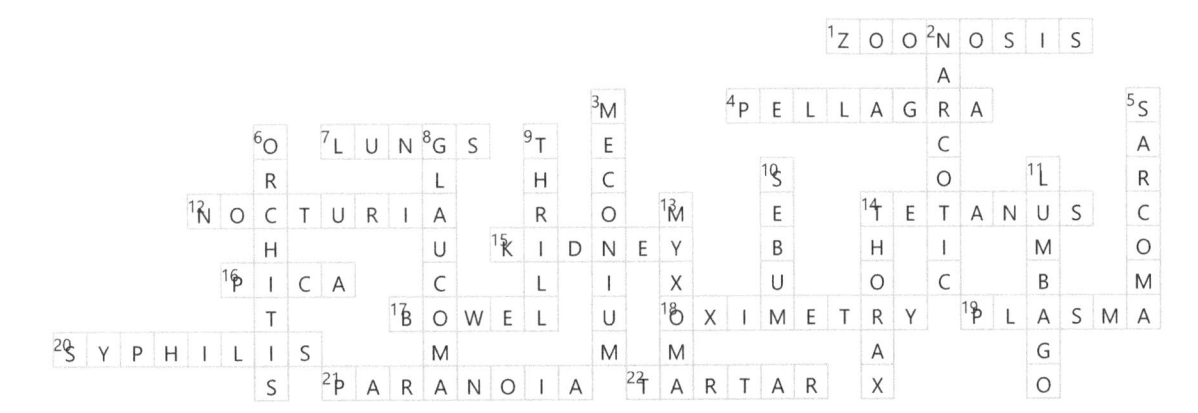

8. Using the Across and Down clues, write the correct words in the numbered grid below.

```
                                              ¹Z O O ²N O S I S
                                                    A
                        ³M         ⁴P E L L A G R A              ⁵S
        ⁶O  ⁷L U N ⁸G S  ⁹T        E          C                  A
        R   L            H         ¹⁰S         O       ¹¹L       R
        ¹²N O C T U R I A   R      ¹³M  E      ¹⁴T E T A N U S   C
        H       U   ¹⁵K I D N E Y   B          H       M         O
        ¹⁶P I C A   L       I      X           O       B         M
        T           ¹⁷B O W E L    ¹⁸O X I M E T R Y   ¹⁹P L A S M A
²⁰S Y P H I L I S       M           M          A       G
        S   ²¹P A R A N O I A      ²²T A R T A R       O
```

ACROSS

1. A parasite-caused or infectious disease in animals that can be transferred to humans
4. A deficiency of the vitamin niacin; causes dermatitis, diarrhea, and mental disorders
7. Two organs in the chest that take in oxygen from the air and release carbon dioxide
12. Urination or a sleep-disturbing need to urinate during the night
14. A sometimes fatal disease affecting the brain and spinal cord
15. One of two organs that are part of the urinary tract
16. A desire to eat materials that are not food
17. Intestine
18. Determination of the amount of oxygen in the blood by measuring the amount of light transmitted through an area of skin
19. The liquid part of the blood, containing substances such as nutrients, salts, and proteins
20. A sexually transmitted disease
21. A disorder in which a person becomes overly suspicious and emotionally sensitive
22. The hard deposit formed on teeth when mineral salts in saliva combine with plaque

DOWN

1. A parasite-caused or infectious disease in animals that can be transferred to humans
4. A deficiency of the vitamin niacin; causes dermatitis, diarrhea, and mental disorders
7. Two organs in the chest that take in oxygen from the air and release carbon dioxide
12. Urination or a sleep-disturbing need to urinate during the night
14. A sometimes fatal disease affecting the brain and spinal cord
15. One of two organs that are part of the urinary tract
16. A desire to eat materials that are not food
17. Intestine
18. Determination of the amount of oxygen in the blood by measuring the amount of light transmitted through an area of skin
19. The liquid part of the blood, containing substances such as nutrients, salts, and proteins
20. A sexually transmitted disease
21. A disorder in which a person becomes overly suspicious and emotionally sensitive
22. The hard deposit formed on teeth when mineral salts in saliva combine with plaque

A. Plasma	B. Myxoma	C. Lumbago	D. Thrill	E. Sebum
F. Lungs	G. Nocturia	H. Narcotic	I. Tartar	J. Bowel
K. Pellagra	L. Thorax	M. Tetanus	N. Pica	O. Kidney
P. Zoonosis	Q. Paranoia	R. Oximetry	S. Sarcoma	T. Syphilis
U. Orchitis	V. Glaucoma	W. Meconium		

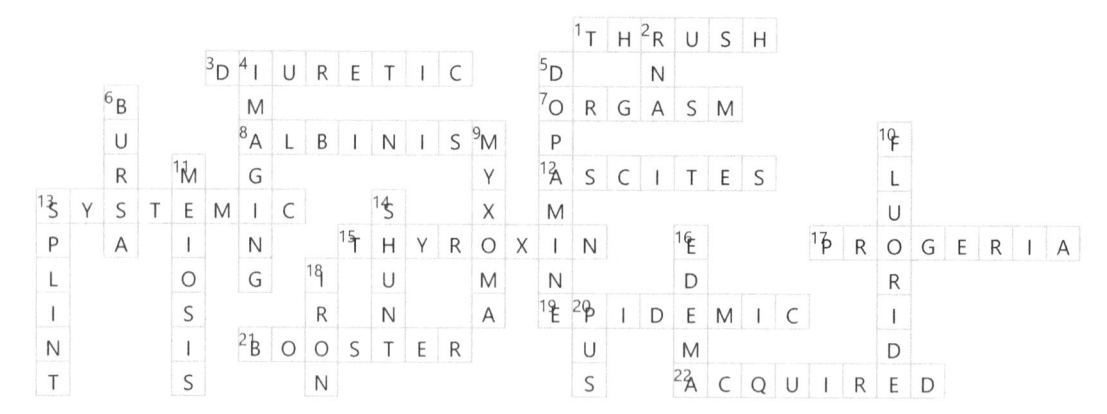

9. Using the Across and Down clues, write the correct words in the numbered grid below.

```
                                    ¹T H ²R U S H
              ³D ⁴I U R E T I C   ⁵D     N
           ⁶B     M               ⁷O R G A S M
           U   ⁸A L B I N I S ⁹M  P                    ¹⁰F
           R  ¹¹M G           Y  ¹²A S C I T E S        L
        ¹³S Y S T E M I C    ¹⁴S  X                     U
           P A I N        ¹⁵T H Y R O X I N  ¹⁶E    ¹⁷P R O G E R I A
           L   O G     ¹⁸I  U   M            D        R
           I   S       R    N   A          ¹⁹E ²⁰P I D E M I C
           N   I      ²¹B O O S T E R        U   M         I
           T   S       N                     S  ²²A C Q U I R E D
```

ACROSS

1. A candidiasis infection
3. A drug that increases the amount of water in the urine, removing excess water from the body
7. Involuntary contraction of genital muscles experienced at the peak of sexual excitement
8. A condition in which people are born with insufficient amounts of the pigment melanin, which is responsible for hair, skin, and eye color
12. Excess fluid in the abdominal cavity, which leads to swelling
13. Affecting the whole body
15. A hormone produced by the thyroid gland that helps regulate energy production in the body
17. An extremely rare condition in which the body ages prematurely
19. A term used to describe a disease that is rare then suddenly affects more people than usually expected
21. An additional dose of a vaccine taken after the first dose to maintain or renew the first one
22. A word describing any condition that is not present at birth, but develops some time during life

DOWN

1. A candidiasis infection
3. A drug that increases the amount of water in the urine, removing excess water from the body
7. Involuntary contraction of genital muscles experienced at the peak of sexual excitement
8. A condition in which people are born with insufficient amounts of the pigment melanin, which is responsible for hair, skin, and eye color
12. Excess fluid in the abdominal cavity, which leads to swelling
13. Affecting the whole body
15. A hormone produced by the thyroid gland that helps regulate energy production in the body
17. An extremely rare condition in which the body ages prematurely
19. A term used to describe a disease that is rare then suddenly affects more people than usually expected
21. An additional dose of a vaccine taken after the first dose to maintain or renew the first one
22. A word describing any condition that is not present at birth, but develops some time during life

A. Imaging	B. Booster	C. Shunt	D. Ascites	E. Dopamine	F. Diuretic
G. RNA	H. Systemic	I. Fluoride	J. Orgasm	K. Bursa	L. Pus
M. Albinism	N. Progeria	O. Thyroxin	P. Edema	Q. Epidemic	R. Thrush
S. Myxoma	T. Acquired	U. Splint	V. Meiosis	W. Iron	

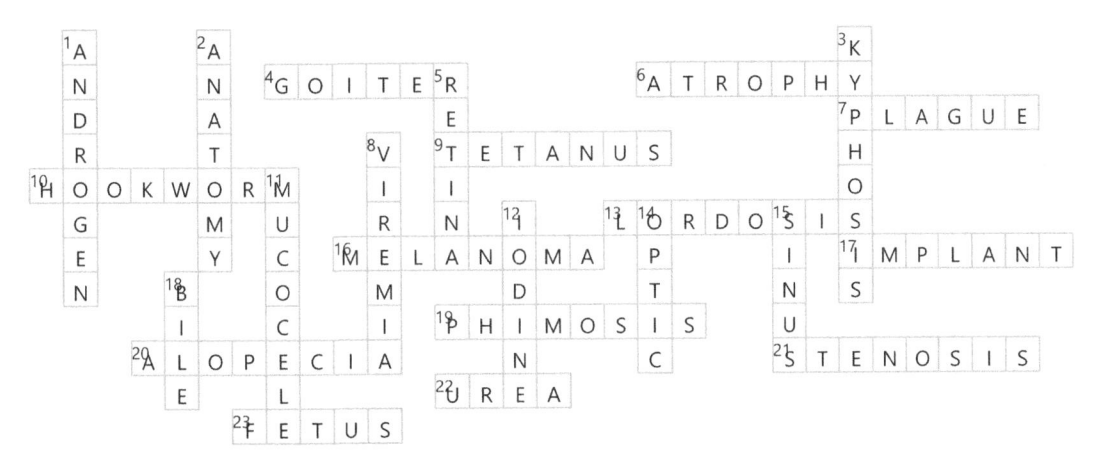

10. Using the Across and Down clues, write the correct words in the numbered grid below.

```
 1A        2A                                              3K
  N         N    4G O I T E 5R         6A T R O P H Y
  D         A              E                            7P L A G U E
  R         T         8V  9T E T A N U S                H
10H O O K W O R 11M   I    I                            O
  G         M    U    R    N   12      13 14O R D O 15S
  E         Y    C    16M E L A N O M A  P       17I M P L A N T
  N        18B   O         M         D    T    N   S
            I         19P H I M O S I S   U  21S T E N O S I S
           20A L O P E C I A         N    C
            E    L         22U R E A
                23F E T U S
```

ACROSS

4. Enlargement of the thyroid gland, which produces a swelling on the neck
6. The shrinkage or near disappearance of a tissue or organ
7. A serious infectious disease transmitted to humans through bites of rodent fleas
9. A sometimes fatal disease affecting the brain and spinal cord
10. Infestation by a small, round, blood-sucking parasite
13. The inward curvature of the spine at the lower back, which is normal to a certain degree
16. A skin tumor composed of cells called melanocytes
17. An organ, tissue, or device surgically inserted and left in the body
19. Tightness of the foreskin, which prevents it from being moved back over the head of the penis
20. Baldness or loss of hair, mainly on the head, either in defined patches or completely
21. Narrowing of a body passageway
22. A waste product of the metabolism of proteins that is formed by the liver and secreted by the kidneys
23. The term used to refer to an unborn child from 8 weeks after fertilization to birth

DOWN

4. Enlargement of the thyroid gland, which produces a swelling on the neck
6. The shrinkage or near disappearance of a tissue or organ
7. A serious infectious disease transmitted to humans through bites of rodent fleas
9. A sometimes fatal disease affecting the brain and spinal cord
10. Infestation by a small, round, blood-sucking parasite
13. The inward curvature of the spine at the lower back, which is normal to a certain degree
16. A skin tumor composed of cells called melanocytes
17. An organ, tissue, or device surgically inserted and left in the body
19. Tightness of the foreskin, which prevents it from being moved back over the head of the penis
20. Baldness or loss of hair, mainly on the head, either in defined patches or completely
21. Narrowing of a body passageway
22. A waste product of the metabolism of proteins that is formed by the liver and secreted by the kidneys
23. The term used to refer to an unborn child from 8 weeks after fertilization to birth

A. Alopecia	B. Androgen	C. Melanoma	D. Mucocele	E. Plague
F. Optic	G. Sinus	H. Iodine	I. Retina	J. Urea
K. Hookworm	L. Bile	M. Stenosis	N. Fetus	O. Kyphosis
P. Atrophy	Q. Goiter	R. Lordosis	S. Phimosis	T. Anatomy
U. Viremia	V. Implant	W. Tetanus		

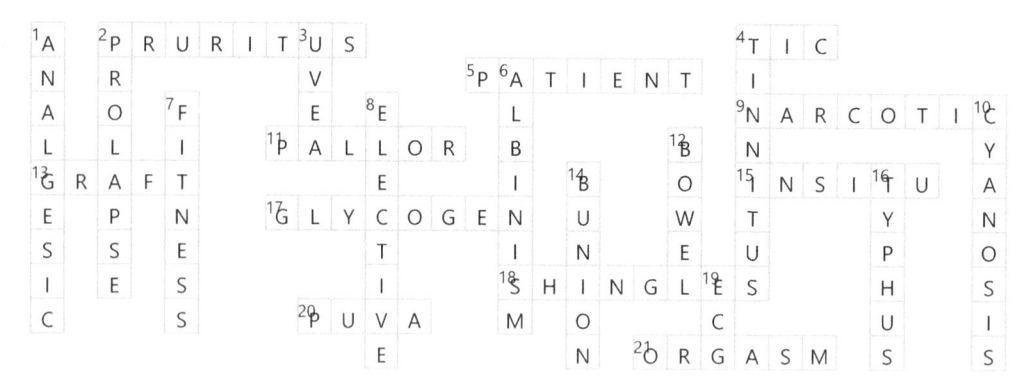

11. Using the Across and Down clues, write the correct words in the numbered grid below.

```
 1A  2P  R  U  R  I  3U  S                      4T  I  C
 N   R         V         5P  6A  T  I  E  N  T  I
 A   O   7F    E    8E       L              9N  A  R  C  O  T  I  10C
 L   L   I    11P A  L  L  O  R   B      12B   N              Y
13G   R  A   F  T         E       I   14B   O  15I  N  S  16I  U   A
 E       P   N       17G L  Y  C  O  G  E  N    U      W   T       Y    N
 S       S   E                T       I       N       E   U       P    O
 I       E   S                I              18S  H  I  N  G  L  19E  S   H   S
 C       S          20P  U  V  A      M       O              C       U    I
                    E                  N      21O  R  G  A  S  M       S    S
```

ACROSS
2. The medical term for itching
4. An involuntary, repetitive movement such as a twitch
5. Controlled analgesia- a system for administering pain-killing drugs in which the amount of drug delivered is controlled by the patient
9. An addictive substance that blunts the senses
11. Abnormally pale skin
13. Healthy tissue that is used to replace diseased or defective tissue
15. "in place"; often describes a cancer that has not spread
17. The main form that glucose, the body's energy source, takes when it is stored
18. A nerve infection caused by the chickenpox virus, causing areas of painful rash covered with blisters
20. A form of phototherapy that combines the use of psoralens and ultraviolet light to treat skin disorders
21. Involuntary contraction of genital muscles experienced at the peak of sexual excitement

DOWN
2. The medical term for itching
4. An involuntary, repetitive movement such as a twitch
5. Controlled analgesia- a system for administering pain-killing drugs in which the amount of drug delivered is controlled by the patient
9. An addictive substance that blunts the senses
11. Abnormally pale skin
13. Healthy tissue that is used to replace diseased or defective tissue
15. "in place"; often describes a cancer that has not spread
17. The main form that glucose, the body's energy source, takes when it is stored
18. A nerve infection caused by the chickenpox virus, causing areas of painful rash covered with blisters
20. A form of phototherapy that combines the use of psoralens and ultraviolet light to treat skin disorders
21. Involuntary contraction of genital muscles experienced at the peak of sexual excitement

A. Bowel   B. Glycogen   C. Albinism   D. Prolapse   E. Patient   F. Bunion
G. ECG   H. Orgasm   I. Tinnitus   J. PUVA   K. Fitness   L. Shingles
M. Tic   N. Uvea   O. Cyanosis   P. Elective   Q. Pallor   R. Narcotic
S. Typhus   T. Pruritus   U. Analgesic   V. Graft   W. In situ

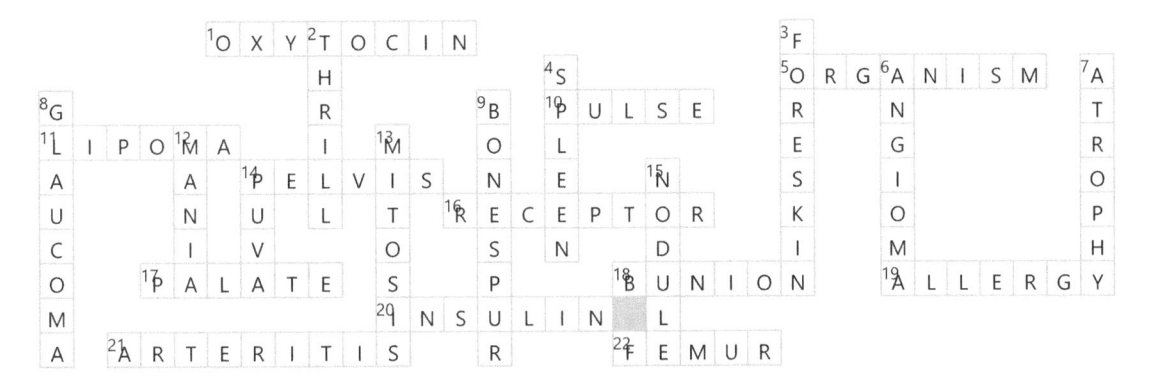

12. Using the Across and Down clues, write the correct words in the numbered grid below.

			¹O	X	Y	²T	O	C	I	N							³F					
						H						⁴S			⁵O	R	G	⁶A	N	I	S	M	⁷A
⁸G						R			⁹B	¹⁰P	U	L	S	E		R		N				T
¹¹L	I	P	O	¹²M	A			¹³M		O		L				E		G				R
A				A		¹⁴P	E	L	V	I	S		T		¹⁵N		S		I				O
U				N		U				L		¹⁶R	E	C	E	P	T	O	R			P
C				I		V				O		S			N			D			I	H
O			¹⁷P	A	L	A	T	E		S		P				¹⁸B	U	N	I	O	N	¹⁹A	L	L	E	R	G	Y
M									²⁰I	N	S	U	L	I	N			L				
A		²¹A	R	T	E	R	I	T	I	S			R		²²F	E	M	U	R			

ACROSS

1. A hormone produced in the pituitary gland that causes contraction of the uterus during childbirth and stimulation of milk flow during breast-feeding.
5. Any single, functioning form of life
10. The expansion and contraction of a blood vessel due to the blood pumped through it
11. A noncancerous tumor of fatty tissue
14. The group of bones in the lower part of the trunk that support the upper body and protect the abdominal organs
16. A nerve cell that responds to a stimulus and produces a nerve impulse
17. The roof of the mouth
18. A hard, fluid-filled pad along the inside joint of the big toe
19. A negative reaction to a substance that in most people causes no reaction
20. A hormone made in the pancreas that plays an important role in the absorption of glucose (the body's main source of energy) into muscle cells
21. Inflammation of the walls of an artery that causes the passageway to become narrower
22. The bone located between the hip and the knee

DOWN

1. A hormone produced in the pituitary gland that causes contraction of the uterus during childbirth and stimulation of milk flow during breast-feeding.
5. Any single, functioning form of life
10. The expansion and contraction of a blood vessel due to the blood pumped through it
11. A noncancerous tumor of fatty tissue
14. The group of bones in the lower part of the trunk that support the upper body and protect the abdominal organs
16. A nerve cell that responds to a stimulus and produces a nerve impulse
17. The roof of the mouth
18. A hard, fluid-filled pad along the inside joint of the big toe
19. A negative reaction to a substance that in most people causes no reaction
20. A hormone made in the pancreas that plays an important role in the absorption of glucose (the body's main source of energy) into muscle cells
21. Inflammation of the walls of an artery that causes the passageway to become narrower
22. The bone located between the hip and the knee

A. Organism	B. Pulse	C. Pelvis	D. Nodule	E. Bone spur	F. Lipoma
G. Allergy	H. Mania	I. Atrophy	J. Insulin	K. Spleen	L. Bunion
M. Foreskin	N. Glaucoma	O. Thrill	P. Femur	Q. Arteritis	R. Receptor
S. Palate	T. Oxytocin	U. PUVA	V. Angioma	W. Mitosis	

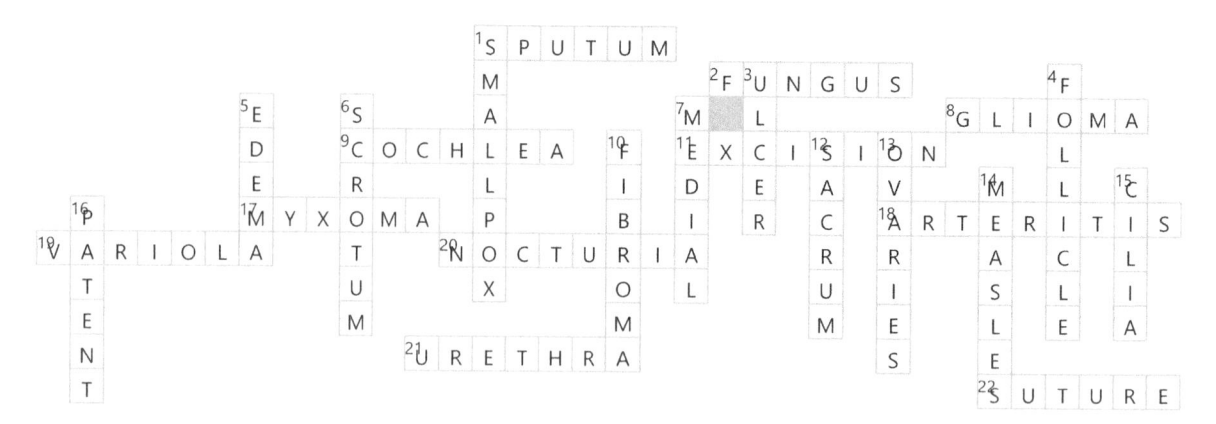

13. Using the Across and Down clues, write the correct words in the numbered grid below.

```
                    ¹S P U T U M
                      M              ²F ³U N G U S      ⁴F
         ⁵E    ⁶S     A              ⁷M  L              ⁸G L I O M A
          D    ⁹C  O  C  H  L  E  A  ¹⁰F ¹¹E X C ¹²S I ¹³O N    L
          E    R     L        I  D     E  A  V  ¹⁴M  L  ¹⁵C
    ¹⁶P       ¹⁷M Y X O M A   P  B     R  C ¹⁸A R T E R I T I S
    ¹⁹V A R I O L A     T     ²⁰N O C T U R I A   R  A  C  L
     T                  U        X           O  L  U  I  S  L  I
     E                  M        M           U  M  E  L  E  A
     N                    ²¹U  R E T H R A      S        E
     T                                                 ²²S U T U R E
```

ACROSS

1. Mucus and other material produced by the lining of the respiratory tract
2. An organism that is dependent on another organism for nourishment
8. A brain tumor arising from cells that support nerve cells
9. A coiled organ in the inner ear that plays a large role in hearing by picking up sound vibrations and transmitting them as electrical signals
11. The surgical removal of diseased tissue
17. A noncancerous tumor made of mucous material and fibrous connective tissue
18. Inflammation of the walls of an artery that causes the passageway to become narrower
19. Another term for smallpox
20. Urination or a sleep-disturbing need to urinate during the night
21. The tube by which urine is released from the bladder
22. A surgical stitch that helps close an incision or wound so that it can heal properly

DOWN

1. Mucus and other material produced by the lining of the respiratory tract
2. An organism that is dependent on another organism for nourishment
8. A brain tumor arising from cells that support nerve cells
9. A coiled organ in the inner ear that plays a large role in hearing by picking up sound vibrations and transmitting them as electrical signals
11. The surgical removal of diseased tissue
17. A noncancerous tumor made of mucous material and fibrous connective tissue
18. Inflammation of the walls of an artery that causes the passageway to become narrower
19. Another term for smallpox
20. Urination or a sleep-disturbing need to urinate during the night
21. The tube by which urine is released from the bladder
22. A surgical stitch that helps close an incision or wound so that it can heal properly

A. Ulcer   B. Myxoma   C. Ovaries   D. Smallpox   E. Excision   F. Glioma
G. Cochlea   H. Medial   I. Edema   J. Nocturia   K. Suture   L. Measles
M. Fungus   N. Follicle   O. Cilia   P. Patent   Q. Arteritis   R. Fibroma
S. Sputum   T. Scrotum   U. Variola   V. Sacrum   W. Urethra

14. Using the Across and Down clues, write the correct words in the numbered grid below.

```
 1A  B  2S  C  E  S  S                      3F  E  M  U  R     4L  5A  Z  Y  E  Y  E
 6S      P                  7B  A  C  8I  L  L  U  S          E                  S
 P       R                  O           N              9S  T  O  M  10A
 A       U    11A  12P      T           F              U              T    13I  N  H  A  L  14E  R
15S  P  L  E  E  N    U    16B  U  R  S  I  T  I  S              R              M              C
 M           E        V     L           S              17L  O  C  K  J  A  W     Z
       18B  U  L  I  M  I  A    I           I              P                       E
              I                  S    19B  O  N  E  S  P  U  R                   M
             20A  N  A  T  O  M  Y  N                 21Z  Y  G  O  T  E          A
```

ACROSS

1. An accumulation of pus in a body tissue, usually caused by a bacterial infection
3. The bone located between the hip and the knee
4. The common name for the visual defect resulting from untreated strabismus, in which the eyes are not correctly aligned
7. Any bacteria that is rod-shaped
9. A surgically formed opening on a body surface
13. A device used to introduce a powdered or misted drug into the lungs through the mouth, usually to treat respiratory disorders such as asthma
15. An organ located in the upper left abdomen behind the ribs that removes and destroys old red blood cells and helps fight infection
16. Inflammation of a bursa due to excessive pressure or friction, or from injury
17. A spasm of the jaw muscles that prevents the mouth from opening, such as that caused by tetanus
18. A disorder in which a person eats large amounts of food then forces vomiting or uses laxatives to prevent weight gain (called binging and purging)
19. An abnormal growth of bone out of another bone, often located on the heel and usually painful
20. The structure of bodies
21. The cell that results when an egg is fertilized by a sperm

DOWN

1. An accumulation of pus in a body tissue, usually caused by a bacterial infection
3. The bone located between the hip and the knee
4. The common name for the visual defect resulting from untreated strabismus, in which the eyes are not correctly aligned
7. Any bacteria that is rod-shaped
9. A surgically formed opening on a body surface
13. A device used to introduce a powdered or misted drug into the lungs through the mouth, usually to treat respiratory disorders such as asthma
15. An organ located in the upper left abdomen behind the ribs that removes and destroys old red blood cells and helps fight infection
16. Inflammation of a bursa due to excessive pressure or friction, or from injury
17. A spasm of the jaw muscles that prevents the mouth from opening, such as that caused by tetanus
18. A disorder in which a person eats large amounts of food then forces vomiting or uses laxatives to prevent weight gain (called binging and purging)
19. An abnormal growth of bone out of another bone, often located on the heel and usually painful
20. The structure of bodies
21. The cell that results when an egg is fertilized by a sperm

A. Atrophy	B. Bursitis	C. Bone spur	D. Infusion	E. Sprue	F. Spasm
G. PUVA	H. Zygote	I. Anatomy	J. Asthma	K. Lockjaw	L. Stoma
M. Eczema	N. Spleen	O. Inhaler	P. Fetus	Q. Bulimia	R. Abscess
S. Femur	T. Bacillus	U. Botulism	V. Lazy eye	W. Anemia	

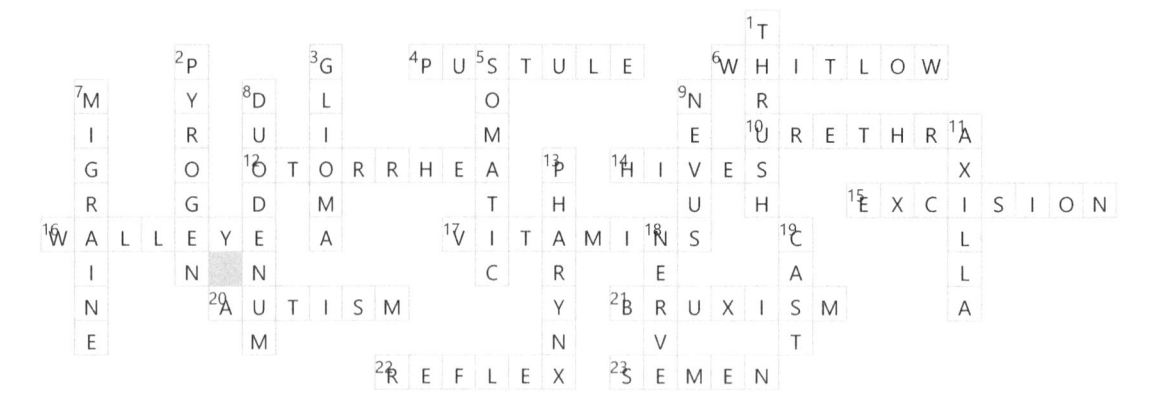

15. Using the Across and Down clues, write the correct words in the numbered grid below.

```
                                    ¹T
              ²P          ³G       ⁴P U ⁵S T U L E        ⁶W H I T L O W
      ⁷M      Y     ⁸D    L              O          ⁹N    R
      I       R     U     I              M          E    ¹⁰U R E T H R ¹¹A
      G       O    ¹²O T  O R R H E A   ¹³P  ¹⁴H I V E S                 X
      R       G     D     M              T    H               ¹⁵E X C I S I O N
     ¹⁶W A L L E Y  E     A       ¹⁷V I T A M I ¹⁸N S    ¹⁹C             L
      I       N     N                    C    R     E    A              L
      N      ²⁰A U  T I S M               Y  ²¹B R U X I  S M            A
      E             M                    N    V     E    T
                         ²²R E F L E X  ²³S E M E N
```

ACROSS
4. A small blister containing pus
6. An abscess on the end of a finger or a toe that is caused by the herpes simplex virus or a bacterial infection
10. The tube by which urine is released from the bladder
12. A discharge from an inflamed ear
14. The common term for urticaria, an itchy, inflamed rash that results from an allergic reaction
15. The surgical removal of diseased tissue
16. A condition in which one eye turns outward
17. Complex substances that are necessary in small amounts to maintain health and ensure proper development and functioning of the body
20. A mental disorder characterized by an inability to relate to other people and extreme withdrawal
21. An unaware clenching or grinding of the teeth, usually during sleep
22. An automatic, involuntary response of the nervous system to a stimulus
23. Fluid released during ejaculation that contains sperm along with fluids produced by the prostate gland and the seminal vesicles

DOWN
4. A small blister containing pus
6. An abscess on the end of a finger or a toe that is caused by the herpes simplex virus or a bacterial infection
10. The tube by which urine is released from the bladder
12. A discharge from an inflamed ear
14. The common term for urticaria, an itchy, inflamed rash that results from an allergic reaction
15. The surgical removal of diseased tissue
16. A condition in which one eye turns outward
17. Complex substances that are necessary in small amounts to maintain health and ensure proper development and functioning of the body
20. A mental disorder characterized by an inability to relate to other people and extreme withdrawal
21. An unaware clenching or grinding of the teeth, usually during sleep
22. An automatic, involuntary response of the nervous system to a stimulus
23. Fluid released during ejaculation that contains sperm along with fluids produced by the prostate gland and the seminal vesicles

A. Otorrhea	B. Hives	C. Reflex	D. Walleye	E. Somatic
F. Pustule	G. Semen	H. Autism	I. Pharynx	J. Cast
K. Nerve	L. Migraine	M. Thrush	N. Duodenum	O. Excision
P. Bruxism	Q. Pyrogen	R. Nevus	S. Urethra	T. Glioma
U. Whitlow	V. Vitamins	W. Axilla		

16. Using the Across and Down clues, write the correct words in the numbered grid below.

ACROSS

3. The throat
5. A sample of cells spread across a glass slide to be examined through a microscope
7. The colored part of the eye
11. A tumor composed of cells not normally found in the part of the body when the tumor occurred
13. Microorganisms that cause several human infections and can be transmitted sexually
17. Death of a tissue because of a lack of blood supply
18. A vibration felt when the hand is placed flat on the chest
19. On one side
20. A mental disorder characterized by extreme excitement, happiness, overactivity, and agitation
21. The medical term for an earache
22. An automatic, involuntary response of the nervous system to a stimulus
23. Inflammation of the uvea

DOWN

3. The throat
5. A sample of cells spread across a glass slide to be examined through a microscope
7. The colored part of the eye
11. A tumor composed of cells not normally found in the part of the body when the tumor occurred
13. Microorganisms that cause several human infections and can be transmitted sexually
17. Death of a tissue because of a lack of blood supply
18. A vibration felt when the hand is placed flat on the chest
19. On one side
20. A mental disorder characterized by extreme excitement, happiness, overactivity, and agitation
21. The medical term for an earache
22. An automatic, involuntary response of the nervous system to a stimulus
23. Inflammation of the uvea

A. Thrill
B. Skull
C. Malaria
D. Abortion
E. Iris
F. Ocular
G. Chlamydia
H. Reflex
I. Mania
J. Teratoma
K. Triage
L. Lipids
M. Keloid
N. Otalgia
O. Plasma
P. Gangrene
Q. Labia
R. Pharynx
S. Plague
T. Lateral
U. Uveitis
V. Smear
W. Zoonosis

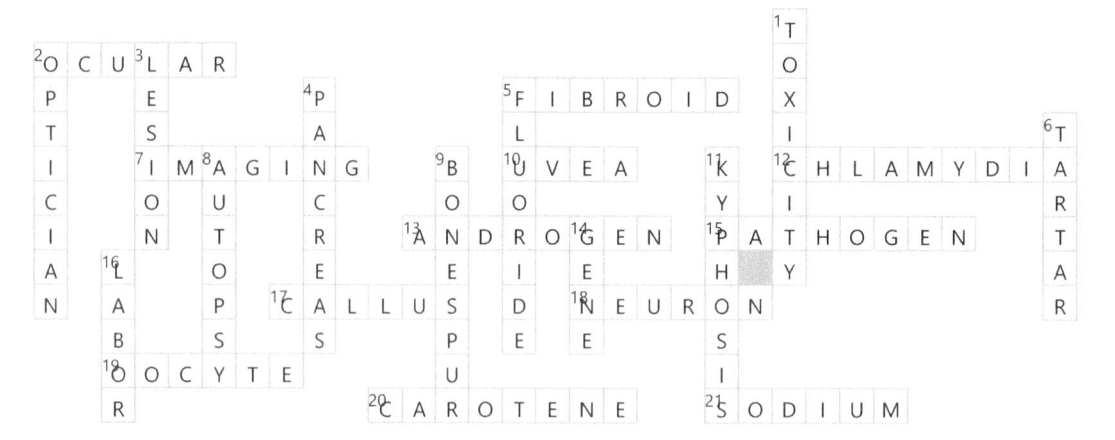

17. Using the Across and Down clues, write the correct words in the numbered grid below.

```
                                              ¹T
²O C U ³L A R                                  O
P     E         ⁴P         ⁵F I B R O I D      X
T     S         A          L                   I           ⁶T
I     ⁷I M ⁸A G I N G   ⁹B ¹⁰U V E A  ¹¹K ¹²C H L A M Y D I A
C       O  U    C          O           Y   I               R
I       N  T    R       ¹³A N D R O ¹⁴G E N ¹⁵P A T H O G E N
A  ¹⁶L     O    E          E         I     H     Y         A
N   A      P  ¹⁷C A L L U S D      ¹⁸N E U R O N           R
    B      S    S          P         E     S
   ¹⁹O O C Y T E           U                I
    R                   ²⁰C A R O T E N E  ²¹S O D I U M
```

ACROSS

2. Describes something related to the eyes
5. A noncancerous tumor of the uterus made up of smooth muscle and connective tissue
7. The technique of creating pictures of structures inside of the body using x-rays, ultrasound waves, or magnetic fields
10. A structure consisting of the colored area of the eye and the middle layer of the eye that contains blood vessels
12. Microorganisms that cause several human infections and can be transmitted sexually
13. A hormone (such as testosterone) that causes development of male characteristics and sex organs
15. Any substance capable of causing a disease
17. A thickened area of skin due to consistent pressure or friction, or the area around a bone break where new bone is formed
18. Another term for a nerve cell
19. An egg cell that has not developed completely
20. An orange pigment present in colored plants such as carrots that is converted by the body to the essential nutrient vitamin a
21. A mineral that plays a role in the body's water balance, heart rhythm, nerve impulses, and muscle contraction

DOWN

2. Describes something related to the eyes
5. A noncancerous tumor of the uterus made up of smooth muscle and connective tissue
7. The technique of creating pictures of structures inside of the body using x-rays, ultrasound waves, or magnetic fields
10. A structure consisting of the colored area of the eye and the middle layer of the eye that contains blood vessels
12. Microorganisms that cause several human infections and can be transmitted sexually
13. A hormone (such as testosterone) that causes development of male characteristics and sex organs
15. Any substance capable of causing a disease
17. A thickened area of skin due to consistent pressure or friction, or the area around a bone break where new bone is formed
18. Another term for a nerve cell
19. An egg cell that has not developed completely
20. An orange pigment present in colored plants such as carrots that is converted by the body to the essential nutrient vitamin a
21. A mineral that plays a role in the body's water balance, heart rhythm, nerve impulses, and muscle contraction

A. Pathogen	B. Toxicity	C. Sodium	D. Imaging	E. Fluoride	F. Callus
G. Lesion	H. Androgen	I. Kyphosis	J. Bone spur	K. Pancreas	L. Autopsy
M. Carotene	N. Ocular	O. Gene	P. Uvea	Q. Optician	R. Tartar
S. Fibroid	T. Oocyte	U. Chlamydia	V. Labor	W. Neuron	

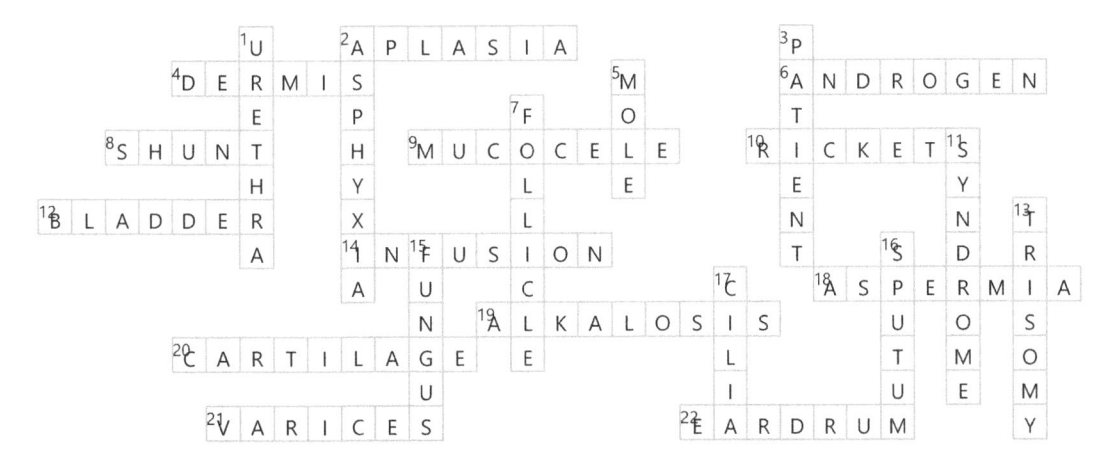

18. Using the Across and Down clues, write the correct words in the numbered grid below.

```
            ¹U      ²A P L A S I A              ³P
        ⁴D  E  R M I S        ⁵M      ⁶A N D R O G E N
            E       P       ⁷F     O      T
        ⁸S  H  U N T         H  ⁹M U C O C E L E    ¹⁰R I C K E T ¹¹S
            H       Y           L     E        E              Y
        ¹²B L  A D D E R   X     L              N          ¹³T
            A           ¹⁴I N ¹⁵F U S I O N     T   ¹⁶S    R
                         A  U       C        ¹⁷C ¹⁸A S P E R M I A
                         N ¹⁹A L K A L O S I S    U  O    S
                    ²⁰C  A  R T I L A G E     L   T  M    O
                         U                    I   U  E    M
                    ²¹V  A  R I C E S        ²²E A R D R U M    Y
```

ACROSS

2. The complete or partial failure of any organ or tissue to grow
4. The inner skin layer
6. A hormone (such as testosterone) that causes development of male characteristics and sex organs
8. An artificially constructed or an abnormal passage connecting two usually separate structures in the body
9. A sac or body cavity that is swollen because of the production of mucus by the cells in its lining
10. A childhood disease in which bones lack calcium and are deformed because of vitamin d deficiency
12. An organ located in the pelvis whose function is to collect and store urine until it is expelled
14. The introduction of a substance, such as a drug or nutrient, into the bloodstream or a body cavity
18. The failure either to produce or to ejaculate sperm
19. Dangerously decreased acidity of the blood, which can be caused by high altitudes, hyperventilation, and excessive vomiting
20. A connective tissue (softer than bone) that is part of the skeletal system, including the joints
21. Enlarged or twisted blood or lymph vessels
22. A thin, oval-shaped membrane that separates the inner ear from the outer ear and is responsible for transmitting sound waves

DOWN

2. The complete or partial failure of any organ or tissue to grow
4. The inner skin layer
6. A hormone (such as testosterone) that causes development of male characteristics and sex organs
8. An artificially constructed or an abnormal passage connecting two usually separate structures in the body
9. A sac or body cavity that is swollen because of the production of mucus by the cells in its lining
10. A childhood disease in which bones lack calcium and are deformed because of vitamin d deficiency
12. An organ located in the pelvis whose function is to collect and store urine until it is expelled
14. The introduction of a substance, such as a drug or nutrient, into the bloodstream or a body cavity
18. The failure either to produce or to ejaculate sperm
19. Dangerously decreased acidity of the blood, which can be caused by high altitudes, hyperventilation, and excessive vomiting
20. A connective tissue (softer than bone) that is part of the skeletal system, including the joints
21. Enlarged or twisted blood or lymph vessels
22. A thin, oval-shaped membrane that separates the inner ear from the outer ear and is responsible for transmitting sound waves

A. Urethra	B. Aplasia	C. Sputum	D. Shunt	E. Cartilage	F. Fungus
G. Mucocele	H. Syndrome	I. Cilia	J. Trisomy	K. Androgen	L. Alkalosis
M. Bladder	N. Follicle	O. Asphyxia	P. Mole	Q. Rickets	R. Infusion
S. Aspermia	T. Eardrum	U. Varices	V. Dermis	W. Patient	

19. Using the Across and Down clues, write the correct words in the numbered grid below.

```
 1C              2P              3H
  L               A        4C A R C I N O M A              5D
  U        6P    R               O              7H O R M O N E
  B         A    E    8O          K         9N    I         X
  F         N    S    X    10R I N G W O R M   11A B S C E S S  T
  O   12A D E N I T I S         O         R    C         R
  O         E    S    M    13S A C R U 14M 15M  C  16M U C U S O 17U
 18T R I S M U S        E         T    M    A    I    O    P         S  V
            I    19M U T A T I O N         N    T    T         20H Y G I E N E
            C         R         O    21E P I D E M I C              A
            Y         L         A         S         C
```

ACROSS

4. A cancer that occurs on the surface or lining of an organ
7. A chemical produced by a gland or tissue that is released into the bloodstream
10. A skin infection caused by a fungus that spreads out in an even circle, characterized by ring- like, scaly patches of red skin
11. An accumulation of pus in a body tissue, usually caused by a bacterial infection
12. Infection and inflammation of a gland, especially a lymph node
13. The triangular bone located at the bottom of the spine that is connected to the tailbone
16. A slippery fluid produced by mucous membranes that lubricates and protects the internal surfaces of the body
18. The medical term for lockjaw
19. A change in the genetic information within a cell
20. The practice, maintenance, and study of health
21. A term used to describe a disease that is rare then suddenly affects more people than usually expected

DOWN

4. A cancer that occurs on the surface or lining of an organ
7. A chemical produced by a gland or tissue that is released into the bloodstream
10. A skin infection caused by a fungus that spreads out in an even circle, characterized by ring- like, scaly patches of red skin
11. An accumulation of pus in a body tissue, usually caused by a bacterial infection
12. Infection and inflammation of a gland, especially a lymph node
13. The triangular bone located at the bottom of the spine that is connected to the tailbone
16. A slippery fluid produced by mucous membranes that lubricates and protects the internal surfaces of the body
18. The medical term for lockjaw
19. A change in the genetic information within a cell
20. The practice, maintenance, and study of health
21. A term used to describe a disease that is rare then suddenly affects more people than usually expected

A. Narcotic	B. Clubfoot	C. Mania	D. Epidemic	E. Pandemic
F. Uvea	G. Oximetry	H. Hookworm	I. Mutation	J. Mucus
K. Trismus	L. Hygiene	M. Dextrose	N. Mites	O. Carcinoma
P. Adenitis	Q. Sacrum	R. Hormone	S. Stool	T. Abscess
U. Ringworm	V. Paresis	W. Hiccup		

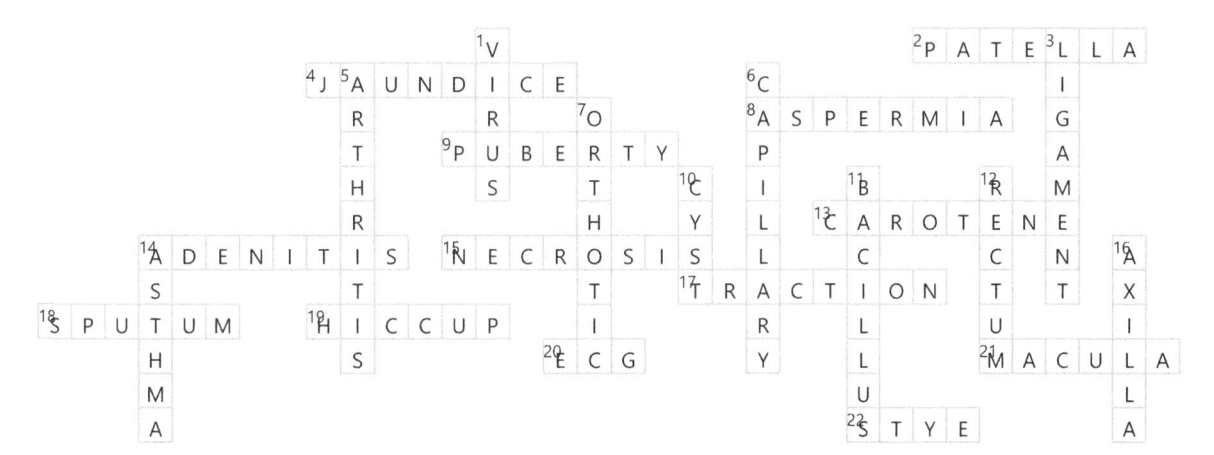

20. Using the Across and Down clues, write the correct words in the numbered grid below.

```
                    ¹V                              ²P A T E ³L L A
          ⁴J ⁵A U N D I C E            ⁶C                   I
             R       R       ⁷O        ⁸A S P E R M I A     G
             T       ⁹P U B E R T Y    P                    A
             H       S       T    ¹⁰C  I   ¹¹B   ¹²R        M
             R               H    Y    L   ¹³C A R O T E N E
       ¹⁴A D E N I T I S  ¹⁵N E C R O S I S  C       C    ¹⁶A
          S         T           T    ¹⁷T R A C T I O N T    X
       ¹⁸S P U T U M  ¹⁹H I C C U P   R       L       U     I
          H         S       ²⁰E C G   Y       L     ²¹M A C U L A
          M                                   U             L
          A                              ²²S  T Y E         A
```

ACROSS

2. The medical term for the kneecap
4. Yellowing of the skin and whites of the eyes because of the presence of excess bilirubin in the blood; usually a sign of a disorder of the liver
8. The failure either to produce or to ejaculate sperm
9. The period during which sexual development occurs
13. An orange pigment present in colored plants such as carrots that is converted by the body to the essential nutrient vitamin a
14. Infection and inflammation of a gland, especially a lymph node
15. The medical term for the death of tissue cells
17. The use of tension to hold a body part in place or to correct or prevent an alignment problem
18. Mucus and other material produced by the lining of the respiratory tract
19. Involuntary sudden contraction of the diaphragm along with the closing of the vocal cords, producing a "hiccup" sound
20. An electrocardiogram, which is a record of the electrical impulses that trigger the heartbeat; used to diagnose heart disorders
21. The area of the retina that allows fine details to be observed at the center of vision
22. A pus- filled abscess in the follicle of an eyelash

DOWN

2. The medical term for the kneecap
4. Yellowing of the skin and whites of the eyes because of the presence of excess bilirubin in the blood; usually a sign of a disorder of the liver
8. The failure either to produce or to ejaculate sperm
9. The period during which sexual development occurs
13. An orange pigment present in colored plants such as carrots that is converted by the body to the essential nutrient vitamin a
14. Infection and inflammation of a gland, especially a lymph node
15. The medical term for the death of tissue cells
17. The use of tension to hold a body part in place or to correct or prevent an alignment problem
18. Mucus and other material produced by the lining of the respiratory tract
19. Involuntary sudden contraction of the diaphragm along with the closing of the vocal cords, producing a "hiccup" sound
20. An electrocardiogram, which is a record of the electrical impulses that trigger the heartbeat; used to diagnose heart disorders
21. The area of the retina that allows fine details to be observed at the center of vision
22. A pus- filled abscess in the follicle of an eyelash

A. Arthritis	B. Rectum	C. Capillary	D. Sputum	E. Jaundice	F. Aspermia
G. Adenitis	H. Hiccup	I. Patella	J. Cyst	K. Carotene	L. Stye
M. Macula	N. Bacillus	O. ECG	P. Ligament	Q. Asthma	R. Puberty
S. Necrosis	T. Traction	U. Orthotic	V. Axilla	W. Virus	

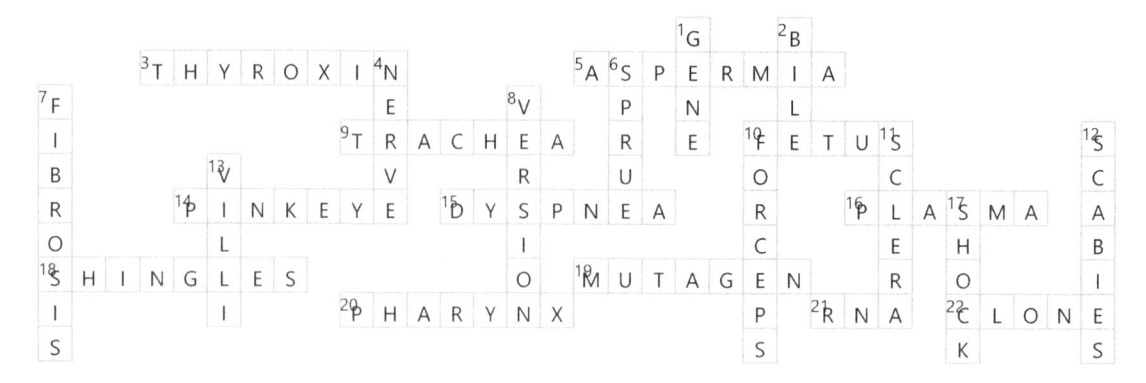

21. Using the Across and Down clues, write the correct words in the numbered grid below.

```
                                                    ¹G    ²B
            ³T H Y R O X I ⁴N           ⁵A ⁶S P E R M I A
      ⁷F                E       ⁸V         P    N    L
       I               ⁹T R A C H E A      R   ¹⁰F E T U ¹¹S              ¹²S
       B          ¹³V      V             R    O         C                 C
       R     ¹⁴P  I  N  K  E  Y  E  ¹⁵D  Y  S  P  N  E  A     ¹⁶P L A ¹⁷S M A
       O          L                  I         C              E    H      B
      ¹⁸S H I N G L E S               O    ¹⁹M U T A G E N    R    O      I
       I          I       ²⁰P H A R Y N X      P      ²¹R N A    ²²C L O N E
       S                                        S             K           S
```

ACROSS

3. A hormone produced by the thyroid gland that helps regulate energy production in the body
5. The failure either to produce or to ejaculate sperm
9. The tube running from the larynx (the voice box) down the neck and into the upper part of the chest
10. The term used to refer to an unborn child from 8 weeks after fertilization to birth
14. Inflammation of the membrane that covers the white of the eyes and lines the eyelids
15. Difficulty breathing
16. The liquid part of the blood, containing substances such as nutrients, salts, and proteins
18. A nerve infection caused by the chickenpox virus, causing areas of painful rash covered with blisters
19. Anything that can increase the rate of abnormal change in cells, which can lead to cancer
20. The throat
21. Ribonucleic acid, which helps to decode and process the information contained in DNA
22. An exact copy of a gene, cell, or organism

DOWN

3. A hormone produced by the thyroid gland that helps regulate energy production in the body
5. The failure either to produce or to ejaculate sperm
9. The tube running from the larynx (the voice box) down the neck and into the upper part of the chest
10. The term used to refer to an unborn child from 8 weeks after fertilization to birth
14. Inflammation of the membrane that covers the white of the eyes and lines the eyelids
15. Difficulty breathing
16. The liquid part of the blood, containing substances such as nutrients, salts, and proteins
18. A nerve infection caused by the chickenpox virus, causing areas of painful rash covered with blisters
19. Anything that can increase the rate of abnormal change in cells, which can lead to cancer
20. The throat
21. Ribonucleic acid, which helps to decode and process the information contained in DNA
22. An exact copy of a gene, cell, or organism

A. Shingles	B. Trachea	C. Aspermia	D. Pharynx	E. RNA	F. Fibrosis
G. Fetus	H. Thyroxin	I. Shock	J. Nerve	K. Villi	L. Gene
M. Sclera	N. Plasma	O. Forceps	P. Mutagen	Q. Sprue	R. Scabies
S. Pinkeye	T. Bile	U. Version	V. Clone	W. Dyspnea	

22. Using the Across and Down clues, write the correct words in the numbered grid below.

ACROSS

1. A long gland located behind the stomach that produces enzymes that help to break down food and hormones (insulin and glucagon) that help to regulate glucose levels in the blood
6. The hollow female reproductive organ in which a fertilized egg is implanted, and a fetus develops
11. Dull, aching pain in the lower back
13. A disease in which eye damage is caused by an increase in the pressure of the fluid within the eye
15. An abnormal swelling of the wall of an artery, caused by a weakening in the vessel wall
16. An element for the formation of thyroid hormones
18. The displacement of an organ from its normal position to a new one
19. A possibly life-threatening condition in which breathing stops, for either a short or long period of time
20. The drooping of the upper eyelid
21. A tunnel-like passage
22. The medical term for lockjaw
23. A sugar that is the main source of energy for the body

DOWN

1. A long gland located behind the stomach that produces enzymes that help to break down food and hormones (insulin and glucagon) that help to regulate glucose levels in the blood
6. The hollow female reproductive organ in which a fertilized egg is implanted, and a fetus develops
11. Dull, aching pain in the lower back
13. A disease in which eye damage is caused by an increase in the pressure of the fluid within the eye
15. An abnormal swelling of the wall of an artery, caused by a weakening in the vessel wall
16. An element for the formation of thyroid hormones
18. The displacement of an organ from its normal position to a new one
19. A possibly life-threatening condition in which breathing stops, for either a short or long period of time
20. The drooping of the upper eyelid
21. A tunnel-like passage
22. The medical term for lockjaw
23. A sugar that is the main source of energy for the body

A. Glaucoma   B. Pancreas   C. Progeria   D. Node   E. Overdose
F. Duodenum   G. Uterus   H. Aneurysm   I. Apnea   J. Silicone
K. Canal   L. Anemia   M. Airways   N. Trismus   O. Prolapse
P. Sputum   Q. Stye   R. Iodine   S. Ptosis   T. Lumbago
U. Parasite   V. Atresia   W. Glucose

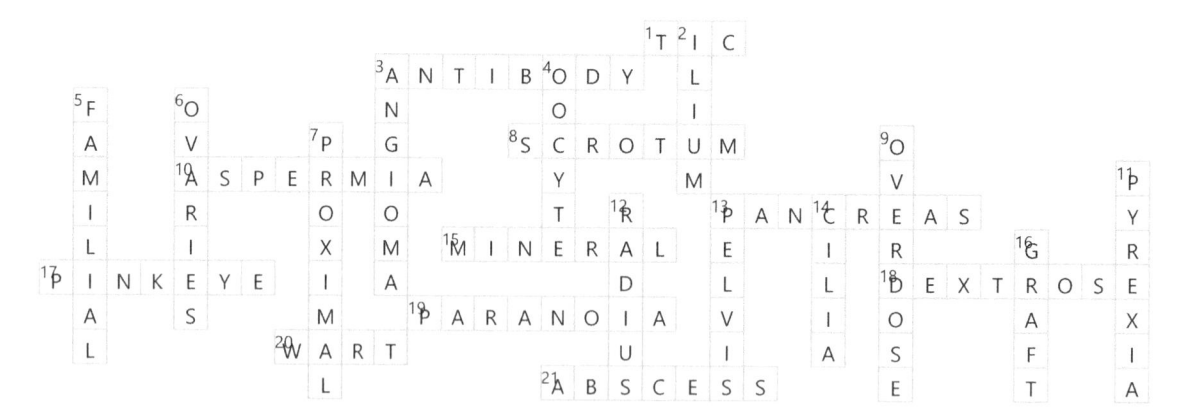

23. Using the Across and Down clues, write the correct words in the numbered grid below.

```
                              ¹T ²I  C
              ³A N T I B ⁴O D Y     L
   ⁵F    ⁶O        N     O         I
    A     V   ⁷P   G    ⁸S C R O T U M      ⁹O
    M    ¹⁰A S P E R M I A     Y   M         V         ¹¹P
    I     R        O     O     T  ¹²R  ¹³P A N ¹⁴C R E A S      Y
    L     I        X     M  ¹⁵M I N E R A L  E    I R    ¹⁶G     R
  ¹⁷P I N K E Y E  I    A           D         L   ¹⁸D E X T R O S E
    A     S        M  ¹⁹P A R A N O I A       V   O        A     X
    L             ²⁰W A R T            U       I   S        F     I
                   L                ²¹A B S C E S S         E     T    A
```

ACROSS

1. An involuntary, repetitive movement such as a twitch
3. A protein made by white blood cells that reacts with a specific foreign protein as part of the immune response
8. The sac containing the testicles
10. The failure either to produce or to ejaculate sperm
13. A long gland located behind the stomach that produces enzymes that help to break down food and hormones (insulin and glucagon) that help to regulate glucose levels in the blood
15. A substance that is a necessary part of a healthy diet (such as potassium, calcium, sodium, phosphorus, and magnesium)
17. Inflammation of the membrane that covers the white of the eyes and lines the eyelids
18. Another name for the sugar glucose
19. A disorder in which a person becomes overly suspicious and emotionally sensitive
20. A contagious, harmless growth caused by a virus that occurs on the skin or a mucous membrane
21. An accumulation of pus in a body tissue, usually caused by a bacterial infection

DOWN

1. An involuntary, repetitive movement such as a twitch
3. A protein made by white blood cells that reacts with a specific foreign protein as part of the immune response
8. The sac containing the testicles
10. The failure either to produce or to ejaculate sperm
13. A long gland located behind the stomach that produces enzymes that help to break down food and hormones (insulin and glucagon) that help to regulate glucose levels in the blood
15. A substance that is a necessary part of a healthy diet (such as potassium, calcium, sodium, phosphorus, and magnesium)
17. Inflammation of the membrane that covers the white of the eyes and lines the eyelids
18. Another name for the sugar glucose
19. A disorder in which a person becomes overly suspicious and emotionally sensitive
20. A contagious, harmless growth caused by a virus that occurs on the skin or a mucous membrane
21. An accumulation of pus in a body tissue, usually caused by a bacterial infection

A. Cilia	B. Paranoia	C. Pinkeye	D. Angioma	E. Pelvis	F. Radius
G. Familial	H. Ovaries	I. Pancreas	J. Graft	K. Oocyte	L. Proximal
M. Mineral	N. Aspermia	O. Overdose	P. Antibody	Q. Abscess	R. Scrotum
S. Tic	T. Wart	U. Pyrexia	V. Dextrose	W. Ilium	

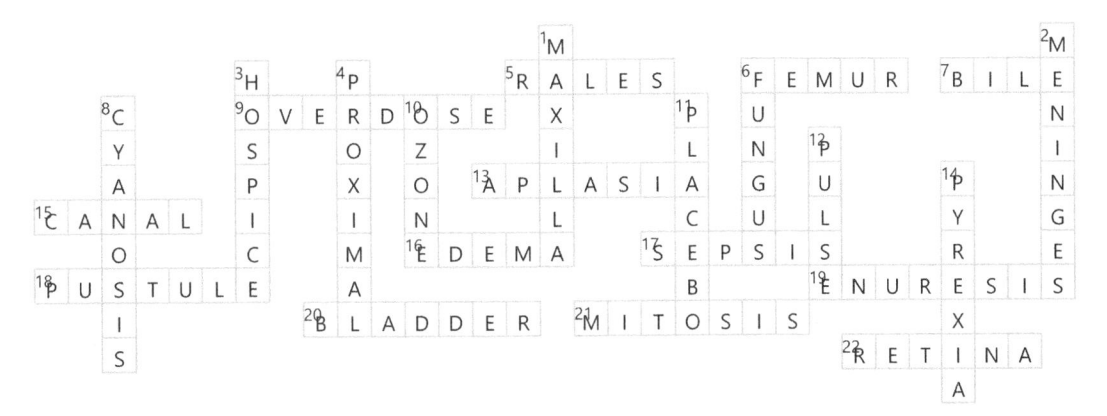

24. Using the Across and Down clues, write the correct words in the numbered grid below.

```
                              ¹M                              ²M
                ³H      ⁴P        ⁵R A L E S      ⁶F E M U R  ⁷B I L E
       ⁸C       ⁹O V E R D ¹⁰O S E      X        ¹¹P          N
        Y        S         O          I         U  ¹²P        I
        A        P         X       ¹³A P L A S I A  U          ¹⁴P    N
       ¹⁵C A N A L         I         N  L         C  U         Y    G
        O                  C        ¹⁶E D E M A   ¹⁷S E P S I S      R  E
       ¹⁸P U S T U L E     A                      B         ¹⁹E N U R E S I S
        I           ²⁰B L A D D E R   ²¹M I T O S I S          X
        S                                                ²²R E T I N A
                                                          A
```

ACROSS

5. Abnormal crackling or bubbling sounds heard in the lungs during breathing
6. The bone located between the hip and the knee
7. A yellow-green liquid produced in the liver whose function is to remove waste from the liver and break down fats as food is digested
9. An excessively large dose of a drug, which can lead to coma and death
13. The complete or partial failure of any organ or tissue to grow
15. A tunnel-like passage
16. Abnormal buildup of fluid in the body, which may cause visible swelling
17. The infection of a wound or tissue with bacteria, causing the spread of the bacteria into the bloodstream
18. A small blister containing pus
19. The medical term for wetting the bed
20. An organ located in the pelvis whose function is to collect and store urine until it is expelled
21. The process by which most cells divide to reproduce
22. A membrane lining the inside of the back of the eye that contains light-sensitive nerve cells that convert focused light into nerve impulses, making vision possible

DOWN

5. Abnormal crackling or bubbling sounds heard in the lungs during breathing
6. The bone located between the hip and the knee
7. A yellow-green liquid produced in the liver whose function is to remove waste from the liver and break down fats as food is digested
9. An excessively large dose of a drug, which can lead to coma and death
13. The complete or partial failure of any organ or tissue to grow
15. A tunnel-like passage
16. Abnormal buildup of fluid in the body, which may cause visible swelling
17. The infection of a wound or tissue with bacteria, causing the spread of the bacteria into the bloodstream
18. A small blister containing pus
19. The medical term for wetting the bed
20. An organ located in the pelvis whose function is to collect and store urine until it is expelled
21. The process by which most cells divide to reproduce
22. A membrane lining the inside of the back of the eye that contains light-sensitive nerve cells that convert focused light into nerve impulses, making vision possible

A. Ozone	B. Sepsis	C. Aplasia
G. Fungus	H. Maxilla	I. Bile
M. Pyrexia	N. Cyanosis	O. Placebo
S. Overdose	T. Edema	U. Mitosis
D. Pulse	E. Meninges	F. Proximal
J. Bladder	K. Rales	L. Femur
P. Pustule	Q. Retina	R. Hospice
V. Canal	W. Enuresis	

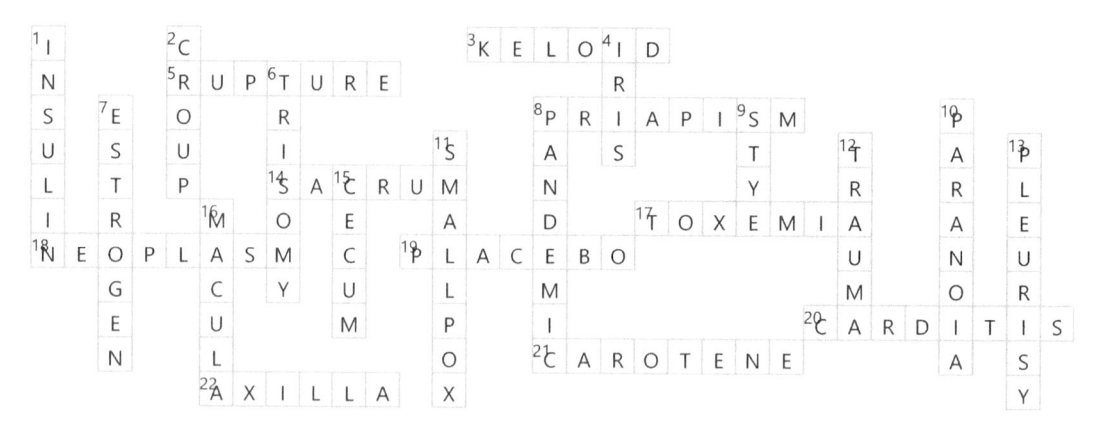

25. Using the Across and Down clues, write the correct words in the numbered grid below.

```
 1I           2C              3K E L O 4I D
  N           5R U P 6T U R E         R
  S   7E      O     R            8P R I A P I 9S M      10P
  U    S      U     I       11S   A        S    12T     A   13P
  L    T      P    14S A 15C R U M   N        Y    R     R   L
  I    R     16M     O     E     A   D    17T O X E M I A   A   E
 18N E O P L  A  S    M     C    19P L A C E B O      U   N   U
  G         C     Y     U    L    M              M   O   R
  E         U           M    P    I          20C A R D I T S
  N         L                O   21C A R O T E N E      A   S
           22A X  I  L L A    X                        Y
```

ACROSS

3. A raised, firm, thick scar that forms because of a defect in the natural healing process
5. A tear or break in an organ or tissue
8. A painful, persistent erection without sexual arousal, requiring emergency treatment
14. The triangular bone located at the bottom of the spine that is connected to the tailbone
17. The presence of bacterial toxins in the blood
18. Another term for a tumor
19. A chemically inactive substance given in place of a drug to test how much of a drug's effectiveness can be attributed to a patient's expectations that the drug will have a positive effect
20. Inflammation of the heart
21. An orange pigment present in colored plants such as carrots that is converted by the body to the essential nutrient vitamin a
22. Medical term for the armpit

DOWN

3. A raised, firm, thick scar that forms because of a defect in the natural healing process
5. A tear or break in an organ or tissue
8. A painful, persistent erection without sexual arousal, requiring emergency treatment
14. The triangular bone located at the bottom of the spine that is connected to the tailbone
17. The presence of bacterial toxins in the blood
18. Another term for a tumor
19. A chemically inactive substance given in place of a drug to test how much of a drug's effectiveness can be attributed to a patient's expectations that the drug will have a positive effect
20. Inflammation of the heart
21. An orange pigment present in colored plants such as carrots that is converted by the body to the essential nutrient vitamin a
22. Medical term for the armpit

A. Neoplasm	B. Cecum	C. Carditis	D. Trauma	E. Pleurisy	F. Pandemic
G. Macula	H. Rupture	I. Stye	J. Priapism	K. Insulin	L. Estrogen
M. Smallpox	N. Toxemia	O. Sacrum	P. Croup	Q. Placebo	R. Trisomy
S. Carotene	T. Paranoia	U. Axilla	V. Iris	W. Keloid	

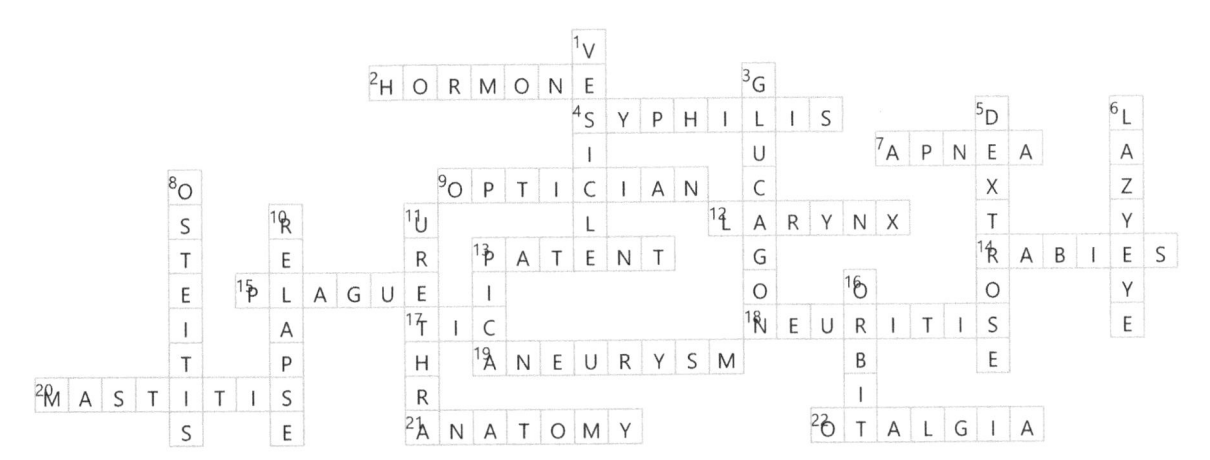

26. Using the Across and Down clues, write the correct words in the numbered grid below.

```
            ¹V
     ²H O R M O N E      ³G              ⁵D        ⁶L
              ⁴S Y P H I L I S     ⁷A P N E A      A
              I           U              X         Z
  ⁸O          ⁹O P T I C I A N          ¹²L A R Y N X    Y
   S  ¹⁰R  ¹¹U    L                      T        ¹⁴R A B I E S
   T   E   R   ¹³P A T E N T   G                  Y
   E ¹⁵P L A G U E   I           ¹⁶O       O       Y
   I   A      ¹⁷T   C           ¹⁸N E U R I T I S  E
   T   P      H  ¹⁹A N E U R Y S M   B      E
  ²⁰M A S T I T I S   R                   I
   S   E     ²¹A N A T O M Y         ²²O T A L G I A
```

ACROSS
2. A chemical produced by a gland or tissue that is released into the bloodstream
4. A sexually transmitted disease
7. A possibly life-threatening condition in which breathing stops, for either a short or long period of time
9. A person who specializes in the making and adjustment of eyeglasses and contact lenses
12. The medical term for the voice box, the organ in the throat that produces voice and prevents food from entering the airway
13. Not obstructed; open
14. An infectious viral disease primarily affecting animals
15. A serious infectious disease transmitted to humans through bites of rodent fleas
17. An involuntary, repetitive movement such as a twitch
18. Inflammation of a nerve, often characterized by pain, numbness, or tingling
19. An abnormal swelling of the wall of an artery, caused by a weakening in the vessel wall
20. Inflammation of the breast, which is usually caused by a bacterial infection
21. The structure of bodies
22. The medical term for an earache

DOWN
2. A chemical produced by a gland or tissue that is released into the bloodstream
4. A sexually transmitted disease
7. A possibly life-threatening condition in which breathing stops, for either a short or long period of time
9. A person who specializes in the making and adjustment of eyeglasses and contact lenses
12. The medical term for the voice box, the organ in the throat that produces voice and prevents food from entering the airway
13. Not obstructed; open
14. An infectious viral disease primarily affecting animals
15. A serious infectious disease transmitted to humans through bites of rodent fleas
17. An involuntary, repetitive movement such as a twitch
18. Inflammation of a nerve, often characterized by pain, numbness, or tingling
19. An abnormal swelling of the wall of an artery, caused by a weakening in the vessel wall
20. Inflammation of the breast, which is usually caused by a bacterial infection
21. The structure of bodies
22. The medical term for an earache

A. Urethra   B. Anatomy   C. Neuritis   D. Tic   E. Aneurysm   F. Rabies
G. Hormone   H. Glucagon   I. Patent   J. Mastitis   K. Larynx   L. Plague
M. Syphilis   N. Lazy eye   O. Osteitis   P. Otalgia   Q. Apnea   R. Vesicle
S. Relapse   T. Dextrose   U. Pica   V. Optician   W. Orbit

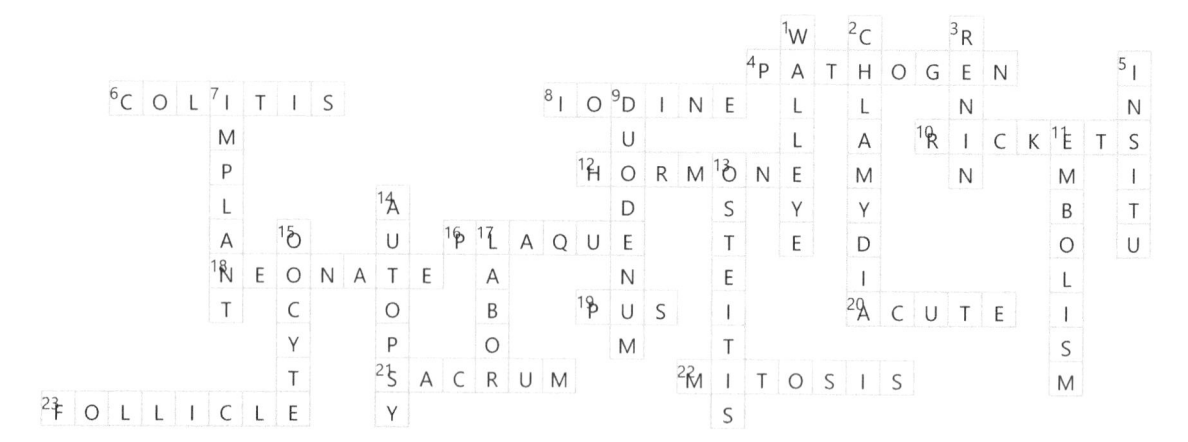

27. Using the Across and Down clues, write the correct words in the numbered grid below.

```
                                              ¹W    ²C          ³R
                                           ⁴P  A  T  H  O  G  E  N            ⁵I
⁶C  O  L  ⁷I  T  I  S           ⁸I  O  ⁹D  I  N  E     L     L              N
         M                              U              L     A     ¹⁰R  I  C  K  ¹¹E  T  S
         P                              ¹²H  O  R  M  ¹³O  N  E     M              N     M     I
         L              ¹⁴A              D              S     Y              Y     B     T
         A     ¹⁵O        U     ¹⁶P  ¹⁷L  A  Q  U  E     T     E              D     O     U
         ¹⁸N  E  O  N  A  T  E     A              N     E                          L
         T     C        O        B        ¹⁹P  U  S     I           ²⁰A  C  U  T  E     I
         Y     P        O                    M     T                          S
         T     ²¹S  A  C  R  U  M           ²²M  I  T  O  S  I  S              M
²³F  O  L  L  I  C  L  E     Y                    S
```

ACROSS

4. Any substance capable of causing a disease
6. Inflammation of the large intestine (the colon), which usually leads to abdominal pain, fever, and diarrhea with blood and mucus
8. An element for the formation of thyroid hormones
10. A childhood disease in which bones lack calcium and are deformed because of vitamin d deficiency
12. A chemical produced by a gland or tissue that is released into the bloodstream
16. An area of buildup of fat deposits in an artery, causing narrowing of the artery and possibly heart disease
18. A term used to describe a newborn infant from birth to 1 month of age
19. A thick, yellowish or greenish fluid that contains dead white blood cells, tissues, and bacteria; occurs at the site of a bacterial infection
20. Describes a condition or illness that begins suddenly and is usually short-lasting
21. The triangular bone located at the bottom of the spine that is connected to the tailbone
22. The process by which most cells divide to reproduce
23. A tiny pouchlike cavity in a structure of the body, such as a hair follicle

DOWN

4. Any substance capable of causing a disease
6. Inflammation of the large intestine (the colon), which usually leads to abdominal pain, fever, and diarrhea with blood and mucus
8. An element for the formation of thyroid hormones
10. A childhood disease in which bones lack calcium and are deformed because of vitamin d deficiency
12. A chemical produced by a gland or tissue that is released into the bloodstream
16. An area of buildup of fat deposits in an artery, causing narrowing of the artery and possibly heart disease
18. A term used to describe a newborn infant from birth to 1 month of age
19. A thick, yellowish or greenish fluid that contains dead white blood cells, tissues, and bacteria; occurs at the site of a bacterial infection
20. Describes a condition or illness that begins suddenly and is usually short-lasting
21. The triangular bone located at the bottom of the spine that is connected to the tailbone
22. The process by which most cells divide to reproduce
23. A tiny pouchlike cavity in a structure of the body, such as a hair follicle

A. Labor	B. Oocyte	C. Pathogen	D. Pus	E. Iodine
F. Duodenum	G. Mitosis	H. In situ	I. Chlamydia	J. Embolism
K. Implant	L. Colitis	M. Osteitis	N. Follicle	O. Sacrum
P. Rickets	Q. Walleye	R. Neonate	S. Acute	T. Autopsy
U. Hormone	V. Renin	W. Plaque		

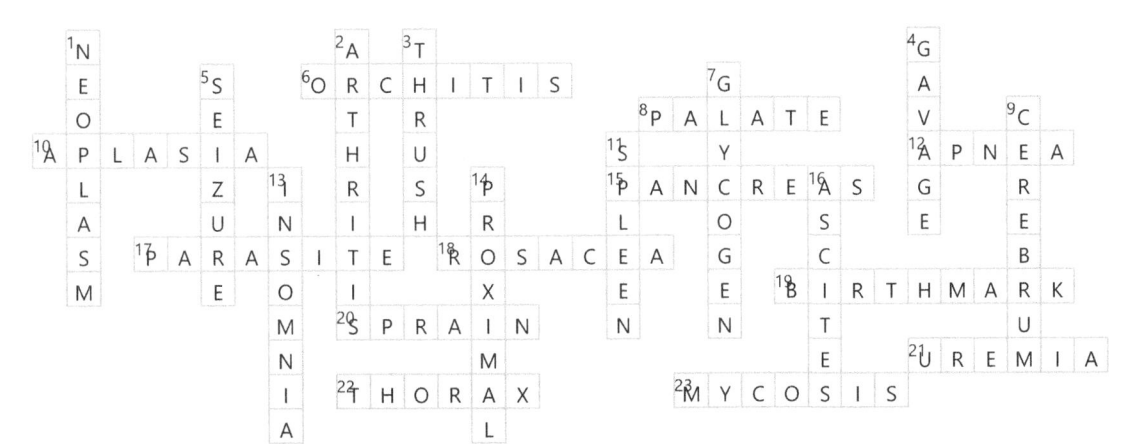

28. Using the Across and Down clues, write the correct words in the numbered grid below.

```
 1N              2A  3T                      4G
  E      5S    6O R C H I T I S      7G       A
  O       E     T   R            8P A L A T E V      9C
10A P L A S I A    H   U         11S         12A P N E A
  L       Z  13I  R   S   14P   15P A N C R E 16A S G      R
  A       U   N   I   H   R      L           S   E      B
  S      17P A R A S I T E  18R O S A C E A  G           B
  M       E   O       X       E              C
               M  20S P R A I N   E    19B I R T H M A R K
               N      M          N       T              U
               I   22T H O R A X       E         21U R E M I A
               A              L    23M Y C O S I S
```

ACROSS

6. Inflammation of a testicle, which can be caused by infection with the mumps virus
8. The roof of the mouth
10. The complete or partial failure of any organ or tissue to grow
12. A possibly life-threatening condition in which breathing stops, for either a short or long period of time
15. A long gland located behind the stomach that produces enzymes that help to break down food and hormones (insulin and glucagon) that help to regulate glucose levels in the blood
17. Organisms that lives on or in other organisms, from which it obtains nutrients
18. A skin disorder that is characterized by patches of red skin on the nose and cheeks and acne- like bumps
19. Any area of discolored skin that is present when a baby is born
20. The tearing or stretching of the ligaments in a joint, characterized by pain, swelling, and an inability to move the joint
21. Abnormally high levels of waste products such as urea in the blood
22. The chest
23. Any disease caused by a fungus

DOWN

6. Inflammation of a testicle, which can be caused by infection with the mumps virus
8. The roof of the mouth
10. The complete or partial failure of any organ or tissue to grow
12. A possibly life-threatening condition in which breathing stops, for either a short or long period of time
15. A long gland located behind the stomach that produces enzymes that help to break down food and hormones (insulin and glucagon) that help to regulate glucose levels in the blood
17. Organisms that lives on or in other organisms, from which it obtains nutrients
18. A skin disorder that is characterized by patches of red skin on the nose and cheeks and acne- like bumps
19. Any area of discolored skin that is present when a baby is born
20. The tearing or stretching of the ligaments in a joint, characterized by pain, swelling, and an inability to move the joint
21. Abnormally high levels of waste products such as urea in the blood
22. The chest
23. Any disease caused by a fungus

A. Birthmark	B. Mycosis	C. Parasite	D. Arthritis	E. Glycogen	F. Seizure
G. Gavage	H. Rosacea	I. Apnea	J. Aplasia	K. Sprain	L. Cerebrum
M. Insomnia	N. Spleen	O. Palate	P. Uremia	Q. Proximal	R. Orchitis
S. Thorax	T. Neoplasm	U. Pancreas	V. Thrush	W. Ascites	

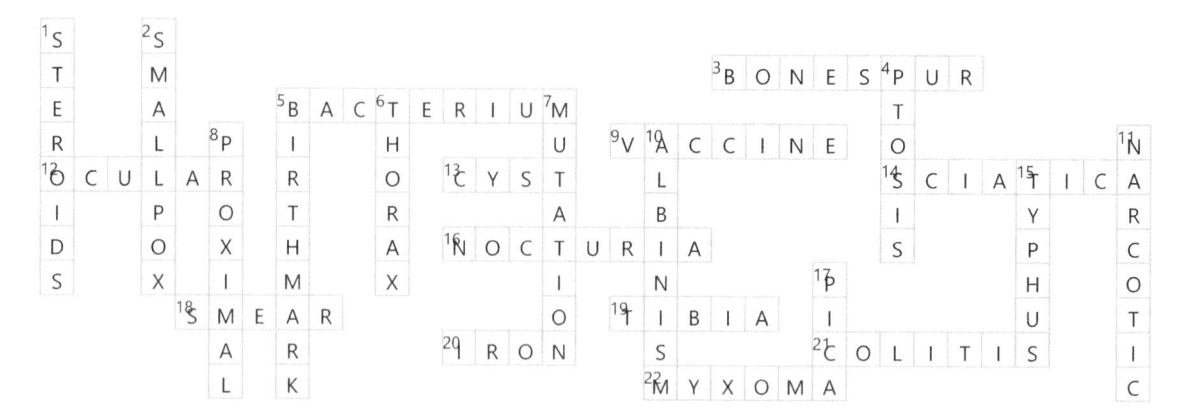

29. Using the Across and Down clues, write the correct words in the numbered grid below.

```
 1S       2S
  T        M                                              3B O N E S 4P U R
  E        A         5B A C 6T E R I U 7M                         T
  R        L    8P   I      H         U     9V 10A C C I N E      O           11N
 12O C U L A R      I      O    13C Y S T       L          14S C I 15T I C A
  I        P        O      T         A         B              I      Y        R
  D        O        X      H         A    16N O C T U R I A   S      P        C
  S        X        I      M                   N       17P           H        O
            18S M E A R                        19T I B I A   I       U        T
                    A      R          20I R O N            S        21C O L I T I S
                    L      K                       22M Y X O M A             C
```

ACROSS

3. An abnormal growth of bone out of another bone, often located on the heel and usually painful
5. A tiny, single- celled microorganism, commonly known as a germ
9. A preparation of weakened microorganisms given to create resistance to a certain disease
12. Describes something related to the eyes
13. A lump filled with either fluid or soft material, occurring in any organ or tissue
14. Pain along the sciatic nerve, which runs down the length of the leg to the foot
16. Urination or a sleep- disturbing need to urinate during the night
18. A sample of cells spread across a glass slide to be examined through a microscope
19. The thicker of the two long bones in the lower leg
20. A mineral necessary for the formation of important biological substances such as hemoglobin, myoglobin, and certain enzymes
21. Inflammation of the large intestine (the colon), which usually leads to abdominal pain, fever, and diarrhea with blood and mucus
22. A noncancerous tumor made of mucous material and fibrous connective tissue

DOWN

3. An abnormal growth of bone out of another bone, often located on the heel and usually painful
5. A tiny, single- celled microorganism, commonly known as a germ
9. A preparation of weakened microorganisms given to create resistance to a certain disease
12. Describes something related to the eyes
13. A lump filled with either fluid or soft material, occurring in any organ or tissue
14. Pain along the sciatic nerve, which runs down the length of the leg to the foot
16. Urination or a sleep- disturbing need to urinate during the night
18. A sample of cells spread across a glass slide to be examined through a microscope
19. The thicker of the two long bones in the lower leg
20. A mineral necessary for the formation of important biological substances such as hemoglobin, myoglobin, and certain enzymes
21. Inflammation of the large intestine (the colon), which usually leads to abdominal pain, fever, and diarrhea with blood and mucus
22. A noncancerous tumor made of mucous material and fibrous connective tissue

A. Albinism	B. Vaccine	C. Ptosis	D. Typhus	E. Ocular	F. Iron
G. Smallpox	H. Myxoma	I. Steroids	J. Colitis	K. Nocturia	L. Thorax
M. Narcotic	N. Birthmark	O. Smear	P. Pica	Q. Proximal	R. Sciatica
S. Bacterium	T. Mutation	U. Cyst	V. Tibia	W. Bone spur	

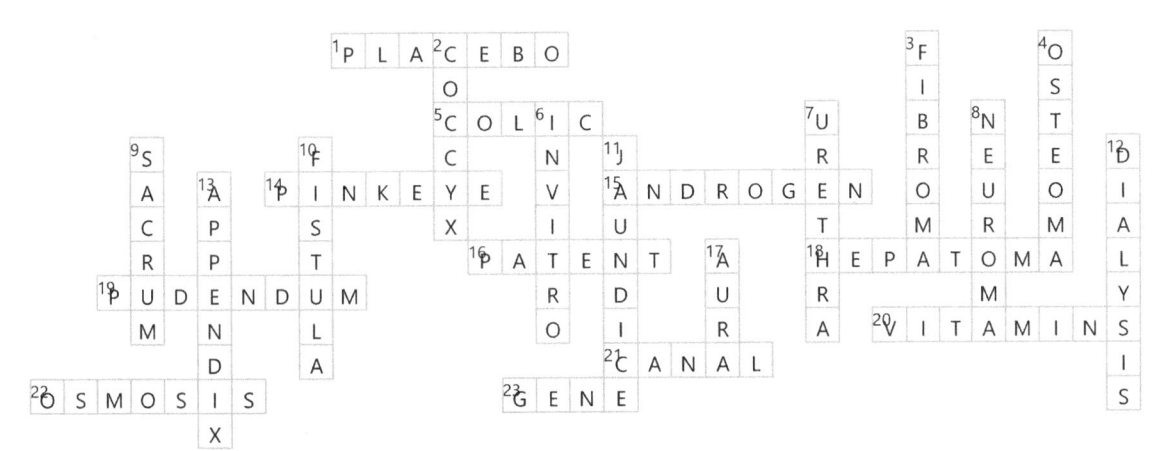

30. Using the Across and Down clues, write the correct words in the numbered grid below.

```
              ¹P L A ²C E B O                    ³F      ⁴O
                    O                             I       S
                    ⁵C O L ⁶I C            ⁷U    B   ⁸N  T
      ⁹S       ¹⁰F    C     N    ¹¹J      R    R   E  ¹²D
       A  ¹³A ¹⁴P I N K E Y E  ¹⁵A N D R O G E N  O   U   O   I
       C   P   S         X     U              T   M   R   M   A
       R   P   T         ¹⁶P A T E N T  ¹⁷A  ¹⁸H E P A T O M A L
   ¹⁹P U D E N D U M     R     D    U   R         M           Y
       M   N   L         O     I    R   A  ²⁰V I T A M I N S
           D   A              ²¹C A N A L                    I
   ²²O S M O S I S       ²³G E N E                           S
           X
```

ACROSS

1. A chemically inactive substance given in place of a drug to test how much of a drug's effectiveness can be attributed to a patient's expectations that the drug will have a positive effect
5. Waves of pain in the abdomen that increase in strength, disappear, and return
14. Inflammation of the membrane that covers the white of the eyes and lines the eyelids
15. A hormone (such as testosterone) that causes development of male characteristics and sex organs
16. Not obstructed; open
18. A cancerous tumor of the liver
19. The external genitals, usually referring to the female
20. Complex substances that are necessary in small amounts to maintain health and ensure proper development and functioning of the body
21. A tunnel-like passage
22. The process of passage of the solvent portion of a lesser- concentrated solution through a semipermeable membrane into a higher- concentrated solution until the two solutions are equal in concentration
23. The basic unit of DNA, which is responsible for passing genetic information

DOWN

2. Four fused bones that form a triangular shape at the base of the spine (also known as the tailbone)
3. A noncancerous tumor of connective tissue
4. A noncancerous bone tumor
6. "in glass"; a biological test or process that is carried out in a laboratory
7. The tube by which urine is released from the bladder
8. A noncancerous tumor occurring in nerve tissue
9. The triangular bone located at the bottom of the spine that is connected to the tailbone
10. An abnormal passageway from one organ to another or from an organ to the body surface
11. Yellowing of the skin and whites of the eyes because of the presence of excess bilirubin in the blood; usually a sign of a disorder of the liver
12. A procedure to treat kidney failure in which artificial means are used to filter waste, maintain acid-base balance, and remove excess fluid from the body
13. A short, tube-like structure that branches off the large intestine
17. A "warning" signal that comes before a migraine headache or an epileptic seizure, which might include emotions or sensations of movement or discomfort

A. Hepatoma   B. Colic   C. Fistula   D. Osmosis   E. Appendix
F. Sacrum   G. Fibroma   H. Pinkeye   I. Dialysis   J. Coccyx
K. Patent   L. Osteoma   M. Neuroma   N. Androgen   O. Canal
P. Aura   Q. Jaundice   R. Vitamins   S. Urethra   T. Gene
U. Placebo   V. In vitro   W. Pudendum

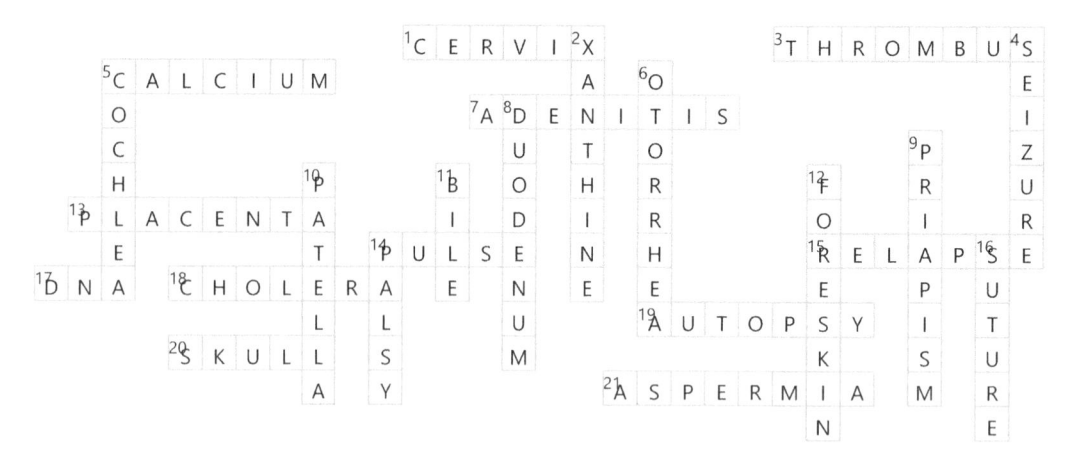

31. Using the Across and Down clues, write the correct words in the numbered grid below.

```
                              ¹C  E  R  V  I  ²X        ³T  H  R  O  M  B  U  ⁴S
         ⁵C  A  L  C  I  U  M              A     ⁶O                            E
            O                      ⁷A ⁸D  E  N  I  T  I  S                     I
            C                          U     T     O              ⁹P           Z
            H           ¹⁰P        ¹¹B O     H     R        ¹²F     R           U
        ¹³P L  A  C  E  N  T  A        I     D     I              O     I      R
            E                    T    ¹⁴P U  L  S  E        ¹⁵R  E  L  A  P ¹⁶S E
        ¹⁷D N           ¹⁸C H  O  L  E  R  A        E            E        P   U
                           L           L     U              ¹⁹A U  T  O  P  S  Y     I        T
                        ²⁰S K  U  L  L  S           M                    K        S     U
                           A              Y                  ²¹A  S  P  E  R  M  I  A    R
                                                                                 N       E
```

ACROSS

1. A small, round organ making up the neck of the uterus and separating it from the vagina
3. A blood clot in a blood vessel
5. A plentiful mineral in the body and the basic component of teeth and bones
7. Infection and inflammation of a gland, especially a lymph node
13. An organ formed in the uterus during pregnancy that links the blood of the mother to the blood of the fetus
14. The expansion and contraction of a blood vessel due to the blood pumped through it
15. The return of a disease or symptom after it had disappeared
17. Deoxyribonucleic acid; responsible for passing genetic information in nearly all organisms
18. A bacterial infection of the small intestine that causes severe watery diarrhea, dehydration, and possibly death
19. The examination of a body following death, possibly to determine the cause of death or for research
20. The bones that form the framework of the head and enclose and protect the brain and other sensory organs
21. The failure either to produce or to ejaculate sperm

DOWN

2. A bronchodilator drug that is used to treat asthma
4. Sudden uncontrolled waves of electrical activity in the brain, causing involuntary movement or loss of consciousness
5. A coiled organ in the inner ear that plays a large role in hearing by picking up sound vibrations and transmitting them as electrical signals
6. A discharge from an inflamed ear
8. The first part of the small intestine, immediately following the stomach
9. A painful, persistent erection without sexual arousal, requiring emergency treatment
10. The medical term for the kneecap
11. A yellow-green liquid produced in the liver whose function is to remove waste from the liver and break down fats as food is digested
12. The loose skin that covers the head of the penis
14. Loss of sensation or ability to move
16. A surgical stitch that helps close an incision or wound so that it can heal properly

A. Aspermia B. Skull   C. Cochlea   D. Relapse   E. Calcium
F. Palsy   G. Seizure   H. Bile   I. Autopsy   J. Placenta
K. DNA   L. Thrombus M. Patella   N. Cholera   O. Pulse
P. Foreskin Q. Suture   R. Priapism S. Xanthine T. Cervix
U. Otorrhea V. Adenitis W. Duodenum

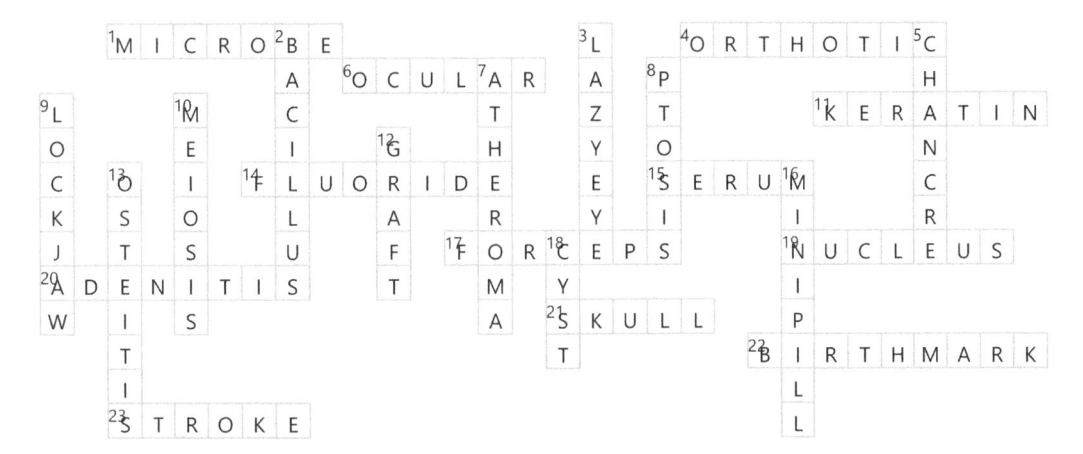

32. Using the Across and Down clues, write the correct words in the numbered grid below.

```
           ¹M I C R O ²B E                    ³L      ⁴O R T H O T I ⁵C
                     A  ⁶O C U L ⁷A R          A  ⁸P                  H
    ⁹L      ¹⁰M       C           T            Z   T          ¹¹K E R A T I N
     O       E       I   ¹²G      H            Y   O                   N
     C  ¹³O  I  ¹⁴F L U O R I D E               E  ¹⁵S E R U ¹⁶M        C
     K   S   O      L   A        R             Y   I          I        R
     J   T   S      U   F  ¹⁷F O R ¹⁸C E P S        ¹⁹N U C L E U S
    ²⁰A  D E N I T I S      T      M             Y        I
     W   I       S          T     ²¹S K U L L              P
         T                  A                     ²²B I R T H M A R K
         I                                        L
        ²³S T R O K E                              L
```

ACROSS

1. Another term for a microorganism, especially one that causes disease
4. A device used to correct or control deformed bones, muscles, or joints
6. Describes something related to the eyes
11. A tough protein found in skin, nails, and hair
14. A mineral that helps protect teeth against decay
15. The clear, watery fluid that separates from clotted blood
17. Instruments resembling tweezers that are used to handle objects or tissue during surgery
19. The center or most important point of an object
20. Infection and inflammation of a gland, especially a lymph node
21. The bones that form the framework of the head and enclose and protect the brain and other sensory organs
22. Any area of discolored skin that is present when a baby is born
23. Damage to part of the brain because of a lack of blood supply or the rupturing of a blood vessel

DOWN

2. Any bacteria that is rod-shaped
3. The common name for the visual defect resulting from untreated strabismus, in which the eyes are not correctly aligned
5. A painless sore that has a thick, rubbery base and a defined edge
7. Fatty deposits on the inner walls of blood vessels, which can cause narrowing and decrease blood flow
8. The drooping of the upper eyelid
9. A spasm of the jaw muscles that prevents the mouth from opening, such as that caused by tetanus
10. The type of cell division that occurs only in the ovaries and testicles, producing cells with half the genes of the original cell
12. Healthy tissue that is used to replace diseased or defective tissue
13. Inflammation of bone
16. An oral contraceptive containing only the synthetic hormone progesterone (birth control pills contain estrogen and progesterone)
18. A lump filled with either fluid or soft material, occurring in any organ or tissue

A. Skull	B. Minipill	C. Nucleus	D. Ptosis	E. Cyst	F. Stroke
G. Serum	H. Bacillus	I. Meiosis	J. Chancre	K. Adenitis	L. Fluoride
M. Keratin	N. Lockjaw	O. Osteitis	P. Graft	Q. Lazy eye	R. Ocular
S. Orthotic	T. Birthmark	U. Forceps	V. Microbe	W. Atheroma	

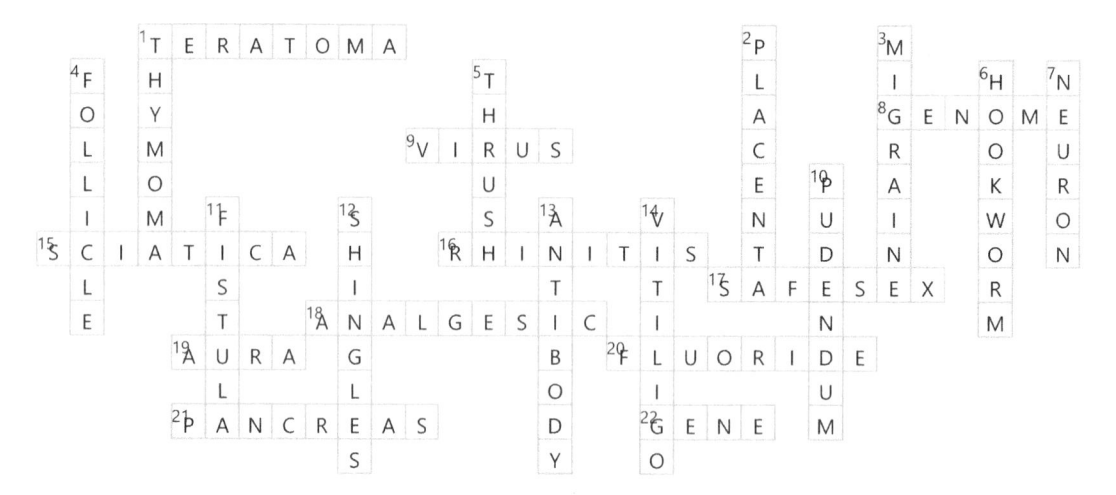

33. Using the Across and Down clues, write the correct words in the numbered grid below.

				¹T	E	R	A	T	O	M	A								²P		³M				⁶H		⁷N
		⁴F		H				⁵T											L		I		⁸G	E	N	O	M	E
		O		Y				H											A		R				O		U
		L		M				⁹V	I	R	U	S							C		A	¹⁰P					R
		L		O				U											E		I				K		O
		I		M	¹¹F		¹²S		S		¹³A		¹⁴V		N		U			W		N
¹⁵S	C	I	A	T	I	C	A		H		¹⁶R	H	I	N	I	T	I	S		¹⁷S	A	F	E	S	E	X
		L			S				I				T		T				N		R
		E			T		¹⁸A	N	A	L	G	E	S	I	C			N			M
				¹⁹A	U	R	A		G				B		²⁰F	L	U	O	R	I	D	E
				L				L				O		I			U
				²¹P	A	N	C	R	E	A	S			D		²²G	E	N	E	M
				S									Y		O

ACROSS

1. A tumor composed of cells not normally found in the part of the body when the tumor occurred
8. The complete set of an organism's genes
9. The smallest known disease-causing microorganism
15. Pain along the sciatic nerve, which runs down the length of the leg to the foot
16. Inflammation of the mucous membrane lining the nose
17. Measures taken to reduce the risk of acquiring a sexually transmitted disease, such as the use of a condom
18. A drug that relieves pain, such as aspirin or acetaminophen
19. A "warning" signal that comes before a migraine headache or an epileptic seizure, which might include emotions or sensations of movement or discomfort
20. A mineral that helps protect teeth against decay
21. A long gland located behind the stomach that produces enzymes that help to break down food and hormones (insulin and glucagon) that help to regulate glucose levels in the blood
22. The basic unit of DNA, which is responsible for passing genetic information

DOWN

1. A tumor of the thymus gland
2. An organ formed in the uterus during pregnancy that links the blood of the mother to the blood of the fetus
3. A severe headache, usually accompanied by vision problems and
4. A tiny pouchlike cavity in a structure of the body, such as a hair follicle
5. A candidiasis infection
6. Infestation by a small, round, blood-sucking parasite
7. Another term for a nerve cell
10. The external genitals, usually referring to the female
11. An abnormal passageway from one organ to another or from an organ to the body surface
12. A nerve infection caused by the chickenpox virus, causing areas of painful rash covered with blisters
13. A protein made by white blood cells that reacts with a specific foreign protein as part of the immune response
14. A condition in which patches of skin on the body lose their color

A. Shingles	B. Fluoride	C. Virus	D. Antibody	E. Sciatica
F. Fistula	G. Aura	H. Rhinitis	I. Hookworm	J. Placenta
K. Gene	L. Follicle	M. Vitiligo	N. Analgesic	O. Pancreas
P. Pudendum	Q. Genome	R. Neuron	S. Thymoma	T. Safe sex
U. Migraine	V. Teratoma	W. Thrush		

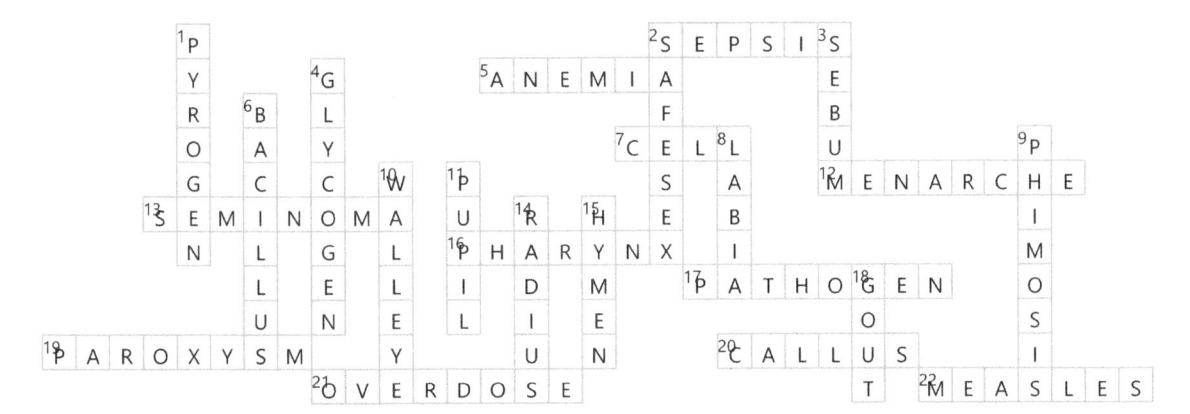

34. Using the Across and Down clues, write the correct words in the numbered grid below.

```
                                    ²S  E  P  S  ³S
    ¹P                              E           E
    Y           ⁴G      ⁵A N E M I  A           B
    R     ⁶B    L                   F           B
    O     A     Y              ⁷C E L ⁸L  U        ⁹P
    G     C     C  ¹⁰W  ¹¹P        S    A   ¹²M E N A R C H  E
  ¹³S E M  I  N  O  M  A   U  ¹⁴R  ¹⁵H  E    B              I
    N     L     G     L  ¹⁶P  H   A  R  Y  N  X             M
          L     E     L     D     M        ¹⁷P A T H O ¹⁸G E N     O
          U     N     E     I     E               O             S
  ¹⁹P A R O X Y S M     Y     U             ²⁰C A L L  U  S      I
                ²¹O V E R D O S E                 T ²²M E A S L E S
```

ACROSS

2. The infection of a wound or tissue with bacteria, causing the spread of the bacteria into the bloodstream
5. A condition in which the blood does not contain enough hemoglobin, the compound that carries oxygen from the lungs to other parts of the body
7. The tiny structures that make up all the tissues of the body and carry out all its functions
12. The beginning of menstruation
13. A type of testicular cancer that is made up of only a single type of cell
16. The throat
17. Any substance capable of causing a disease
19. A sudden attack or worsening of a disease's symptoms
20. A thickened area of skin due to consistent pressure or friction, or the area around a bone break where new bone is formed
21. An excessively large dose of a drug, which can lead to coma and death
22. An illness caused by a viral infection, causing a characteristic rash and a fever

DOWN

1. Any substance that causes a fever
2. Measures taken to reduce the risk of acquiring a sexually transmitted disease, such as the use of a condom
3. The oily, lubricating substance that is secreted by glands in the skin
4. The main form that glucose, the body's energy source, takes when it is stored
6. Any bacteria that is rod-shaped
8. The two pairs of skinfolds that protect the opening of the vagina
9. Tightness of the foreskin, which prevents it from being moved back over the head of the penis
10. A condition in which one eye turns outward
11. The opening at the center of the iris in the eye that constricts (contracts) and dilates (widens) in response to light
14. One of the two long bones of the forearm located on the thumb side of the arm
15. A thin fold of membrane partly closing the opening of the vagina
18. A disorder marked by high levels of uric acid in the blood

A. Sepsis	B. Pupil	C. Paroxysm	D. Callus	E. Bacillus
F. Seminoma	G. Pathogen	H. Anemia	I. Pharynx	J. Pyrogen
K. Overdose	L. Measles	M. Menarche	N. Safe sex	O. Phimosis
P. Walleye	Q. Sebum	R. Glycogen	S. Gout	T. Cell
U. Labia	V. Hymen	W. Radius		

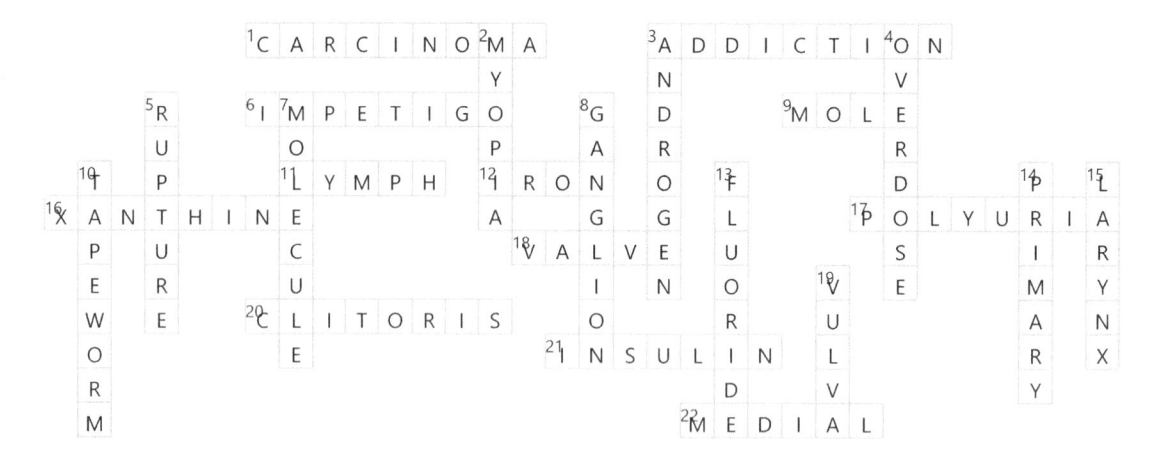

35. Using the Across and Down clues, write the correct words in the numbered grid below.

						¹C	A	R	C	I	N	O	²M	A				³A	D	D	I	C	T	I	⁴O	N		
													Y					N							V			
				⁵R		⁶I	⁷M	P	E	T	I	G	O		⁸G			D				⁹M	O	L	E			
				U			O						P		A			R							R			
	¹⁰T			P		¹¹L	Y	M	P	H		¹²I	R	O	N		¹³F								D		¹⁴P	¹⁵L
¹⁶X	A	N	T	H	I	N	E						A		G		L					¹⁷P	O	L	Y	U	R	I	A
	P			U		C					¹⁸V	A	L	V	E		U					S				I	R
	E			R		U						I			N		O		¹⁹V			E				M	Y
	W			E		²⁰C	L	I	T	O	R	I	S				R		U						A	N
	O					E						O			²¹I	N	S	U	L	I	N			R	X
	R											D							V						Y	
	M											²²M	E	D	I	A	L									

ACROSS

1. A cancer that occurs on the surface or lining of an organ
3. Dependence on a substance (such as alcohol or other drugs) or an activity, to the point that stopping is very difficult and causes severe physical and mental reactions
6. A highly contagious skin infection caused by bacteria, usually occurring around the nose and mouth
9. A brown to dark-brown spot on the skin that can be flat or raised
11. A milky fluid containing white blood cells, proteins, and fats
12. A mineral necessary for the formation of important biological substances such as hemoglobin, myoglobin, and certain enzymes
16. A bronchodilator drug that is used to treat asthma
17. The excessive production of urine
18. A structure that allows fluid flow in only one direction
20. A small female organ located near the opening of the vagina that swells when sexually aroused
21. A hormone made in the pancreas that plays an important role in the absorption of glucose (the body's main source of energy) into muscle cells
22. A term used to describe something situated on or near the midline of the body or a body structure

DOWN

2. The medical term for nearsightedness
3. A hormone (such as testosterone) that causes development of male characteristics and sex organs
4. An excessively large dose of a drug, which can lead to coma and death
5. A tear or break in an organ or tissue
7. The smallest unit of a substance that possesses its characteristics
8. A fluid-filled cyst attached to a tendon sheath or joint
10. A parasitic worm that lives in the intestines
13. A mineral that helps protect teeth against decay
14. A disease that began in the affected location
15. The medical term for the voice box, the organ in the throat that produces voice and prevents food from entering the airway
19. The outer, visible portion of the female genitals

A. Xanthine
B. Addiction
C. Valve
D. Androgen
E. Larynx
F. Lymph
G. Insulin
H. Iron
I. Impetigo
J. Rupture
K. Polyuria
L. Myopia
M. Molecule
N. Overdose
O. Fluoride
P. Ganglion
Q. Carcinoma
R. Mole
S. Medial
T. Clitoris
U. Vulva
V. Primary
W. Tapeworm

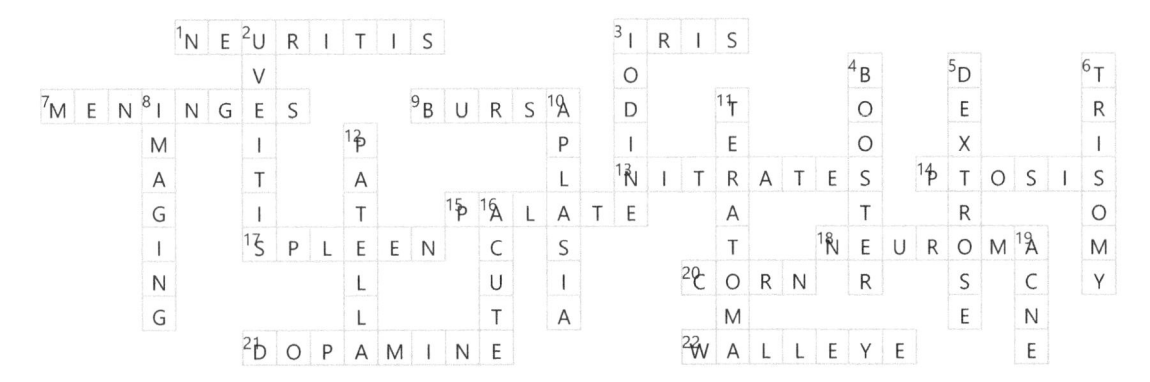

36. Using the Across and Down clues, write the correct words in the numbered grid below.

ACROSS

1. Inflammation of a nerve, often characterized by pain, numbness, or tingling
3. The colored part of the eye
7. The three membranes that surround and protect the spinal cord and brain
9. A fluid-filled sac that cushions and reduces friction in certain parts of the body
13. A group of drugs that widen blood vessels
14. The drooping of the upper eyelid
15. The roof of the mouth
17. An organ located in the upper left abdomen behind the ribs that removes and destroys old red blood cells and helps fight infection
18. A noncancerous tumor occurring in nerve tissue
20. A thickened callus on the foot that is caused by an improperly fitting shoe
21. A chemical that transmits messages in the brain and plays a role in movement
22. A condition in which one eye turns outward

DOWN

2. Inflammation of the uvea
3. An element for the formation of thyroid hormones
4. An additional dose of a vaccine taken after the first dose to maintain or renew the first one
5. Another name for the sugar glucose
6. The presence in the cells of three copies of a certain chromosome instead of the normal two copies
8. The technique of creating pictures of structures inside of the body using x-rays, ultrasound waves, or magnetic fields
10. The complete or partial failure of any organ or tissue to grow
11. A tumor composed of cells not normally found in the part of the body when the tumor occurred
12. The medical term for the kneecap
16. Describes a condition or illness that begins suddenly and is usually short-lasting
19. A skin condition characterized by inflamed, pus-filled areas that occur on the skin's surface, most commonly occurring during adolescence

A. Ptosis
B. Iris
C. Bursa
D. Uveitis
E. Acne
F. Walleye
G. Palate
H. Acute
I. Imaging
J. Neuritis
K. Nitrates
L. Booster
M. Iodine
N. Dopamine
O. Spleen
P. Patella
Q. Neuroma
R. Dextrose
S. Trisomy
T. Meninges
U. Teratoma
V. Aplasia
W. Corn

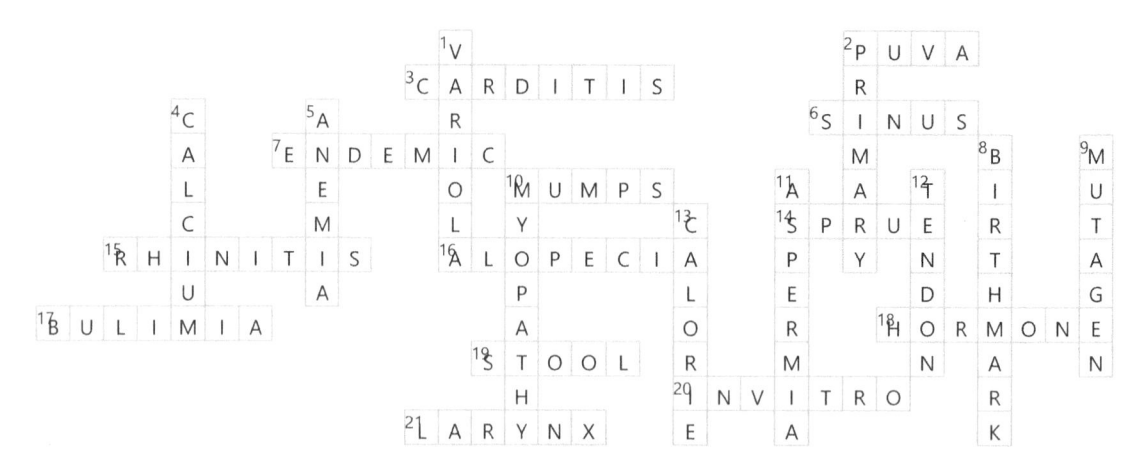

37. Using the Across and Down clues, write the correct words in the numbered grid below.

```
                              ¹V                          ²P  U  V  A
                           ³C  A  R  D  I  T  I  S        R
              ⁴C        ⁵A  R                          ⁶S  I  N  U  S
              A      ⁷E  N  D  E  M  I  C              M           ⁸B        ⁹M
              L         E     O    ¹⁰M  U  M  P  S  ¹¹A     ¹²T     I           U
              C         M     L           Y      ¹³C  S  P  R  U  E     R           T
        ¹⁵R  H  I  N  I  T  I  S   ¹⁶A  L  O  P  E  C  I  A     Y     N           T           A
              U              A        P           L     E           D           H           G
        ¹⁷B  U  L  I  M  I  A        A           O     R        ¹⁸H  O  R  M  O  N  E
                                  ¹⁹S  T  O  O  L     M                    A           N
                                        H        ²⁰I  N  V  I  T  R  O     R
                                  ²¹L  A  R  Y  N  X        E        A              K
```

ACROSS

2. A form of phototherapy that combines the use of psoralens and ultraviolet light to treat skin disorders
3. Inflammation of the heart
6. A cavity within bone or a channel that contains blood
7. Describes a disease that is always present in a certain population of people
10. A viral infection that causes inflammation of salivary glands
14. A digestive disorder in which nutrients cannot be properly absorbed from food, causing weakness and loss of weight
15. Inflammation of the mucous membrane lining the nose
16. Baldness or loss of hair, mainly on the head, either in defined patches or completely
17. A disorder in which a person eats large amounts of food then forces vomiting or uses laxatives to prevent weight gain (called binging and purging)
18. A chemical produced by a gland or tissue that is released into the bloodstream
19. Another term for feces
20. "in glass"; a biological test or process that is carried out in a laboratory
21. The medical term for the voice box, the organ in the throat that produces voice and prevents food from entering the airway

DOWN

1. Another term for smallpox
2. A disease that began in the affected location
4. A plentiful mineral in the body and the basic component of teeth and bones
5. A condition in which the blood does not contain enough hemoglobin, the compound that carries oxygen from the lungs to other parts of the body
8. Any area of discolored skin that is present when a baby is born
9. Anything that can increase the rate of abnormal change in cells, which can lead to cancer
10. A muscle disease, usually one that results in the deterioration of muscle
11. The failure either to produce or to ejaculate sperm
12. Strong connective tissue cords that attach muscle to bone or muscle to muscle
13. A unit that is used to measure the energy content in food

A. Calorie	B. Alopecia	C. PUVA	D. Hormone	E. Bulimia	F. Endemic
G. Tendon	H. Mumps	I. Sinus	J. Carditis	K. Stool	L. Mutagen
M. Primary	N. Anemia	O. Sprue	P. Larynx	Q. Calcium	R. Myopathy
S. In vitro	T. Aspermia	U. Variola	V. Rhinitis	W. Birthmark	

38. Using the Across and Down clues, write the correct words in the numbered grid below.

		¹B		²F	I	B	R	³O	S	I	S		⁴P	E	N	I	S							
		A						T					A								⁵K			
		C						O					R								E		⁶P	
		T		⁷M	⁸A	L	A	R	I	A		⁹E	A	R	D	R	U	M		¹⁰V	L		U	
¹¹W	H	E	E	Z	E			R				S					¹²F			E	O		L	
		R			T			R			¹³G	I		¹⁴V	A	¹⁵S	C	U	L	A	R		S	
		I			R		¹⁶M	E	A	S	L	E	S			T			U		¹⁷N	O	D	U	¹⁸L	E
¹⁹N	O	C	T	U	R	I	A				I					E			K		I			A	
		M			I		²⁰F	O	R	E	S	K	I	N		E			X				B	
											M					T					²¹S	O	D	I	U	M
							²²T	H	A	L	A	M	U	S							A		

ACROSS

2. Abnormal formation of connective or scar tissue
4. The external male reproductive organ, which passes urine and semen out of the body
7. A parasitic disease spread by mosquitos that causes chills and fever
9. A thin, oval-shaped membrane that separates the inner ear from the outer ear and is responsible for transmitting sound waves
11. A high-pitched sound produced during breathing because of narrowing of the airways
14. Pertaining to blood vessels
16. An illness caused by a viral infection, causing a characteristic rash and a fever
17. A small lump of tissue that is usually abnormal
19. Urination or a sleep-disturbing need to urinate during the night
20. The loose skin that covers the head of the penis
21. A mineral that plays a role in the body's water balance, heart rhythm, nerve impulses, and muscle contraction
22. A structure in the brain that relays and processes incoming sensory information from the eyes and ears and from pressure and pain receptors

DOWN

1. A tiny, single-celled microorganism, commonly known as a germ
3. A discharge from an inflamed ear
4. Partial paralysis
5. A raised, firm, thick scar that forms because of a defect in the natural healing process
6. The expansion and contraction of a blood vessel due to the blood pumped through it
8. The two upper chambers of the heart
10. The thick, greasy substance that covers the skin of a newborn baby
12. A parasitic flatworm that can infest humans
13. A brain tumor arising from cells that support nerve cells
15. A device used to hold tissues in place, such as to support a skin graft
18. The two pairs of skinfolds that protect the opening of the vagina

A. Stent	B. Nodule	C. Eardrum	D. Vascular	E. Bacterium	F. Sodium
G. Foreskin	H. Pulse	I. Vernix	J. Fibrosis	K. Keloid	L. Paresis
M. Thalamus	N. Labia	O. Glioma	P. Atria	Q. Otorrhea	R. Penis
S. Malaria	T. Fluke	U. Measles	V. Wheeze	W. Nocturia	

39. Using the Across and Down clues, write the correct words in the numbered grid below.

		¹N			²Z			³P											
		E		⁴O	X	Y	T	O	C	I	N	⁵M	I	N	I	P	I	⁶L	L	⁷M
		U			G			C								I		I	⁸A
		R			O		⁹R	A	D	O	¹⁰N					G		O	B
	¹⁰O	X	¹²M	E	T	R	Y				E		¹³P			A		T	¹⁴S	E	L	E	N	I	U	M
		N	N		E				¹⁵G	¹⁶L	U	C	A	G	O	N		M		I	C
			V							A		R				L	¹⁷V	E	S	I	C	L	E
		¹⁸A	I	R	W	A	Y	S		Z		O				Y	N			S
			S							Y		S	¹⁹M	U	T	A	T	I	O	N	S
²⁰O	P	T	I	C	I	A	N		²¹F	L	U	K	E			R				
			V							Y		S	²²B	I	R	T	H	M	A	R	K
			E		²³G	E	N	O	M	E			A							

ACROSS

4. A hormone produced in the pituitary gland that causes contraction of the uterus during childbirth and stimulation of milk flow during breast-feeding.
5. An oral contraceptive containing only the synthetic hormone progesterone (birth control pills contain estrogen and progesterone)
9. A colorless, odorless, tasteless radioactive gas that is produced by materials in soil, rocks, and building materials; suspected of causing cancer
11. Determination of the amount of oxygen in the blood by measuring the amount of light transmitted through an area of skin
14. An element needed by the body only in very small amounts that helps maintain tissue elasticity
15. A hormone produced by the pancreas that converts stored carbohydrates (glycogen) into glucose, the body's energy source
17. A small skin blister, or any sac in the body, that contains fluid
18. The passageways that air moves through while traveling in and out of the lungs during breathing
19. A change in the genetic information within a cell
20. A person who specializes in the making and adjustment of eyeglasses and contact lenses
21. A parasitic flatworm that can infest humans
22. Any area of discolored skin that is present when a baby is born
23. The complete set of an organism's genes

DOWN

1. Another term for a nerve cell
2. The cell that results when an egg is fertilized by a sperm
3. A desire to eat materials that are not food
6. A tough, elastic band of tissue that connects bones and supports organs
7. A drug that causes the pupil to constrict
8. An accumulation of pus in a body tissue, usually caused by a bacterial infection
10. The medical term for the death of tissue cells
12. Describes something that spreads throughout body tissues, such as a tumor or microorganism
13. The excessive production of urine
16. The common name for the visual defect resulting from untreated strabismus, in which the eyes are not correctly aligned

A. Airways	B. Oxytocin	C. Ligament	D. Genome	E. Radon	F. Vesicle
G. Birthmark	H. Optician	I. Lazy eye	J. Polyuria	K. Neuron	L. Abscess
M. Necrosis	N. Selenium	O. Zygote	P. Glucagon	Q. Pica	R. Mutation
S. Fluke	T. Oximetry	U. Minipill	V. Invasive	W. Miotic	

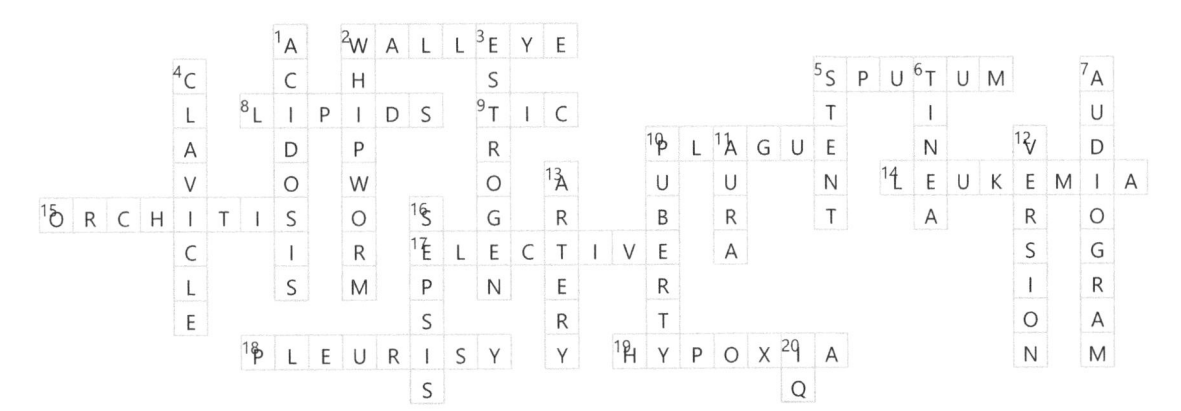

40. Using the Across and Down clues, write the correct words in the numbered grid below.

```
                    ¹A  ²W  A   L   L   ³E  Y   E
         ⁴C         C       H           S                           ⁵S  P   U   ⁶T  U   M           ⁷A
                ⁸L  I   P   I   D   S   ⁹T  I   C                   T           I                   U
         L          D       P           R                       ¹⁰P L   ¹¹A G   U   E   N       ¹²V D
         A          O       W           O           ¹³A             U       U           ¹⁴L E   U   K   E   M   I   A
    ¹⁵O  R   C   H  I   T   I   S       O       ¹⁶S G   R           B       R           A           R   O
         C          I       R       ¹⁷E L   E   C   T   I   V   E   A                           S   G
         L          S       M           N           E           R                               I   R
         E                  S           R           T                                           O   A
                ¹⁸P L   E   U   R   I   S   Y       ¹⁹H Y   P   O   X   ²⁰A                     N   M
                                        S                           Q
```

ACROSS

2. A condition in which one eye turns outward
5. Mucus and other material produced by the lining of the respiratory tract
8. A group of fats stored in the body and used for energy
9. An involuntary, repetitive movement such as a twitch
10. A serious infectious disease transmitted to humans through bites of rodent fleas
14. A group of bone marrow cancers in which white blood cells divide uncontrollably, affecting the production of normal white blood cells, red blood cells, and platelets
15. Inflammation of a testicle, which can be caused by infection with the mumps virus
17. Describes a treatment or procedure that is not urgent and can be arranged at the patient's convenience
18. Inflammation of the lining of the lungs and chest cavity usually caused by a lung infection
19. A reduced level of oxygen in tissues

DOWN

1. A condition marked by abnormally high acid levels in the blood, associated with some forms of diabetes, lung disease, and severe kidney disease
2. A small, parasitic worm that can live in the intestines of a human and may cause diarrhea, abdominal pain, and anemia
3. A group of hormones (produced mainly in the ovaries) that are necessary for female sexual development and reproductive functioning
4. The medical term for the collarbone
5. A device used to hold tissues in place, such as to support a skin graft
6. A group of common infections occurring on the skin, hair, and nails that are caused by a fungus
7. A graph showing a person's hearing ability, determined from a set of tests examining hearing acuity of different sound frequencies
10. The period during which sexual development occurs
11. A "warning" signal that comes before a migraine headache or an epileptic seizure, which might include emotions or sensations of movement or discomfort
12. A shift in the position of the fetus inside of the uterus, either occurring naturally or as performed by a doctor to facilitate delivery
13. A large blood vessel that carries blood from the heart to tissues and organs in the body
16. The infection of a wound or tissue with bacteria, causing the spread of the bacteria into the bloodstream
20. Intelligence quotient; a measure of a person's intelligence as determined by specific tests

A. Audiogram
B. Puberty
C. Sepsis
D. Leukemia
E. Hypoxia
F. Acidosis
G. Orchitis
H. Whipworm
I. Clavicle
J. Aura
K. Tic
L. Elective
M. Lipids
N. Version
O. Plague
P. Tinea
Q. Sputum
R. Pleurisy
S. Stent
T. Estrogen
U. Walleye
V. IQ
W. Artery

Multiple Choice

From the words provided for each clue, provide the letter of the word which best matches the clue.

1. _____ An abnormal mass that occurs when cells in a certain area reproduce unchecked
   A. Glycogen   B. Cochlea   C. Tumor   D. Rhinitis

2. _____ An enzyme that plays a role in increasing a low blood pressure
   A. Renin   B. Fungus   C. Osteoma   D. Traction

3. _____ A muscle disease, usually one that results in the deterioration of muscle
   A. Antibody   B. Virus   C. Myopathy   D. Thrombus

4. _____ A mineral that plays a role in the body's water balance, heart rhythm, nerve impulses, and muscle contraction
   A. Sodium   B. Ocular   C. Urea   D. Orchitis

5. _____ A term describing something related to or caused by a virus
   A. Vesicle   B. Viral   C. Version   D. Vitamins

6. _____ The use of tension to hold a body part in place or to correct or prevent an alignment problem
   A. Cyst   B. Traction   C. Apnea   D. Myelitis

7. _____ A candidiasis infection
   A. Menarche   B. Thrush   C. Thrombus   D. Pleurisy

8. _____ Anything that can increase the rate of abnormal change in cells, which can lead to cancer
   A. Sepsis   B. Mutagen   C. Lymph   D. Clavicle

9. _____ The extent to which a substance is poisonous
   A. Osteoma   B. Myelitis   C. B cell   D. Toxicity

10. _____ A term used to describe a newborn infant from birth to 1 month of age
    A. Dementia   B. Neonate   C. Nucleus   D. Strain

11. _____ The foreskin
    A. Urethra   B. Toxin   C. Erythema   D. Prepuce

12. _____ Any bacteria that is rod-shaped
    A. Rales   B. Apnea   C. Bacillus   D. Clavicle

13. _____ An extremely rare condition in which the body ages prematurely
    A. Progeria   B. Stoma   C. Anatomy   D. Gene

14. _____ A small skin blister, or any sac in the body, that contains fluid
    A. Fibroma   B. Abscess   C. Vesicle   D. B cell

15. _____ A yellow-green liquid produced in the liver whose function is to remove waste from the liver and break down fats as food is digested
    A. ECG   B. Bile   C. Trauma   D. Gene

16. _____ An involuntary, repetitive movement such as a twitch
    A. Endemic   B. Tic   C. Botulism   D. Glycogen

17. _____ The long, flat bone located at the center of the chest
    A. Sternum   B. Spasm   C. Endemic   D. Carcinoma

18. A noncancerous tumor of connective tissue
    A. Ectopic B. Vascular C. Cochlea D. Fibroma

19. A chemical produced by a gland or tissue that is released into the bloodstream
    A. Pellagra B. Vitamins C. Ticks D. Hormone

20. The medical term for nearsightedness
    A. Myopia B. Aplasia C. Patient D. Cyst

21. A term used to describe something related to a fever, such as febrile seizures (seizures occurring in a child who has a fever)
    A. Venom B. Osteoma C. Insulin D. Febrile

22. An organism that is dependent on another organism for nourishment
    A. Thrush B. Fungus C. Anatomy D. Enuresis

23. An excessively large dose of a drug, which can lead to coma and death
    A. Cochlea B. Thrombus C. Culture D. Overdose

24. A group of drugs that widen blood vessels
    A. Nitrates B. Mole C. Rales D. Trismus

25. A genetic disorder in which the foot is twisted and misshapen
    A. Ocular B. Clubfoot C. Ovaries D. Nephrons

26. A discharge from an inflamed ear
    A. Urethra B. Fetus C. Anatomy D. Otorrhea

27. A person who specializes in the making and adjustment of eyeglasses and contact lenses
    A. Emetic B. Spasm C. Optician D. Syndrome

28. A condition in which a tissue or organ does not receive enough supply of blood
    A. Bladder B. Walleye C. Appendix D. Ischemia

29. The loose skin that covers the head of the penis
    A. Foreskin B. Coccyx C. Birthmark D. Axilla

30. A blood clot in a blood vessel
    A. Vitamins B. Ischemia C. Thrombus D. Saline

31. The three membranes that surround and protect the spinal cord and brain
    A. Seizure B. Meninges C. Fibroma D. Coma

32. The thicker of the two long bones in the lower leg
    A. Radon B. Tibia C. Osteoma D. Iron

33. The bones that form the framework of the head and enclose and protect the brain and other sensory organs
    A. Bruxism B. Skull C. Erythema D. Androgen

34. An organ located in the pelvis whose function is to collect and store urine until it is expelled
    A. Bladder B. Lymph C. Walleye D. Emetic

35. Abnormal crackling or bubbling sounds heard in the lungs during breathing
    A. Progeria B. Clone C. Rales D. Abscess

36. A protein made by white blood cells that reacts with a specific foreign protein as part of the immune response
A. Antibody   B. Saline   C. Clavicle   D. Fetus

37. The medical term for lockjaw
A. Lactose   B. Ligation   C. Trismus   D. Rectum

38. Poisoning from poorly preserved food contaminated with a dangerous bacterial toxin that results in paralysis
A. Fibroma   B. Viral   C. Botulism   D. Pleura

39. Any one of the 33 bones that make up the spine
A. Emetic   B. Vulvitis   C. Vertebra   D. Myopathy

40. Any area of discolored skin that is present when a baby is born
A. Birthmark   B. Strain   C. Excision   D. Emetic

41. A marking on the skin; can be present at birth (birthmark) or develop later (such as a mole)
A. Nevus   B. Microbe   C. Hookworm   D. Anatomy

42. A negative reaction to a substance that in most people causes no reaction
A. Pupil   B. PUVA   C. Allergy   D. Mitosis

43. A possibly life-threatening condition in which breathing stops, for either a short or long period of time
A. Nerve   B. Mineral   C. Clone   D. Apnea

44. Four fused bones that form a triangular shape at the base of the spine (also known as the tailbone)
A. Addiction   B. Coccyx   C. Hysteria   D. Myopia

45. A chemically inactive substance given in place of a drug to test how much of a drug's effectiveness can be attributed to a patient's expectations that the drug will have a positive effect
A. Placebo   B. Dementia   C. Pruritus   D. Somatic

46. A slippery fluid produced by mucous membranes that lubricates and protects the internal surfaces of the body
A. Neuritis   B. Seizure   C. Mucus   D. Pellagra

47. A term describing a condition that affects both sides of the body or two paired organs, such as bilateral deafness (deafness in both ears)
A. Ringworm   B. Bilateral   C. Viremia   D. Nucleus

48. The common term for urticaria, an itchy, inflamed rash that results from an allergic reaction
A. Carcinoma   B. Hives   C. Clubfoot   D. Rectum

49. A shift in the position of the fetus inside of the uterus, either occurring naturally or as performed by a doctor to facilitate delivery
A. Bilateral   B. Myopia   C. In vivo   D. Version

50. Another name for the sugar glucose
A. Carditis   B. Iron   C. Dextrose   D. Pleurisy

51. Mucus and other material produced by the lining of the respiratory tract
A. Aneurysm   B. Phlegm   C. Sebum   D. Pellagra

52. Inflammation of a nerve, often characterized by pain, numbness, or tingling
A. Neuritis   B. Sepsis   C. Radon   D. Phimosis

53. Pertaining to blood vessels
A. Fibroma   B. Enuresis   C. Hepatic   D. Vascular

54. The medical term for itching
A. Microbe B. Fibroma C. Fungus D. Pruritus

55. An electrocardiogram, which is a record of the electrical impulses that trigger the heartbeat; used to diagnose heart disorders
A. Thrush B. Sciatica C. Allergy D. ECG

56. A short, tube-like structure that branches off the large intestine
A. Enuresis B. Graft C. Appendix D. Audiogram

57. Dependence on a substance (such as alcohol or other drugs) or an activity, to the point that stopping is very difficult and causes severe physical and mental reactions
A. Erythema B. Addiction C. Rales D. Patient

58. Small, eight-legged animals that can attach to humans and animals and feed on blood
A. Scrotum B. Walleye C. Ticks D. Fibroma

59. A system used to classify sick or injured people according to the severity of their conditions
A. Thrush B. Sternum C. Aplasia D. Triage

60. A cancer in connective tissue, fibrous tissue, or blood vessels
A. Spasm B. Sarcoma C. Mineral D. Sternum

61. Another term for a microorganism, especially one that causes disease
A. Safe sex B. Vesicle C. Microbe D. Patent

62. Pertaining to the body
A. Enuresis B. Somatic C. Menarche D. Optic

63. A tiny pouchlike cavity in a structure of the body, such as a hair follicle
A. Follicle B. Anatomy C. Kidney D. Dextrose

64. A noncancerous bone tumor
A. Toxin B. Vagina C. Renin D. Osteoma

65. A lump filled with either fluid or soft material, occurring in any organ or tissue
A. Cyst B. Microbe C. Bilateral D. Mutagen

66. The blockage of a blood vessel by an embolus- something previously circulating in the blood (such as a blood clot, gas bubble, tissue, bacteria, bone marrow, cholesterol, fat, etc.)
A. Tetanus B. Embolism C. Vesicle D. Emetic

67. The infection of a wound or tissue with bacteria, causing the spread of the bacteria into the bloodstream
A. Stoma B. Toxicity C. Sepsis D. Birthmark

68. Dangerously decreased acidity of the blood, which can be caused by high altitudes, hyperventilation, and excessive vomiting
A. Chlamydia B. Alkalosis C. Hives D. Sternum

69. A highly contagious skin disorder caused by a mite that burrows into the skin and produces an intense, itchy rash
A. Liver B. Clavicle C. Rubella D. Scabies

70. The basic unit of DNA, which is responsible for passing genetic information
A. Tibia B. Ringworm C. Selenium D. Gene

71. A drug that causes the pupil to constrict
   A. Botulism   B. Miotic   C. Insulin   D. Emetic

72. A body temperature of above 98.6°f in the mouth or 99.8°f in the rectum
   A. Keratin   B. Pyrexia   C. Antibody   D. Tibia

73. Healthy tissue that is used to replace diseased or defective tissue
   A. Bilateral   B. Urea   C. Graft   D. Receptor

74. Inflammation of a testicle, which can be caused by infection with the mumps virus
   A. Fibroma   B. Orchitis   C. Cyst   D. Varices

75. Physical injury or emotional shock
   A. Pleurisy   B. Trauma   C. Pellagra   D. Ligation

76. The sugar found in dairy products
   A. Radon   B. Scabies   C. Lactose   D. Androgen

77. A coiled organ in the inner ear that plays a large role in hearing by picking up sound vibrations and transmitting them as electrical signals
   A. Tendon   B. Nitrates   C. Cochlea   D. Embolism

78. Redness of the skin
   A. Erythema   B. Pupil   C. Ocular   D. Infusion

79. The structure of bodies
   A. Rectum   B. Anatomy   C. Embolism   D. Myositis

80. A sometimes fatal disease affecting the brain and spinal cord
   A. Tetanus   B. In vivo   C. Rales   D. Lymph

81. Controlled analgesia- a system for administering pain- killing drugs in which the amount of drug delivered is controlled by the patient
   A. Patient   B. Clone   C. Allergy   D. Thrombus

82. A reduced level of oxygen in tissues
   A. Polyuria   B. Hypoxia   C. Clubfoot   D. Urea

83. The process by which most cells divide to reproduce
   A. Aplasia   B. Systemic   C. Mitosis   D. Anatomy

84. A colorless, odorless, tasteless radioactive gas that is produced by materials in soil, rocks, and building materials; suspected of causing cancer
   A. Mutagen   B. Birthmark   C. Radon   D. Rectum

85. Measures taken to reduce the risk of acquiring a sexually transmitted disease, such as the use of a condom
   A. Safe sex   B. Infusion   C. Gene   D. Syndrome

86. A tumor of the thymus gland
   A. Androgen   B. Rubella   C. Mutagen   D. Thymoma

87. A hospital or an area of a hospital dedicated to treating people who are dying, often of a specific cause
   A. Systemic   B. Silicone   C. Tibia   D. Hospice

88. The smallest known disease- causing microorganism
   A. Virus   B. Rubella   C. Nodule   D. Somatic

89. A brown to dark-brown spot on the skin that can be flat or raised
    A. Mucus   B. Mole   C. Infusion   D. Fibroma

90. A bundle of fibers that transmit electrical messages between the brain and areas of the body
    A. Stoma   B. Nerve   C. Enuresis   D. Vagina

91. Inflammation of the lining of the lungs and chest cavity usually caused by a lung infection
    A. Pleurisy   B. Botulism   C. Hospice   D. Clone

92. One of two organs that are part of the urinary tract
    A. Kidney   B. Triage   C. Rectum   D. Appendix

93. Inflammation of the mucous membrane lining the nose
    A. Rhinitis   B. Erythema   C. Uveitis   D. Hospice

94. A growth that occurs on mucous membranes such as those in the nose and intestine
    A. Optician   B. Ringworm   C. Hysteria   D. Polyp

95. A bacterial infection of the small intestine that causes severe watery diarrhea, dehydration, and possibly death
    A. Trisomy   B. Cholera   C. Insulin   D. Clone

96. A tough protein found in skin, nails, and hair
    A. Ticks   B. Aneurysm   C. Lymph   D. Keratin

97. A cancer that occurs on the surface or lining of an organ
    A. Carcinoma   B. Iron   C. Miotic   D. Axilla

98. A serious infectious disease transmitted to humans through bites of rodent fleas
    A. Infusion   B. Plague   C. Toxin   D. Sepsis

99. A short tube located at the end of the large intestine, which connects the intestine to the anus
    A. Vertebra   B. Thymoma   C. Myopathy   D. Rectum

100. The sac containing the testicles
     A. Sciatica   B. Scrotum   C. Hysteria   D. Sodium

From the words provided for each clue, provide the letter of the word which best matches the clue.

101. A thin, oval-shaped membrane that separates the inner ear from the outer ear and is responsible for transmitting sound waves
     A. Bile   B. Thalamus   C. Keratin   D. Eardrum

102. A small lump of tissue that is usually abnormal
     A. Otorrhea   B. Medulla   C. Nodule   D. Scabies

103. The interval from onset of contractions to birth of a baby
     A. Scabies   B. Pancreas   C. Labor   D. Tonsils

104. A condition in which people are born with insufficient amounts of the pigment melanin, which is responsible for hair, skin, and eye color
     A. Osteoma   B. Keratin   C. Albinism   D. DNA

105. Twisting and obstruction of an area of intestine
     A. Zygote   B. Lipoma   C. Volvulus   D. Dementia

106. The period during which sexual development occurs
A. Reflex   B. Thrombus   C. Tetanus   D. Puberty

107. A disease caused by a lack of vitamin c, characterized by weakness, bleeding and pain in joints and muscles, bleeding gums, and abnormal bone and tooth growth
A. Scurvy   B. Orthotic   C. Osmosis   D. Silicone

108. Thick, sticky, greenish-brown stool passed by a postmature fetus, or one experiencing fetal distress, into the amniotic fluid, or by an infant during the first couple of days after birth
A. Vulvitis   B. Meconium   C. Villi   D. Appendix

109. Describes a disease that is always present in a certain population of people
A. Scrotum   B. Endemic   C. Aura   D. Aplasia

110. The medical term for the collarbone
A. Renin   B. Pancreas   C. Vesicle   D. Clavicle

111. The socket in the skull that contains the eyeball, along with its blood vessels, nerves, and muscles
A. Sprue   B. Tonsils   C. Orbit   D. Palate

112. The long, flat bone located at the center of the chest
A. Hookworm   B. Sternum   C. Urea   D. Thorax

113. A group of compounds of silicon and oxygen
A. Rubeola   B. Orthotic   C. Silicone   D. Version

114. The medical term for an earache
A. IQ   B. Lipoma   C. Otalgia   D. Reflex

115. A lump filled with either fluid or soft material, occurring in any organ or tissue
A. Neurosis   B. Cyst   C. Dermis   D. Seminoma

116. An additional dose of a vaccine taken after the first dose to maintain or renew the first one
A. Hookworm   B. Booster   C. Tremor   D. Optic

117. The column of bones and cartilage running along the midline of the back that surrounds and protects the spinal cord and supports the head
A. Spine   B. Polyp   C. Hookworm   D. Splint

118. The inner skin layer
A. Dermis   B. Eardrum   C. Vertebra   D. Hepatoma

119. Intestine
A. Bowel   B. Scabies   C. Dialysis   D. Pulse

120. A growth that occurs on mucous membranes such as those in the nose and intestine
A. Reflex   B. Atheroma   C. Kidney   D. Polyp

121. A hormone that stimulates the release of gastric acid in the stomach
A. Bursitis   B. Forceps   C. Gastrin   D. Osmosis

122. A childhood disease in which bones lack calcium and are deformed because of vitamin d deficiency
A. Receptor   B. Impetigo   C. Rickets   D. Hookworm

123. A disorder marked by high levels of uric acid in the blood
A. Zygote   B. Thalamus   C. Gout   D. Pleurisy

124. A hormone produced by the thyroid gland that helps regulate energy production in the body
A. Thrush   B. Medulla   C. Thyroxin   D. Hookworm

125. Relatively mild emotional disorders (such as mild depression and phobias)
A. Renin   B. Rubeola   C. Uterus   D. Neurosis

126. The presence of viruses in the blood
A. Oximetry   B. Thalamus   C. Impetigo   D. Viremia

127. A brain tumor arising from cells that support nerve cells
A. Sprue   B. Ptosis   C. Phlegm   D. Glioma

128. Controlled analgesia- a system for administering pain- killing drugs in which the amount of drug delivered is controlled by the patient
A. Traction   B. Dementia   C. Patient   D. Melanoma

129. "in the living body"; a biological process that occurs inside of the body
A. Pyrogen   B. Boil   C. In vivo   D. Platelet

130. Inflammation of the lining of the lungs and chest cavity usually caused by a lung infection
A. Labor   B. Viremia   C. Splint   D. Pleurisy

131. A drug that relieves pain, such as aspirin or acetaminophen
A. Osmosis   B. Analgesic   C. Radon   D. Lordosis

132. The presence in the cells of three copies of a certain chromosome instead of the normal two copies
A. Renin   B. Trisomy   C. Ozone   D. Melanin

133. An egg cell that has not developed completely
A. Stool   B. Numbness   C. Oocyte   D. Axilla

134. Another term for a nerve cell
A. Coitus   B. Shock   C. Neuron   D. Cataract

135. A "warning" signal that comes before a migraine headache or an epileptic seizure, which might include emotions or sensations of movement or discomfort
A. Tumor   B. Systemic   C. Lipoma   D. Aura

136. A vitamin important in many chemical processes in the body; also known as vitamin b3
A. Appendix   B. Niacin   C. Rickets   D. Platelet

137. The introduction of a substance, such as a drug or nutrient, into the bloodstream or a body cavity
A. Fistula   B. Ticks   C. Orthotic   D. Infusion

138. A sudden attack or worsening of a disease's symptoms
A. Hypoxia   B. Paroxysm   C. Shock   D. Whitlow

139. A discharge from an inflamed ear
A. In vivo   B. Dementia   C. Whitlow   D. Otorrhea

140. A disorder in which a person becomes overly suspicious and emotionally sensitive
A. Fluke   B. Mitosis   C. Carotene   D. Paranoia

141. A salt solution or any substance that contains salt
A. Rectum   B. Tetanus   C. Saline   D. Ptosis

142. A vibration felt when the hand is placed flat on the chest
    A. Zygote   B. Thrill   C. Reflex   D. In vivo

143. Any substance that the body can use to maintain its health
    A. Volvulus   B. Nutrient   C. Patient   D. Zygote

144. The muscular passage connecting the uterus with the outside genitals
    A. Rubeola   B. Labia   C. Vagina   D. Menarche

145. The opening through which feces are passed from the body
    A. Fibroma   B. Anus   C. Impetigo   D. Labia

146. The sac containing the testicles
    A. Meconium   B. Scrotum   C. Melanoma   D. Thyroxin

147. A noncancerous bone tumor
    A. Sprain   B. Chronic   C. Osteoma   D. Miotic

148. A connective tissue (softer than bone) that is part of the skeletal system, including the joints
    A. Cartilage   B. Melanoma   C. Osteitis   D. Osteoma

149. An abscess on the end of a finger or a toe that is caused by the herpes simplex virus or a bacterial infection
    A. Whitlow   B. Vulvitis   C. Mitosis   D. Keratin

150. A sometimes fatal disease affecting the brain and spinal cord
    A. Wart   B. Fistula   C. Tetanus   D. Phimosis

151. A gradual decline in mental ability usually caused by a brain disease, such as Alzheimer's disease
    A. Oocyte   B. Allergen   C. Dementia   D. Gastrin

152. A waste product of the metabolism of proteins that is formed by the liver and secreted by the kidneys
    A. Atheroma   B. Paranoia   C. Urea   D. Vagina

153. Any disease caused by a fungus
    A. Receptor   B. Radon   C. Mycosis   D. Ligation

154. The complete set of an organism's genes
    A. Atheroma   B. Larynx   C. Organism   D. Genome

155. An abnormal mass that occurs when cells in a certain area reproduce unchecked
    A. Tumor   B. Paranoia   C. Aspermia   D. Rectum

156. A marking on the skin; can be present at birth (birthmark) or develop later (such as a mole)
    A. Otalgia   B. Labor   C. Myopia   D. Nevus

157. A chemical, originating in a cell, that regulates reactions in the body
    A. Endemic   B. Polyp   C. Lobe   D. Enzyme

158. Inflammation of a testicle, which can be caused by infection with the mumps virus
    A. Renin   B. Pinkeye   C. Orchitis   D. Otalgia

159. Inflammation of the membrane that covers the white of the eyes and lines the eyelids
    A. Pinkeye   B. Thalamus   C. Reflex   D. Pepsin

160. An inflamed, raised area of skin that is pus-filled; usually an infected hair follicle
A. Plasma   B. Toxicity   C. Lobe   D. Boil

161. The millions of fingerlike projections on the lining of the small intestine that aid in the absorption of food
A. Villi   B. Neuron   C. Rubeola   D. Orthotic

162. A tough, elastic band of tissue that connects bones and supports organs
A. Niacin   B. Acne   C. Myopia   D. Ligament

163. The lack of sensation in a part of the body because of interruption of nerve impulses
A. Oocyte   B. Alopecia   C. Numbness   D. Vertebra

164. Masses of lymphoid tissue located at either side of the back of the throat
A. Variola   B. Hookworm   C. Implant   D. Tonsils

165. Baldness or loss of hair, mainly on the head, either in defined patches or completely
A. Thrill   B. Alopecia   C. Spine   D. Ectopic

166. The extent to which a substance is poisonous
A. Hepatoma   B. Gastrin   C. Mycosis   D. Toxicity

167. Infestation by a small, round, blood-sucking parasite
A. Immunity   B. Pinkeye   C. Tetanus   D. Hookworm

168. An automatic, involuntary response of the nervous system to a stimulus
A. Paranoia   B. Reflex   C. Numbness   D. pH

169. A poisonous form of oxygen that is present in the earth's upper atmosphere, where it helps to screen the earth from damaging ultraviolet rays
A. Ozone   B. Allergen   C. Receptor   D. Atheroma

170. Mucus and other material produced by the lining of the respiratory tract
A. Cyst   B. Phlegm   C. Miotic   D. Vertebra

171. An artificial feeding technique in which liquids are passed into the stomach by way of a tube inserted through the nose
A. Tonsils   B. Sternum   C. Sepsis   D. Gavage

172. Fatty deposits on the inner walls of blood vessels, which can cause narrowing and decrease blood flow
A. Polyp   B. Vertebra   C. Atheroma   D. Plasma

173. The inward curvature of the spine at the lower back, which is normal to a certain degree
A. Lordosis   B. Endemic   C. Larynx   D. Ectopic

174. Pertaining to the eyes
A. Analgesic   B. Villi   C. Splint   D. Optic

175. Occurring at an abnormal position or time
A. Thrill   B. Ectopic   C. Fluoride   D. Pancreas

176. The examination of a body following death, possibly to determine the cause of death or for research
A. Iron   B. Gavage   C. Ectopic   D. Autopsy

177. Affecting the whole body
A. Systemic   B. Rubella   C. Rectum   D. Otalgia

178. A hormone made in the pancreas that plays an important role in the absorption of glucose (the body's main source of energy) into muscle cells
A. Pyrexia   B. Keloid   C. Insulin   D. Bunion

179. Medical term for the armpit
A. Axilla   B. Labor   C. Pepsin   D. Numbness

180. The enzyme found in gastric juice that helps digest protein
A. Pepsin   B. Hepatic   C. Node   D. Platelet

181. A reduced level of oxygen in tissues
A. Rubella   B. Skull   C. Hypoxia   D. Maxilla

182. A term used to describe something that is related to the liver
A. Keratin   B. Ocular   C. Glucose   D. Hepatic

183. A shift in the position of the fetus inside of the uterus, either occurring naturally or as performed by a doctor to facilitate delivery
A. Hepatic   B. Endemic   C. Pinkeye   D. Version

184. A device used to correct or control deformed bones, muscles, or joints
A. Forceps   B. Rectum   C. Implant   D. Orthotic

185. One of two organs that are part of the urinary tract
A. Implant   B. Paranoia   C. Kidney   D. Volvulus

186. The medical term for the voice box, the organ in the throat that produces voice and prevents food from entering the airway
A. Diuretic   B. Hepatoma   C. Systemic   D. Larynx

187. Instruments resembling tweezers that are used to handle objects or tissue during surgery
A. Pellagra   B. Audiogram   C. Bowel   D. Forceps

188. The process of passage of the solvent portion of a lesser-concentrated solution through a semipermeable membrane into a higher-concentrated solution until the two solutions are equal in concentration
A. Atrophy   B. Hepatoma   C. Osmosis   D. Viremia

189. A thickened callus on the foot that is caused by an improperly fitting shoe
A. Maxilla   B. Osmosis   C. Iron   D. Corn

190. A well-defined, separate part of an organ
A. Toxin   B. Kidney   C. Lobe   D. Bile

191. Tightness of the foreskin, which prevents it from being moved back over the head of the penis
A. Nodule   B. Ptosis   C. Fluoride   D. Phimosis

192. Describes a disorder that continues for a long period of time
A. Skull   B. Bile   C. Pathogen   D. Chronic

193. The two pairs of skinfolds that protect the opening of the vagina
A. Labia   B. Necrosis   C. Nevus   D. Polyp

194. A mineral that helps protect teeth against decay
A. Fluoride   B. Polyp   C. Variola   D. pH

195. _____ A term describing something related to or caused by a virus
A. Otalgia B. Ocular C. Viral D. Sternum

196. _____ A negative reaction to a substance that in most people causes no reaction
A. Lipoma B. Allergy C. Radon D. Volvulus

197. _____ A highly contagious skin infection caused by bacteria, usually occurring around the nose and mouth
A. Impetigo B. Menarche C. Infusion D. Toxin

198. _____ The shrinkage or near disappearance of a tissue or organ
A. Atrophy B. In vivo C. Tumor D. Pinkeye

199. _____ A disorder in which the lens of the eye becomes less transparent and, in some cases, a milky white, making vision less clear
A. Analgesic B. Enzyme C. Cataract D. Palsy

200. _____ A cancerous tumor of the liver
A. Ligation B. Clavicle C. Glioma D. Hepatoma

From the words provided for each clue, provide the letter of the word which best matches the clue.

201. _____ An area of buildup of fat deposits in an artery, causing narrowing of the artery and possibly heart disease
A. Bulimia B. Fistula C. Acne D. Plaque

202. _____ The process of passage of the solvent portion of a lesser-concentrated solution through a semipermeable membrane into a higher-concentrated solution until the two solutions are equal in concentration
A. Ectopic B. Whipworm C. Nevus D. Osmosis

203. _____ Another term for a microorganism, especially one that causes disease
A. Macula B. Atheroma C. Microbe D. Migraine

204. _____ A group of cells or an organ that produces substances (such as hormones and enzyme) that are used by the body
A. Ileum B. Stye C. Gland D. Iodine

205. _____ A term describing something related to or caused by a virus
A. Maxilla B. Toxin C. Labia D. Viral

206. _____ A chemical produced by a gland or tissue that is released into the bloodstream
A. Trachoma B. Plasma C. Pancreas D. Hormone

207. _____ A form of phototherapy that combines the use of psoralens and ultraviolet light to treat skin disorders
A. Dopamine B. Retinoid C. PUVA D. Sclera

208. _____ The expansion and contraction of a blood vessel due to the blood pumped through it
A. Aorta B. Pulse C. Nutrient D. Thrombus

209. _____ A nerve infection caused by the chickenpox virus, causing areas of painful rash covered with blisters
A. Colon B. Shingles C. Orchitis D. Pancreas

210. _____ A measure of the acidic or basic character of a substance
A. pH B. Patent C. Coma D. Insulin

211. Abnormally pale skin
    A. pH   B. Trachoma   C. Pallor   D. Labia

212. Abnormal formation of connective or scar tissue
    A. Fibrosis   B. Callus   C. Lesion   D. Retina

213. The interval from onset of contractions to birth of a baby
    A. Labor   B. Cervix   C. Placenta   D. Pallor

214. A highly contagious and often fatal viral infection that has been completely eradicated by immunization
    A. Nevus   B. Orchitis   C. Pruritus   D. Smallpox

215. The clear, watery fluid that separates from clotted blood
    A. Thymoma   B. Virus   C. Serum   D. Rhinitis

216. Not obstructed; open
    A. Bile   B. Patent   C. Familial   D. Macula

217. An illness caused by a viral infection, causing a characteristic rash and a fever
    A. Sternum   B. Prion   C. Iodine   D. Measles

218. Loss of sensation or ability to move
    A. Dopamine   B. Palsy   C. Meiosis   D. Myelitis

219. Mucus and other material produced by the lining of the respiratory tract
    A. DNA   B. Sputum   C. Strain   D. Ascites

220. A device used to hold tissues in place, such as to support a skin graft
    A. Placebo   B. Stent   C. DNA   D. Palsy

221. Controlled analgesia- a system for administering pain- killing drugs in which the amount of drug delivered is controlled by the patient
    A. Patient   B. Ozone   C. Cholera   D. Syndrome

222. A sugar that is the main source of energy for the body
    A. Plaque   B. Placebo   C. Polyp   D. Glucose

223. The presence in the cells of three copies of a certain chromosome instead of the normal two copies
    A. Syndrome   B. Sepsis   C. Trisomy   D. Fungus

224. Enlargement of the thyroid gland, which produces a swelling on the neck
    A. Microbe   B. Aorta   C. Goiter   D. Fracture

225. An agent that is believed to cause several degenerative brain diseases
    A. Keloid   B. Prion   C. Polyuria   D. Rabies

226. A tunnel-like passage
    A. Smear   B. Tonsils   C. Smallpox   D. Canal

227. Partial paralysis
    A. Niacin   B. Osmosis   C. Bifocal   D. Paresis

228. The type of cell division that occurs only in the ovaries and testicles, producing cells with half the genes of the original cell
    A. Meiosis   B. Minipill   C. Fungus   D. Measles

229. A small, parasitic worm that can live in the intestines of a human and may cause diarrhea, abdominal pain, and anemia
A. Primary B. Dermis C. Mandible D. Whipworm

230. The passageways that air moves through while traveling in and out of the lungs during breathing
A. Plaque B. Varices C. Airways D. Lumbago

231. An addictive substance that blunts the senses
A. Macula B. Seizure C. Nausea D. Narcotic

232. A surgically formed opening on a body surface
A. IQ B. Mandible C. Aorta D. Stoma

233. A cancer that occurs on the surface or lining of an organ
A. Meniscus B. Ozone C. Nausea D. Carcinoma

234. A measure of a person's physical strength, flexibility, and endurance
A. Fibrosis B. Fitness C. DNA D. Myositis

235. A lens that corrects both near and distant vision by having two parts with different focusing strengths
A. Imaging B. Kidney C. Murmur D. Bifocal

236. Small, eight-legged animals that can attach to humans and animals and feed on blood
A. Ticks B. Teratoma C. Ulcer D. Saline

237. A sometimes fatal disease affecting the brain and spinal cord
A. Tetanus B. Aspermia C. Osmosis D. Fistula

238. An element for the formation of thyroid hormones
A. Iodine B. Patient C. Familial D. Tetanus

239. Two tubes that carry urine from the kidneys to the bladder
A. Ureters B. Bifocal C. Thymoma D. Genome

240. A cancer in connective tissue, fibrous tissue, or blood vessels
A. Primary B. Apnea C. Sarcoma D. Nutrient

241. A small, round organ making up the neck of the uterus and separating it from the vagina
A. Numbness B. Hysteria C. Cervix D. Tonsils

242. The lowest section of the small intestine, which attaches to the large intestine
A. Measles B. Chlamydia C. Ileum D. Nutrient

243. A blood vessel that carries blood toward the heart
A. Anatomy B. Vein C. pH D. Syndrome

244. A poisonous substance
A. Toxin B. Aorta C. Sepsis D. Rabies

245. The tough, white coating that covers and protects the inner structures of the eye
A. Platelet B. Fluoride C. Sclera D. Cholera

246. A substance resembling vitamin a that is used to treat skin conditions such as acne and has been reported to reduce skin wrinkling
A. Sprue B. Retinoid C. Genome D. Bile

247. The infection of a wound or tissue with bacteria, causing the spread of the bacteria into the bloodstream
A. Coitus   B. Sepsis   C. Penis   D. Bacterium

248. Masses of lymphoid tissue located at either side of the back of the throat
A. Meiosis   B. Cholera   C. Tonsils   D. Imaging

249. A tiny blood vessel that connects the smallest arteries to the smallest veins and allows exchange of oxygen and other materials between blood cells and body tissue cells
A. Shingles   B. Familial   C. Niacin   D. Capillary

250. Inflammation of a testicle, which can be caused by infection with the mumps virus
A. Cecum   B. Orchitis   C. Seizure   D. PUVA

251. A term describing a disorder or characteristic (such as male pattern baldness) that occurs within a family more often than would be expected
A. ECG   B. Familial   C. Androgen   D. Teratoma

252. A tear or break in an organ or tissue
A. Polyp   B. Rupture   C. Minipill   D. Pyrogen

253. A thickened area of skin due to consistent pressure or friction, or the area around a bone break where new bone is formed
A. Callus   B. Neuritis   C. Sinus   D. Coitus

254. A characteristic sound of blood flowing irregularly through the heart
A. Murmur   B. Primary   C. Vertigo   D. Syndrome

255. Any substance that causes a fever
A. Foreskin   B. Silicone   C. Pyrogen   D. Rupture

256. A group of compounds of silicon and oxygen
A. Narcotic   B. Gene   C. Nausea   D. Silicone

257. A term used to describe something situated on or near the midline of the body or a body structure
A. Colitis   B. Myelitis   C. Niacin   D. Medial

258. A marking on the skin; can be present at birth (birthmark) or develop later (such as a mole)
A. Nevus   B. Syndrome   C. Plasma   D. Genome

259. Muscle inflammation, causing pain and weakness
A. Sprue   B. Phimosis   C. Autopsy   D. Myositis

260. The roof of the mouth
A. Pyrogen   B. Polyp   C. Paresis   D. Palate

261. A shift in the position of the fetus inside of the uterus, either occurring naturally or as performed by a doctor to facilitate delivery
A. Fungus   B. Foreskin   C. Capillary   D. Version

262. One of two bones that form the upper jaw, the roof of the mouth, and the center portion of the face
A. DNA   B. Villi   C. Maxilla   D. Genome

263. A term used to describe a disease that is rare then suddenly affects more people than usually expected
A. Epidemic   B. Hormone   C. Myelitis   D. Ureters

264. An open sore that occurs on the skin or on a mucous membrane because of the destruction of surface tissue
A. Version B. Murmur C. Ulcer D. Nausea

265. A severe headache, usually accompanied by vision problems and
A. Eardrum B. Ozone C. Migraine D. Pharynx

266. A vitamin important in many chemical processes in the body; also known as vitamin b3
A. Fluoride B. Airways C. Niacin D. Vertigo

267. "in glass"; a biological test or process that is carried out in a laboratory
A. Patent B. Bifocal C. In vitro D. Fibrosis

268. The sticky, brown substance in cigarettes that coats the lungs; causes lung and other cancers
A. Tar B. Glycogen C. Insulin D. Callus

269. Pertaining to the eyes
A. Palate B. Parasite C. Migraine D. Optic

270. A persistent, contagious form of conjunctivitis that can lead to complications such as blindness if untreated
A. Pancreas B. Bacterium C. Trachoma D. Murmur

271. Muscle damage resulting from excessive stretching or forceful contraction
A. Palsy B. Vein C. Villi D. Strain

272. The lack of sensation in a part of the body because of interruption of nerve impulses
A. Myelitis B. Pharynx C. Shingles D. Numbness

273. An electrocardiogram, which is a record of the electrical impulses that trigger the heartbeat; used to diagnose heart disorders
A. ECG B. Myopathy C. Osmosis D. Maxilla

274. A tumor of the thymus gland
A. Coma B. Strain C. Thymoma D. Bulimia

275. Feeling the need to vomit
A. Patient B. Nausea C. Genome D. Palsy

276. Narrowing of a body passageway
A. Callus B. Epidemic C. Ureters D. Stenosis

277. A tiny pouchlike cavity in a structure of the body, such as a hair follicle
A. Nausea B. Pyrogen C. Follicle D. Polyp

278. A blood clot in a blood vessel
A. Maxilla B. Sputum C. Thrombus D. Virus

279. A group of symptoms that indicate a certain disorder when they occur together
A. Fibrosis B. Niacin C. Syndrome D. Patent

280. A disorder in which a person becomes overly suspicious and emotionally sensitive
A. Fitness B. Pancreas C. Paranoia D. Impetigo

281. An organ formed in the uterus during pregnancy that links the blood of the mother to the blood of the fetus
A. Ulcer B. Meiosis C. Imaging D. Placenta

282. Dependence on a substance (such as alcohol or other drugs) or an activity, to the point that stopping is very difficult and causes severe physical and mental reactions
A. Stent   B. Genome   C. Virus   D. Addiction

283. An oral contraceptive containing only the synthetic hormone progesterone (birth control pills contain estrogen and progesterone)
A. Minipill   B. Polyp   C. Xanthine   D. Keratin

284. A hormone (such as testosterone) that causes development of male characteristics and sex organs
A. Smallpox   B. Androgen   C. Follicle   D. Orbit

285. The millions of fingerlike projections on the lining of the small intestine that aid in the absorption of food
A. Imaging   B. Villi   C. Airways   D. Strain

286. A raised, firm, thick scar that forms because of a defect in the natural healing process
A. Febrile   B. Numbness   C. Keloid   D. Acne

287. The hollow female reproductive organ in which a fertilized egg is implanted, and a fetus develops
A. Aorta   B. Insulin   C. Uterus   D. Plaque

288. The muscular passage connecting the uterus with the outside genitals
A. Coronary   B. Fistula   C. Vagina   D. Fibroid

289. Inflammation of the mucous membrane lining the nose
A. Airways   B. Hematoma   C. Rhinitis   D. Trachoma

290. A colorless, odorless, tasteless radioactive gas that is produced by materials in soil, rocks, and building materials; suspected of causing cancer
A. Radon   B. Pustule   C. Meiosis   D. Myelitis

291. A term used to describe symptoms that are caused by mental stress and occur in someone who does not have a mental disorder
A. Hysteria   B. DNA   C. Patent   D. Saline

292. A digestive disorder in which nutrients cannot be properly absorbed from food, causing weakness and loss of weight
A. Stoma   B. Optic   C. Sprue   D. Coma

293. A hormone made in the pancreas that plays an important role in the absorption of glucose (the body's main source of energy) into muscle cells
A. Sputum   B. Stye   C. Insulin   D. Tar

294. Sudden uncontrolled waves of electrical activity in the brain, causing involuntary movement or loss of consciousness
A. Labia   B. Erythema   C. Nevus   D. Seizure

295. The socket in the skull that contains the eyeball, along with its blood vessels, nerves, and muscles
A. Numbness   B. Orbit   C. Imaging   D. Tar

296. An accumulation of blood from a broken blood vessel
A. Autopsy   B. Hematoma   C. Palsy   D. Glioma

297. A bacterial infection of the small intestine that causes severe watery diarrhea, dehydration, and possibly death
A. Cholera   B. Seizure   C. Pharynx   D. Macula

298. A growth that occurs on mucous membranes such as those in the nose and intestine
A. Gene   B. Polyp   C. Goiter   D. Genome

299. ___ Another term for a tumor
A. Meniscus B. Maxilla C. Neoplasm D. Mucocele

300. ___ Intelligence quotient; a measure of a person's intelligence as determined by specific tests
A. Vertigo B. Somatic C. Kidney D. IQ

From the words provided for each clue, provide the letter of the word which best matches the clue.

301. ___ Pertaining to blood vessels
A. Dermis B. Polyuria C. Osteoma D. Vascular

302. ___ Another term for a microorganism, especially one that causes disease
A. Microbe B. Carcinoma C. Sperm D. Pharynx

303. ___ A hormone that stimulates the release of gastric acid in the stomach
A. Bursa B. Orgasm C. Hygiene D. Gastrin

304. ___ A disease that began in the affected location
A. Mucus B. Version C. Vein D. Primary

305. ___ An abnormal mass that occurs when cells in a certain area reproduce unchecked
A. Pruritus B. Ischemia C. Tumor D. Overdose

306. ___ A bacterial infection of the small intestine that causes severe watery diarrhea, dehydration, and possibly death
A. Sciatica B. Cholera C. Foreskin D. Scurvy

307. ___ A chemically inactive substance given in place of a drug to test how much of a drug's effectiveness can be attributed to a patient's expectations that the drug will have a positive effect
A. Cilia B. Villi C. Placebo D. Clone

308. ___ An excessively large dose of a drug, which can lead to coma and death
A. Carcinoma B. Rhinitis C. Airways D. Overdose

309. ___ The colored part of the eye
A. Pudendum B. Spleen C. Fitness D. Iris

310. ___ The foreskin
A. Microbe B. Prepuce C. Inhaler D. Orthotic

311. ___ A thin, oval-shaped membrane that separates the inner ear from the outer ear and is responsible for transmitting sound waves
A. Varices B. Eardrum C. Ulcer D. Organism

312. ___ An open sore that occurs on the skin or on a mucous membrane because of the destruction of surface tissue
A. Osteitis B. Ulcer C. Atrophy D. Tartar

313. ___ The two upper chambers of the heart
A. Atria B. Neurosis C. Mucus D. Audiogram

314. ___ A slippery fluid produced by mucous membranes that lubricates and protects the internal surfaces of the body
A. Rhinitis B. Colic C. Version D. Mucus

315. A hormone made in the pancreas that plays an important role in the absorption of glucose (the body's main source of energy) into muscle cells
A. Ozone   B. Syndrome   C. Insulin   D. Nephrons

316. A condition in which a tissue or organ does not receive enough supply of blood
A. Ticks   B. Ischemia   C. Asthma   D. Menarche

317. A person who specializes in the making and adjustment of eyeglasses and contact lenses
A. Optician   B. Cell   C. Cataract   D. Spleen

318. A poisonous form of oxygen that is present in the earth's upper atmosphere, where it helps to screen the earth from damaging ultraviolet rays
A. Niacin   B. Ozone   C. Angioma   D. Cholera

319. A thickened area of skin due to consistent pressure or friction, or the area around a bone break where new bone is formed
A. Coccyx   B. Maxilla   C. Callus   D. Colic

320. The displacement of an organ from its normal position to a new one
A. Ulcer   B. Prolapse   C. In vitro   D. Plague

321. A tumor composed of cells not normally found in the part of the body when the tumor occurred
A. Neuron   B. Fitness   C. Valve   D. Teratoma

322. The column of bones and cartilage running along the midline of the back that surrounds and protects the spinal cord and supports the head
A. Spine   B. Placebo   C. Varices   D. Cilia

323. Instruments resembling tweezers that are used to handle objects or tissue during surgery
A. Bilateral   B. Atheroma   C. Forceps   D. Audiogram

324. An abnormal passageway from one organ to another or from an organ to the body surface
A. Retina   B. Pulse   C. Calcium   D. Fistula

325. Inflammation of the uvea
A. Uveitis   B. Palsy   C. Paresis   D. Aorta

326. The excessive production of urine
A. Numbness   B. Syndrome   C. Atrophy   D. Polyuria

327. The medical term for nearsightedness
A. Booster   B. Myopia   C. Microbe   D. Orbit

328. The medical term for itching
A. Fluke   B. Calcium   C. Coccyx   D. Pruritus

329. An organ located in the upper left abdomen behind the ribs that removes and destroys old red blood cells and helps fight infection
A. Organism   B. Spleen   C. Vascular   D. Cell

330. The inner skin layer
A. Dermis   B. Vitamins   C. Orthotic   D. Colitis

331. Another term for a nerve cell
A. Semen   B. Hypoxia   C. Neuron   D. Vascular

332. A device used to correct or control deformed bones, muscles, or joints
A. Neuron B. Foreskin C. Uterus D. Orthotic

333. A cancer that occurs on the surface or lining of an organ
A. Dermis B. Bilateral C. Carcinoma D. Forceps

334. Damage to part of the brain because of a lack of blood supply or the rupturing of a blood vessel
A. Stroke B. Iodine C. Atrophy D. Microbe

335. The male sex cell produced in the testicles
A. Pinworm B. Sperm C. Villi D. Hematoma

336. A cavity within bone or a channel that contains blood
A. Embryo B. Plaque C. Cast D. Sinus

337. A serious infectious disease transmitted to humans through bites of rodent fleas
A. Paroxysm B. Plague C. Bacillus D. Suture

338. A brain tumor arising from cells that support nerve cells
A. Viremia B. Glioma C. Familial D. Prion

339. A negative reaction to a substance that in most people causes no reaction
A. Sprain B. Allergy C. Fistula D. Nodule

340. An abnormal growth of bone out of another bone, often located on the heel and usually painful
A. Vesicle B. Coma C. Rosacea D. Bone spur

341. The expansion and contraction of a blood vessel due to the blood pumped through it
A. Villi B. Bladder C. Uveitis D. Pulse

342. A hormone produced by the thyroid gland that helps regulate energy production in the body
A. Cyanosis B. Paroxysm C. Vein D. Thyroxin

343. The extent to which a substance is poisonous
A. Paresis B. Hepatoma C. Orbit D. Toxicity

344. A vitamin important in many chemical processes in the body; also known as vitamin b3
A. Ozone B. Ischemia C. Niacin D. Viremia

345. The main form that glucose, the body's energy source, takes when it is stored
A. Spine B. Glycogen C. Pelvis D. Primary

346. Small spots that float across the field of vision, caused by debris floating in the gel-like substance that fills the eye
A. Androgen B. Thorax C. Floaters D. Booster

347. A disorder in which the lens of the eye becomes less transparent and, in some cases, a milky white, making vision less clear
A. Familial B. Gastrin C. Minipill D. Cataract

348. An automatic, involuntary response of the nervous system to a stimulus
A. Erythema B. Reflex C. Bladder D. Allergen

349. Partial paralysis
A. Necrosis B. Paresis C. Booster D. Vascular

350. Inflammation of the heart
A. Fistula   B. Carditis   C. Tapeworm   D. Cyst

351. A substance that causes vomiting
A. Sciatica   B. Croup   C. pH   D. Emetic

352. The orange-yellow pigment in bile, causing jaundice if it builds up in the blood and skin
A. Bilirubin   B. Sperm   C. Pharynx   D. Atrophy

353. A short, tube-like structure that branches off the large intestine
A. Tumor   B. Calcium   C. Appendix   D. Abscess

354. A poisonous substance produced by certain animals
A. Eczema   B. Ischemia   C. Venom   D. Speculum

355. A group of symptoms that indicate a certain disorder when they occur together
A. Croup   B. Rectum   C. Syndrome   D. Uterus

356. The sugar found in dairy products
A. Lactose   B. Dopamine   C. Overdose   D. Hypoxia

357. Redness of the skin
A. Erythema   B. Abscess   C. Vascular   D. Selenium

358. A deficiency of the vitamin niacin; causes dermatitis, diarrhea, and mental disorders
A. Osteitis   B. Pellagra   C. Plaque   D. Androgen

359. The presence of bacterial toxins in the blood
A. Toxemia   B. Viremia   C. Graft   D. Orthotic

360. The passageways that air moves through while traveling in and out of the lungs during breathing
A. Vesicle   B. Sperm   C. Airways   D. Pharynx

361. Abnormal crackling or bubbling sounds heard in the lungs during breathing
A. Glioma   B. Rales   C. Coma   D. Selenium

362. An orange pigment present in colored plants such as carrots that is converted by the body to the essential nutrient vitamin a
A. Rosacea   B. Niacin   C. Carotene   D. Plaque

363. A lump filled with either fluid or soft material, occurring in any organ or tissue
A. Shock   B. Bacterium   C. Cyst   D. Antacid

364. A fluid-filled sac that cushions and reduces friction in certain parts of the body
A. Bursa   B. Atria   C. Allergen   D. Placenta

365. The practice, maintenance, and study of health
A. Hygiene   B. Carotene   C. Graft   D. Ischemia

366. Any bacteria that is rod-shaped
A. Lockjaw   B. Bacillus   C. Chlamydia   D. Hematoma

367. A possibly life-threatening condition in which breathing stops, for either a short or long period of time
A. Apnea   B. Hypoxia   C. Sprain   D. Hematoma

368. Healthy tissue that is used to replace diseased or defective tissue
A. Glycogen B. Smear C. Vitamins D. Graft

369. Any one of the 33 bones that make up the spine
A. Vertebra B. Ptosis C. Uterus D. Palsy

370. An element needed by the body only in very small amounts that helps maintain tissue elasticity
A. Coma B. Erythema C. Trauma D. Selenium

371. An involuntary, repetitive movement such as a twitch
A. Coccyx B. Tic C. In situ D. Neuroma

372. A painless sore that has a thick, rubbery base and a defined edge
A. Nephrons B. Typhus C. Chancre D. Carotene

373. A spasm of the jaw muscles that prevents the mouth from opening, such as that caused by tetanus
A. Lockjaw B. Erythema C. Nephrons D. Optic

374. "in glass"; a biological test or process that is carried out in a laboratory
A. In vitro B. Orgasm C. Pus D. Allergy

375. An additional dose of a vaccine taken after the first dose to maintain or renew the first one
A. Calcium B. Maxilla C. Booster D. Optician

376. An element for the formation of thyroid hormones
A. Iodine B. Floaters C. Dopamine D. Sperm

377. A condition in which people are born with insufficient amounts of the pigment melanin, which is responsible for hair, skin, and eye color
A. Toxicity B. Ectopic C. Fluke D. Albinism

378. Microorganisms that cause several human infections and can be transmitted sexually
A. Mucus B. Embryo C. Appendix D. Chlamydia

379. The introduction of a substance, such as a drug or nutrient, into the bloodstream or a body cavity
A. Lactose B. Excision C. Hypoxia D. Infusion

380. An organ located in the pelvis whose function is to collect and store urine until it is expelled
A. Bladder B. Smear C. Iodine D. Appendix

381. The loose skin that covers the head of the penis
A. Foreskin B. Infusion C. Vein D. Cell

382. Fatty deposits on the inner walls of blood vessels, which can cause narrowing and decrease blood flow
A. Atheroma B. Carcinoma C. Molecule D. Vesicle

383. Inflammation of the mucous membrane lining the nose
A. Vascular B. Orbit C. Steroids D. Rhinitis

384. An area of buildup of fat deposits in an artery, causing narrowing of the artery and possibly heart disease
A. Plaque B. Syndrome C. Estrogen D. Orbit

385. A group of diseases caused by the microorganism rickettsia, spread by the bites of fleas, mites, or ticks
A. Numbness B. Typhus C. Pus D. Calcium

386. A noncancerous bone tumor
A. Orthotic   B. Osteoma   C. Albinism   D. Numbness

387. The return of a disease or symptom after it had disappeared
A. Relapse   B. Palsy   C. Glioma   D. Graft

388. A graph showing a person's hearing ability, determined from a set of tests examining hearing acuity of different sound frequencies
A. Fitness   B. Apnea   C. Prion   D. Audiogram

389. Pertaining to the eyes
A. Optic   B. Teratoma   C. Overdose   D. Plaque

390. A thick, yellowish or greenish fluid that contains dead white blood cells, tissues, and bacteria; occurs at the site of a bacterial infection
A. Numbness   B. Pus   C. Molecule   D. Optic

391. Loss of sensation or ability to move
A. Palsy   B. Node   C. Valve   D. Tartar

392. Abnormal formation of connective or scar tissue
A. Bacillus   B. Osteitis   C. Hematoma   D. Fibrosis

393. A disorder characterized by inflamed airways and difficulty breathing
A. Plaque   B. Ozone   C. Glioma   D. Asthma

394. Difficulty breathing
A. Macula   B. Dyspnea   C. Valve   D. Glioma

395. A shift in the position of the fetus inside of the uterus, either occurring naturally or as performed by a doctor to facilitate delivery
A. Plaque   B. Orgasm   C. Spine   D. Version

396. A parasitic flatworm that can infest humans
A. Audiogram   B. Insulin   C. Rosacea   D. Fluke

397. A sudden attack or worsening of a disease's symptoms
A. Appendix   B. Syndrome   C. Paroxysm   D. Inhaler

398. The smallest unit of a substance that possesses its characteristics
A. Inhaler   B. Gene   C. In vitro   D. Molecule

399. The tiny filtering units of the kidney
A. pH   B. Hematoma   C. Neuroma   D. Nephrons

400. A group of drugs which resemble hormones produced by the adrenal glands, and anabolic steroids, which are like the hormones produced by the male sex organs
A. Paroxysm   B. Steroids   C. Selenium   D. Appendix

From the words provided for each clue, provide the letter of the word which best matches the clue.

401. The first part of the small intestine, immediately following the stomach
A. Lateral   B. Duodenum   C. Nutrient   D. Axilla

402. Inflammation of a testicle, which can be caused by infection with the mumps virus
A. Cerebrum   B. Toxin   C. Insomnia   D. Orchitis

403. The medical term for the kneecap
A. Patella   B. Rubeola   C. Cochlea   D. Nutrient

404. A noncancerous bone tumor
A. Pleura   B. Mutation   C. Rubella   D. Osteoma

405. A drug that neutralizes stomach acids
A. Immunity   B. Tic   C. Antacid   D. Duodenum

406. An artificially constructed or an abnormal passage connecting two usually separate structures in the body
A. Retina   B. Triage   C. Shunt   D. Sclera

407. Describes a treatment or procedure that is not urgent and can be arranged at the patient's convenience
A. Enuresis   B. Elective   C. Aplasia   D. Osteoma

408. Two almond-shaped glands located at the opening of the fallopian tubes on both sides of the uterus
A. Ovaries   B. Scrotum   C. Mumps   D. Pandemic

409. An excessively large dose of a drug, which can lead to coma and death
A. Embryo   B. Numbness   C. Antacid   D. Overdose

410. The medical term for lockjaw
A. Trismus   B. Callus   C. Pallor   D. Retina

411. Medical term for the armpit
A. Nucleus   B. Axilla   C. Toxin   D. Tonsils

412. The process by which most cells divide to reproduce
A. Meiosis   B. Mitosis   C. Thymoma   D. Hematoma

413. A group of fats stored in the body and used for energy
A. Toxicity   B. Pelvis   C. Pancreas   D. Lipids

414. A connective tissue (softer than bone) that is part of the skeletal system, including the joints
A. Miotic   B. Orchitis   C. Colon   D. Cartilage

415. A characteristic sound of blood flowing irregularly through the heart
A. Hysteria   B. Murmur   C. Duodenum   D. Rabies

416. The clear, watery fluid that separates from clotted blood
A. Fitness   B. Osteoma   C. Nephrons   D. Serum

417. Infestation by a small, round, blood-sucking parasite
A. Vein   B. Hookworm   C. Typhus   D. Enzyme

418. The oily, lubricating substance that is secreted by glands in the skin
A. Enuresis   B. Pandemic   C. Sebum   D. Bulimia

419. The smallest particle found in the blood, which plays a major role in forming blood clots
A. Platelet   B. Trismus   C. Bilateral   D. Nitrates

420. A group of drugs which resemble hormones produced by the adrenal glands, and anabolic steroids, which are like the hormones produced by the male sex organs
A. Patent   B. Steroids   C. Thrombus   D. Pandemic

421. A term used to describe a child in the womb from fertilization to 8 weeks following fertilization
A. Cerebrum   B. Impetigo   C. Vertebra   D. Embryo

422. A coiled organ in the inner ear that plays a large role in hearing by picking up sound vibrations and transmitting them as electrical signals
A. Fitness   B. Cochlea   C. Implant   D. Nephrons

423. Small eight-legged animals, many of which burrow and feed on blood
A. Numbness   B. Mites   C. Uveitis   D. Graft

424. A sudden attack or worsening of a disease's symptoms
A. Toxin   B. Bilateral   C. Paroxysm   D. Penis

425. An infectious viral disease primarily affecting animals
A. Renin   B. Thymoma   C. Arteritis   D. Rabies

426. The extent to which a substance is poisonous
A. Stent   B. Bacillus   C. In situ   D. Toxicity

427. The double-layered membrane that lines the lungs and chest cavity and allows for lung movement during breathing
A. Neuroma   B. Canal   C. Pleura   D. Embryo

428. A discharge from an inflamed ear
A. Bulimia   B. Molecule   C. Otorrhea   D. Penis

429. The common term for urticaria, an itchy, inflamed rash that results from an allergic reaction
A. Gangrene   B. Fibroid   C. Hives   D. Hematoma

430. A painful, persistent erection without sexual arousal, requiring emergency treatment
A. Aplasia   B. Priapism   C. Excision   D. Carcinoma

431. Another term for a microorganism, especially one that causes disease
A. Chancre   B. Progeria   C. Microbe   D. Volvulus

432. An organ formed in the uterus during pregnancy that links the blood of the mother to the blood of the fetus
A. Rabies   B. Thalamus   C. Placenta   D. Pudendum

433. The term used to refer to an unborn child from 8 weeks after fertilization to birth
A. Fetus   B. Oocyte   C. Birthmark   D. Serum

434. A tear or break in an organ or tissue
A. Rupture   B. Tapeworm   C. Ilium   D. Cochlea

435. The tough, white coating that covers and protects the inner structures of the eye
A. Vitiligo   B. Sclera   C. Walleye   D. Bilateral

436. Another term for measles
A. Receptor   B. Pelvis   C. Rubeola   D. Calorie

437. The tiny structures that make up all the tissues of the body and carry out all its functions
A. Thrombus   B. Vertebra   C. Cell   D. Bilateral

438. The beginning of menstruation
A. Pulse B. Colon C. Menarche D. Molecule

439. A crescent-shaped pad of cartilage in joints that helps to reduce friction
A. Meniscus B. Rubeola C. Trachoma D. Virus

440. A high- pitched sound produced during breathing because of narrowing of the airways
A. Erythema B. Tonsils C. Wheeze D. Nucleus

441. Describes a condition or illness that begins suddenly and is usually short- lasting
A. Cholera B. Vulva C. Acute D. Shunt

442. A parasite- caused or infectious disease in animals that can be transferred to humans
A. Zoonosis B. Rabies C. Mineral D. Osteoma

443. A short tube located at the end of the large intestine, which connects the intestine to the anus
A. Rectum B. Dextrose C. Epilepsy D. Mucus

444. The sac containing the testicles
A. Scrotum B. Ilium C. Mites D. Fibroid

445. The outer, visible portion of the female genitals
A. Cochlea B. Glucose C. Vulva D. Bulimia

446. The three membranes that surround and protect the spinal cord and brain
A. Meninges B. DNA C. Mutation D. Tremor

447. An organ, tissue, or device surgically inserted and left in the body
A. Implant B. Scrotum C. Bladder D. Toxin

448. Baldness or loss of hair, mainly on the head, either in defined patches or completely
A. Microbe B. In vitro C. Alopecia D. Serum

449. A measure of a person's physical strength, flexibility, and endurance
A. Platelet B. Pelvis C. Mucus D. Fitness

450. Healthy tissue that is used to replace diseased or defective tissue
A. Volvulus B. Whipworm C. Graft D. Aspermia

451. A disease of the joints characterized by inflammation, pain, stiffness, and redness
A. Bifocal B. Arthritis C. Orchitis D. Molecule

452. The presence of bacterial toxins in the blood
A. Walleye B. Toxemia C. Traction D. Overdose

453. Redness of the skin
A. Cartilage B. Erythema C. Placenta D. Rupture

454. A bacterial infection of the small intestine that causes severe watery diarrhea, dehydration, and possibly death
A. Paroxysm B. Cholera C. Wart D. Duodenum

455. An organ located in the pelvis whose function is to collect and store urine until it is expelled
A. Bladder B. Sclera C. Lipids D. Spasm

456. A disorder in which a person eats large amounts of food then forces vomiting or uses laxatives to prevent weight gain (called binging and purging)
A. Bulimia   B. Carcinoma   C. Rabies   D. Dextrose

457. Difficulty breathing
A. Nucleus   B. DNA   C. Progeria   D. Dyspnea

458. A widespread epidemic
A. Seminoma   B. Plasma   C. Pandemic   D. Thalamus

459. A small parasite worm that can live in the intestines
A. Cochlea   B. Menarche   C. Fitness   D. Pinworm

460. A system used to classify sick or injured people according to the severity of their conditions
A. Necrosis   B. Vein   C. Volvulus   D. Triage

461. Resistance to a specific disease because of the responses of the immune system
A. Paroxysm   B. Immunity   C. Birthmark   D. Cholera

462. Death of a tissue because of a lack of blood supply
A. Embryo   B. Gangrene   C. Rectum   D. Nodule

463. An involuntary, rhythmic, shaking movement caused by alternating contraction and relaxation of muscles
A. Tremor   B. Traction   C. Menarche   D. Nephrons

464. Relatively mild emotional disorders (such as mild depression and phobias)
A. Menarche   B. Wheeze   C. Neurosis   D. Appendix

465. The liquid part of the blood, containing substances such as nutrients, salts, and proteins
A. Plasma   B. Embryo   C. In situ   D. Lipids

466. A long gland located behind the stomach that produces enzymes that help to break down food and hormones (insulin and glucagon) that help to regulate glucose levels in the blood
A. Invasive   B. Myositis   C. Pancreas   D. DNA

467. A disorder in which a person becomes overly suspicious and emotionally sensitive
A. Fracture   B. Nephrons   C. Paranoia   D. Glucose

468. The type of cell division that occurs only in the ovaries and testicles, producing cells with half the genes of the original cell
A. Meiosis   B. Arteritis   C. Zoonosis   D. Ovum

469. A viral infection that causes inflammation of salivary glands
A. Mumps   B. Strain   C. Tonsils   D. Bone spur

470. A cancer that occurs on the surface or lining of an organ
A. Carcinoma   B. Birthmark   C. Measles   D. Erythema

471. A lens that corrects both near and distant vision by having two parts with different focusing strengths
A. Osteoma   B. Impetigo   C. Phlegm   D. Bifocal

472. The external male reproductive organ, which passes urine and semen out of the body
A. Epidemic   B. Penis   C. Thalamus   D. Whipworm

473. The lack of sensation in a part of the body because of interruption of nerve impulses
A. Numbness   B. Dialysis   C. Rash   D. Osteoma

474. The roof of the mouth
A. Toxemia B. Palate C. Autopsy D. Mites

475. One of two bones that form the upper jaw, the roof of the mouth, and the center portion of the face
A. Maxilla B. Neuroma C. Zoonosis D. Patent

476. Inflammation of bone
A. Nodule B. Osteitis C. Toxemia D. Placebo

477. "in glass"; a biological test or process that is carried out in a laboratory
A. Cyst B. In vitro C. Triage D. Parasite

478. The two upper chambers of the heart
A. Toxicity B. Atria C. Erythema D. Aspermia

479. The period during which sexual development occurs
A. Puberty B. Plasma C. Lateral D. Strain

480. Abnormally pale skin
A. Pulse B. Neuroma C. Pallor D. Rubella

481. A procedure to treat kidney failure in which artificial means are used to filter waste, maintain acid-base balance, and remove excess fluid from the body
A. Toxemia B. Wart C. Retina D. Dialysis

482. A blood clot in a blood vessel
A. Trismus B. Prepuce C. Thrombus D. Follicle

483. A noncancerous tumor occurring in nerve tissue
A. Enuresis B. Invasive C. Patella D. Neuroma

484. Not obstructed; open
A. Scrotum B. Patent C. Walleye D. Arteritis

485. An enzyme that plays a role in increasing a low blood pressure
A. Renin B. Insomnia C. Menarche D. Trachoma

486. Dull, aching pain in the lower back
A. Overdose B. Embryo C. Lumbago D. Palate

487. "in place"; often describes a cancer that has not spread
A. Neuroma B. In situ C. Appendix D. Measles

488. The medical term for wetting the bed
A. Palate B. Enuresis C. Pyrexia D. Thalamus

489. Describes something that spreads throughout body tissues, such as a tumor or microorganism
A. Invasive B. Cecum C. Sebum D. Bifocal

490. A drug that causes the pupil to constrict
A. Patent B. Miotic C. Ilium D. Osteoma

491. A substance that is a necessary part of a healthy diet (such as potassium, calcium, sodium, phosphorus, and magnesium)
A. Mineral B. Otorrhea C. Axilla D. Excision

492. A short, tube-like structure that branches off the large intestine
A. Phlegm B. Appendix C. Steroids D. Fissure

493. A shift in the position of the fetus inside of the uterus, either occurring naturally or as performed by a doctor to facilitate delivery
A. Cochlea B. Ovaries C. Version D. Triage

494. A contagious, harmless growth caused by a virus that occurs on the skin or a mucous membrane
A. Dextrose B. Pandemic C. Neurosis D. Wart

495. Any one of the 33 bones that make up the spine
A. Vertebra B. Antacid C. Triage D. Paroxysm

496. A group of diseases caused by the microorganism rickettsia, spread by the bites of fleas, mites, or ticks
A. Thrush B. Stent C. Typhus D. Palate

497. The group of bones in the lower part of the trunk that support the upper body and protect the abdominal organs
A. Bladder B. Plasma C. Vertebra D. Pelvis

498. The external genitals, usually referring to the female
A. Shunt B. Wart C. Lactose D. Pudendum

499. A condition in which patches of skin on the body lose their color
A. Virus B. Vitiligo C. Meninges D. Tapeworm

500. An additional dose of a vaccine taken after the first dose to maintain or renew the first one
A. Cerebrum B. Booster C. Toxin D. Nephrons

From the words provided for each clue, provide the letter of the word which best matches the clue.

1. __C__ An abnormal mass that occurs when cells in a certain area reproduce unchecked
   A. Glycogen   B. Cochlea   C. Tumor   D. Rhinitis

2. __A__ An enzyme that plays a role in increasing a low blood pressure
   A. Renin   B. Fungus   C. Osteoma   D. Traction

3. __C__ A muscle disease, usually one that results in the deterioration of muscle
   A. Antibody   B. Virus   C. Myopathy   D. Thrombus

4. __A__ A mineral that plays a role in the body's water balance, heart rhythm, nerve impulses, and muscle contraction
   A. Sodium   B. Ocular   C. Urea   D. Orchitis

5. __B__ A term describing something related to or caused by a virus
   A. Vesicle   B. Viral   C. Version   D. Vitamins

6. __B__ The use of tension to hold a body part in place or to correct or prevent an alignment problem
   A. Cyst   B. Traction   C. Apnea   D. Myelitis

7. __B__ A candidiasis infection
   A. Menarche   B. Thrush   C. Thrombus   D. Pleurisy

8. __B__ Anything that can increase the rate of abnormal change in cells, which can lead to cancer
   A. Sepsis   B. Mutagen   C. Lymph   D. Clavicle

9. __D__ The extent to which a substance is poisonous
   A. Osteoma   B. Myelitis   C. B cell   D. Toxicity

10. __B__ A term used to describe a newborn infant from birth to 1 month of age
    A. Dementia   B. Neonate   C. Nucleus   D. Strain

11. __D__ The foreskin
    A. Urethra   B. Toxin   C. Erythema   D. Prepuce

12. __C__ Any bacteria that is rod-shaped
    A. Rales   B. Apnea   C. Bacillus   D. Clavicle

13. __A__ An extremely rare condition in which the body ages prematurely
    A. Progeria   B. Stoma   C. Anatomy   D. Gene

14. __C__ A small skin blister, or any sac in the body, that contains fluid
    A. Fibroma   B. Abscess   C. Vesicle   D. B cell

15. __B__ A yellow-green liquid produced in the liver whose function is to remove waste from the liver and break down fats as food is digested
    A. ECG   B. Bile   C. Trauma   D. Gene

16. __B__ An involuntary, repetitive movement such as a twitch
    A. Endemic   B. Tic   C. Botulism   D. Glycogen

17. __A__ The long, flat bone located at the center of the chest
    A. Sternum   B. Spasm   C. Endemic   D. Carcinoma

18. __D__ A noncancerous tumor of connective tissue
A. Ectopic B. Vascular C. Cochlea D. Fibroma

19. __D__ A chemical produced by a gland or tissue that is released into the bloodstream
A. Pellagra B. Vitamins C. Ticks D. Hormone

20. __A__ The medical term for nearsightedness
A. Myopia B. Aplasia C. Patient D. Cyst

21. __D__ A term used to describe something related to a fever, such as febrile seizures (seizures occurring in a child who has a fever)
A. Venom B. Osteoma C. Insulin D. Febrile

22. __B__ An organism that is dependent on another organism for nourishment
A. Thrush B. Fungus C. Anatomy D. Enuresis

23. __D__ An excessively large dose of a drug, which can lead to coma and death
A. Cochlea B. Thrombus C. Culture D. Overdose

24. __A__ A group of drugs that widen blood vessels
A. Nitrates B. Mole C. Rales D. Trismus

25. __B__ A genetic disorder in which the foot is twisted and misshapen
A. Ocular B. Clubfoot C. Ovaries D. Nephrons

26. __D__ A discharge from an inflamed ear
A. Urethra B. Fetus C. Anatomy D. Otorrhea

27. __C__ A person who specializes in the making and adjustment of eyeglasses and contact lenses
A. Emetic B. Spasm C. Optician D. Syndrome

28. __D__ A condition in which a tissue or organ does not receive enough supply of blood
A. Bladder B. Walleye C. Appendix D. Ischemia

29. __A__ The loose skin that covers the head of the penis
A. Foreskin B. Coccyx C. Birthmark D. Axilla

30. __C__ A blood clot in a blood vessel
A. Vitamins B. Ischemia C. Thrombus D. Saline

31. __B__ The three membranes that surround and protect the spinal cord and brain
A. Seizure B. Meninges C. Fibroma D. Coma

32. __B__ The thicker of the two long bones in the lower leg
A. Radon B. Tibia C. Osteoma D. Iron

33. __B__ The bones that form the framework of the head and enclose and protect the brain and other sensory organs
A. Bruxism B. Skull C. Erythema D. Androgen

34. __A__ An organ located in the pelvis whose function is to collect and store urine until it is expelled
A. Bladder B. Lymph C. Walleye D. Emetic

35. __C__ Abnormal crackling or bubbling sounds heard in the lungs during breathing
A. Progeria B. Clone C. Rales D. Abscess

36. __A__ A protein made by white blood cells that reacts with a specific foreign protein as part of the immune response
A. Antibody   B. Saline   C. Clavicle   D. Fetus

37. __C__ The medical term for lockjaw
A. Lactose   B. Ligation   C. Trismus   D. Rectum

38. __C__ Poisoning from poorly preserved food contaminated with a dangerous bacterial toxin that results in paralysis
A. Fibroma   B. Viral   C. Botulism   D. Pleura

39. __C__ Any one of the 33 bones that make up the spine
A. Emetic   B. Vulvitis   C. Vertebra   D. Myopathy

40. __A__ Any area of discolored skin that is present when a baby is born
A. Birthmark   B. Strain   C. Excision   D. Emetic

41. __A__ A marking on the skin; can be present at birth (birthmark) or develop later (such as a mole)
A. Nevus   B. Microbe   C. Hookworm   D. Anatomy

42. __C__ A negative reaction to a substance that in most people causes no reaction
A. Pupil   B. PUVA   C. Allergy   D. Mitosis

43. __D__ A possibly life-threatening condition in which breathing stops, for either a short or long period of time
A. Nerve   B. Mineral   C. Clone   D. Apnea

44. __B__ Four fused bones that form a triangular shape at the base of the spine (also known as the tailbone)
A. Addiction   B. Coccyx   C. Hysteria   D. Myopia

45. __A__ A chemically inactive substance given in place of a drug to test how much of a drug's effectiveness can be attributed to a patient's expectations that the drug will have a positive effect
A. Placebo   B. Dementia   C. Pruritus   D. Somatic

46. __C__ A slippery fluid produced by mucous membranes that lubricates and protects the internal surfaces of the body
A. Neuritis   B. Seizure   C. Mucus   D. Pellagra

47. __B__ A term describing a condition that affects both sides of the body or two paired organs, such as bilateral deafness (deafness in both ears)
A. Ringworm   B. Bilateral   C. Viremia   D. Nucleus

48. __B__ The common term for urticaria, an itchy, inflamed rash that results from an allergic reaction
A. Carcinoma   B. Hives   C. Clubfoot   D. Rectum

49. __D__ A shift in the position of the fetus inside of the uterus, either occurring naturally or as performed by a doctor to facilitate delivery
A. Bilateral   B. Myopia   C. In vivo   D. Version

50. __C__ Another name for the sugar glucose
A. Carditis   B. Iron   C. Dextrose   D. Pleurisy

51. __B__ Mucus and other material produced by the lining of the respiratory tract
A. Aneurysm   B. Phlegm   C. Sebum   D. Pellagra

52. __A__ Inflammation of a nerve, often characterized by pain, numbness, or tingling
A. Neuritis   B. Sepsis   C. Radon   D. Phimosis

53. __D__ Pertaining to blood vessels
A. Fibroma   B. Enuresis   C. Hepatic   D. Vascular

54. **D** The medical term for itching
   A. Microbe   B. Fibroma   C. Fungus   D. Pruritus

55. **D** An electrocardiogram, which is a record of the electrical impulses that trigger the heartbeat; used to diagnose heart disorders
   A. Thrush   B. Sciatica   C. Allergy   D. ECG

56. **C** A short, tube-like structure that branches off the large intestine
   A. Enuresis   B. Graft   C. Appendix   D. Audiogram

57. **B** Dependence on a substance (such as alcohol or other drugs) or an activity, to the point that stopping is very difficult and causes severe physical and mental reactions
   A. Erythema   B. Addiction   C. Rales   D. Patient

58. **C** Small, eight-legged animals that can attach to humans and animals and feed on blood
   A. Scrotum   B. Walleye   C. Ticks   D. Fibroma

59. **D** A system used to classify sick or injured people according to the severity of their conditions
   A. Thrush   B. Sternum   C. Aplasia   D. Triage

60. **B** A cancer in connective tissue, fibrous tissue, or blood vessels
   A. Spasm   B. Sarcoma   C. Mineral   D. Sternum

61. **C** Another term for a microorganism, especially one that causes disease
   A. Safe sex   B. Vesicle   C. Microbe   D. Patent

62. **B** Pertaining to the body
   A. Enuresis   B. Somatic   C. Menarche   D. Optic

63. **A** A tiny pouchlike cavity in a structure of the body, such as a hair follicle
   A. Follicle   B. Anatomy   C. Kidney   D. Dextrose

64. **D** A noncancerous bone tumor
   A. Toxin   B. Vagina   C. Renin   D. Osteoma

65. **A** A lump filled with either fluid or soft material, occurring in any organ or tissue
   A. Cyst   B. Microbe   C. Bilateral   D. Mutagen

66. **B** The blockage of a blood vessel by an embolus- something previously circulating in the blood (such as a blood clot, gas bubble, tissue, bacteria, bone marrow, cholesterol, fat, etc.)
   A. Tetanus   B. Embolism   C. Vesicle   D. Emetic

67. **C** The infection of a wound or tissue with bacteria, causing the spread of the bacteria into the bloodstream
   A. Stoma   B. Toxicity   C. Sepsis   D. Birthmark

68. **B** Dangerously decreased acidity of the blood, which can be caused by high altitudes, hyperventilation, and excessive vomiting
   A. Chlamydia   B. Alkalosis   C. Hives   D. Sternum

69. **D** A highly contagious skin disorder caused by a mite that burrows into the skin and produces an intense, itchy rash
   A. Liver   B. Clavicle   C. Rubella   D. Scabies

70. **D** The basic unit of DNA, which is responsible for passing genetic information
   A. Tibia   B. Ringworm   C. Selenium   D. Gene

71. B A drug that causes the pupil to constrict
    A. Botulism   B. Miotic   C. Insulin   D. Emetic

72. B A body temperature of above 98.6°f in the mouth or 99.8°f in the rectum
    A. Keratin   B. Pyrexia   C. Antibody   D. Tibia

73. C Healthy tissue that is used to replace diseased or defective tissue
    A. Bilateral   B. Urea   C. Graft   D. Receptor

74. B Inflammation of a testicle, which can be caused by infection with the mumps virus
    A. Fibroma   B. Orchitis   C. Cyst   D. Varices

75. B Physical injury or emotional shock
    A. Pleurisy   B. Trauma   C. Pellagra   D. Ligation

76. C The sugar found in dairy products
    A. Radon   B. Scabies   C. Lactose   D. Androgen

77. C A coiled organ in the inner ear that plays a large role in hearing by picking up sound vibrations and transmitting them as electrical signals
    A. Tendon   B. Nitrates   C. Cochlea   D. Embolism

78. A Redness of the skin
    A. Erythema   B. Pupil   C. Ocular   D. Infusion

79. B The structure of bodies
    A. Rectum   B. Anatomy   C. Embolism   D. Myositis

80. A A sometimes fatal disease affecting the brain and spinal cord
    A. Tetanus   B. In vivo   C. Rales   D. Lymph

81. A Controlled analgesia- a system for administering pain- killing drugs in which the amount of drug delivered is controlled by the patient
    A. Patient   B. Clone   C. Allergy   D. Thrombus

82. B A reduced level of oxygen in tissues
    A. Polyuria   B. Hypoxia   C. Clubfoot   D. Urea

83. C The process by which most cells divide to reproduce
    A. Aplasia   B. Systemic   C. Mitosis   D. Anatomy

84. C A colorless, odorless, tasteless radioactive gas that is produced by materials in soil, rocks, and building materials; suspected of causing cancer
    A. Mutagen   B. Birthmark   C. Radon   D. Rectum

85. A Measures taken to reduce the risk of acquiring a sexually transmitted disease, such as the use of a condom
    A. Safe sex   B. Infusion   C. Gene   D. Syndrome

86. D A tumor of the thymus gland
    A. Androgen   B. Rubella   C. Mutagen   D. Thymoma

87. D A hospital or an area of a hospital dedicated to treating people who are dying, often of a specific cause
    A. Systemic   B. Silicone   C. Tibia   D. Hospice

88. A The smallest known disease- causing microorganism
    A. Virus   B. Rubella   C. Nodule   D. Somatic

89. __B__ A brown to dark-brown spot on the skin that can be flat or raised
A. Mucus B. Mole C. Infusion D. Fibroma

90. __B__ A bundle of fibers that transmit electrical messages between the brain and areas of the body
A. Stoma B. Nerve C. Enuresis D. Vagina

91. __A__ Inflammation of the lining of the lungs and chest cavity usually caused by a lung infection
A. Pleurisy B. Botulism C. Hospice D. Clone

92. __A__ One of two organs that are part of the urinary tract
A. Kidney B. Triage C. Rectum D. Appendix

93. __A__ Inflammation of the mucous membrane lining the nose
A. Rhinitis B. Erythema C. Uveitis D. Hospice

94. __D__ A growth that occurs on mucous membranes such as those in the nose and intestine
A. Optician B. Ringworm C. Hysteria D. Polyp

95. __B__ A bacterial infection of the small intestine that causes severe watery diarrhea, dehydration, and possibly death
A. Trisomy B. Cholera C. Insulin D. Clone

96. __D__ A tough protein found in skin, nails, and hair
A. Ticks B. Aneurysm C. Lymph D. Keratin

97. __A__ A cancer that occurs on the surface or lining of an organ
A. Carcinoma B. Iron C. Miotic D. Axilla

98. __B__ A serious infectious disease transmitted to humans through bites of rodent fleas
A. Infusion B. Plague C. Toxin D. Sepsis

99. __D__ A short tube located at the end of the large intestine, which connects the intestine to the anus
A. Vertebra B. Thymoma C. Myopathy D. Rectum

100. __B__ The sac containing the testicles
A. Sciatica B. Scrotum C. Hysteria D. Sodium

From the words provided for each clue, provide the letter of the word which best matches the clue.

101. __D__ A thin, oval-shaped membrane that separates the inner ear from the outer ear and is responsible for transmitting sound waves
A. Bile B. Thalamus C. Keratin D. Eardrum

102. __C__ A small lump of tissue that is usually abnormal
A. Otorrhea B. Medulla C. Nodule D. Scabies

103. __C__ The interval from onset of contractions to birth of a baby
A. Scabies B. Pancreas C. Labor D. Tonsils

104. __C__ A condition in which people are born with insufficient amounts of the pigment melanin, which is responsible for hair, skin, and eye color
A. Osteoma B. Keratin C. Albinism D. DNA

105. __C__ Twisting and obstruction of an area of intestine
A. Zygote B. Lipoma C. Volvulus D. Dementia

106. __D__ The period during which sexual development occurs
A. Reflex B. Thrombus C. Tetanus D. Puberty

107. __A__ A disease caused by a lack of vitamin c, characterized by weakness, bleeding and pain in joints and muscles, bleeding gums, and abnormal bone and tooth growth
A. Scurvy B. Orthotic C. Osmosis D. Silicone

108. __B__ Thick, sticky, greenish-brown stool passed by a postmature fetus, or one experiencing fetal distress, into the amniotic fluid, or by an infant during the first couple of days after birth
A. Vulvitis B. Meconium C. Villi D. Appendix

109. __B__ Describes a disease that is always present in a certain population of people
A. Scrotum B. Endemic C. Aura D. Aplasia

110. __D__ The medical term for the collarbone
A. Renin B. Pancreas C. Vesicle D. Clavicle

111. __C__ The socket in the skull that contains the eyeball, along with its blood vessels, nerves, and muscles
A. Sprue B. Tonsils C. Orbit D. Palate

112. __B__ The long, flat bone located at the center of the chest
A. Hookworm B. Sternum C. Urea D. Thorax

113. __C__ A group of compounds of silicon and oxygen
A. Rubeola B. Orthotic C. Silicone D. Version

114. __C__ The medical term for an earache
A. IQ B. Lipoma C. Otalgia D. Reflex

115. __B__ A lump filled with either fluid or soft material, occurring in any organ or tissue
A. Neurosis B. Cyst C. Dermis D. Seminoma

116. __B__ An additional dose of a vaccine taken after the first dose to maintain or renew the first one
A. Hookworm B. Booster C. Tremor D. Optic

117. __A__ The column of bones and cartilage running along the midline of the back that surrounds and protects the spinal cord and supports the head
A. Spine B. Polyp C. Hookworm D. Splint

118. __A__ The inner skin layer
A. Dermis B. Eardrum C. Vertebra D. Hepatoma

119. __A__ Intestine
A. Bowel B. Scabies C. Dialysis D. Pulse

120. __D__ A growth that occurs on mucous membranes such as those in the nose and intestine
A. Reflex B. Atheroma C. Kidney D. Polyp

121. __C__ A hormone that stimulates the release of gastric acid in the stomach
A. Bursitis B. Forceps C. Gastrin D. Osmosis

122. __C__ A childhood disease in which bones lack calcium and are deformed because of vitamin d deficiency
A. Receptor B. Impetigo C. Rickets D. Hookworm

123. __C__ A disorder marked by high levels of uric acid in the blood
A. Zygote B. Thalamus C. Gout D. Pleurisy

124. C A hormone produced by the thyroid gland that helps regulate energy production in the body
   A. Thrush   B. Medulla   C. Thyroxin   D. Hookworm

125. D Relatively mild emotional disorders (such as mild depression and phobias)
   A. Renin   B. Rubeola   C. Uterus   D. Neurosis

126. D The presence of viruses in the blood
   A. Oximetry   B. Thalamus   C. Impetigo   D. Viremia

127. D A brain tumor arising from cells that support nerve cells
   A. Sprue   B. Ptosis   C. Phlegm   D. Glioma

128. C Controlled analgesia- a system for administering pain- killing drugs in which the amount of drug delivered is controlled by the patient
   A. Traction   B. Dementia   C. Patient   D. Melanoma

129. C "in the living body"; a biological process that occurs inside of the body
   A. Pyrogen   B. Boil   C. In vivo   D. Platelet

130. D Inflammation of the lining of the lungs and chest cavity usually caused by a lung infection
   A. Labor   B. Viremia   C. Splint   D. Pleurisy

131. B A drug that relieves pain, such as aspirin or acetaminophen
   A. Osmosis   B. Analgesic   C. Radon   D. Lordosis

132. B The presence in the cells of three copies of a certain chromosome instead of the normal two copies
   A. Renin   B. Trisomy   C. Ozone   D. Melanin

133. C An egg cell that has not developed completely
   A. Stool   B. Numbness   C. Oocyte   D. Axilla

134. C Another term for a nerve cell
   A. Coitus   B. Shock   C. Neuron   D. Cataract

135. D A "warning" signal that comes before a migraine headache or an epileptic seizure, which might include emotions or sensations of movement or discomfort
   A. Tumor   B. Systemic   C. Lipoma   D. Aura

136. B A vitamin important in many chemical processes in the body; also known as vitamin b3
   A. Appendix   B. Niacin   C. Rickets   D. Platelet

137. D The introduction of a substance, such as a drug or nutrient, into the bloodstream or a body cavity
   A. Fistula   B. Ticks   C. Orthotic   D. Infusion

138. B A sudden attack or worsening of a disease's symptoms
   A. Hypoxia   B. Paroxysm   C. Shock   D. Whitlow

139. D A discharge from an inflamed ear
   A. In vivo   B. Dementia   C. Whitlow   D. Otorrhea

140. D A disorder in which a person becomes overly suspicious and emotionally sensitive
   A. Fluke   B. Mitosis   C. Carotene   D. Paranoia

141. C A salt solution or any substance that contains salt
   A. Rectum   B. Tetanus   C. Saline   D. Ptosis

142. __B__ A vibration felt when the hand is placed flat on the chest
A. Zygote   B. Thrill   C. Reflex   D. In vivo

143. __B__ Any substance that the body can use to maintain its health
A. Volvulus   B. Nutrient   C. Patient   D. Zygote

144. __C__ The muscular passage connecting the uterus with the outside genitals
A. Rubeola   B. Labia   C. Vagina   D. Menarche

145. __B__ The opening through which feces are passed from the body
A. Fibroma   B. Anus   C. Impetigo   D. Labia

146. __B__ The sac containing the testicles
A. Meconium   B. Scrotum   C. Melanoma   D. Thyroxin

147. __C__ A noncancerous bone tumor
A. Sprain   B. Chronic   C. Osteoma   D. Miotic

148. __A__ A connective tissue (softer than bone) that is part of the skeletal system, including the joints
A. Cartilage   B. Melanoma   C. Osteitis   D. Osteoma

149. __A__ An abscess on the end of a finger or a toe that is caused by the herpes simplex virus or a bacterial infection
A. Whitlow   B. Vulvitis   C. Mitosis   D. Keratin

150. __C__ A sometimes fatal disease affecting the brain and spinal cord
A. Wart   B. Fistula   C. Tetanus   D. Phimosis

151. __C__ A gradual decline in mental ability usually caused by a brain disease, such as Alzheimer's disease
A. Oocyte   B. Allergen   C. Dementia   D. Gastrin

152. __C__ A waste product of the metabolism of proteins that is formed by the liver and secreted by the kidneys
A. Atheroma   B. Paranoia   C. Urea   D. Vagina

153. __C__ Any disease caused by a fungus
A. Receptor   B. Radon   C. Mycosis   D. Ligation

154. __D__ The complete set of an organism's genes
A. Atheroma   B. Larynx   C. Organism   D. Genome

155. __A__ An abnormal mass that occurs when cells in a certain area reproduce unchecked
A. Tumor   B. Paranoia   C. Aspermia   D. Rectum

156. __D__ A marking on the skin; can be present at birth (birthmark) or develop later (such as a mole)
A. Otalgia   B. Labor   C. Myopia   D. Nevus

157. __D__ A chemical, originating in a cell, that regulates reactions in the body
A. Endemic   B. Polyp   C. Lobe   D. Enzyme

158. __C__ Inflammation of a testicle, which can be caused by infection with the mumps virus
A. Renin   B. Pinkeye   C. Orchitis   D. Otalgia

159. __A__ Inflammation of the membrane that covers the white of the eyes and lines the eyelids
A. Pinkeye   B. Thalamus   C. Reflex   D. Pepsin

160. D An inflamed, raised area of skin that is pus-filled; usually an infected hair follicle
A. Plasma   B. Toxicity   C. Lobe   D. Boil

161. A The millions of fingerlike projections on the lining of the small intestine that aid in the absorption of food
A. Villi   B. Neuron   C. Rubeola   D. Orthotic

162. D A tough, elastic band of tissue that connects bones and supports organs
A. Niacin   B. Acne   C. Myopia   D. Ligament

163. C The lack of sensation in a part of the body because of interruption of nerve impulses
A. Oocyte   B. Alopecia   C. Numbness   D. Vertebra

164. D Masses of lymphoid tissue located at either side of the back of the throat
A. Variola   B. Hookworm   C. Implant   D. Tonsils

165. B Baldness or loss of hair, mainly on the head, either in defined patches or completely
A. Thrill   B. Alopecia   C. Spine   D. Ectopic

166. D The extent to which a substance is poisonous
A. Hepatoma   B. Gastrin   C. Mycosis   D. Toxicity

167. D Infestation by a small, round, blood-sucking parasite
A. Immunity   B. Pinkeye   C. Tetanus   D. Hookworm

168. B An automatic, involuntary response of the nervous system to a stimulus
A. Paranoia   B. Reflex   C. Numbness   D. pH

169. A A poisonous form of oxygen that is present in the earth's upper atmosphere, where it helps to screen the earth from damaging ultraviolet rays
A. Ozone   B. Allergen   C. Receptor   D. Atheroma

170. B Mucus and other material produced by the lining of the respiratory tract
A. Cyst   B. Phlegm   C. Miotic   D. Vertebra

171. D An artificial feeding technique in which liquids are passed into the stomach by way of a tube inserted through the nose
A. Tonsils   B. Sternum   C. Sepsis   D. Gavage

172. C Fatty deposits on the inner walls of blood vessels, which can cause narrowing and decrease blood flow
A. Polyp   B. Vertebra   C. Atheroma   D. Plasma

173. A The inward curvature of the spine at the lower back, which is normal to a certain degree
A. Lordosis   B. Endemic   C. Larynx   D. Ectopic

174. D Pertaining to the eyes
A. Analgesic   B. Villi   C. Splint   D. Optic

175. B Occurring at an abnormal position or time
A. Thrill   B. Ectopic   C. Fluoride   D. Pancreas

176. D The examination of a body following death, possibly to determine the cause of death or for research
A. Iron   B. Gavage   C. Ectopic   D. Autopsy

177. A Affecting the whole body
A. Systemic   B. Rubella   C. Rectum   D. Otalgia

178. C A hormone made in the pancreas that plays an important role in the absorption of glucose (the body's main source of energy) into muscle cells
A. Pyrexia   B. Keloid   C. Insulin   D. Bunion

179. A Medical term for the armpit
A. Axilla   B. Labor   C. Pepsin   D. Numbness

180. A The enzyme found in gastric juice that helps digest protein
A. Pepsin   B. Hepatic   C. Node   D. Platelet

181. C A reduced level of oxygen in tissues
A. Rubella   B. Skull   C. Hypoxia   D. Maxilla

182. D A term used to describe something that is related to the liver
A. Keratin   B. Ocular   C. Glucose   D. Hepatic

183. D A shift in the position of the fetus inside of the uterus, either occurring naturally or as performed by a doctor to facilitate delivery
A. Hepatic   B. Endemic   C. Pinkeye   D. Version

184. D A device used to correct or control deformed bones, muscles, or joints
A. Forceps   B. Rectum   C. Implant   D. Orthotic

185. C One of two organs that are part of the urinary tract
A. Implant   B. Paranoia   C. Kidney   D. Volvulus

186. D The medical term for the voice box, the organ in the throat that produces voice and prevents food from entering the airway
A. Diuretic   B. Hepatoma   C. Systemic   D. Larynx

187. D Instruments resembling tweezers that are used to handle objects or tissue during surgery
A. Pellagra   B. Audiogram   C. Bowel   D. Forceps

188. C The process of passage of the solvent portion of a lesser-concentrated solution through a semipermeable membrane into a higher-concentrated solution until the two solutions are equal in concentration
A. Atrophy   B. Hepatoma   C. Osmosis   D. Viremia

189. D A thickened callus on the foot that is caused by an improperly fitting shoe
A. Maxilla   B. Osmosis   C. Iron   D. Corn

190. C A well-defined, separate part of an organ
A. Toxin   B. Kidney   C. Lobe   D. Bile

191. D Tightness of the foreskin, which prevents it from being moved back over the head of the penis
A. Nodule   B. Ptosis   C. Fluoride   D. Phimosis

192. D Describes a disorder that continues for a long period of time
A. Skull   B. Bile   C. Pathogen   D. Chronic

193. A The two pairs of skinfolds that protect the opening of the vagina
A. Labia   B. Necrosis   C. Nevus   D. Polyp

194. A A mineral that helps protect teeth against decay
A. Fluoride   B. Polyp   C. Variola   D. pH

195. __C__ A term describing something related to or caused by a virus
　　A. Otalgia　B. Ocular　C. Viral　D. Sternum

196. __B__ A negative reaction to a substance that in most people causes no reaction
　　A. Lipoma　B. Allergy　C. Radon　D. Volvulus

197. __A__ A highly contagious skin infection caused by bacteria, usually occurring around the nose and mouth
　　A. Impetigo　B. Menarche　C. Infusion　D. Toxin

198. __A__ The shrinkage or near disappearance of a tissue or organ
　　A. Atrophy　B. In vivo　C. Tumor　D. Pinkeye

199. __C__ A disorder in which the lens of the eye becomes less transparent and, in some cases, a milky white, making vision less clear
　　A. Analgesic　B. Enzyme　C. Cataract　D. Palsy

200. __D__ A cancerous tumor of the liver
　　A. Ligation　B. Clavicle　C. Glioma　D. Hepatoma

From the words provided for each clue, provide the letter of the word which best matches the clue.

201. __D__ An area of buildup of fat deposits in an artery, causing narrowing of the artery and possibly heart disease
　　A. Bulimia　B. Fistula　C. Acne　D. Plaque

202. __D__ The process of passage of the solvent portion of a lesser-concentrated solution through a semipermeable membrane into a higher-concentrated solution until the two solutions are equal in concentration
　　A. Ectopic　B. Whipworm　C. Nevus　D. Osmosis

203. __C__ Another term for a microorganism, especially one that causes disease
　　A. Macula　B. Atheroma　C. Microbe　D. Migraine

204. __C__ A group of cells or an organ that produces substances (such as hormones and enzyme) that are used by the body
　　A. Ileum　B. Stye　C. Gland　D. Iodine

205. __D__ A term describing something related to or caused by a virus
　　A. Maxilla　B. Toxin　C. Labia　D. Viral

206. __D__ A chemical produced by a gland or tissue that is released into the bloodstream
　　A. Trachoma　B. Plasma　C. Pancreas　D. Hormone

207. __C__ A form of phototherapy that combines the use of psoralens and ultraviolet light to treat skin disorders
　　A. Dopamine　B. Retinoid　C. PUVA　D. Sclera

208. __B__ The expansion and contraction of a blood vessel due to the blood pumped through it
　　A. Aorta　B. Pulse　C. Nutrient　D. Thrombus

209. __B__ A nerve infection caused by the chickenpox virus, causing areas of painful rash covered with blisters
　　A. Colon　B. Shingles　C. Orchitis　D. Pancreas

210. __A__ A measure of the acidic or basic character of a substance
　　A. pH　B. Patent　C. Coma　D. Insulin

211. __C__ Abnormally pale skin
A. pH   B. Trachoma   C. Pallor   D. Labia

212. __A__ Abnormal formation of connective or scar tissue
A. Fibrosis   B. Callus   C. Lesion   D. Retina

213. __A__ The interval from onset of contractions to birth of a baby
A. Labor   B. Cervix   C. Placenta   D. Pallor

214. __D__ A highly contagious and often fatal viral infection that has been completely eradicated by immunization
A. Nevus   B. Orchitis   C. Pruritus   D. Smallpox

215. __C__ The clear, watery fluid that separates from clotted blood
A. Thymoma   B. Virus   C. Serum   D. Rhinitis

216. __B__ Not obstructed; open
A. Bile   B. Patent   C. Familial   D. Macula

217. __D__ An illness caused by a viral infection, causing a characteristic rash and a fever
A. Sternum   B. Prion   C. Iodine   D. Measles

218. __B__ Loss of sensation or ability to move
A. Dopamine   B. Palsy   C. Meiosis   D. Myelitis

219. __B__ Mucus and other material produced by the lining of the respiratory tract
A. DNA   B. Sputum   C. Strain   D. Ascites

220. __B__ A device used to hold tissues in place, such as to support a skin graft
A. Placebo   B. Stent   C. DNA   D. Palsy

221. __A__ Controlled analgesia- a system for administering pain- killing drugs in which the amount of drug delivered is controlled by the patient
A. Patient   B. Ozone   C. Cholera   D. Syndrome

222. __D__ A sugar that is the main source of energy for the body
A. Plaque   B. Placebo   C. Polyp   D. Glucose

223. __C__ The presence in the cells of three copies of a certain chromosome instead of the normal two copies
A. Syndrome   B. Sepsis   C. Trisomy   D. Fungus

224. __C__ Enlargement of the thyroid gland, which produces a swelling on the neck
A. Microbe   B. Aorta   C. Goiter   D. Fracture

225. __B__ An agent that is believed to cause several degenerative brain diseases
A. Keloid   B. Prion   C. Polyuria   D. Rabies

226. __D__ A tunnel-like passage
A. Smear   B. Tonsils   C. Smallpox   D. Canal

227. __D__ Partial paralysis
A. Niacin   B. Osmosis   C. Bifocal   D. Paresis

228. __A__ The type of cell division that occurs only in the ovaries and testicles, producing cells with half the genes of the original cell
A. Meiosis   B. Minipill   C. Fungus   D. Measles

229. D A small, parasitic worm that can live in the intestines of a human and may cause diarrhea, abdominal pain, and anemia
A. Primary   B. Dermis   C. Mandible   D. Whipworm

230. C The passageways that air moves through while traveling in and out of the lungs during breathing
A. Plaque   B. Varices   C. Airways   D. Lumbago

231. D An addictive substance that blunts the senses
A. Macula   B. Seizure   C. Nausea   D. Narcotic

232. D A surgically formed opening on a body surface
A. IQ   B. Mandible   C. Aorta   D. Stoma

233. D A cancer that occurs on the surface or lining of an organ
A. Meniscus   B. Ozone   C. Nausea   D. Carcinoma

234. B A measure of a person's physical strength, flexibility, and endurance
A. Fibrosis   B. Fitness   C. DNA   D. Myositis

235. D A lens that corrects both near and distant vision by having two parts with different focusing strengths
A. Imaging   B. Kidney   C. Murmur   D. Bifocal

236. A Small, eight-legged animals that can attach to humans and animals and feed on blood
A. Ticks   B. Teratoma   C. Ulcer   D. Saline

237. A A sometimes fatal disease affecting the brain and spinal cord
A. Tetanus   B. Aspermia   C. Osmosis   D. Fistula

238. A An element for the formation of thyroid hormones
A. Iodine   B. Patient   C. Familial   D. Tetanus

239. A Two tubes that carry urine from the kidneys to the bladder
A. Ureters   B. Bifocal   C. Thymoma   D. Genome

240. C A cancer in connective tissue, fibrous tissue, or blood vessels
A. Primary   B. Apnea   C. Sarcoma   D. Nutrient

241. C A small, round organ making up the neck of the uterus and separating it from the vagina
A. Numbness   B. Hysteria   C. Cervix   D. Tonsils

242. C The lowest section of the small intestine, which attaches to the large intestine
A. Measles   B. Chlamydia   C. Ileum   D. Nutrient

243. B A blood vessel that carries blood toward the heart
A. Anatomy   B. Vein   C. pH   D. Syndrome

244. A A poisonous substance
A. Toxin   B. Aorta   C. Sepsis   D. Rabies

245. C The tough, white coating that covers and protects the inner structures of the eye
A. Platelet   B. Fluoride   C. Sclera   D. Cholera

246. B A substance resembling vitamin a that is used to treat skin conditions such as acne and has been reported to reduce skin wrinkling
A. Sprue   B. Retinoid   C. Genome   D. Bile

247. B The infection of a wound or tissue with bacteria, causing the spread of the bacteria into the bloodstream
A. Coitus B. Sepsis C. Penis D. Bacterium

248. C Masses of lymphoid tissue located at either side of the back of the throat
A. Meiosis B. Cholera C. Tonsils D. Imaging

249. D A tiny blood vessel that connects the smallest arteries to the smallest veins and allows exchange of oxygen and other materials between blood cells and body tissue cells
A. Shingles B. Familial C. Niacin D. Capillary

250. B Inflammation of a testicle, which can be caused by infection with the mumps virus
A. Cecum B. Orchitis C. Seizure D. PUVA

251. B A term describing a disorder or characteristic (such as male pattern baldness) that occurs within a family more often than would be expected
A. ECG B. Familial C. Androgen D. Teratoma

252. B A tear or break in an organ or tissue
A. Polyp B. Rupture C. Minipill D. Pyrogen

253. A A thickened area of skin due to consistent pressure or friction, or the area around a bone break where new bone is formed
A. Callus B. Neuritis C. Sinus D. Coitus

254. A A characteristic sound of blood flowing irregularly through the heart
A. Murmur B. Primary C. Vertigo D. Syndrome

255. C Any substance that causes a fever
A. Foreskin B. Silicone C. Pyrogen D. Rupture

256. D A group of compounds of silicon and oxygen
A. Narcotic B. Gene C. Nausea D. Silicone

257. D A term used to describe something situated on or near the midline of the body or a body structure
A. Colitis B. Myelitis C. Niacin D. Medial

258. A A marking on the skin; can be present at birth (birthmark) or develop later (such as a mole)
A. Nevus B. Syndrome C. Plasma D. Genome

259. D Muscle inflammation, causing pain and weakness
A. Sprue B. Phimosis C. Autopsy D. Myositis

260. D The roof of the mouth
A. Pyrogen B. Polyp C. Paresis D. Palate

261. D A shift in the position of the fetus inside of the uterus, either occurring naturally or as performed by a doctor to facilitate delivery
A. Fungus B. Foreskin C. Capillary D. Version

262. C One of two bones that form the upper jaw, the roof of the mouth, and the center portion of the face
A. DNA B. Villi C. Maxilla D. Genome

263. A A term used to describe a disease that is rare then suddenly affects more people than usually expected
A. Epidemic B. Hormone C. Myelitis D. Ureters

264. C An open sore that occurs on the skin or on a mucous membrane because of the destruction of surface tissue
    A. Version B. Murmur C. Ulcer D. Nausea

265. C A severe headache, usually accompanied by vision problems and
    A. Eardrum B. Ozone C. Migraine D. Pharynx

266. C A vitamin important in many chemical processes in the body; also known as vitamin b3
    A. Fluoride B. Airways C. Niacin D. Vertigo

267. C "in glass"; a biological test or process that is carried out in a laboratory
    A. Patent B. Bifocal C. In vitro D. Fibrosis

268. A The sticky, brown substance in cigarettes that coats the lungs; causes lung and other cancers
    A. Tar B. Glycogen C. Insulin D. Callus

269. D Pertaining to the eyes
    A. Palate B. Parasite C. Migraine D. Optic

270. C A persistent, contagious form of conjunctivitis that can lead to complications such as blindness if untreated
    A. Pancreas B. Bacterium C. Trachoma D. Murmur

271. D Muscle damage resulting from excessive stretching or forceful contraction
    A. Palsy B. Vein C. Villi D. Strain

272. D The lack of sensation in a part of the body because of interruption of nerve impulses
    A. Myelitis B. Pharynx C. Shingles D. Numbness

273. A An electrocardiogram, which is a record of the electrical impulses that trigger the heartbeat; used to diagnose heart disorders
    A. ECG B. Myopathy C. Osmosis D. Maxilla

274. C A tumor of the thymus gland
    A. Coma B. Strain C. Thymoma D. Bulimia

275. B Feeling the need to vomit
    A. Patient B. Nausea C. Genome D. Palsy

276. D Narrowing of a body passageway
    A. Callus B. Epidemic C. Ureters D. Stenosis

277. C A tiny pouchlike cavity in a structure of the body, such as a hair follicle
    A. Nausea B. Pyrogen C. Follicle D. Polyp

278. C A blood clot in a blood vessel
    A. Maxilla B. Sputum C. Thrombus D. Virus

279. C A group of symptoms that indicate a certain disorder when they occur together
    A. Fibrosis B. Niacin C. Syndrome D. Patent

280. C A disorder in which a person becomes overly suspicious and emotionally sensitive
    A. Fitness B. Pancreas C. Paranoia D. Impetigo

281. D An organ formed in the uterus during pregnancy that links the blood of the mother to the blood of the fetus
    A. Ulcer B. Meiosis C. Imaging D. Placenta

282. __D__ Dependence on a substance (such as alcohol or other drugs) or an activity, to the point that stopping is very difficult and causes severe physical and mental reactions
A. Stent   B. Genome   C. Virus   D. Addiction

283. __A__ An oral contraceptive containing only the synthetic hormone progesterone (birth control pills contain estrogen and progesterone)
A. Minipill   B. Polyp   C. Xanthine   D. Keratin

284. __B__ A hormone (such as testosterone) that causes development of male characteristics and sex organs
A. Smallpox   B. Androgen   C. Follicle   D. Orbit

285. __B__ The millions of fingerlike projections on the lining of the small intestine that aid in the absorption of food
A. Imaging   B. Villi   C. Airways   D. Strain

286. __C__ A raised, firm, thick scar that forms because of a defect in the natural healing process
A. Febrile   B. Numbness   C. Keloid   D. Acne

287. __C__ The hollow female reproductive organ in which a fertilized egg is implanted, and a fetus develops
A. Aorta   B. Insulin   C. Uterus   D. Plaque

288. __C__ The muscular passage connecting the uterus with the outside genitals
A. Coronary   B. Fistula   C. Vagina   D. Fibroid

289. __C__ Inflammation of the mucous membrane lining the nose
A. Airways   B. Hematoma   C. Rhinitis   D. Trachoma

290. __A__ A colorless, odorless, tasteless radioactive gas that is produced by materials in soil, rocks, and building materials; suspected of causing cancer
A. Radon   B. Pustule   C. Meiosis   D. Myelitis

291. __A__ A term used to describe symptoms that are caused by mental stress and occur in someone who does not have a mental disorder
A. Hysteria   B. DNA   C. Patent   D. Saline

292. __C__ A digestive disorder in which nutrients cannot be properly absorbed from food, causing weakness and loss of weight
A. Stoma   B. Optic   C. Sprue   D. Coma

293. __C__ A hormone made in the pancreas that plays an important role in the absorption of glucose (the body's main source of energy) into muscle cells
A. Sputum   B. Stye   C. Insulin   D. Tar

294. __D__ Sudden uncontrolled waves of electrical activity in the brain, causing involuntary movement or loss of consciousness
A. Labia   B. Erythema   C. Nevus   D. Seizure

295. __B__ The socket in the skull that contains the eyeball, along with its blood vessels, nerves, and muscles
A. Numbness   B. Orbit   C. Imaging   D. Tar

296. __B__ An accumulation of blood from a broken blood vessel
A. Autopsy   B. Hematoma   C. Palsy   D. Glioma

297. __A__ A bacterial infection of the small intestine that causes severe watery diarrhea, dehydration, and possibly death
A. Cholera   B. Seizure   C. Pharynx   D. Macula

298. __B__ A growth that occurs on mucous membranes such as those in the nose and intestine
A. Gene   B. Polyp   C. Goiter   D. Genome

299. C Another term for a tumor
A. Meniscus   B. Maxilla   C. Neoplasm   D. Mucocele

300. D Intelligence quotient; a measure of a person's intelligence as determined by specific tests
A. Vertigo   B. Somatic   C. Kidney   D. IQ

From the words provided for each clue, provide the letter of the word which best matches the clue.

301. D Pertaining to blood vessels
A. Dermis   B. Polyuria   C. Osteoma   D. Vascular

302. A Another term for a microorganism, especially one that causes disease
A. Microbe   B. Carcinoma   C. Sperm   D. Pharynx

303. D A hormone that stimulates the release of gastric acid in the stomach
A. Bursa   B. Orgasm   C. Hygiene   D. Gastrin

304. D A disease that began in the affected location
A. Mucus   B. Version   C. Vein   D. Primary

305. C An abnormal mass that occurs when cells in a certain area reproduce unchecked
A. Pruritus   B. Ischemia   C. Tumor   D. Overdose

306. B A bacterial infection of the small intestine that causes severe watery diarrhea, dehydration, and possibly death
A. Sciatica   B. Cholera   C. Foreskin   D. Scurvy

307. C A chemically inactive substance given in place of a drug to test how much of a drug's effectiveness can be attributed to a patient's expectations that the drug will have a positive effect
A. Cilia   B. Villi   C. Placebo   D. Clone

308. D An excessively large dose of a drug, which can lead to coma and death
A. Carcinoma   B. Rhinitis   C. Airways   D. Overdose

309. D The colored part of the eye
A. Pudendum   B. Spleen   C. Fitness   D. Iris

310. B The foreskin
A. Microbe   B. Prepuce   C. Inhaler   D. Orthotic

311. B A thin, oval-shaped membrane that separates the inner ear from the outer ear and is responsible for transmitting sound waves
A. Varices   B. Eardrum   C. Ulcer   D. Organism

312. B An open sore that occurs on the skin or on a mucous membrane because of the destruction of surface tissue
A. Osteitis   B. Ulcer   C. Atrophy   D. Tartar

313. A The two upper chambers of the heart
A. Atria   B. Neurosis   C. Mucus   D. Audiogram

314. D A slippery fluid produced by mucous membranes that lubricates and protects the internal surfaces of the body
A. Rhinitis   B. Colic   C. Version   D. Mucus

315. C A hormone made in the pancreas that plays an important role in the absorption of glucose (the body's main source of energy) into muscle cells
A. Ozone B. Syndrome C. Insulin D. Nephrons

316. B A condition in which a tissue or organ does not receive enough supply of blood
A. Ticks B. Ischemia C. Asthma D. Menarche

317. A A person who specializes in the making and adjustment of eyeglasses and contact lenses
A. Optician B. Cell C. Cataract D. Spleen

318. B A poisonous form of oxygen that is present in the earth's upper atmosphere, where it helps to screen the earth from damaging ultraviolet rays
A. Niacin B. Ozone C. Angioma D. Cholera

319. C A thickened area of skin due to consistent pressure or friction, or the area around a bone break where new bone is formed
A. Coccyx B. Maxilla C. Callus D. Colic

320. B The displacement of an organ from its normal position to a new one
A. Ulcer B. Prolapse C. In vitro D. Plague

321. D A tumor composed of cells not normally found in the part of the body when the tumor occurred
A. Neuron B. Fitness C. Valve D. Teratoma

322. A The column of bones and cartilage running along the midline of the back that surrounds and protects the spinal cord and supports the head
A. Spine B. Placebo C. Varices D. Cilia

323. C Instruments resembling tweezers that are used to handle objects or tissue during surgery
A. Bilateral B. Atheroma C. Forceps D. Audiogram

324. D An abnormal passageway from one organ to another or from an organ to the body surface
A. Retina B. Pulse C. Calcium D. Fistula

325. A Inflammation of the uvea
A. Uveitis B. Palsy C. Paresis D. Aorta

326. D The excessive production of urine
A. Numbness B. Syndrome C. Atrophy D. Polyuria

327. B The medical term for nearsightedness
A. Booster B. Myopia C. Microbe D. Orbit

328. D The medical term for itching
A. Fluke B. Calcium C. Coccyx D. Pruritus

329. B An organ located in the upper left abdomen behind the ribs that removes and destroys old red blood cells and helps fight infection
A. Organism B. Spleen C. Vascular D. Cell

330. A The inner skin layer
A. Dermis B. Vitamins C. Orthotic D. Colitis

331. C Another term for a nerve cell
A. Semen B. Hypoxia C. Neuron D. Vascular

332. D A device used to correct or control deformed bones, muscles, or joints
    A. Neuron   B. Foreskin   C. Uterus   D. Orthotic

333. C A cancer that occurs on the surface or lining of an organ
    A. Dermis   B. Bilateral   C. Carcinoma   D. Forceps

334. A Damage to part of the brain because of a lack of blood supply or the rupturing of a blood vessel
    A. Stroke   B. Iodine   C. Atrophy   D. Microbe

335. B The male sex cell produced in the testicles
    A. Pinworm   B. Sperm   C. Villi   D. Hematoma

336. D A cavity within bone or a channel that contains blood
    A. Embryo   B. Plaque   C. Cast   D. Sinus

337. B A serious infectious disease transmitted to humans through bites of rodent fleas
    A. Paroxysm   B. Plague   C. Bacillus   D. Suture

338. B A brain tumor arising from cells that support nerve cells
    A. Viremia   B. Glioma   C. Familial   D. Prion

339. B A negative reaction to a substance that in most people causes no reaction
    A. Sprain   B. Allergy   C. Fistula   D. Nodule

340. D An abnormal growth of bone out of another bone, often located on the heel and usually painful
    A. Vesicle   B. Coma   C. Rosacea   D. Bone spur

341. D The expansion and contraction of a blood vessel due to the blood pumped through it
    A. Villi   B. Bladder   C. Uveitis   D. Pulse

342. D A hormone produced by the thyroid gland that helps regulate energy production in the body
    A. Cyanosis   B. Paroxysm   C. Vein   D. Thyroxin

343. D The extent to which a substance is poisonous
    A. Paresis   B. Hepatoma   C. Orbit   D. Toxicity

344. C A vitamin important in many chemical processes in the body; also known as vitamin b3
    A. Ozone   B. Ischemia   C. Niacin   D. Viremia

345. B The main form that glucose, the body's energy source, takes when it is stored
    A. Spine   B. Glycogen   C. Pelvis   D. Primary

346. C Small spots that float across the field of vision, caused by debris floating in the gel-like substance that fills the eye
    A. Androgen   B. Thorax   C. Floaters   D. Booster

347. D A disorder in which the lens of the eye becomes less transparent and, in some cases, a milky white, making vision less clear
    A. Familial   B. Gastrin   C. Minipill   D. Cataract

348. B An automatic, involuntary response of the nervous system to a stimulus
    A. Erythema   B. Reflex   C. Bladder   D. Allergen

349. B Partial paralysis
    A. Necrosis   B. Paresis   C. Booster   D. Vascular

350. __B__ Inflammation of the heart
A. Fistula   B. Carditis   C. Tapeworm   D. Cyst

351. __D__ A substance that causes vomiting
A. Sciatica   B. Croup   C. pH   D. Emetic

352. __A__ The orange-yellow pigment in bile, causing jaundice if it builds up in the blood and skin
A. Bilirubin   B. Sperm   C. Pharynx   D. Atrophy

353. __C__ A short, tube-like structure that branches off the large intestine
A. Tumor   B. Calcium   C. Appendix   D. Abscess

354. __C__ A poisonous substance produced by certain animals
A. Eczema   B. Ischemia   C. Venom   D. Speculum

355. __C__ A group of symptoms that indicate a certain disorder when they occur together
A. Croup   B. Rectum   C. Syndrome   D. Uterus

356. __A__ The sugar found in dairy products
A. Lactose   B. Dopamine   C. Overdose   D. Hypoxia

357. __A__ Redness of the skin
A. Erythema   B. Abscess   C. Vascular   D. Selenium

358. __B__ A deficiency of the vitamin niacin; causes dermatitis, diarrhea, and mental disorders
A. Osteitis   B. Pellagra   C. Plaque   D. Androgen

359. __A__ The presence of bacterial toxins in the blood
A. Toxemia   B. Viremia   C. Graft   D. Orthotic

360. __C__ The passageways that air moves through while traveling in and out of the lungs during breathing
A. Vesicle   B. Sperm   C. Airways   D. Pharynx

361. __B__ Abnormal crackling or bubbling sounds heard in the lungs during breathing
A. Glioma   B. Rales   C. Coma   D. Selenium

362. __C__ An orange pigment present in colored plants such as carrots that is converted by the body to the essential nutrient vitamin a
A. Rosacea   B. Niacin   C. Carotene   D. Plaque

363. __C__ A lump filled with either fluid or soft material, occurring in any organ or tissue
A. Shock   B. Bacterium   C. Cyst   D. Antacid

364. __A__ A fluid-filled sac that cushions and reduces friction in certain parts of the body
A. Bursa   B. Atria   C. Allergen   D. Placenta

365. __A__ The practice, maintenance, and study of health
A. Hygiene   B. Carotene   C. Graft   D. Ischemia

366. __B__ Any bacteria that is rod-shaped
A. Lockjaw   B. Bacillus   C. Chlamydia   D. Hematoma

367. __A__ A possibly life-threatening condition in which breathing stops, for either a short or long period of time
A. Apnea   B. Hypoxia   C. Sprain   D. Hematoma

368. D Healthy tissue that is used to replace diseased or defective tissue
A. Glycogen   B. Smear   C. Vitamins   D. Graft

369. A Any one of the 33 bones that make up the spine
A. Vertebra   B. Ptosis   C. Uterus   D. Palsy

370. D An element needed by the body only in very small amounts that helps maintain tissue elasticity
A. Coma   B. Erythema   C. Trauma   D. Selenium

371. B An involuntary, repetitive movement such as a twitch
A. Coccyx   B. Tic   C. In situ   D. Neuroma

372. C A painless sore that has a thick, rubbery base and a defined edge
A. Nephrons   B. Typhus   C. Chancre   D. Carotene

373. A A spasm of the jaw muscles that prevents the mouth from opening, such as that caused by tetanus
A. Lockjaw   B. Erythema   C. Nephrons   D. Optic

374. A "in glass"; a biological test or process that is carried out in a laboratory
A. In vitro   B. Orgasm   C. Pus   D. Allergy

375. C An additional dose of a vaccine taken after the first dose to maintain or renew the first one
A. Calcium   B. Maxilla   C. Booster   D. Optician

376. A An element for the formation of thyroid hormones
A. Iodine   B. Floaters   C. Dopamine   D. Sperm

377. D A condition in which people are born with insufficient amounts of the pigment melanin, which is responsible for hair, skin, and eye color
A. Toxicity   B. Ectopic   C. Fluke   D. Albinism

378. D Microorganisms that cause several human infections and can be transmitted sexually
A. Mucus   B. Embryo   C. Appendix   D. Chlamydia

379. D The introduction of a substance, such as a drug or nutrient, into the bloodstream or a body cavity
A. Lactose   B. Excision   C. Hypoxia   D. Infusion

380. A An organ located in the pelvis whose function is to collect and store urine until it is expelled
A. Bladder   B. Smear   C. Iodine   D. Appendix

381. A The loose skin that covers the head of the penis
A. Foreskin   B. Infusion   C. Vein   D. Cell

382. A Fatty deposits on the inner walls of blood vessels, which can cause narrowing and decrease blood flow
A. Atheroma   B. Carcinoma   C. Molecule   D. Vesicle

383. D Inflammation of the mucous membrane lining the nose
A. Vascular   B. Orbit   C. Steroids   D. Rhinitis

384. A An area of buildup of fat deposits in an artery, causing narrowing of the artery and possibly heart disease
A. Plaque   B. Syndrome   C. Estrogen   D. Orbit

385. B A group of diseases caused by the microorganism rickettsia, spread by the bites of fleas, mites, or ticks
A. Numbness   B. Typhus   C. Pus   D. Calcium

386. __B__ A noncancerous bone tumor
   A. Orthotic   B. Osteoma   C. Albinism   D. Numbness

387. __A__ The return of a disease or symptom after it had disappeared
   A. Relapse   B. Palsy   C. Glioma   D. Graft

388. __D__ A graph showing a person's hearing ability, determined from a set of tests examining hearing acuity of different sound frequencies
   A. Fitness   B. Apnea   C. Prion   D. Audiogram

389. __A__ Pertaining to the eyes
   A. Optic   B. Teratoma   C. Overdose   D. Plaque

390. __B__ A thick, yellowish or greenish fluid that contains dead white blood cells, tissues, and bacteria; occurs at the site of a bacterial infection
   A. Numbness   B. Pus   C. Molecule   D. Optic

391. __A__ Loss of sensation or ability to move
   A. Palsy   B. Node   C. Valve   D. Tartar

392. __D__ Abnormal formation of connective or scar tissue
   A. Bacillus   B. Osteitis   C. Hematoma   D. Fibrosis

393. __D__ A disorder characterized by inflamed airways and difficulty breathing
   A. Plaque   B. Ozone   C. Glioma   D. Asthma

394. __B__ Difficulty breathing
   A. Macula   B. Dyspnea   C. Valve   D. Glioma

395. __D__ A shift in the position of the fetus inside of the uterus, either occurring naturally or as performed by a doctor to facilitate delivery
   A. Plaque   B. Orgasm   C. Spine   D. Version

396. __D__ A parasitic flatworm that can infest humans
   A. Audiogram   B. Insulin   C. Rosacea   D. Fluke

397. __C__ A sudden attack or worsening of a disease's symptoms
   A. Appendix   B. Syndrome   C. Paroxysm   D. Inhaler

398. __D__ The smallest unit of a substance that possesses its characteristics
   A. Inhaler   B. Gene   C. In vitro   D. Molecule

399. __D__ The tiny filtering units of the kidney
   A. pH   B. Hematoma   C. Neuroma   D. Nephrons

400. __B__ A group of drugs which resemble hormones produced by the adrenal glands, and anabolic steroids, which are like the hormones produced by the male sex organs
   A. Paroxysm   B. Steroids   C. Selenium   D. Appendix

From the words provided for each clue, provide the letter of the word which best matches the clue.

401. __B__ The first part of the small intestine, immediately following the stomach
   A. Lateral   B. Duodenum   C. Nutrient   D. Axilla

402. D Inflammation of a testicle, which can be caused by infection with the mumps virus
   A. Cerebrum   B. Toxin   C. Insomnia   D. Orchitis

403. A The medical term for the kneecap
   A. Patella   B. Rubeola   C. Cochlea   D. Nutrient

404. D A noncancerous bone tumor
   A. Pleura   B. Mutation   C. Rubella   D. Osteoma

405. C A drug that neutralizes stomach acids
   A. Immunity   B. Tic   C. Antacid   D. Duodenum

406. C An artificially constructed or an abnormal passage connecting two usually separate structures in the body
   A. Retina   B. Triage   C. Shunt   D. Sclera

407. B Describes a treatment or procedure that is not urgent and can be arranged at the patient's convenience
   A. Enuresis   B. Elective   C. Aplasia   D. Osteoma

408. A Two almond-shaped glands located at the opening of the fallopian tubes on both sides of the uterus
   A. Ovaries   B. Scrotum   C. Mumps   D. Pandemic

409. D An excessively large dose of a drug, which can lead to coma and death
   A. Embryo   B. Numbness   C. Antacid   D. Overdose

410. A The medical term for lockjaw
   A. Trismus   B. Callus   C. Pallor   D. Retina

411. B Medical term for the armpit
   A. Nucleus   B. Axilla   C. Toxin   D. Tonsils

412. B The process by which most cells divide to reproduce
   A. Meiosis   B. Mitosis   C. Thymoma   D. Hematoma

413. D A group of fats stored in the body and used for energy
   A. Toxicity   B. Pelvis   C. Pancreas   D. Lipids

414. D A connective tissue (softer than bone) that is part of the skeletal system, including the joints
   A. Miotic   B. Orchitis   C. Colon   D. Cartilage

415. B A characteristic sound of blood flowing irregularly through the heart
   A. Hysteria   B. Murmur   C. Duodenum   D. Rabies

416. D The clear, watery fluid that separates from clotted blood
   A. Fitness   B. Osteoma   C. Nephrons   D. Serum

417. B Infestation by a small, round, blood-sucking parasite
   A. Vein   B. Hookworm   C. Typhus   D. Enzyme

418. C The oily, lubricating substance that is secreted by glands in the skin
   A. Enuresis   B. Pandemic   C. Sebum   D. Bulimia

419. A The smallest particle found in the blood, which plays a major role in forming blood clots
   A. Platelet   B. Trismus   C. Bilateral   D. Nitrates

420. __B__ A group of drugs which resemble hormones produced by the adrenal glands, and anabolic steroids, which are like the hormones produced by the male sex organs
A. Patent   B. Steroids   C. Thrombus   D. Pandemic

421. __D__ A term used to describe a child in the womb from fertilization to 8 weeks following fertilization
A. Cerebrum   B. Impetigo   C. Vertebra   D. Embryo

422. __B__ A coiled organ in the inner ear that plays a large role in hearing by picking up sound vibrations and transmitting them as electrical signals
A. Fitness   B. Cochlea   C. Implant   D. Nephrons

423. __B__ Small eight-legged animals, many of which burrow and feed on blood
A. Numbness   B. Mites   C. Uveitis   D. Graft

424. __C__ A sudden attack or worsening of a disease's symptoms
A. Toxin   B. Bilateral   C. Paroxysm   D. Penis

425. __D__ An infectious viral disease primarily affecting animals
A. Renin   B. Thymoma   C. Arteritis   D. Rabies

426. __D__ The extent to which a substance is poisonous
A. Stent   B. Bacillus   C. In situ   D. Toxicity

427. __C__ The double-layered membrane that lines the lungs and chest cavity and allows for lung movement during breathing
A. Neuroma   B. Canal   C. Pleura   D. Embryo

428. __C__ A discharge from an inflamed ear
A. Bulimia   B. Molecule   C. Otorrhea   D. Penis

429. __C__ The common term for urticaria, an itchy, inflamed rash that results from an allergic reaction
A. Gangrene   B. Fibroid   C. Hives   D. Hematoma

430. __B__ A painful, persistent erection without sexual arousal, requiring emergency treatment
A. Aplasia   B. Priapism   C. Excision   D. Carcinoma

431. __C__ Another term for a microorganism, especially one that causes disease
A. Chancre   B. Progeria   C. Microbe   D. Volvulus

432. __C__ An organ formed in the uterus during pregnancy that links the blood of the mother to the blood of the fetus
A. Rabies   B. Thalamus   C. Placenta   D. Pudendum

433. __A__ The term used to refer to an unborn child from 8 weeks after fertilization to birth
A. Fetus   B. Oocyte   C. Birthmark   D. Serum

434. __A__ A tear or break in an organ or tissue
A. Rupture   B. Tapeworm   C. Ilium   D. Cochlea

435. __B__ The tough, white coating that covers and protects the inner structures of the eye
A. Vitiligo   B. Sclera   C. Walleye   D. Bilateral

436. __C__ Another term for measles
A. Receptor   B. Pelvis   C. Rubeola   D. Calorie

437. __C__ The tiny structures that make up all the tissues of the body and carry out all its functions
A. Thrombus   B. Vertebra   C. Cell   D. Bilateral

438. C The beginning of menstruation
A. Pulse   B. Colon   C. Menarche   D. Molecule

439. A A crescent-shaped pad of cartilage in joints that helps to reduce friction
A. Meniscus   B. Rubeola   C. Trachoma   D. Virus

440. C A high- pitched sound produced during breathing because of narrowing of the airways
A. Erythema   B. Tonsils   C. Wheeze   D. Nucleus

441. C Describes a condition or illness that begins suddenly and is usually short- lasting
A. Cholera   B. Vulva   C. Acute   D. Shunt

442. A A parasite- caused or infectious disease in animals that can be transferred to humans
A. Zoonosis   B. Rabies   C. Mineral   D. Osteoma

443. A A short tube located at the end of the large intestine, which connects the intestine to the anus
A. Rectum   B. Dextrose   C. Epilepsy   D. Mucus

444. A The sac containing the testicles
A. Scrotum   B. Ilium   C. Mites   D. Fibroid

445. C The outer, visible portion of the female genitals
A. Cochlea   B. Glucose   C. Vulva   D. Bulimia

446. A The three membranes that surround and protect the spinal cord and brain
A. Meninges   B. DNA   C. Mutation   D. Tremor

447. A An organ, tissue, or device surgically inserted and left in the body
A. Implant   B. Scrotum   C. Bladder   D. Toxin

448. C Baldness or loss of hair, mainly on the head, either in defined patches or completely
A. Microbe   B. In vitro   C. Alopecia   D. Serum

449. D A measure of a person's physical strength, flexibility, and endurance
A. Platelet   B. Pelvis   C. Mucus   D. Fitness

450. C Healthy tissue that is used to replace diseased or defective tissue
A. Volvulus   B. Whipworm   C. Graft   D. Aspermia

451. B A disease of the joints characterized by inflammation, pain, stiffness, and redness
A. Bifocal   B. Arthritis   C. Orchitis   D. Molecule

452. B The presence of bacterial toxins in the blood
A. Walleye   B. Toxemia   C. Traction   D. Overdose

453. B Redness of the skin
A. Cartilage   B. Erythema   C. Placenta   D. Rupture

454. B A bacterial infection of the small intestine that causes severe watery diarrhea, dehydration, and possibly death
A. Paroxysm   B. Cholera   C. Wart   D. Duodenum

455. A An organ located in the pelvis whose function is to collect and store urine until it is expelled
A. Bladder   B. Sclera   C. Lipids   D. Spasm

456. A — A disorder in which a person eats large amounts of food then forces vomiting or uses laxatives to prevent weight gain (called binging and purging)
A. Bulimia   B. Carcinoma   C. Rabies   D. Dextrose

457. D — Difficulty breathing
A. Nucleus   B. DNA   C. Progeria   D. Dyspnea

458. C — A widespread epidemic
A. Seminoma   B. Plasma   C. Pandemic   D. Thalamus

459. D — A small parasite worm that can live in the intestines
A. Cochlea   B. Menarche   C. Fitness   D. Pinworm

460. D — A system used to classify sick or injured people according to the severity of their conditions
A. Necrosis   B. Vein   C. Volvulus   D. Triage

461. B — Resistance to a specific disease because of the responses of the immune system
A. Paroxysm   B. Immunity   C. Birthmark   D. Cholera

462. B — Death of a tissue because of a lack of blood supply
A. Embryo   B. Gangrene   C. Rectum   D. Nodule

463. A — An involuntary, rhythmic, shaking movement caused by alternating contraction and relaxation of muscles
A. Tremor   B. Traction   C. Menarche   D. Nephrons

464. C — Relatively mild emotional disorders (such as mild depression and phobias)
A. Menarche   B. Wheeze   C. Neurosis   D. Appendix

465. A — The liquid part of the blood, containing substances such as nutrients, salts, and proteins
A. Plasma   B. Embryo   C. In situ   D. Lipids

466. C — A long gland located behind the stomach that produces enzymes that help to break down food and hormones (insulin and glucagon) that help to regulate glucose levels in the blood
A. Invasive   B. Myositis   C. Pancreas   D. DNA

467. C — A disorder in which a person becomes overly suspicious and emotionally sensitive
A. Fracture   B. Nephrons   C. Paranoia   D. Glucose

468. A — The type of cell division that occurs only in the ovaries and testicles, producing cells with half the genes of the original cell
A. Meiosis   B. Arteritis   C. Zoonosis   D. Ovum

469. A — A viral infection that causes inflammation of salivary glands
A. Mumps   B. Strain   C. Tonsils   D. Bone spur

470. A — A cancer that occurs on the surface or lining of an organ
A. Carcinoma   B. Birthmark   C. Measles   D. Erythema

471. D — A lens that corrects both near and distant vision by having two parts with different focusing strengths
A. Osteoma   B. Impetigo   C. Phlegm   D. Bifocal

472. B — The external male reproductive organ, which passes urine and semen out of the body
A. Epidemic   B. Penis   C. Thalamus   D. Whipworm

473. A — The lack of sensation in a part of the body because of interruption of nerve impulses
A. Numbness   B. Dialysis   C. Rash   D. Osteoma

474. B The roof of the mouth
A. Toxemia B. Palate C. Autopsy D. Mites

475. A One of two bones that form the upper jaw, the roof of the mouth, and the center portion of the face
A. Maxilla B. Neuroma C. Zoonosis D. Patent

476. B Inflammation of bone
A. Nodule B. Osteitis C. Toxemia D. Placebo

477. B "in glass"; a biological test or process that is carried out in a laboratory
A. Cyst B. In vitro C. Triage D. Parasite

478. B The two upper chambers of the heart
A. Toxicity B. Atria C. Erythema D. Aspermia

479. A The period during which sexual development occurs
A. Puberty B. Plasma C. Lateral D. Strain

480. C Abnormally pale skin
A. Pulse B. Neuroma C. Pallor D. Rubella

481. D A procedure to treat kidney failure in which artificial means are used to filter waste, maintain acid-base balance, and remove excess fluid from the body
A. Toxemia B. Wart C. Retina D. Dialysis

482. C A blood clot in a blood vessel
A. Trismus B. Prepuce C. Thrombus D. Follicle

483. D A noncancerous tumor occurring in nerve tissue
A. Enuresis B. Invasive C. Patella D. Neuroma

484. B Not obstructed; open
A. Scrotum B. Patent C. Walleye D. Arteritis

485. A An enzyme that plays a role in increasing a low blood pressure
A. Renin B. Insomnia C. Menarche D. Trachoma

486. C Dull, aching pain in the lower back
A. Overdose B. Embryo C. Lumbago D. Palate

487. B "in place"; often describes a cancer that has not spread
A. Neuroma B. In situ C. Appendix D. Measles

488. B The medical term for wetting the bed
A. Palate B. Enuresis C. Pyrexia D. Thalamus

489. A Describes something that spreads throughout body tissues, such as a tumor or microorganism
A. Invasive B. Cecum C. Sebum D. Bifocal

490. B A drug that causes the pupil to constrict
A. Patent B. Miotic C. Ilium D. Osteoma

491. A A substance that is a necessary part of a healthy diet (such as potassium, calcium, sodium, phosphorus, and magnesium)
A. Mineral B. Otorrhea C. Axilla D. Excision

492. __B__ A short, tube-like structure that branches off the large intestine
A. Phlegm B. Appendix C. Steroids D. Fissure

493. __C__ A shift in the position of the fetus inside of the uterus, either occurring naturally or as performed by a doctor to facilitate delivery
A. Cochlea B. Ovaries C. Version D. Triage

494. __D__ A contagious, harmless growth caused by a virus that occurs on the skin or a mucous membrane
A. Dextrose B. Pandemic C. Neurosis D. Wart

495. __A__ Any one of the 33 bones that make up the spine
A. Vertebra B. Antacid C. Triage D. Paroxysm

496. __C__ A group of diseases caused by the microorganism rickettsia, spread by the bites of fleas, mites, or ticks
A. Thrush B. Stent C. Typhus D. Palate

497. __D__ The group of bones in the lower part of the trunk that support the upper body and protect the abdominal organs
A. Bladder B. Plasma C. Vertebra D. Pelvis

498. __D__ The external genitals, usually referring to the female
A. Shunt B. Wart C. Lactose D. Pudendum

499. __B__ A condition in which patches of skin on the body lose their color
A. Virus B. Vitiligo C. Meninges D. Tapeworm

500. __B__ An additional dose of a vaccine taken after the first dose to maintain or renew the first one
A. Cerebrum B. Booster C. Toxin D. Nephrons

Matching

A. Provide the word that best matches each clue.

1. _____ An illness caused by a viral infection, causing a characteristic rash and a fever

2. _____ A coiled organ in the inner ear that plays a large role in hearing by picking up sound vibrations and transmitting them as electrical signals

3. _____ A surgical stitch that helps close an incision or wound so that it can heal properly

4. _____ The soft tissue inside of a tooth that contains blood vessels and nerves

5. _____ A short, tube-like structure that branches off the large intestine

6. _____ A waste product of the metabolism of proteins that is formed by the liver and secreted by the kidneys

7. _____ Involuntary sudden contraction of the diaphragm along with the closing of the vocal cords, producing a "hiccup" sound

8. _____ A structure in the brain that relays and processes incoming sensory information from the eyes and ears and from pressure and pain receptors

9. _____ A tumor composed of cells not normally found in the part of the body when the tumor occurred

10. _____ The medical term for the collarbone

11. _____ The roof of the mouth

12. _____ The outer, visible portion of the female genitals

13. _____ The medical term for the voice box, the organ in the throat that produces voice and prevents food from entering the airway

14. _____ The center part of an organ or body structure

15. _____ The sticky, brown substance in cigarettes that coats the lungs; causes lung and other cancers

16. _____ A substance that causes vomiting

17. _____ The tiny structures that make up all the tissues of the body and carry out all its functions

18. _____ The group of bones in the lower part of the trunk that support the upper body and protect the abdominal organs

19. _____ A drug that increases the amount of water in the urine, removing excess water from the body

20. _____ A procedure to treat kidney failure in which artificial means are used to filter waste, maintain acid-base balance, and remove excess fluid from the body

21. _____ Sudden uncontrolled waves of electrical activity in the brain, causing involuntary movement or loss of consciousness

22. _____ Two almond-shaped glands located at the opening of the fallopian tubes on both sides of the uterus

23. _____ On one side

24. _____ A small female organ located near the opening of the vagina that swells when sexually aroused

25. _____ The main part of the large intestine, between the cecum and the rectum

A. Cell	B. Teratoma	C. Palate	D. Medulla	E. Clitoris	F. Pulp
G. Ovaries	H. Cochlea	I. Suture	J. Pelvis	K. Thalamus	L. Lateral
M. Seizure	N. Urea	O. Larynx	P. Tar	Q. Diuretic	R. Appendix
S. Measles	T. Clavicle	U. Dialysis	V. Vulva	W. Colon	X. Emetic
Y. Hiccup					

B. Provide the word that best matches each clue.

1. _____ The socket in the skull that contains the eyeball, along with its blood vessels, nerves, and muscles

2. _____ A group of common infections occurring on the skin, hair, and nails that are caused by a fungus

3. _____ Sudden uncontrolled waves of electrical activity in the brain, causing involuntary movement or loss of consciousness

4. _____ The process of passage of the solvent portion of a lesser-concentrated solution through a semipermeable membrane into a higher-concentrated solution until the two solutions are equal in concentration

5. _____ A term describing something related to or caused by a virus

6. _____ The largest organ in the body, producing many essential chemicals and regulating the levels of most vital substances in the blood

7. _____ Healthy tissue that is used to replace diseased or defective tissue

8. _____ Any area of discolored skin that is present when a baby is born

9. _____ The return of a disease or symptom after it had disappeared

10. _____ The presence of white blood cells in the urine

11. _____ The smallest particle found in the blood, which plays a major role in forming blood clots

12. _____ A negative reaction to a substance that in most people causes no reaction

13. _____ A sometimes fatal disease affecting the brain and spinal cord

14. _____ The practice, maintenance, and study of health

15. _____ A cavity within bone or a channel that contains blood

16. _____ Inflammation of the heart

17. _____ Masses of lymphoid tissue located at either side of the back of the throat

18. _____ A reduced level of oxygen in tissues

19. _____ A system used to classify sick or injured people according to the severity of their conditions

20. _____ A small, parasitic worm that can live in the intestines of a human and may cause diarrhea, abdominal pain, and anemia

21. _____ A procedure to treat kidney failure in which artificial means are used to filter waste, maintain acid-base balance, and remove excess fluid from the body

22. _____ An abnormal growth of bone out of another bone, often located on the heel and usually painful

23. _____ A membrane lining the inside of the back of the eye that contains light-sensitive nerve cells that convert focused light into nerve impulses, making vision possible

24. _____ The double-layered membrane that lines the lungs and chest cavity and allows for lung movement during breathing

25. _____ Infestation by a small, round, blood-sucking parasite

A. Hookworm	B. Hygiene	C. Seizure	D. Platelet	E. Viral	F. Bone spur
G. Birthmark	H. Retina	I. Whipworm	J. Liver	K. Sinus	L. Dialysis
M. Hypoxia	N. Relapse	O. Tetanus	P. Tinea	Q. Pyuria	R. Triage
S. Graft	T. Osmosis	U. Pleura	V. Carditis	W. Tonsils	X. Allergy
Y. Orbit					

C. Provide the word that best matches each clue.

1. _____ Inflammation of the uvea

2. _____ The thick, greasy substance that covers the skin of a newborn baby

3. _____ A drug that causes the pupil to constrict

4. _____ A tear or break in an organ or tissue

5. _____ A gradual decline in mental ability usually caused by a brain disease, such as Alzheimer's disease

6. _____ An artificially constructed or an abnormal passage connecting two usually separate structures in the body

7. _____ A drug (or other chemical) induced drowsiness or stupor

8. _____ The muscular passage connecting the uterus with the outside genitals

9. _____ One of the two bones that form the hip on either side of the body

10. _____ The group of bones in the lower part of the trunk that support the upper body and protect the abdominal organs

11. _____ An abnormal growth of bone out of another bone, often located on the heel and usually painful

12. _____ An egg cell that has not developed completely

13. _____ Another term for a nerve cell

14. _____ Sexual intercourse

15. _____ Any one of the 33 bones that make up the spine

16. _____ A white blood cell that makes antibodies to fight infections caused by foreign proteins

17. _____ A substance that causes vomiting

18. _____ A hormone produced by the pancreas that converts stored carbohydrates (glycogen) into glucose, the body's energy source

19. _____ Inflammation of the breast, which is usually caused by a bacterial infection

20. _____ Damage to part of the brain because of a lack of blood supply or the rupturing of a blood vessel

21. _____ An organism that is dependent on another organism for nourishment

22. _____ An organ, tissue, or device surgically inserted and left in the body

23. _____ A severe headache, usually accompanied by vision problems and

24. _____ The process of closing a blood vessel or duct by tying it off

25. _____ A plentiful mineral in the body and the basic component of teeth and bones

A. Miotic	B. Calcium	C. B cell	D. Vagina	E. Neuron	F. Uveitis
G. Emetic	H. Coitus	I. Glucagon	J. Pelvis	K. Fungus	L. Stroke
M. Rupture	N. Ligation	O. Ilium	P. Bone spur	Q. Vertebra	R. Vernix
S. Shunt	T. Migraine	U. Implant	V. Dementia	W. Mastitis	X. Narcosis
Y. Oocyte					

D. Provide the word that best matches each clue.

1. _____ A measure of the acidic or basic character of a substance

2. _____ The hard deposit formed on teeth when mineral salts in saliva combine with plaque

3. _____ One of the two bones that form the hip on either side of the body

4. _____ The hollow female reproductive organ in which a fertilized egg is implanted, and a fetus develops

5. _____ The beginning of menstruation

6. _____ A bluish discoloration of the skin caused by low levels of oxygen in the blood

7. _____ Damage to part of the brain because of a lack of blood supply or the rupturing of a blood vessel

8. _____ A drug that neutralizes stomach acids

9. _____ The foreskin

10. _____ Inflammation of a testicle, which can be caused by infection with the mumps virus

11. _____ The sac containing the testicles

12. _____ Any one of the 33 bones that make up the spine

13. _____ Excessive curvature of the spine, which usually affects the top part of the spine and causes a hump

14. _____ The medical term for muscle pain

15. _____ A usually mild and temporary condition common in children under the age of 4 in which the walls of the airways become inflamed and narrow, resulting in wheezing and coughing

16. _____ Two tubes that carry urine from the kidneys to the bladder

17. _____ A disorder of the nervous system in which abnormal electrical activity in the brain causes seizures

18. _____ The opening through which feces are passed from the body

19. _____ The inward curvature of the spine at the lower back, which is normal to a certain degree

20. _____ Small spots that float across the field of vision, caused by debris floating in the gel-like substance that fills the eye

21. _____ A slippery fluid produced by mucous membranes that lubricates and protects the internal surfaces of the body

22. _____ A mental disorder characterized by an inability to relate to other people and extreme withdrawal

23. _____ A skin tumor composed of cells called melanocytes

24. _____ The artificial growth of cells, tissue, or microorganisms such as bacteria in a laboratory

25. _____ Dangerously decreased acidity of the blood, which can be caused by high altitudes, hyperventilation, and excessive vomiting

A. Orchitis   B. Ureters   C. Myalgia   D. Epilepsy   E. Autism   F. Lordosis
G. Culture   H. Prepuce   I. Croup   J. Anus   K. Cyanosis   L. Vertebra
M. Floaters   N. Menarche   O. Uterus   P. Alkalosis   Q. Mucus   R. pH
S. Ilium   T. Melanoma   U. Tartar   V. Kyphosis   W. Stroke   X. Antacid
Y. Scrotum

E. Provide the word that best matches each clue.

1. _____ A disorder in which the lens of the eye becomes less transparent and, in some cases, a milky white, making vision less clear

2. _____ A "warning" signal that comes before a migraine headache or an epileptic seizure, which might include emotions or sensations of movement or discomfort

3. _____ The excessive production of urine

4. _____ Infection and inflammation of a gland, especially a lymph node

5. _____ Any disease caused by a fungus

6. _____ Occurring at an abnormal position or time

7. _____ A skin infection caused by a fungus that spreads out in an even circle, characterized by ring-like, scaly patches of red skin

8. _____ A hormone produced by the thyroid gland that helps regulate energy production in the body

9. _____ Describes a disorder that continues for a long period of time

10. _____ The hard deposit formed on teeth when mineral salts in saliva combine with plaque

11. _____ An illness caused by a viral infection, causing a characteristic rash and a fever

12. _____ An involuntary, repetitive movement such as a twitch

13. _____ A vibration felt when the hand is placed flat on the chest

14. _____ The two pairs of skinfolds that protect the opening of the vagina

15. _____ The beginning of the large intestine, which is connected to the appendix at its lower end

16. _____ An additional dose of a vaccine taken after the first dose to maintain or renew the first one

17. _____ The technique of creating pictures of structures inside of the body using x-rays, ultrasound waves, or magnetic fields

18. _____ A hospital or an area of a hospital dedicated to treating people who are dying, often of a specific cause

19. _____ The main part of the large intestine, between the cecum and the rectum

20. _____ An abnormal growth of bone out of another bone, often located on the heel and usually painful

21. _____ A term used to describe a newborn infant from birth to 1 month of age

22. _____ The oily, lubricating substance that is secreted by glands in the skin

23. _____ A negative reaction to a substance that in most people causes no reaction

24. _____ The clear, dome-shaped front portion of the eye's outer covering

25. _____ Instruments resembling tweezers that are used to handle objects or tissue during surgery

A. Aura   B. Cornea   C. Cecum   D. Sebum   E. Bone spur   F. Forceps
G. Ringworm   H. Ectopic   I. Imaging   J. Hospice   K. Measles   L. Booster
M. Cataract   N. Polyuria   O. Neonate   P. Adenitis   Q. Thrill   R. Colon
S. Thyroxin   T. Tartar   U. Mycosis   V. Allergy   W. Tic   X. Labia
Y. Chronic

F. Provide the word that best matches each clue.

1. _____ Abnormally pale skin

2. _____ A tiny blood vessel that connects the smallest arteries to the smallest veins and allows exchange of oxygen and other materials between blood cells and body tissue cells

3. _____ Inflammation of the mucous membrane lining the nose

4. _____ A thickened callus on the foot that is caused by an improperly fitting shoe

5. _____ Difficulty falling or remaining asleep

6. _____ A white blood cell that makes antibodies to fight infections caused by foreign proteins

7. _____ The tough, white coating that covers and protects the inner structures of the eye

8. _____ Sudden uncontrolled waves of electrical activity in the brain, causing involuntary movement or loss of consciousness

9. _____ The tube by which urine is released from the bladder

10. _____ A poisonous substance produced by certain animals

11. _____ The presence of bacterial toxins in the blood

12. _____ An additional dose of a vaccine taken after the first dose to maintain or renew the first one

13. _____ A tumor of the thymus gland

14. _____ The process by which most cells divide to reproduce

15. _____ A hard plaster or fiberglass shell that molds to a body part such as an arm and holds it in place for proper healing

16. _____ The smallest known disease-causing microorganism

17. _____ A drug that causes the pupil to constrict

18. _____ An area of buildup of fat deposits in an artery, causing narrowing of the artery and possibly heart disease

19. _____ The smallest unit of a substance that possesses its characteristics

20. _____ Inflammation of the lining of the lungs and chest cavity usually caused by a lung infection

21. _____ The male sex cell produced in the testicles

22. _____ The term used to refer to an unborn child from 8 weeks after fertilization to birth

23. _____ A skin infection caused by a fungus that spreads out in an even circle, characterized by ring-like, scaly patches of red skin

24. _____ The orange-yellow pigment in bile, causing jaundice if it builds up in the blood and skin

25. _____ An element for the formation of thyroid hormones

A. Sperm	B. Venom	C. Rhinitis	D. Toxemia	E. Pleurisy	F. Bilirubin
G. Booster	H. Insomnia	I. Seizure	J. Virus	K. Urethra	L. Miotic
M. Capillary	N. Molecule	O. Iodine	P. Mitosis	Q. Corn	R. Fetus
S. Plaque	T. Thymoma	U. Cast	V. B cell	W. Pallor	X. Ringworm
Y. Sclera					

G. Provide the word that best matches each clue.

1. _____ Muscle damage resulting from excessive stretching or forceful contraction

2. _____ Two tubes that carry urine from the kidneys to the bladder

3. _____ One of the two long bones of the forearm located on the thumb side of the arm

4. _____ The external male reproductive organ, which passes urine and semen out of the body

5. _____ The type of cell division that occurs only in the ovaries and testicles, producing cells with half the genes of the original cell

6. _____ A poisonous substance

7. _____ The opening at the center of the iris in the eye that constricts (contracts) and dilates (widens) in response to light

8. _____ Masses of lymphoid tissue located at either side of the back of the throat

9. _____ The drooping of the upper eyelid

10. _____ The medical term for suffocation

11. _____ A fluid-filled cyst attached to a tendon sheath or joint

12. _____ Partial paralysis

13. _____ Another term for a tumor

14. _____ A term describing a disorder or characteristic (such as male pattern baldness) that occurs within a family more often than would be expected

15. _____ A persistent, contagious form of conjunctivitis that can lead to complications such as blindness if untreated

16. _____ Fluid released during ejaculation that contains sperm along with fluids produced by the prostate gland and the seminal vesicles

17. _____ A group of fats stored in the body and used for energy

18. _____ Controlled analgesia- a system for administering pain- killing drugs in which the amount of drug delivered is controlled by the patient

19. _____ An organism that is dependent on another organism for nourishment

20. _____ A parasitic disease spread by mosquitos that causes chills and fever

21. _____ The cell that results when an egg is fertilized by a sperm

22. _____ The bulging of an organ or tissue through a weakened area in the muscle wall

23. _____ A lump filled with either fluid or soft material, occurring in any organ or tissue

24. _____ An oral contraceptive containing only the synthetic hormone progesterone (birth control pills contain estrogen and progesterone)

25. _____ Large molecules made up of amino acids that play many major roles in the body, including forming the basis of body structures.

A. Meiosis	B. Lipids	C. Semen	D. Penis	E. Ureters	F. Radius
G. Proteins	H. Strain	I. Familial	J. Neoplasm	K. Patient	L. Pupil
M. Tonsils	N. Ptosis	O. Toxin	P. Minipill	Q. Malaria	R. Trachoma
S. Ganglion	T. Cyst	U. Hernia	V. Asphyxia	W. Paresis	X. Zygote
Y. Fungus					

H. Provide the word that best matches each clue.

1. _____ A condition in which the blood does not contain enough hemoglobin, the compound that carries oxygen from the lungs to other parts of the body

2. _____ Inflammation of bone

3. _____ Small eight-legged animals, many of which burrow and feed on blood

4. _____ A substance that causes vomiting

5. _____ The long, flat bone located at the center of the chest

6. _____ A severe headache, usually accompanied by vision problems and

7. _____ Twisting and obstruction of an area of intestine

8. _____ The opening at the center of the iris in the eye that constricts (contracts) and dilates (widens) in response to light

9. _____ A waste product of the metabolism of proteins that is formed by the liver and secreted by the kidneys

10. _____ Inflammation of the spinal cord, which can cause headaches, fever, muscle stiffness, pain, weakness, and eventually paralysis

11. _____ An automatic, involuntary response of the nervous system to a stimulus

12. _____ The presence in the cells of three copies of a certain chromosome instead of the normal two copies

13. _____ The triangular bone located at the bottom of the spine that is connected to the tailbone

14. _____ Sudden uncontrolled waves of electrical activity in the brain, causing involuntary movement or loss of consciousness

15. _____ A gradual decline in mental ability usually caused by a brain disease, such as Alzheimer's disease

16. _____ An abnormal swelling of the wall of an artery, caused by a weakening in the vessel wall

17. _____ A cancer affecting cells in the bone marrow

18. _____ The shrinkage or near disappearance of a tissue or organ

19. _____ An agent that is believed to cause several degenerative brain diseases

20. _____ A chemically inactive substance given in place of a drug to test how much of a drug's effectiveness can be attributed to a patient's expectations that the drug will have a positive effect

21. _____ A parasitic worm that lives in the intestines

22. _____ A brain tumor arising from cells that support nerve cells

23. _____ A term describing a disorder or characteristic (such as male pattern baldness) that occurs within a family more often than would be expected

24. _____ A poisonous form of oxygen that is present in the earth's upper atmosphere, where it helps to screen the earth from damaging ultraviolet rays

25. _____ A thick, yellowish or greenish fluid that contains dead white blood cells, tissues, and bacteria; occurs at the site of a bacterial infection

A. Pupil	B. Sternum	C. Anemia	D. Urea	E. Myelitis	F. Trisomy
G. Aneurysm	H. Atrophy	I. Ozone	J. Prion	K. Tapeworm	L. Sacrum
M. Mites	N. Osteitis	O. Pus	P. Glioma	Q. Emetic	R. Seizure
S. Migraine	T. Reflex	U. Volvulus	V. Dementia	W. Familial	X. Myeloma
Y. Placebo					

I. Provide the word that best matches each clue.

1. _____ An artificially constructed or an abnormal passage connecting two usually separate structures in the body

2. _____ A blood clot in a blood vessel

3. _____ The main artery in the body, carrying oxygenated blood from the heart to other arteries in the body

4. _____ An infectious viral disease primarily affecting animals

5. _____ Another term for the lower jaw

6. _____ A fluid-filled sac that cushions and reduces friction in certain parts of the body

7. _____ The main form that glucose, the body's energy source, takes when it is stored

8. _____ A group of common infections occurring on the skin, hair, and nails that are caused by a fungus

9. _____ Any substance capable of causing a disease

10. _____ A salt solution or any substance that contains salt

11. _____ Dependence on a substance (such as alcohol or other drugs) or an activity, to the point that stopping is very difficult and causes severe physical and mental reactions

12. _____ A surgical technique in which the flow of blood or another body fluid is redirected around a blockage

13. _____ Sudden uncontrolled waves of electrical activity in the brain, causing involuntary movement or loss of consciousness

14. _____ A disorder in which the lens of the eye becomes less transparent and, in some cases, a milky white, making vision less clear

15. _____ A hormone (such as testosterone) that causes development of male characteristics and sex organs

16. _____ Small, eight-legged animals that can attach to humans and animals and feed on blood

17. _____ A parasitic worm that lives in the intestines

18. _____ The bone located between the hip and the knee

19. _____ The process by which most cells divide to reproduce

20. _____ A discharge from an inflamed ear

21. _____ A gradual decline in mental ability usually caused by a brain disease, such as Alzheimer's disease

22. _____ An electrocardiogram, which is a record of the electrical impulses that trigger the heartbeat; used to diagnose heart disorders

23. _____ Organisms that lives on or in other organisms, from which it obtains nutrients

24. _____ The infection of a wound or tissue with bacteria, causing the spread of the bacteria into the bloodstream

25. _____ A coiled organ in the inner ear that plays a large role in hearing by picking up sound vibrations and transmitting them as electrical signals

A. Parasite	B. Femur	C. Shunt	D. Tinea	E. Saline	F. Rabies
G. Addiction	H. Pathogen	I. Seizure	J. Otorrhea	K. Cochlea	L. Mitosis
M. Bypass	N. Bursa	O. Aorta	P. Cataract	Q. Glycogen	R. Thrombus
S. ECG	T. Tapeworm	U. Dementia	V. Ticks	W. Androgen	X. Mandible
Y. Sepsis					

J. Provide the word that best matches each clue.

1. _____ A tiny pouchlike cavity in a structure of the body, such as a hair follicle

2. _____ The oily, lubricating substance that is secreted by glands in the skin

3. _____ A membrane lining the inside of the back of the eye that contains light-sensitive nerve cells that convert focused light into nerve impulses, making vision possible

4. _____ The introduction of a substance, such as a drug or nutrient, into the bloodstream or a body cavity

5. _____ A group of compounds of silicon and oxygen

6. _____ A usually mild and temporary condition common in children under the age of 4 in which the walls of the airways become inflamed and narrow, resulting in wheezing and coughing

7. _____ A condition in which one eye turns outward

8. _____ Dangerously decreased acidity of the blood, which can be caused by high altitudes, hyperventilation, and excessive vomiting

9. _____ A small female organ located near the opening of the vagina that swells when sexually aroused

10. _____ Inflammation of the spinal cord, which can cause headaches, fever, muscle stiffness, pain, weakness, and eventually paralysis

11. _____ The tube running from the larynx (the voice box) down the neck and into the upper part of the chest

12. _____ Located nearer to a central point of reference on the body, such as the trunk

13. _____ Feeling the need to vomit

14. _____ "in the living body"; a biological process that occurs inside of the body

15. _____ An abnormal growth of bone out of another bone, often located on the heel and usually painful

16. _____ The muscular passage connecting the uterus with the outside genitals

17. _____ A term used to describe a disease that is rare then suddenly affects more people than usually expected

18. _____ Small eight-legged animals, many of which burrow and feed on blood

19. _____ Determination of the amount of oxygen in the blood by measuring the amount of light transmitted through an area of skin

20. _____ The center part of an organ or body structure

21. _____ Damage to part of the brain because of a lack of blood supply or the rupturing of a blood vessel

22. _____ Infection and inflammation of a gland, especially a lymph node

23. _____ The colored part of the eye

24. _____ Inflammation of the large intestine (the colon), which usually leads to abdominal pain, fever, and diarrhea with blood and mucus

25. _____ A poisonous form of oxygen that is present in the earth's upper atmosphere, where it helps to screen the earth from damaging ultraviolet rays

A. Trachea   B. Follicle   C. Retina   D. Alkalosis E. Nausea   F. Stroke
G. Colitis   H. Ozone   I. Bone spur J. Adenitis   K. In vivo   L. Croup
M. Oximetry N. Iris   O. Vagina   P. Walleye   Q. Myelitis R. Silicone
S. Mites   T. Infusion   U. Epidemic V. Proximal   W. Medulla   X. Clitoris
Y. Sebum

K. Provide the word that best matches each clue.

1. _____ A deficiency of the vitamin niacin; causes dermatitis, diarrhea, and mental disorders

2. _____ The structure of bodies

3. _____ A cancer that occurs on the surface or lining of an organ

4. _____ A term describing a disorder or characteristic (such as male pattern baldness) that occurs within a family more often than would be expected

5. _____ A shift in the position of the fetus inside of the uterus, either occurring naturally or as performed by a doctor to facilitate delivery

6. _____ Inflammation of the vulva

7. _____ A thickened area of skin due to consistent pressure or friction, or the area around a bone break where new bone is formed

8. _____ The presence of bacterial toxins in the blood

9. _____ An extremely rare condition in which the body ages prematurely

10. _____ The foreskin

11. _____ A drug that increases the amount of water in the urine, removing excess water from the body

12. _____ The hollow female reproductive organ in which a fertilized egg is implanted, and a fetus develops

13. _____ The expansion and contraction of a blood vessel due to the blood pumped through it

14. _____ The outer, visible portion of the female genitals

15. _____ A sac or body cavity that is swollen because of the production of mucus by the cells in its lining

16. _____ An organ located in the upper left abdomen behind the ribs that removes and destroys old red blood cells and helps fight infection

17. _____ Dangerously decreased acidity of the blood, which can be caused by high altitudes, hyperventilation, and excessive vomiting

18. _____ A colorless, odorless, tasteless radioactive gas that is produced by materials in soil, rocks, and building materials; suspected of causing cancer

19. _____ The process of passage of the solvent portion of a lesser-concentrated solution through a semipermeable membrane into a higher-concentrated solution until the two solutions are equal in concentration

20. _____ Located nearer to a central point of reference on the body, such as the trunk

21. _____ A hospital or an area of a hospital dedicated to treating people who are dying, often of a specific cause

22. _____ A term used to describe a newborn infant from birth to 1 month of age

23. _____ A hormone (such as testosterone) that causes development of male characteristics and sex organs

24. _____ The medical term for muscle pain

25. _____ A group of hormones (produced mainly in the ovaries) that are necessary for female sexual development and reproductive functioning

A. Carcinoma	B. Diuretic	C. Proximal	D. Callus	E. Spleen	F. Osmosis
G. Radon	H. Anatomy	I. Toxemia	J. Mucocele	K. Version	L. Vulvitis
M. Vulva	N. Pellagra	O. Pulse	P. Androgen	Q. Uterus	R. Alkalosis
S. Myalgia	T. Prepuce	U. Familial	V. Estrogen	W. Hospice	X. Progeria
Y. Neonate					

L. Provide the word that best matches each clue.

1. _____ A device used to hold tissues in place, such as to support a skin graft

2. _____ The common term for urticaria, an itchy, inflamed rash that results from an allergic reaction

3. _____ Four fused bones that form a triangular shape at the base of the spine (also known as the tailbone)

4. _____ Tightness of the foreskin, which prevents it from being moved back over the head of the penis

5. _____ Sexual intercourse

6. _____ A surgically formed opening on a body surface

7. _____ A characteristic sound of blood flowing irregularly through the heart

8. _____ A serious infectious disease transmitted to humans through bites of rodent fleas

9. _____ An accumulation of blood from a broken blood vessel

10. _____ The structure of bodies

11. _____ The complete set of an organism's genes

12. _____ A membrane lining the inside of the back of the eye that contains light-sensitive nerve cells that convert focused light into nerve impulses, making vision possible

13. _____ Two organs in the chest that take in oxygen from the air and release carbon dioxide

14. _____ The sac containing the testicles

15. _____ Inflammation of the lining of the lungs and chest cavity usually caused by a lung infection

16. _____ A skin condition characterized by inflamed, pus-filled areas that occur on the skin's surface, most commonly occurring during adolescence

17. _____ A parasitic disease spread by mosquitos that causes chills and fever

18. _____ A widespread epidemic

19. _____ The term used to refer to an unborn child from 8 weeks after fertilization to birth

20. _____ A term used to describe symptoms that are caused by mental stress and occur in someone who does not have a mental disorder

21. _____ A noncancerous bone tumor

22. _____ A poisonous substance produced by certain animals

23. _____ The tiny structures that make up all the tissues of the body and carry out all its functions

24. _____ A hormone produced by the pancreas that converts stored carbohydrates (glycogen) into glucose, the body's energy source

25. _____ A plentiful mineral in the body and the basic component of teeth and bones

A. Glucagon	B. Pandemic	C. Anatomy	D. Acne	E. Stoma	F. Stent
G. Calcium	H. Lungs	I. Pleurisy	J. Retina	K. Murmur	L. Cell
M. Phimosis	N. Coitus	O. Coccyx	P. Hives	Q. Osteoma	R. Hysteria
S. Plague	T. Genome	U. Hematoma	V. Malaria	W. Venom	X. Scrotum
Y. Fetus					

M. Provide the word that best matches each clue.

1. _____ The two upper chambers of the heart

2. _____ The long, flat bone located at the center of the chest

3. _____ A type of testicular cancer that is made up of only a single type of cell

4. _____ Physical injury or emotional shock

5. _____ A disorder marked by high levels of uric acid in the blood

6. _____ The opening at the center of the iris in the eye that constricts (contracts) and dilates (widens) in response to light

7. _____ A usually mild and temporary condition common in children under the age of 4 in which the walls of the airways become inflamed and narrow, resulting in wheezing and coughing

8. _____ A growth that occurs on mucous membranes such as those in the nose and intestine

9. _____ The column of bones and cartilage running along the midline of the back that surrounds and protects the spinal cord and supports the head

10. _____ A word describing any condition that is not present at birth, but develops some time during life

11. _____ The three membranes that surround and protect the spinal cord and brain

12. _____ A group of symptoms that indicate a certain disorder when they occur together

13. _____ A term used to describe a disease that is rare then suddenly affects more people than usually expected

14. _____ Excess fluid in the abdominal cavity, which leads to swelling

15. _____ A mental disorder characterized by extreme excitement, happiness, overactivity, and agitation

16. _____ Any substance that causes a fever

17. _____ Determination of the amount of oxygen in the blood by measuring the amount of light transmitted through an area of skin

18. _____ Mucus and other material produced by the lining of the respiratory tract

19. _____ A system used to classify sick or injured people according to the severity of their conditions

20. _____ Describes a condition or illness that begins suddenly and is usually short-lasting

21. _____ An abnormal swelling of the wall of an artery, caused by a weakening in the vessel wall

22. _____ Another term for a microorganism, especially one that causes disease

23. _____ A brain tumor arising from cells that support nerve cells

24. _____ Small eight-legged animals, many of which burrow and feed on blood

25. _____ Describes structures that encircle another structure

A. Epidemic	B. Ascites	C. Coronary	D. Microbe	E. Croup	F. Oximetry
G. Meninges	H. Mites	I. Polyp	J. Atria	K. Syndrome	L. Mania
M. Phlegm	N. Trauma	O. Spine	P. Aneurysm	Q. Acquired	R. Pupil
S. Sternum	T. Gout	U. Glioma	V. Seminoma	W. Triage	X. Acute
Y. Pyrogen					

N. Provide the word that best matches each clue.

1. _____ A disorder in which the lens of the eye becomes less transparent and, in some cases, a milky white, making vision less clear

2. _____ An involuntary, repetitive movement such as a twitch

3. _____ A hormone that stimulates the release of gastric acid in the stomach

4. _____ A group of drugs which resemble hormones produced by the adrenal glands, and anabolic steroids, which are like the hormones produced by the male sex organs

5. _____ A contagious, harmless growth caused by a virus that occurs on the skin or a mucous membrane

6. _____ A parasitic worm that lives in the intestines

7. _____ Inflammation of the heart

8. _____ Organisms that lives on or in other organisms, from which it obtains nutrients

9. _____ The three membranes that surround and protect the spinal cord and brain

10. _____ A hormone produced by the thyroid gland that helps regulate energy production in the body

11. _____ Tiny, hair like structures on the outside of some cells, providing mobility

12. _____ An organ formed in the uterus during pregnancy that links the blood of the mother to the blood of the fetus

13. _____ A structure that allows fluid flow in only one direction

14. _____ A slippery fluid produced by mucous membranes that lubricates and protects the internal surfaces of the body

15. _____ A reduced level of oxygen in tissues

16. _____ An organ located in the pelvis whose function is to collect and store urine until it is expelled

17. _____ A surgical stitch that helps close an incision or wound so that it can heal properly

18. _____ The two pairs of skinfolds that protect the opening of the vagina

19. _____ The period during which sexual development occurs

20. _____ A painless sore that has a thick, rubbery base and a defined edge

21. _____ The loose skin that covers the head of the penis

22. _____ A hormone produced in the pituitary gland that causes contraction of the uterus during childbirth and stimulation of milk flow during breast- feeding.

23. _____ An organism that is dependent on another organism for nourishment

24. _____ The blockage of a blood vessel by an embolus- something previously circulating in the blood (such as a blood clot, gas bubble, tissue, bacteria, bone marrow, cholesterol, fat, etc.)

25. _____ Anything that can increase the rate of abnormal change in cells, which can lead to cancer

A. Mucus   B. Tic   C. Valve   D. Mutagen   E. Suture   F. Embolism
G. Oxytocin   H. Carditis   I. Fungus   J. Steroids   K. Placenta   L. Labia
M. Thyroxin   N. Chancre   O. Cataract   P. Cilia   Q. Parasite   R. Bladder
S. Foreskin   T. Tapeworm   U. Meninges   V. Gastrin   W. Wart   X. Hypoxia
Y. Puberty

O. Provide the word that best matches each clue.

1. _____ The presence of viruses in the blood

2. _____ A painless sore that has a thick, rubbery base and a defined edge

3. _____ One of the two bones that form the hip on either side of the body

4. _____ The loose skin that covers the head of the penis

5. _____ Dangerously decreased acidity of the blood, which can be caused by high altitudes, hyperventilation, and excessive vomiting

6. _____ A poisonous form of oxygen that is present in the earth's upper atmosphere, where it helps to screen the earth from damaging ultraviolet rays

7. _____ A bluish discoloration of the skin caused by low levels of oxygen in the blood

8. _____ A small lump of tissue that is usually abnormal

9. _____ Describes a treatment or procedure that is not urgent and can be arranged at the patient's convenience

10. _____ The group of bones in the lower part of the trunk that support the upper body and protect the abdominal organs

11. _____ A salt solution or any substance that contains salt

12. _____ Partial paralysis

13. _____ Any bacteria that is rod-shaped

14. _____ A persisting fear of and desire to avoid something

15. _____ Ribonucleic acid, which helps to decode and process the information contained in DNA

16. _____ A persistent, contagious form of conjunctivitis that can lead to complications such as blindness if untreated

17. _____ The presence in the cells of three copies of a certain chromosome instead of the normal two copies

18. _____ The largest part of the brain and the site of most of its activity, including sensory and motor functions

19. _____ Inflammation of bone

20. _____ An organ, tissue, or device surgically inserted and left in the body

21. _____ A highly contagious skin disorder caused by a mite that burrows into the skin and produces an intense, itchy rash

22. _____ A genetic disorder in which the foot is twisted and misshapen

23. _____ The common term for urticaria, an itchy, inflamed rash that results from an allergic reaction

24. _____ A mild viral infection (also known as German measles) that produces a rash and fever

25. _____ The smallest unit of a substance that possesses its characteristics

A. Trisomy	B. Bacillus	C. Nodule	D. Saline	E. Trachoma	F. Clubfoot
G. Hives	H. Cyanosis	I. Paresis	J. Elective	K. Cerebrum	L. Scabies
M. Ilium	N. Implant	O. Osteitis	P. Foreskin	Q. Molecule	R. Pelvis
S. Chancre	T. Ozone	U. Alkalosis	V. Viremia	W. Rubella	X. RNA
Y. Phobia					

P. Provide the word that best matches each clue.

1. _____ Any substance that the body can use to maintain its health

2. _____ The artificial growth of cells, tissue, or microorganisms such as bacteria in a laboratory

3. _____ A bronchodilator drug that is used to treat asthma

4. _____ The muscular passage connecting the uterus with the outside genitals

5. _____ A unit that is used to measure the energy content in food

6. _____ A disease caused by a lack of vitamin c, characterized by weakness, bleeding and pain in joints and muscles, bleeding gums, and abnormal bone and tooth growth

7. _____ A device used to correct or control deformed bones, muscles, or joints

8. _____ Healthy tissue that is used to replace diseased or defective tissue

9. _____ The bone located between the hip and the knee

10. _____ The drooping of the upper eyelid

11. _____ A parasitic disease spread by mosquitos that causes chills and fever

12. _____ The three membranes that surround and protect the spinal cord and brain

13. _____ The presence of viruses in the blood

14. _____ A fluid-filled cyst attached to a tendon sheath or joint

15. _____ A mental disorder characterized by an inability to relate to other people and extreme withdrawal

16. _____ Pertaining to the eyes

17. _____ A skin condition characterized by inflamed, pus-filled areas that occur on the skin's surface, most commonly occurring during adolescence

18. _____ A white blood cell that makes antibodies to fight infections caused by foreign proteins

19. _____ A preparation of weakened microorganisms given to create resistance to a certain disease

20. _____ A widespread epidemic

21. _____ A hormone (such as testosterone) that causes development of male characteristics and sex organs

22. _____ A bone break

23. _____ One of the two long bones of the forearm located on the thumb side of the arm

24. _____ An area of buildup of fat deposits in an artery, causing narrowing of the artery and possibly heart disease

25. _____ "in glass"; a biological test or process that is carried out in a laboratory

A. Androgen	B. Optic	C. Ganglion	D. Culture	E. Vaccine	F. Calorie
G. Malaria	H. B cell	I. Scurvy	J. Fracture	K. Femur	L. Vagina
M. Meninges	N. Plaque	O. Nutrient	P. Ptosis	Q. Radius	R. Viremia
S. Autism	T. Orthotic	U. In vitro	V. Graft	W. Pandemic	X. Xanthine
Y. Acne					

Q. Provide the word that best matches each clue.

1. _____ A body temperature of above 98.6°f in the mouth or 99.8°f in the rectum

2. _____ An element for the formation of thyroid hormones

3. _____ The medical term for wetting the bed

4. _____ The introduction of a substance, such as a drug or nutrient, into the bloodstream or a body cavity

5. _____ A plentiful mineral in the body and the basic component of teeth and bones

6. _____ The medical term for muscle pain

7. _____ A group of fats stored in the body and used for energy

8. _____ The foreskin

9. _____ The smallest particle found in the blood, which plays a major role in forming blood clots

10. _____ A parasitic flatworm that can infest humans

11. _____ "in the living body"; a biological process that occurs inside of the body

12. _____ Masses of lymphoid tissue located at either side of the back of the throat

13. _____ Measures taken to reduce the risk of acquiring a sexually transmitted disease, such as the use of a condom

14. _____ An abnormal passageway from one organ to another or from an organ to the body surface

15. _____ An abnormal mass that occurs when cells in a certain area reproduce unchecked

16. _____ The largest part of the brain and the site of most of its activity, including sensory and motor functions

17. _____ The external male reproductive organ, which passes urine and semen out of the body

18. _____ The male sex cell produced in the testicles

19. _____ The first part of the small intestine, immediately following the stomach

20. _____ A constituent of plants that cannot be digested, which helps maintain healthy functioning of the bowels

21. _____ A disorder marked by high levels of uric acid in the blood

22. _____ A change in the genetic information within a cell

23. _____ Inflammation of the vulva

24. _____ Describes a disorder that continues for a long period of time

25. _____ Excessive curvature of the spine, which usually affects the top part of the spine and causes a hump

A. Pyrexia	B. In vivo	C. Chronic	D. Gout	E. Fluke
F. Calcium	G. Penis	H. Infusion	I. Tonsils	J. Cerebrum
K. Enuresis	L. Prepuce	M. Sperm	N. Fiber	O. Mutation
P. Lipids	Q. Myalgia	R. Fistula	S. Vulvitis	T. Tumor
U. Safe sex	V. Kyphosis	W. Duodenum	X. Iodine	Y. Platelet

R. Provide the word that best matches each clue.

1. _____ Narrowing of a body passageway

2. _____ Dangerously decreased acidity of the blood, which can be caused by high altitudes, hyperventilation, and excessive vomiting

3. _____ A fluid-filled cyst attached to a tendon sheath or joint

4. _____ A blood clot in a blood vessel

5. _____ A hormone produced in the pituitary gland that causes contraction of the uterus during childbirth and stimulation of milk flow during breast-feeding.

6. _____ A white blood cell that makes antibodies to fight infections caused by foreign proteins

7. _____ The triangular bone located at the bottom of the spine that is connected to the tailbone

8. _____ A unit that is used to measure the energy content in food

9. _____ Inflammation of the heart

10. _____ The throat

11. _____ A hard, fluid-filled pad along the inside joint of the big toe

12. _____ A group of drugs that widen blood vessels

13. _____ A device used to introduce a powdered or misted drug into the lungs through the mouth, usually to treat respiratory disorders such as asthma

14. _____ A sexually transmitted disease

15. _____ The beginning of menstruation

16. _____ A noncancerous tumor of connective tissue

17. _____ A term used to describe a disease that is rare then suddenly affects more people than usually expected

18. _____ A group of symptoms that indicate a certain disorder when they occur together

19. _____ An exact copy of a gene, cell, or organism

20. _____ Physical injury or emotional shock

21. _____ Inflammation of a testicle, which can be caused by infection with the mumps virus

22. _____ The tube running from the larynx (the voice box) down the neck and into the upper part of the chest

23. _____ The two upper chambers of the heart

24. _____ A bundle of fibers that transmit electrical messages between the brain and areas of the body

25. _____ The type of cell division that occurs only in the ovaries and testicles, producing cells with half the genes of the original cell

A. Trachea B. Alkalosis C. B cell D. Syndrome E. Inhaler F. Carditis
G. Ganglion H. Thrombus I. Nerve J. Menarche K. Pharynx L. Orchitis
M. Sacrum N. Fibroma O. Epidemic P. Nitrates Q. Calorie R. Bunion
S. Syphilis T. Stenosis U. Clone V. Meiosis W. Atria X. Trauma
Y. Oxytocin

S. Provide the word that best matches each clue.

1. _____ Inflammation of a nerve, often characterized by pain, numbness, or tingling

2. _____ The medical term for an earache

3. _____ One of the two bones that form the hip on either side of the body

4. _____ A small parasite worm that can live in the intestines

5. _____ An orange pigment present in colored plants such as carrots that is converted by the body to the essential nutrient vitamin a

6. _____ A tough, elastic band of tissue that connects bones and supports organs

7. _____ The process by which most cells divide to reproduce

8. _____ A genetic disorder in which the foot is twisted and misshapen

9. _____ A disorder in which a person eats large amounts of food then forces vomiting or uses laxatives to prevent weight gain (called binging and purging)

10. _____ A raised, firm, thick scar that forms because of a defect in the natural healing process

11. _____ The largest part of the brain and the site of most of its activity, including sensory and motor functions

12. _____ The tiny filtering units of the kidney

13. _____ An illness caused by a viral infection, causing a characteristic rash and a fever

14. _____ A spasm of the jaw muscles that prevents the mouth from opening, such as that caused by tetanus

15. _____ An agent that is believed to cause several degenerative brain diseases

16. _____ A tiny, single-celled microorganism, commonly known as a germ

17. _____ A structure that allows fluid flow in only one direction

18. _____ A chemical that transmits messages in the brain and plays a role in movement

19. _____ The extent to which a substance is poisonous

20. _____ A thickened callus on the foot that is caused by an improperly fitting shoe

21. _____ A highly contagious and often fatal viral infection that has been completely eradicated by immunization

22. _____ A skin infection caused by a fungus that spreads out in an even circle, characterized by ring-like, scaly patches of red skin

23. _____ A cancer affecting cells in the bone marrow

24. _____ Strong connective tissue cords that attach muscle to bone or muscle to muscle

25. _____ Inflammation of a testicle, which can be caused by infection with the mumps virus

A. Otalgia	B. Cerebrum	C. Lockjaw	D. Keloid	E. Valve	F. Bulimia
G. Mitosis	H. Myeloma	I. Smallpox	J. Toxicity	K. Neuritis	L. Ringworm
M. Nephrons	N. Pinworm	O. Measles	P. Prion	Q. Dopamine	R. Ilium
S. Carotene	T. Bacterium	U. Ligament	V. Tendon	W. Orchitis	X. Clubfoot
Y. Corn					

T. Provide the word that best matches each clue.

1. _____ Redness of the skin

2. _____ A possibly life-threatening condition in which breathing stops, for either a short or long period of time

3. _____ A short tube located at the end of the large intestine, which connects the intestine to the anus

4. _____ Abnormally pale skin

5. _____ A group of cells or an organ that produces substances (such as hormones and enzyme) that are used by the body

6. _____ A large blood vessel that carries blood from the heart to tissues and organs in the body

7. _____ The column of bones and cartilage running along the midline of the back that surrounds and protects the spinal cord and supports the head

8. _____ A term describing a condition that affects both sides of the body or two paired organs, such as bilateral deafness (deafness in both ears)

9. _____ A small, parasitic worm that can live in the intestines of a human and may cause diarrhea, abdominal pain, and anemia

10. _____ A tiny pouchlike cavity in a structure of the body, such as a hair follicle

11. _____ A crescent-shaped pad of cartilage in joints that helps to reduce friction

12. _____ A hormone produced by the pancreas that converts stored carbohydrates (glycogen) into glucose, the body's energy source

13. _____ The medical term for the death of tissue cells

14. _____ On one side

15. _____ The clear, watery fluid that separates from clotted blood

16. _____ Describes structures that encircle another structure

17. _____ A small parasite worm that can live in the intestines

18. _____ A lump filled with either fluid or soft material, occurring in any organ or tissue

19. _____ The presence in the cells of three copies of a certain chromosome instead of the normal two copies

20. _____ A painless sore that has a thick, rubbery base and a defined edge

21. _____ A type of testicular cancer that is made up of only a single type of cell

22. _____ Microorganisms that cause several human infections and can be transmitted sexually

23. _____ Describes a disease that is always present in a certain population of people

24. _____ An excessively large dose of a drug, which can lead to coma and death

25. _____ The hard deposit formed on teeth when mineral salts in saliva combine with plaque

A. Serum	B. Apnea	C. Follicle	D. Tartar	E. Lateral	F. Necrosis
G. Meniscus	H. Whipworm	I. Pallor	J. Rectum	K. Chlamydia	L. Spine
M. Pinworm	N. Seminoma	O. Trisomy	P. Endemic	Q. Gland	R. Erythema
S. Glucagon	T. Artery	U. Coronary	V. Overdose	W. Chancre	X. Cyst
Y. Bilateral					

A. Provide the word that best matches each clue.

1. MEASLES — An illness caused by a viral infection, causing a characteristic rash and a fever
2. COCHLEA — A coiled organ in the inner ear that plays a large role in hearing by picking up sound vibrations and transmitting them as electrical signals
3. SUTURE — A surgical stitch that helps close an incision or wound so that it can heal properly
4. PULP — The soft tissue inside of a tooth that contains blood vessels and nerves
5. APPENDIX — A short, tube-like structure that branches off the large intestine
6. UREA — A waste product of the metabolism of proteins that is formed by the liver and secreted by the kidneys
7. HICCUP — Involuntary sudden contraction of the diaphragm along with the closing of the vocal cords, producing a "hiccup" sound
8. THALAMUS — A structure in the brain that relays and processes incoming sensory information from the eyes and ears and from pressure and pain receptors
9. TERATOMA — A tumor composed of cells not normally found in the part of the body when the tumor occurred
10. CLAVICLE — The medical term for the collarbone
11. PALATE — The roof of the mouth
12. VULVA — The outer, visible portion of the female genitals
13. LARYNX — The medical term for the voice box, the organ in the throat that produces voice and prevents food from entering the airway
14. MEDULLA — The center part of an organ or body structure
15. TAR — The sticky, brown substance in cigarettes that coats the lungs; causes lung and other cancers
16. EMETIC — A substance that causes vomiting
17. CELL — The tiny structures that make up all the tissues of the body and carry out all its functions
18. PELVIS — The group of bones in the lower part of the trunk that support the upper body and protect the abdominal organs
19. DIURETIC — A drug that increases the amount of water in the urine, removing excess water from the body
20. DIALYSIS — A procedure to treat kidney failure in which artificial means are used to filter waste, maintain acid-base balance, and remove excess fluid from the body

21. SEIZURE — Sudden uncontrolled waves of electrical activity in the brain, causing involuntary movement or loss of consciousness

22. OVARIES — Two almond- shaped glands located at the opening of the fallopian tubes on both sides of the uterus

23. LATERAL — On one side

24. CLITORIS — A small female organ located near the opening of the vagina that swells when sexually aroused

25. COLON — The main part of the large intestine, between the cecum and the rectum

A. Cell	B. Teratoma	C. Palate	D. Medulla	E. Clitoris	F. Pulp
G. Ovaries	H. Cochlea	I. Suture	J. Pelvis	K. Thalamus	L. Lateral
M. Seizure	N. Urea	O. Larynx	P. Tar	Q. Diuretic	R. Appendix
S. Measles	T. Clavicle	U. Dialysis	V. Vulva	W. Colon	X. Emetic
Y. Hiccup					

B. Provide the word that best matches each clue.

1. ORBIT — The socket in the skull that contains the eyeball, along with its blood vessels, nerves, and muscles

2. TINEA — A group of common infections occurring on the skin, hair, and nails that are caused by a fungus

3. SEIZURE — Sudden uncontrolled waves of electrical activity in the brain, causing involuntary movement or loss of consciousness

4. OSMOSIS — The process of passage of the solvent portion of a lesser- concentrated solution through a semipermeable membrane into a higher- concentrated solution until the two solutions are equal in concentration

5. VIRAL — A term describing something related to or caused by a virus

6. LIVER — The largest organ in the body, producing many essential chemicals and regulating the levels of most vital substances in the blood

7. GRAFT — Healthy tissue that is used to replace diseased or defective tissue

8. BIRTHMARK — Any area of discolored skin that is present when a baby is born

9. RELAPSE — The return of a disease or symptom after it had disappeared

10. PYURIA — The presence of white blood cells in the urine

11. PLATELET — The smallest particle found in the blood, which plays a major role in forming blood clots

12. ALLERGY — A negative reaction to a substance that in most people causes no reaction

13. TETANUS — A sometimes fatal disease affecting the brain and spinal cord

14. HYGIENE   The practice, maintenance, and study of health

15. SINUS   A cavity within bone or a channel that contains blood

16. CARDITIS   Inflammation of the heart

17. TONSILS   Masses of lymphoid tissue located at either side of the back of the throat

18. HYPOXIA   A reduced level of oxygen in tissues

19. TRIAGE   A system used to classify sick or injured people according to the severity of their conditions

20. WHIPWORM   A small, parasitic worm that can live in the intestines of a human and may cause diarrhea, abdominal pain, and anemia

21. DIALYSIS   A procedure to treat kidney failure in which artificial means are used to filter waste, maintain acid-base balance, and remove excess fluid from the body

22. BONE SPUR   An abnormal growth of bone out of another bone, often located on the heel and usually painful

23. RETINA   A membrane lining the inside of the back of the eye that contains light-sensitive nerve cells that convert focused light into nerve impulses, making vision possible

24. PLEURA   The double-layered membrane that lines the lungs and chest cavity and allows for lung movement during breathing

25. HOOKWORM   Infestation by a small, round, blood-sucking parasite

A. Hookworm	B. Hygiene	C. Seizure	D. Platelet	E. Viral	F. Bone spur
G. Birthmark	H. Retina	I. Whipworm	J. Liver	K. Sinus	L. Dialysis
M. Hypoxia	N. Relapse	O. Tetanus	P. Tinea	Q. Pyuria	R. Triage
S. Graft	T. Osmosis	U. Pleura	V. Carditis	W. Tonsils	X. Allergy
Y. Orbit					

C. Provide the word that best matches each clue.

1. UVEITIS   Inflammation of the uvea

2. VERNIX   The thick, greasy substance that covers the skin of a newborn baby

3. MIOTIC   A drug that causes the pupil to constrict

4. RUPTURE   A tear or break in an organ or tissue

5. DEMENTIA   A gradual decline in mental ability usually caused by a brain disease, such as Alzheimer's disease

6. SHUNT   An artificially constructed or an abnormal passage connecting two usually separate structures in the body

7. NARCOSIS   A drug (or other chemical) induced drowsiness or stupor

8. VAGINA   The muscular passage connecting the uterus with the outside genitals

9. ILIUM   One of the two bones that form the hip on either side of the body

10. PELVIS   The group of bones in the lower part of the trunk that support the upper body and protect the abdominal organs

11. BONE SPUR   An abnormal growth of bone out of another bone, often located on the heel and usually painful

12. OOCYTE   An egg cell that has not developed completely

13. NEURON   Another term for a nerve cell

14. COITUS   Sexual intercourse

15. VERTEBRA   Any one of the 33 bones that make up the spine

16. B CELL   A white blood cell that makes antibodies to fight infections caused by foreign proteins

17. EMETIC   A substance that causes vomiting

18. GLUCAGON   A hormone produced by the pancreas that converts stored carbohydrates (glycogen) into glucose, the body's energy source

19. MASTITIS   Inflammation of the breast, which is usually caused by a bacterial infection

20. STROKE   Damage to part of the brain because of a lack of blood supply or the rupturing of a blood vessel

21. FUNGUS   An organism that is dependent on another organism for nourishment

22. IMPLANT   An organ, tissue, or device surgically inserted and left in the body

23. MIGRAINE   A severe headache, usually accompanied by vision problems and

24. LIGATION   The process of closing a blood vessel or duct by tying it off

25. CALCIUM   A plentiful mineral in the body and the basic component of teeth and bones

A. Miotic	B. Calcium	C. B cell	D. Vagina	E. Neuron	F. Uveitis
G. Emetic	H. Coitus	I. Glucagon	J. Pelvis	K. Fungus	L. Stroke
M. Rupture	N. Ligation	O. Ilium	P. Bone spur	Q. Vertebra	R. Vernix
S. Shunt	T. Migraine	U. Implant	V. Dementia	W. Mastitis	X. Narcosis
Y. Oocyte					

D. Provide the word that best matches each clue.

1. PH   A measure of the acidic or basic character of a substance

2. TARTAR   The hard deposit formed on teeth when mineral salts in saliva combine with plaque

3. ILIUM — One of the two bones that form the hip on either side of the body

4. UTERUS — The hollow female reproductive organ in which a fertilized egg is implanted, and a fetus develops

5. MENARCHE — The beginning of menstruation

6. CYANOSIS — A bluish discoloration of the skin caused by low levels of oxygen in the blood

7. STROKE — Damage to part of the brain because of a lack of blood supply or the rupturing of a blood vessel

8. ANTACID — A drug that neutralizes stomach acids

9. PREPUCE — The foreskin

10. ORCHITIS — Inflammation of a testicle, which can be caused by infection with the mumps virus

11. SCROTUM — The sac containing the testicles

12. VERTEBRA — Any one of the 33 bones that make up the spine

13. KYPHOSIS — Excessive curvature of the spine, which usually affects the top part of the spine and causes a hump

14. MYALGIA — The medical term for muscle pain

15. CROUP — A usually mild and temporary condition common in children under the age of 4 in which the walls of the airways become inflamed and narrow, resulting in wheezing and coughing

16. URETERS — Two tubes that carry urine from the kidneys to the bladder

17. EPILEPSY — A disorder of the nervous system in which abnormal electrical activity in the brain causes seizures

18. ANUS — The opening through which feces are passed from the body

19. LORDOSIS — The inward curvature of the spine at the lower back, which is normal to a certain degree

20. FLOATERS — Small spots that float across the field of vision, caused by debris floating in the gel-like substance that fills the eye

21. MUCUS — A slippery fluid produced by mucous membranes that lubricates and protects the internal surfaces of the body

22. AUTISM — A mental disorder characterized by an inability to relate to other people and extreme withdrawal

23. MELANOMA — A skin tumor composed of cells called melanocytes

24. CULTURE — The artificial growth of cells, tissue, or microorganisms such as bacteria in a laboratory

25. ALKALOSIS — Dangerously decreased acidity of the blood, which can be caused by high altitudes, hyperventilation, and excessive vomiting

A. Orchitis	B. Ureters	C. Myalgia	D. Epilepsy	E. Autism	F. Lordosis
G. Culture	H. Prepuce	I. Croup	J. Anus	K. Cyanosis	L. Vertebra
M. Floaters	N. Menarche	O. Uterus	P. Alkalosis	Q. Mucus	R. pH
S. Ilium	T. Melanoma	U. Tartar	V. Kyphosis	W. Stroke	X. Antacid
Y. Scrotum					

E. Provide the word that best matches each clue.

1. **CATARACT** — A disorder in which the lens of the eye becomes less transparent and, in some cases, a milky white, making vision less clear

2. **AURA** — A "warning" signal that comes before a migraine headache or an epileptic seizure, which might include emotions or sensations of movement or discomfort

3. **POLYURIA** — The excessive production of urine

4. **ADENITIS** — Infection and inflammation of a gland, especially a lymph node

5. **MYCOSIS** — Any disease caused by a fungus

6. **ECTOPIC** — Occurring at an abnormal position or time

7. **RINGWORM** — A skin infection caused by a fungus that spreads out in an even circle, characterized by ring-like, scaly patches of red skin

8. **THYROXIN** — A hormone produced by the thyroid gland that helps regulate energy production in the body

9. **CHRONIC** — Describes a disorder that continues for a long period of time

10. **TARTAR** — The hard deposit formed on teeth when mineral salts in saliva combine with plaque

11. **MEASLES** — An illness caused by a viral infection, causing a characteristic rash and a fever

12. **TIC** — An involuntary, repetitive movement such as a twitch

13. **THRILL** — A vibration felt when the hand is placed flat on the chest

14. **LABIA** — The two pairs of skinfolds that protect the opening of the vagina

15. **CECUM** — The beginning of the large intestine, which is connected to the appendix at its lower end

16. **BOOSTER** — An additional dose of a vaccine taken after the first dose to maintain or renew the first one

17. **IMAGING** — The technique of creating pictures of structures inside of the body using x-rays, ultrasound waves, or magnetic fields

18. **HOSPICE** — A hospital or an area of a hospital dedicated to treating people who are dying, often of a specific cause

19. **COLON** — The main part of the large intestine, between the cecum and the rectum

20. BONE SPUR   An abnormal growth of bone out of another bone, often located on the heel and usually painful

21. NEONATE   A term used to describe a newborn infant from birth to 1 month of age

22. SEBUM   The oily, lubricating substance that is secreted by glands in the skin

23. ALLERGY   A negative reaction to a substance that in most people causes no reaction

24. CORNEA   The clear, dome-shaped front portion of the eye's outer covering

25. FORCEPS   Instruments resembling tweezers that are used to handle objects or tissue during surgery

A. Aura	B. Cornea	C. Cecum	D. Sebum	E. Bone spur	F. Forceps
G. Ringworm	H. Ectopic	I. Imaging	J. Hospice	K. Measles	L. Booster
M. Cataract	N. Polyuria	O. Neonate	P. Adenitis	Q. Thrill	R. Colon
S. Thyroxin	T. Tartar	U. Mycosis	V. Allergy	W. Tic	X. Labia
Y. Chronic					

F. Provide the word that best matches each clue.

1. PALLOR   Abnormally pale skin

2. CAPILLARY   A tiny blood vessel that connects the smallest arteries to the smallest veins and allows exchange of oxygen and other materials between blood cells and body tissue cells

3. RHINITIS   Inflammation of the mucous membrane lining the nose

4. CORN   A thickened callus on the foot that is caused by an improperly fitting shoe

5. INSOMNIA   Difficulty falling or remaining asleep

6. B CELL   A white blood cell that makes antibodies to fight infections caused by foreign proteins

7. SCLERA   The tough, white coating that covers and protects the inner structures of the eye

8. SEIZURE   Sudden uncontrolled waves of electrical activity in the brain, causing involuntary movement or loss of consciousness

9. URETHRA   The tube by which urine is released from the bladder

10. VENOM   A poisonous substance produced by certain animals

11. TOXEMIA   The presence of bacterial toxins in the blood

12. BOOSTER   An additional dose of a vaccine taken after the first dose to maintain or renew the first one

13. THYMOMA   A tumor of the thymus gland

14. MITOSIS   The process by which most cells divide to reproduce

15. CAST — A hard plaster or fiberglass shell that molds to a body part such as an arm and holds it in place for proper healing

16. VIRUS — The smallest known disease- causing microorganism

17. MIOTIC — A drug that causes the pupil to constrict

18. PLAQUE — An area of buildup of fat deposits in an artery, causing narrowing of the artery and possibly heart disease

19. MOLECULE — The smallest unit of a substance that possesses its characteristics

20. PLEURISY — Inflammation of the lining of the lungs and chest cavity usually caused by a lung infection

21. SPERM — The male sex cell produced in the testicles

22. FETUS — The term used to refer to an unborn child from 8 weeks after fertilization to birth

23. RINGWORM — A skin infection caused by a fungus that spreads out in an even circle, characterized by ring- like, scaly patches of red skin

24. BILIRUBIN — The orange-yellow pigment in bile, causing jaundice if it builds up in the blood and skin

25. IODINE — An element for the formation of thyroid hormones

A. Sperm	B. Venom	C. Rhinitis	D. Toxemia	E. Pleurisy	F. Bilirubin
G. Booster	H. Insomnia	I. Seizure	J. Virus	K. Urethra	L. Miotic
M. Capillary	N. Molecule	O. Iodine	P. Mitosis	Q. Corn	R. Fetus
S. Plaque	T. Thymoma	U. Cast	V. B cell	W. Pallor	X. Ringworm
Y. Sclera					

G. Provide the word that best matches each clue.

1. STRAIN — Muscle damage resulting from excessive stretching or forceful contraction

2. URETERS — Two tubes that carry urine from the kidneys to the bladder

3. RADIUS — One of the two long bones of the forearm located on the thumb side of the arm

4. PENIS — The external male reproductive organ, which passes urine and semen out of the body

5. MEIOSIS — The type of cell division that occurs only in the ovaries and testicles, producing cells with half the genes of the original cell

6. TOXIN — A poisonous substance

7. PUPIL — The opening at the center of the iris in the eye that constricts (contracts) and dilates (widens) in response to light

8. TONSILS — Masses of lymphoid tissue located at either side of the back of the throat

9. PTOSIS — The drooping of the upper eyelid

10. ASPHYXIA — The medical term for suffocation

11. GANGLION — A fluid-filled cyst attached to a tendon sheath or joint

12. PARESIS — Partial paralysis

13. NEOPLASM — Another term for a tumor

14. FAMILIAL — A term describing a disorder or characteristic (such as male pattern baldness) that occurs within a family more often than would be expected

15. TRACHOMA — A persistent, contagious form of conjunctivitis that can lead to complications such as blindness if untreated

16. SEMEN — Fluid released during ejaculation that contains sperm along with fluids produced by the prostate gland and the seminal vesicles

17. LIPIDS — A group of fats stored in the body and used for energy

18. PATIENT — Controlled analgesia- a system for administering pain- killing drugs in which the amount of drug delivered is controlled by the patient

19. FUNGUS — An organism that is dependent on another organism for nourishment

20. MALARIA — A parasitic disease spread by mosquitos that causes chills and fever

21. ZYGOTE — The cell that results when an egg is fertilized by a sperm

22. HERNIA — The bulging of an organ or tissue through a weakened area in the muscle wall

23. CYST — A lump filled with either fluid or soft material, occurring in any organ or tissue

24. MINIPILL — An oral contraceptive containing only the synthetic hormone progesterone (birth control pills contain estrogen and progesterone)

25. PROTEINS — Large molecules made up of amino acids that play many major roles in the body, including forming the basis of body structures.

A. Meiosis	B. Lipids	C. Semen	D. Penis	E. Ureters	F. Radius
G. Proteins	H. Strain	I. Familial	J. Neoplasm	K. Patient	L. Pupil
M. Tonsils	N. Ptosis	O. Toxin	P. Minipill	Q. Malaria	R. Trachoma
S. Ganglion	T. Cyst	U. Hernia	V. Asphyxia	W. Paresis	X. Zygote
Y. Fungus					

H. Provide the word that best matches each clue.

1. ANEMIA — A condition in which the blood does not contain enough hemoglobin, the compound that carries oxygen from the lungs to other parts of the body

2. OSTEITIS — Inflammation of bone

3. MITES — Small eight-legged animals, many of which burrow and feed on blood

4. EMETIC — A substance that causes vomiting

5. STERNUM — The long, flat bone located at the center of the chest

6. MIGRAINE — A severe headache, usually accompanied by vision problems and

7. VOLVULUS — Twisting and obstruction of an area of intestine

8. PUPIL — The opening at the center of the iris in the eye that constricts (contracts) and dilates (widens) in response to light

9. UREA — A waste product of the metabolism of proteins that is formed by the liver and secreted by the kidneys

10. MYELITIS — Inflammation of the spinal cord, which can cause headaches, fever, muscle stiffness, pain, weakness, and eventually paralysis

11. REFLEX — An automatic, involuntary response of the nervous system to a stimulus

12. TRISOMY — The presence in the cells of three copies of a certain chromosome instead of the normal two copies

13. SACRUM — The triangular bone located at the bottom of the spine that is connected to the tailbone

14. SEIZURE — Sudden uncontrolled waves of electrical activity in the brain, causing involuntary movement or loss of consciousness

15. DEMENTIA — A gradual decline in mental ability usually caused by a brain disease, such as Alzheimer's disease

16. ANEURYSM — An abnormal swelling of the wall of an artery, caused by a weakening in the vessel wall

17. MYELOMA — A cancer affecting cells in the bone marrow

18. ATROPHY — The shrinkage or near disappearance of a tissue or organ

19. PRION — An agent that is believed to cause several degenerative brain diseases

20. PLACEBO — A chemically inactive substance given in place of a drug to test how much of a drug's effectiveness can be attributed to a patient's expectations that the drug will have a positive effect

21. TAPEWORM — A parasitic worm that lives in the intestines

22. GLIOMA — A brain tumor arising from cells that support nerve cells

23. FAMILIAL — A term describing a disorder or characteristic (such as male pattern baldness) that occurs within a family more often than would be expected

24. OZONE — A poisonous form of oxygen that is present in the earth's upper atmosphere, where it helps to screen the earth from damaging ultraviolet rays

25. PUS — A thick, yellowish or greenish fluid that contains dead white blood cells, tissues, and bacteria; occurs at the site of a bacterial infection

A. Pupil	B. Sternum	C. Anemia	D. Urea	E. Myelitis	F. Trisomy
G. Aneurysm	H. Atrophy	I. Ozone	J. Prion	K. Tapeworm	L. Sacrum
M. Mites	N. Osteitis	O. Pus	P. Glioma	Q. Emetic	R. Seizure
S. Migraine	T. Reflex	U. Volvulus	V. Dementia	W. Familial	X. Myeloma
Y. Placebo					

I. Provide the word that best matches each clue.

1. SHUNT — An artificially constructed or an abnormal passage connecting two usually separate structures in the body

2. THROMBUS — A blood clot in a blood vessel

3. AORTA — The main artery in the body, carrying oxygenated blood from the heart to other arteries in the body

4. RABIES — An infectious viral disease primarily affecting animals

5. MANDIBLE — Another term for the lower jaw

6. BURSA — A fluid-filled sac that cushions and reduces friction in certain parts of the body

7. GLYCOGEN — The main form that glucose, the body's energy source, takes when it is stored

8. TINEA — A group of common infections occurring on the skin, hair, and nails that are caused by a fungus

9. PATHOGEN — Any substance capable of causing a disease

10. SALINE — A salt solution or any substance that contains salt

11. ADDICTION — Dependence on a substance (such as alcohol or other drugs) or an activity, to the point that stopping is very difficult and causes severe physical and mental reactions

12. BYPASS — A surgical technique in which the flow of blood or another body fluid is redirected around a blockage

13. SEIZURE — Sudden uncontrolled waves of electrical activity in the brain, causing involuntary movement or loss of consciousness

14. CATARACT — A disorder in which the lens of the eye becomes less transparent and, in some cases, a milky white, making vision less clear

15. ANDROGEN — A hormone (such as testosterone) that causes development of male characteristics and sex organs

16. TICKS — Small, eight-legged animals that can attach to humans and animals and feed on blood

17. TAPEWORM — A parasitic worm that lives in the intestines

18. FEMUR — The bone located between the hip and the knee

19. MITOSIS — The process by which most cells divide to reproduce

20. OTORRHEA — A discharge from an inflamed ear

21. DEMENTIA — A gradual decline in mental ability usually caused by a brain disease, such as Alzheimer's disease

22. ECG — An electrocardiogram, which is a record of the electrical impulses that trigger the heartbeat; used to diagnose heart disorders

23. PARASITE — Organisms that lives on or in other organisms, from which it obtains nutrients

24. SEPSIS — The infection of a wound or tissue with bacteria, causing the spread of the bacteria into the bloodstream

25. COCHLEA — A coiled organ in the inner ear that plays a large role in hearing by picking up sound vibrations and transmitting them as electrical signals

A. Parasite	B. Femur	C. Shunt	D. Tinea	E. Saline	F. Rabies
G. Addiction	H. Pathogen	I. Seizure	J. Otorrhea	K. Cochlea	L. Mitosis
M. Bypass	N. Bursa	O. Aorta	P. Cataract	Q. Glycogen	R. Thrombus
S. ECG	T. Tapeworm	U. Dementia	V. Ticks	W. Androgen	X. Mandible
Y. Sepsis					

J. Provide the word that best matches each clue.

1. FOLLICLE — A tiny pouchlike cavity in a structure of the body, such as a hair follicle

2. SEBUM — The oily, lubricating substance that is secreted by glands in the skin

3. RETINA — A membrane lining the inside of the back of the eye that contains light-sensitive nerve cells that convert focused light into nerve impulses, making vision possible

4. INFUSION — The introduction of a substance, such as a drug or nutrient, into the bloodstream or a body cavity

5. SILICONE — A group of compounds of silicon and oxygen

6. CROUP — A usually mild and temporary condition common in children under the age of 4 in which the walls of the airways become inflamed and narrow, resulting in wheezing and coughing

7. WALLEYE — A condition in which one eye turns outward

8. ALKALOSIS — Dangerously decreased acidity of the blood, which can be caused by high altitudes, hyperventilation, and excessive vomiting

9. CLITORIS — A small female organ located near the opening of the vagina that swells when sexually aroused

10. MYELITIS — Inflammation of the spinal cord, which can cause headaches, fever, muscle stiffness, pain, weakness, and eventually paralysis

11. TRACHEA — The tube running from the larynx (the voice box) down the neck and into the upper part of the chest

12. PROXIMAL — Located nearer to a central point of reference on the body, such as the trunk

13. NAUSEA — Feeling the need to vomit

14. IN VIVO — "in the living body"; a biological process that occurs inside of the body

15. BONE SPUR — An abnormal growth of bone out of another bone, often located on the heel and usually painful

16. VAGINA — The muscular passage connecting the uterus with the outside genitals

17. EPIDEMIC — A term used to describe a disease that is rare then suddenly affects more people than usually expected

18. MITES — Small eight-legged animals, many of which burrow and feed on blood

19. OXIMETRY — Determination of the amount of oxygen in the blood by measuring the amount of light transmitted through an area of skin

20. MEDULLA — The center part of an organ or body structure

21. STROKE — Damage to part of the brain because of a lack of blood supply or the rupturing of a blood vessel

22. ADENITIS — Infection and inflammation of a gland, especially a lymph node

23. IRIS — The colored part of the eye

24. COLITIS — Inflammation of the large intestine (the colon), which usually leads to abdominal pain, fever, and diarrhea with blood and mucus

25. OZONE — A poisonous form of oxygen that is present in the earth's upper atmosphere, where it helps to screen the earth from damaging ultraviolet rays

A. Trachea	B. Follicle	C. Retina	D. Alkalosis	E. Nausea	F. Stroke
G. Colitis	H. Ozone	I. Bone spur	J. Adenitis	K. In vivo	L. Croup
M. Oximetry	N. Iris	O. Vagina	P. Walleye	Q. Myelitis	R. Silicone
S. Mites	T. Infusion	U. Epidemic	V. Proximal	W. Medulla	X. Clitoris
Y. Sebum					

K. Provide the word that best matches each clue.

1. PELLAGRA — A deficiency of the vitamin niacin; causes dermatitis, diarrhea, and mental disorders

2. ANATOMY — The structure of bodies

3. CARCINOMA — A cancer that occurs on the surface or lining of an organ

4. FAMILIAL — A term describing a disorder or characteristic (such as male pattern baldness) that occurs within a family more often than would be expected

5. VERSION — A shift in the position of the fetus inside of the uterus, either occurring naturally or as performed by a doctor to facilitate delivery

6. VULVITIS — Inflammation of the vulva

7. CALLUS — A thickened area of skin due to consistent pressure or friction, or the area around a bone break where new bone is formed

8. TOXEMIA — The presence of bacterial toxins in the blood

9. PROGERIA — An extremely rare condition in which the body ages prematurely

10. PREPUCE — The foreskin

11. DIURETIC — A drug that increases the amount of water in the urine, removing excess water from the body

12. UTERUS — The hollow female reproductive organ in which a fertilized egg is implanted, and a fetus develops

13. PULSE — The expansion and contraction of a blood vessel due to the blood pumped through it

14. VULVA — The outer, visible portion of the female genitals

15. MUCOCELE — A sac or body cavity that is swollen because of the production of mucus by the cells in its lining

16. SPLEEN — An organ located in the upper left abdomen behind the ribs that removes and destroys old red blood cells and helps fight infection

17. ALKALOSIS — Dangerously decreased acidity of the blood, which can be caused by high altitudes, hyperventilation, and excessive vomiting

18. RADON — A colorless, odorless, tasteless radioactive gas that is produced by materials in soil, rocks, and building materials; suspected of causing cancer

19. OSMOSIS — The process of passage of the solvent portion of a lesser-concentrated solution through a semipermeable membrane into a higher-concentrated solution until the two solutions are equal in concentration

20. PROXIMAL — Located nearer to a central point of reference on the body, such as the trunk

21. HOSPICE — A hospital or an area of a hospital dedicated to treating people who are dying, often of a specific cause

22. **NEONATE** — A term used to describe a newborn infant from birth to 1 month of age

23. **ANDROGEN** — A hormone (such as testosterone) that causes development of male characteristics and sex organs

24. **MYALGIA** — The medical term for muscle pain

25. **ESTROGEN** — A group of hormones (produced mainly in the ovaries) that are necessary for female sexual development and reproductive functioning

A. Carcinoma	B. Diuretic	C. Proximal	D. Callus	E. Spleen	F. Osmosis
G. Radon	H. Anatomy	I. Toxemia	J. Mucocele	K. Version	L. Vulvitis
M. Vulva	N. Pellagra	O. Pulse	P. Androgen	Q. Uterus	R. Alkalosis
S. Myalgia	T. Prepuce	U. Familial	V. Estrogen	W. Hospice	X. Progeria
Y. Neonate					

L. Provide the word that best matches each clue.

1. **STENT** — A device used to hold tissues in place, such as to support a skin graft

2. **HIVES** — The common term for urticaria, an itchy, inflamed rash that results from an allergic reaction

3. **COCCYX** — Four fused bones that form a triangular shape at the base of the spine (also known as the tailbone)

4. **PHIMOSIS** — Tightness of the foreskin, which prevents it from being moved back over the head of the penis

5. **COITUS** — Sexual intercourse

6. **STOMA** — A surgically formed opening on a body surface

7. **MURMUR** — A characteristic sound of blood flowing irregularly through the heart

8. **PLAGUE** — A serious infectious disease transmitted to humans through bites of rodent fleas

9. **HEMATOMA** — An accumulation of blood from a broken blood vessel

10. **ANATOMY** — The structure of bodies

11. **GENOME** — The complete set of an organism's genes

12. **RETINA** — A membrane lining the inside of the back of the eye that contains light-sensitive nerve cells that convert focused light into nerve impulses, making vision possible

13. **LUNGS** — Two organs in the chest that take in oxygen from the air and release carbon dioxide

14. **SCROTUM** — The sac containing the testicles

15. **PLEURISY** — Inflammation of the lining of the lungs and chest cavity usually caused by a lung infection

16. ACNE — A skin condition characterized by inflamed, pus-filled areas that occur on the skin's surface, most commonly occurring during adolescence

17. MALARIA — A parasitic disease spread by mosquitos that causes chills and fever

18. PANDEMIC — A widespread epidemic

19. FETUS — The term used to refer to an unborn child from 8 weeks after fertilization to birth

20. HYSTERIA — A term used to describe symptoms that are caused by mental stress and occur in someone who does not have a mental disorder

21. OSTEOMA — A noncancerous bone tumor

22. VENOM — A poisonous substance produced by certain animals

23. CELL — The tiny structures that make up all the tissues of the body and carry out all its functions

24. GLUCAGON — A hormone produced by the pancreas that converts stored carbohydrates (glycogen) into glucose, the body's energy source

25. CALCIUM — A plentiful mineral in the body and the basic component of teeth and bones

A. Glucagon	B. Pandemic	C. Anatomy	D. Acne	E. Stoma	F. Stent
G. Calcium	H. Lungs	I. Pleurisy	J. Retina	K. Murmur	L. Cell
M. Phimosis	N. Coitus	O. Coccyx	P. Hives	Q. Osteoma	R. Hysteria
S. Plague	T. Genome	U. Hematoma	V. Malaria	W. Venom	X. Scrotum
Y. Fetus					

M. Provide the word that best matches each clue.

1. ATRIA — The two upper chambers of the heart

2. STERNUM — The long, flat bone located at the center of the chest

3. SEMINOMA — A type of testicular cancer that is made up of only a single type of cell

4. TRAUMA — Physical injury or emotional shock

5. GOUT — A disorder marked by high levels of uric acid in the blood

6. PUPIL — The opening at the center of the iris in the eye that constricts (contracts) and dilates (widens) in response to light

7. CROUP — A usually mild and temporary condition common in children under the age of 4 in which the walls of the airways become inflamed and narrow, resulting in wheezing and coughing

8. POLYP — A growth that occurs on mucous membranes such as those in the nose and intestine

9. SPINE — The column of bones and cartilage running along the midline of the back that surrounds and protects the spinal cord and supports the head

10. ACQUIRED — A word describing any condition that is not present at birth, but develops some time during life

11. MENINGES — The three membranes that surround and protect the spinal cord and brain

12. SYNDROME — A group of symptoms that indicate a certain disorder when they occur together

13. EPIDEMIC — A term used to describe a disease that is rare then suddenly affects more people than usually expected

14. ASCITES — Excess fluid in the abdominal cavity, which leads to swelling

15. MANIA — A mental disorder characterized by extreme excitement, happiness, overactivity, and agitation

16. PYROGEN — Any substance that causes a fever

17. OXIMETRY — Determination of the amount of oxygen in the blood by measuring the amount of light transmitted through an area of skin

18. PHLEGM — Mucus and other material produced by the lining of the respiratory tract

19. TRIAGE — A system used to classify sick or injured people according to the severity of their conditions

20. ACUTE — Describes a condition or illness that begins suddenly and is usually short-lasting

21. ANEURYSM — An abnormal swelling of the wall of an artery, caused by a weakening in the vessel wall

22. MICROBE — Another term for a microorganism, especially one that causes disease

23. GLIOMA — A brain tumor arising from cells that support nerve cells

24. MITES — Small eight-legged animals, many of which burrow and feed on blood

25. CORONARY — Describes structures that encircle another structure

A. Epidemic   B. Ascites   C. Coronary   D. Microbe   E. Croup   F. Oximetry
G. Meninges   H. Mites   I. Polyp   J. Atria   K. Syndrome   L. Mania
M. Phlegm   N. Trauma   O. Spine   P. Aneurysm   Q. Acquired   R. Pupil
S. Sternum   T. Gout   U. Glioma   V. Seminoma   W. Triage   X. Acute
Y. Pyrogen

N. Provide the word that best matches each clue.

1. CATARACT — A disorder in which the lens of the eye becomes less transparent and, in some cases, a milky white, making vision less clear

2. TIC — An involuntary, repetitive movement such as a twitch

3. GASTRIN — A hormone that stimulates the release of gastric acid in the stomach

4. STEROIDS — A group of drugs which resemble hormones produced by the adrenal glands, and anabolic steroids, which are like the hormones produced by the male sex organs

5. WART — A contagious, harmless growth caused by a virus that occurs on the skin or a mucous membrane

6. TAPEWORM — A parasitic worm that lives in the intestines

7. CARDITIS — Inflammation of the heart

8. PARASITE — Organisms that lives on or in other organisms, from which it obtains nutrients

9. MENINGES — The three membranes that surround and protect the spinal cord and brain

10. THYROXIN — A hormone produced by the thyroid gland that helps regulate energy production in the body

11. CILIA — Tiny, hair like structures on the outside of some cells, providing mobility

12. PLACENTA — An organ formed in the uterus during pregnancy that links the blood of the mother to the blood of the fetus

13. VALVE — A structure that allows fluid flow in only one direction

14. MUCUS — A slippery fluid produced by mucous membranes that lubricates and protects the internal surfaces of the body

15. HYPOXIA — A reduced level of oxygen in tissues

16. BLADDER — An organ located in the pelvis whose function is to collect and store urine until it is expelled

17. SUTURE — A surgical stitch that helps close an incision or wound so that it can heal properly

18. LABIA — The two pairs of skinfolds that protect the opening of the vagina

19. PUBERTY — The period during which sexual development occurs

20. CHANCRE — A painless sore that has a thick, rubbery base and a defined edge

21. FORESKIN — The loose skin that covers the head of the penis

22. OXYTOCIN — A hormone produced in the pituitary gland that causes contraction of the uterus during childbirth and stimulation of milk flow during breast-feeding.

23. FUNGUS — An organism that is dependent on another organism for nourishment

24. EMBOLISM — The blockage of a blood vessel by an embolus- something previously circulating in the blood (such as a blood clot, gas bubble, tissue, bacteria, bone marrow, cholesterol, fat, etc.)

25. MUTAGEN — Anything that can increase the rate of abnormal change in cells, which can lead to cancer

A. Mucus	B. Tic	C. Valve	D. Mutagen	E. Suture	F. Embolism
G. Oxytocin	H. Carditis	I. Fungus	J. Steroids	K. Placenta	L. Labia
M. Thyroxin	N. Chancre	O. Cataract	P. Cilia	Q. Parasite	R. Bladder
S. Foreskin	T. Tapeworm	U. Meninges	V. Gastrin	W. Wart	X. Hypoxia
Y. Puberty					

O. Provide the word that best matches each clue.

1. VIREMIA — The presence of viruses in the blood

2. CHANCRE — A painless sore that has a thick, rubbery base and a defined edge

3. ILIUM — One of the two bones that form the hip on either side of the body

4. FORESKIN — The loose skin that covers the head of the penis

5. ALKALOSIS — Dangerously decreased acidity of the blood, which can be caused by high altitudes, hyperventilation, and excessive vomiting

6. OZONE — A poisonous form of oxygen that is present in the earth's upper atmosphere, where it helps to screen the earth from damaging ultraviolet rays

7. CYANOSIS — A bluish discoloration of the skin caused by low levels of oxygen in the blood

8. NODULE — A small lump of tissue that is usually abnormal

9. ELECTIVE — Describes a treatment or procedure that is not urgent and can be arranged at the patient's convenience

10. PELVIS — The group of bones in the lower part of the trunk that support the upper body and protect the abdominal organs

11. SALINE — A salt solution or any substance that contains salt

12. PARESIS — Partial paralysis

13. BACILLUS — Any bacteria that is rod-shaped

14. PHOBIA — A persisting fear of and desire to avoid something

15. RNA — Ribonucleic acid, which helps to decode and process the information contained in DNA

16. TRACHOMA — A persistent, contagious form of conjunctivitis that can lead to complications such as blindness if untreated

17. TRISOMY — The presence in the cells of three copies of a certain chromosome instead of the normal two copies

18. CEREBRUM — The largest part of the brain and the site of most of its activity, including sensory and motor functions

19. OSTEITIS — Inflammation of bone

20. IMPLANT — An organ, tissue, or device surgically inserted and left in the body

21. SCABIES — A highly contagious skin disorder caused by a mite that burrows into the skin and produces an intense, itchy rash

22. CLUBFOOT — A genetic disorder in which the foot is twisted and misshapen

23. HIVES — The common term for urticaria, an itchy, inflamed rash that results from an allergic reaction

24. RUBELLA — A mild viral infection (also known as German measles) that produces a rash and fever

25. MOLECULE — The smallest unit of a substance that possesses its characteristics

A. Trisomy	B. Bacillus	C. Nodule	D. Saline	E. Trachoma	F. Clubfoot
G. Hives	H. Cyanosis	I. Paresis	J. Elective	K. Cerebrum	L. Scabies
M. Ilium	N. Implant	O. Osteitis	P. Foreskin	Q. Molecule	R. Pelvis
S. Chancre	T. Ozone	U. Alkalosis	V. Viremia	W. Rubella	X. RNA
Y. Phobia					

P. Provide the word that best matches each clue.

1. NUTRIENT — Any substance that the body can use to maintain its health

2. CULTURE — The artificial growth of cells, tissue, or microorganisms such as bacteria in a laboratory

3. XANTHINE — A bronchodilator drug that is used to treat asthma

4. VAGINA — The muscular passage connecting the uterus with the outside genitals

5. CALORIE — A unit that is used to measure the energy content in food

6. SCURVY — A disease caused by a lack of vitamin c, characterized by weakness, bleeding and pain in joints and muscles, bleeding gums, and abnormal bone and tooth growth

7. ORTHOTIC — A device used to correct or control deformed bones, muscles, or joints

8. GRAFT — Healthy tissue that is used to replace diseased or defective tissue

9. FEMUR — The bone located between the hip and the knee

10. PTOSIS — The drooping of the upper eyelid

11. MALARIA — A parasitic disease spread by mosquitos that causes chills and fever

12. MENINGES — The three membranes that surround and protect the spinal cord and brain

13. VIREMIA — The presence of viruses in the blood

14. GANGLION   A fluid-filled cyst attached to a tendon sheath or joint

15. AUTISM   A mental disorder characterized by an inability to relate to other people and extreme withdrawal

16. OPTIC   Pertaining to the eyes

17. ACNE   A skin condition characterized by inflamed, pus-filled areas that occur on the skin's surface, most commonly occurring during adolescence

18. B CELL   A white blood cell that makes antibodies to fight infections caused by foreign proteins

19. VACCINE   A preparation of weakened microorganisms given to create resistance to a certain disease

20. PANDEMIC   A widespread epidemic

21. ANDROGEN   A hormone (such as testosterone) that causes development of male characteristics and sex organs

22. FRACTURE   A bone break

23. RADIUS   One of the two long bones of the forearm located on the thumb side of the arm

24. PLAQUE   An area of buildup of fat deposits in an artery, causing narrowing of the artery and possibly heart disease

25. IN VITRO   "in glass"; a biological test or process that is carried out in a laboratory

A. Androgen	B. Optic	C. Ganglion	D. Culture	E. Vaccine	F. Calorie
G. Malaria	H. B cell	I. Scurvy	J. Fracture	K. Femur	L. Vagina
M. Meninges	N. Plaque	O. Nutrient	P. Ptosis	Q. Radius	R. Viremia
S. Autism	T. Orthotic	U. In vitro	V. Graft	W. Pandemic	X. Xanthine
Y. Acne					

Q. Provide the word that best matches each clue.

1. PYREXIA   A body temperature of above 98.6°f in the mouth or 99.8°f in the rectum

2. IODINE   An element for the formation of thyroid hormones

3. ENURESIS   The medical term for wetting the bed

4. INFUSION   The introduction of a substance, such as a drug or nutrient, into the bloodstream or a body cavity

5. CALCIUM   A plentiful mineral in the body and the basic component of teeth and bones

6. MYALGIA   The medical term for muscle pain

7. LIPIDS   A group of fats stored in the body and used for energy

8. PREPUCE   The foreskin

9. PLATELET — The smallest particle found in the blood, which plays a major role in forming blood clots

10. FLUKE — A parasitic flatworm that can infest humans

11. IN VIVO — "in the living body"; a biological process that occurs inside of the body

12. TONSILS — Masses of lymphoid tissue located at either side of the back of the throat

13. SAFE SEX — Measures taken to reduce the risk of acquiring a sexually transmitted disease, such as the use of a condom

14. FISTULA — An abnormal passageway from one organ to another or from an organ to the body surface

15. TUMOR — An abnormal mass that occurs when cells in a certain area reproduce unchecked

16. CEREBRUM — The largest part of the brain and the site of most of its activity, including sensory and motor functions

17. PENIS — The external male reproductive organ, which passes urine and semen out of the body

18. SPERM — The male sex cell produced in the testicles

19. DUODENUM — The first part of the small intestine, immediately following the stomach

20. FIBER — A constituent of plants that cannot be digested, which helps maintain healthy functioning of the bowels

21. GOUT — A disorder marked by high levels of uric acid in the blood

22. MUTATION — A change in the genetic information within a cell

23. VULVITIS — Inflammation of the vulva

24. CHRONIC — Describes a disorder that continues for a long period of time

25. KYPHOSIS — Excessive curvature of the spine, which usually affects the top part of the spine and causes a hump

A. Pyrexia	B. In vivo	C. Chronic	D. Gout	E. Fluke
F. Calcium	G. Penis	H. Infusion	I. Tonsils	J. Cerebrum
K. Enuresis	L. Prepuce	M. Sperm	N. Fiber	O. Mutation
P. Lipids	Q. Myalgia	R. Fistula	S. Vulvitis	T. Tumor
U. Safe sex	V. Kyphosis	W. Duodenum	X. Iodine	Y. Platelet

R. Provide the word that best matches each clue.

1. STENOSIS — Narrowing of a body passageway

2. ALKALOSIS — Dangerously decreased acidity of the blood, which can be caused by high altitudes, hyperventilation, and excessive vomiting

3. GANGLION — A fluid-filled cyst attached to a tendon sheath or joint

4. THROMBUS — A blood clot in a blood vessel

5. OXYTOCIN — A hormone produced in the pituitary gland that causes contraction of the uterus during childbirth and stimulation of milk flow during breast-feeding.

6. B CELL — A white blood cell that makes antibodies to fight infections caused by foreign proteins

7. SACRUM — The triangular bone located at the bottom of the spine that is connected to the tailbone

8. CALORIE — A unit that is used to measure the energy content in food

9. CARDITIS — Inflammation of the heart

10. PHARYNX — The throat

11. BUNION — A hard, fluid-filled pad along the inside joint of the big toe

12. NITRATES — A group of drugs that widen blood vessels

13. INHALER — A device used to introduce a powdered or misted drug into the lungs through the mouth, usually to treat respiratory disorders such as asthma

14. SYPHILIS — A sexually transmitted disease

15. MENARCHE — The beginning of menstruation

16. FIBROMA — A noncancerous tumor of connective tissue

17. EPIDEMIC — A term used to describe a disease that is rare then suddenly affects more people than usually expected

18. SYNDROME — A group of symptoms that indicate a certain disorder when they occur together

19. CLONE — An exact copy of a gene, cell, or organism

20. TRAUMA — Physical injury or emotional shock

21. ORCHITIS — Inflammation of a testicle, which can be caused by infection with the mumps virus

22. TRACHEA — The tube running from the larynx (the voice box) down the neck and into the upper part of the chest

23. ATRIA — The two upper chambers of the heart

24. NERVE — A bundle of fibers that transmit electrical messages between the brain and areas of the body

25. MEIOSIS — The type of cell division that occurs only in the ovaries and testicles, producing cells with half the genes of the original cell

A. Trachea   B. Alkalosis   C. B cell   D. Syndrome   E. Inhaler   F. Carditis
G. Ganglion   H. Thrombus   I. Nerve   J. Menarche   K. Pharynx   L. Orchitis
M. Sacrum   N. Fibroma   O. Epidemic   P. Nitrates   Q. Calorie   R. Bunion
S. Syphilis   T. Stenosis   U. Clone   V. Meiosis   W. Atria   X. Trauma
Y. Oxytocin

S. Provide the word that best matches each clue.

1. NEURITIS — Inflammation of a nerve, often characterized by pain, numbness, or tingling

2. OTALGIA — The medical term for an earache

3. ILIUM — One of the two bones that form the hip on either side of the body

4. PINWORM — A small parasite worm that can live in the intestines

5. CAROTENE — An orange pigment present in colored plants such as carrots that is converted by the body to the essential nutrient vitamin a

6. LIGAMENT — A tough, elastic band of tissue that connects bones and supports organs

7. MITOSIS — The process by which most cells divide to reproduce

8. CLUBFOOT — A genetic disorder in which the foot is twisted and misshapen

9. BULIMIA — A disorder in which a person eats large amounts of food then forces vomiting or uses laxatives to prevent weight gain (called binging and purging)

10. KELOID — A raised, firm, thick scar that forms because of a defect in the natural healing process

11. CEREBRUM — The largest part of the brain and the site of most of its activity, including sensory and motor functions

12. NEPHRONS — The tiny filtering units of the kidney

13. MEASLES — An illness caused by a viral infection, causing a characteristic rash and a fever

14. LOCKJAW — A spasm of the jaw muscles that prevents the mouth from opening, such as that caused by tetanus

15. PRION — An agent that is believed to cause several degenerative brain diseases

16. BACTERIUM — A tiny, single-celled microorganism, commonly known as a germ

17. VALVE — A structure that allows fluid flow in only one direction

18. DOPAMINE — A chemical that transmits messages in the brain and plays a role in movement

19. TOXICITY — The extent to which a substance is poisonous

20. CORN — A thickened callus on the foot that is caused by an improperly fitting shoe

21. SMALLPOX — A highly contagious and often fatal viral infection that has been completely eradicated by immunization

22. RINGWORM — A skin infection caused by a fungus that spreads out in an even circle, characterized by ring-like, scaly patches of red skin

23. MYELOMA — A cancer affecting cells in the bone marrow

24. TENDON — Strong connective tissue cords that attach muscle to bone or muscle to muscle

25. ORCHITIS — Inflammation of a testicle, which can be caused by infection with the mumps virus

A. Otalgia	B. Cerebrum	C. Lockjaw	D. Keloid	E. Valve	F. Bulimia
G. Mitosis	H. Myeloma	I. Smallpox	J. Toxicity	K. Neuritis	L. Ringworm
M. Nephrons	N. Pinworm	O. Measles	P. Prion	Q. Dopamine	R. Ilium
S. Carotene	T. Bacterium	U. Ligament	V. Tendon	W. Orchitis	X. Clubfoot
Y. Corn					

T. Provide the word that best matches each clue.

1. ERYTHEMA — Redness of the skin

2. APNEA — A possibly life-threatening condition in which breathing stops, for either a short or long period of time

3. RECTUM — A short tube located at the end of the large intestine, which connects the intestine to the anus

4. PALLOR — Abnormally pale skin

5. GLAND — A group of cells or an organ that produces substances (such as hormones and enzyme) that are used by the body

6. ARTERY — A large blood vessel that carries blood from the heart to tissues and organs in the body

7. SPINE — The column of bones and cartilage running along the midline of the back that surrounds and protects the spinal cord and supports the head

8. BILATERAL — A term describing a condition that affects both sides of the body or two paired organs, such as bilateral deafness (deafness in both ears)

9. WHIPWORM — A small, parasitic worm that can live in the intestines of a human and may cause diarrhea, abdominal pain, and anemia

10. FOLLICLE — A tiny pouchlike cavity in a structure of the body, such as a hair follicle

11. MENISCUS — A crescent-shaped pad of cartilage in joints that helps to reduce friction

12. GLUCAGON   A hormone produced by the pancreas that converts stored carbohydrates (glycogen) into glucose, the body's energy source

13. NECROSIS   The medical term for the death of tissue cells

14. LATERAL   On one side

15. SERUM   The clear, watery fluid that separates from clotted blood

16. CORONARY   Describes structures that encircle another structure

17. PINWORM   A small parasite worm that can live in the intestines

18. CYST   A lump filled with either fluid or soft material, occurring in any organ or tissue

19. TRISOMY   The presence in the cells of three copies of a certain chromosome instead of the normal two copies

20. CHANCRE   A painless sore that has a thick, rubbery base and a defined edge

21. SEMINOMA   A type of testicular cancer that is made up of only a single type of cell

22. CHLAMYDIA   Microorganisms that cause several human infections and can be transmitted sexually

23. ENDEMIC   Describes a disease that is always present in a certain population of people

24. OVERDOSE   An excessively large dose of a drug, which can lead to coma and death

25. TARTAR   The hard deposit formed on teeth when mineral salts in saliva combine with plaque

A. Serum	B. Apnea	C. Follicle	D. Tartar	E. Lateral	F. Necrosis
G. Meniscus	H. Whipworm	I. Pallor	J. Rectum	K. Chlamydia	L. Spine
M. Pinworm	N. Seminoma	O. Trisomy	P. Endemic	Q. Gland	R. Erythema
S. Glucagon	T. Artery	U. Coronary	V. Overdose	W. Chancre	X. Cyst
Y. Bilateral					

Word Search

A. Find the hidden words. The words have been placed horizontally, vertically, or diagonally. When you locate a word, draw an ellipse around it.

W	U	B	I	R	T	H	M	A	R	K	U	A	X	I	L	L	A	F	X	Z	Q	O
O	C	T	F	W	F	W	R	A	N	O	A	M	D	B	N	U	P	C	U	K	F	L
O	J	E	I	U	E	P	Y	R	O	G	E	N	Z	A	B	U	N	I	O	N	P	Y
V	E	N	O	M	M	A	K	X	N	C	E	A	R	D	R	U	M	O	A	W	X	T
E	F	B	P	T	T	H	L	H	W	V	D	I	Q	E	W	R	W	C	M	A	M	Z
C	I	P	U	B	E	R	T	Y	Z	G	A	S	T	R	I	N	D	R	Q	G	N	N
U	B	N	I	S	J	I	P	P	B	X	O	S	S	D	I	R	T	S	R	L	S	Y
K	E	W	G	F	Y	P	Q	B	T	H	O	R	A	X	R	F	S	U	J	B	Q	A
Y	R	V	N	G	L	A	U	C	O	M	A	I	B	H	P	F	P	A	A	N	U	S
K	D	Y	S	P	N	E	A	O	M	U	G	M	P	Z	H	I	R	Q	L	Y	X	O
I	C	V	K	E	R	A	T	I	N	V	C	M	I	L	I	B	A	M	E	J	Z	Y
D	Z	G	A	L	K	A	L	O	S	I	S	U	N	J	M	R	I	S	E	M	E	N
N	Y	J	B	S	R	U	X	D	J	K	X	N	K	W	O	O	N	K	L	Y	Z	Z
E	E	D	T	Q	R	N	F	N	O	L	R	I	E	E	S	S	B	I	B	H	C	V
Y	X	X	U	D	Z	L	T	K	Y	G	T	Y	A	I	I	A	F	J	Z	T	V
M	S	G	V	W	E	C	J	G	Z	H	B	Y	E	W	S	S	O	H	Q	B	C	C

1. Medical term for the armpit
2. A thin, oval-shaped membrane that separates the inner ear from the outer ear and is responsible for transmitting sound waves
3. A poisonous substance produced by certain animals
4. Tightness of the foreskin, which prevents it from being moved back over the head of the penis
5. A constituent of plants that cannot be digested, which helps maintain healthy functioning of the bowels
6. A hard, fluid-filled pad along the inside joint of the big toe
7. A hormone that stimulates the release of gastric acid in the stomach
8. One of two organs that are part of the urinary tract
9. Abnormal formation of connective or scar tissue
10. A disease in which eye damage is caused by an increase in the pressure of the fluid within the eye
11. The tearing or stretching of the ligaments in a joint, characterized by pain, swelling, and an inability to move the joint
12. A tough protein found in skin, nails, and hair
13. The opening through which feces are passed from the body
14. Dangerously decreased acidity of the blood, which can be caused by high altitudes, hyperventilation, and excessive vomiting
15. The chest
16. Resistance to a specific disease because of the responses of the immune system
17. Any substance that causes a fever
18. Any area of discolored skin that is present when a baby is born
19. Difficulty breathing
20. Fluid released during ejaculation that contains sperm along with fluids produced by the prostate gland and the seminal vesicles
21. The period during which sexual development occurs
22. Inflammation of the membrane that covers the white of the eyes and lines the eyelids

A. Semen	B. Pinkeye	C. Glaucoma	D. Axilla	E. Alkalosis	F. Fibrosis
G. Eardrum	H. Anus	I. Sprain	J. Birthmark	K. Fiber	L. Dyspnea
M. Puberty	N. Bunion	O. Kidney	P. Immunity	Q. Keratin	R. Venom
S. Thorax	T. Phimosis	U. Pyrogen	V. Gastrin		

B. Find the hidden words. The words have been placed horizontally, vertically, or diagonally. When you locate a word, draw an ellipse around it.

N	Y	D	A	T	P	Z	W	Z	G	L	S	E	I	Z	U	R	E	H	Y	M	E	Q
E	Y	A	W	G	K	V	A	R	I	C	E	S	I	Q	M	J	O	O	L	B	I	I
J	P	T	U	Y	E	S	L	B	N	S	Q	L	H	L	M	W	H	O	W	B	K	K
E	K	H	C	F	H	U	T	E	R	U	S	R	Q	E	E	X	N	K	H	Q	X	W
F	S	G	L	I	N	V	A	S	I	V	E	M	N	Z	I	O	T	W	E	X	J	A
X	S	D	A	H	Y	G	I	E	N	E	C	O	M	A	Y	Y	E	O	E	E	L	R
T	N	E	C	R	O	S	I	S	X	A	U	W	J	U	D	U	J	R	Z	P	G	D
B	P	Y	W	F	C	T	I	I	X	R	T	M	D	B	X	P	S	M	E	S	R	U
A	M	O	L	H	C	A	R	D	I	T	I	S	N	I	M	P	E	T	I	G	O	T
C	Y	T	Q	E	C	E	N	Z	Y	M	E	Z	A	K	Q	P	E	N	I	S	O	B
K	Z	B	P	P	Z	P	B	O	W	E	L	E	S	T	R	O	G	E	N	C	R	J
K	Z	J	E	A	B	Y	K	I	W	O	B	R	Y	M	D	O	A	N	D	C	D	Z
S	F	Y	L	T	G	U	D	E	L	E	C	T	I	V	E	X	N	I	A	C	I	N
Z	M	P	V	O	R	R	S	O	C	R	B	P	C	S	S	Q	X	B	B	H	M	D
L	M	K	I	M	M	I	X	X	Z	S	Q	F	A	C	X	M	I	J	Z	J	Y	J
K	L	N	S	A	L	A	L	L	J	M	C	R	E	Q	U	Z	M	M	C	D	T	V

1. Describes a treatment or procedure that is not urgent and can be arranged at the patient's convenience
2. The presence of white blood cells in the urine
3. A group of hormones (produced mainly in the ovaries) that are necessary for female sexual development and reproductive functioning
4. The hollow female reproductive organ in which a fertilized egg is implanted, and a fetus develops
5. Inflammation of the heart
6. Infestation by a small, round, blood-sucking parasite
7. Deoxyribonucleic acid; responsible for passing genetic information in nearly all organisms
8. The practice, maintenance, and study of health
9. A condition in which the area of the brain involved in maintaining consciousness is somehow affected, resulting in a state of unconsciousness in which the patient does not respond to stimulation
10. Sudden uncontrolled waves of electrical activity in the brain, causing involuntary movement or loss of consciousness
11. The group of bones in the lower part of the trunk that support the upper body and protect the abdominal organs
12. A highly contagious skin infection caused by bacteria, usually occurring around the nose and mouth
13. Intestine
14. Describes something that spreads throughout body tissues, such as a tumor or microorganism
15. Enlarged or twisted blood or lymph vessels
16. A chemical, originating in a cell, that regulates reactions in the body
17. A vitamin important in many chemical processes in the body; also known as vitamin b3
18. The external male reproductive organ, which passes urine and semen out of the body
19. A cancerous tumor of the liver
20. A high-pitched sound produced during breathing because of narrowing of the airways
21. The medical term for the death of tissue cells

A. Enzyme
B. Seizure
C. Hookworm
D. DNA
E. Elective
F. Niacin
G. Impetigo
H. Invasive
I. Pyuria
J. Hepatoma
K. Pelvis
L. Varices
M. Wheeze
N. Coma
O. Penis
P. Uterus
Q. Carditis
R. Estrogen
S. Hygiene
T. Bowel
U. Necrosis

C. Find the hidden words. The words have been placed horizontally, vertically, or diagonally. When you locate a word, draw an ellipse around it.

P	J	A	W	O	Z	U	G	I	N	C	R	I	D	T	C	Z	Z	Y	A	M	O	M
Q	Z	A	K	H	Y	C	O	M	A	Z	V	H	V	M	A	B	H	I	V	E	S	Q
D	O	F	T	P	A	K	Q	S	C	U	R	V	Y	E	R	I	X	L	R	C	D	P
O	X	R	M	Y	H	R	G	M	N	D	V	C	H	D	D	R	G	C	T	B	V	D
S	Y	A	V	U	G	N	O	D	E	M	E	F	G	U	I	T	B	F	J	S	O	J
B	G	C	P	R	U	L	I	I	Q	B	S	K	N	L	T	H	C	Q	S	N	I	D
T	E	T	I	I	X	Q	G	J	U	T	I	T	G	L	I	M	S	V	D	V	R	J
I	N	U	L	A	C	H	N	X	E	C	C	E	L	A	S	A	A	N	E	M	V	U
S	W	R	R	H	B	B	D	T	E	C	L	C	I	N	M	R	R	S	X	H	T	L
F	A	E	O	I	V	Z	P	R	R	C	E	Z	O	A	C	K	C	A	T	J	E	P
E	L	H	E	P	A	T	I	C	B	G	W	E	M	R	P	B	O	W	R	O	S	N
R	L	S	S	C	M	H	V	T	U	O	C	M	A	C	U	S	M	Q	O	T	R	N
F	E	C	A	P	F	B	R	Z	E	A	A	A	G	O	S	V	A	F	S	W	X	N
B	Y	Q	D	H	A	L	O	P	E	C	I	A	N	T	F	K	G	I	E	F	V	C
W	E	O	H	P	J	W	U	N	D	H	Q	A	S	I	X	M	G	P	X	O	R	E
F	O	D	N	F	R	X	P	I	X	V	W	W	I	C	M	S	R	M	J	C	J	J

1. A thick, yellowish or greenish fluid that contains dead white blood cells, tissues, and bacteria; occurs at the site of a bacterial infection
2. Inflammation of the heart
3. A gas that is colorless, odorless, and tasteless
4. A condition in which one eye turns outward
5. A term used to describe something that is related to the liver
6. Inflammation of the skin, usually causing itchiness and sometimes blisters and scaling
7. A bone break
8. The presence of white blood cells in the urine
9. A brain tumor arising from cells that support nerve cells
10. Intelligence quotient; a measure of a person's intelligence as determined by specific tests
11. Any area of discolored skin that is present when a baby is born
12. The common term for urticaria, an itchy, inflamed rash that results from an allergic reaction
13. A cancer in connective tissue, fibrous tissue, or blood vessels
14. Another name for the sugar glucose
15. A condition in which the area of the brain involved in maintaining consciousness is somehow affected, resulting in a state of unconsciousness in which the patient does not respond to stimulation
16. A small, rounded tissue mass
17. Baldness or loss of hair, mainly on the head, either in defined patches or completely
18. A disease caused by a lack of vitamin c, characterized by weakness, bleeding and pain in joints and muscles, bleeding gums, and abnormal bone and tooth growth
19. An addictive substance that blunts the senses
20. A small skin blister, or any sac in the body, that contains fluid
21. The center part of an organ or body structure

A. Alopecia   B. Hives   C. Node   D. Eczema   E. Birthmark   F. Glioma
G. Narcotic   H. Fracture   I. Hepatic   J. Pyuria   K. Pus   L. Dextrose
M. Carditis   N. Coma   O. Oxygen   P. Vesicle   Q. Walleye   R. Medulla
S. Scurvy   T. Sarcoma   U. IQ

D. Find the hidden words. The words have been placed horizontally, vertically, or diagonally. When you locate a word, draw an ellipse around it.

T	Z	D	O	Q	S	D	Q	L	Q	E	X	R	Z	E	B	D	N	E	W	X	U	K
U	D	W	P	A	B	U	L	I	M	I	A	O	Y	K	F	O	I	V	V	U	D	K
R	B	E	L	M	S	M	F	S	Z	Q	M	N	P	J	E	F	A	L	P	J	E	Z
S	A	G	U	S	P	M	U	C	O	C	E	L	E	S	A	L	C	P	B	W	E	B
R	L	E	M	C	R	L	C	H	Y	P	L	W	G	Y	N	A	I	I	B	A	H	I
K	F	N	B	K	Y	K	Z	O	B	M	W	A	L	L	U	D	N	X	M	U	I	I
M	Y	E	A	N	O	D	E	R	X	B	O	Z	U	A	C	U	T	E	E	N	V	L
P	N	V	G	B	E	O	T	M	J	Y	K	G	C	R	Q	T	C	G	L	L	E	B
F	P	C	O	M	V	I	I	O	Z	E	F	O	A	K	D	Z	U	K	A	S	S	Z
J	X	E	Z	H	I	Q	C	N	M	J	W	F	G	E	O	J	S	L	N	Z	E	I
K	G	L	I	O	M	A	L	E	Z	T	F	V	O	X	Z	Z	Z	V	O	L	C	L
G	X	U	T	M	Y	O	S	I	T	I	S	I	N	H	C	X	G	L	M	Z	T	L
L	T	Z	Q	F	R	R	Z	L	A	H	M	I	N	I	P	I	L	L	A	Z	O	P
R	I	B	I	I	R	R	Y	K	Y	G	U	Q	J	E	X	L	D	Z	R	A	P	H
T	B	I	N	V	A	S	I	V	E	X	Z	O	O	N	O	S	I	S	N	I	I	U
A	U	T	O	P	S	Y	H	E	L	Z	C	Y	S	T	G	Q	U	D	A	R	C	Y

1. A skin tumor composed of cells called melanocytes
2. Describes a condition or illness that begins suddenly and is usually short- lasting
3. A chemical produced by a gland or tissue that is released into the bloodstream
4. A brain tumor arising from cells that support nerve cells
5. An oral contraceptive containing only the synthetic hormone progesterone (birth control pills contain estrogen and progesterone)
6. A sac or body cavity that is swollen because of the production of mucus by the cells in its lining
7. Ribonucleic acid, which helps to decode and process the information contained in DNA
8. A hormone produced by the pancreas that converts stored carbohydrates (glycogen) into glucose, the body's energy source
9. Dull, aching pain in the lower back
10. A lump filled with either fluid or soft material, occurring in any organ or tissue
11. Describes something that spreads throughout body tissues, such as a tumor or microorganism
12. The common term for urticaria, an itchy, inflamed rash that results from an allergic reaction
13. Muscle inflammation, causing pain and weakness
14. The examination of a body following death, possibly to determine the cause of death or for research
15. Occurring at an abnormal position or time
16. The basic unit of DNA, which is responsible for passing genetic information
17. A vitamin important in many chemical processes in the body; also known as vitamin b3
18. A disorder in which a person eats large amounts of food then forces vomiting or uses laxatives to prevent weight gain (called binging and purging)
19. A small, rounded tissue mass
20. An involuntary, repetitive movement such as a twitch
21. A parasite- caused or infectious disease in animals that can be transferred to humans

A. Lumbago	B. Mucocele	C. Tic	D. Ectopic	E. Hives	F. Hormone
G. Bulimia	H. Node	I. Niacin	J. Cyst	K. Glucagon	L. RNA
M. Myositis	N. Acute	O. Melanoma	P. Minipill	Q. Glioma	R. Invasive
S. Gene	T. Autopsy	U. Zoonosis			

E. Find the hidden words. The words have been placed horizontally, vertically, or diagonally. When you locate a word, draw an ellipse around it.

B	P	Y	T	I	M	B	V	R	T	W	O	H	N	C	A	X	H	Z	H	Y	G	D
Z	N	K	S	P	E	R	M	I	N	N	K	S	S	E	M	E	N	P	Z	N	S	F
P	H	I	M	O	S	I	S	C	W	V	E	P	B	I	L	I	R	U	B	I	N	G
S	V	F	S	G	E	S	M	K	G	Z	Q	U	J	A	T	R	E	S	I	A	Z	I
I	V	E	V	S	S	T	X	E	P	K	J	D	U	Z	H	E	P	A	T	O	M	A
Q	C	T	D	X	B	R	P	T	H	G	E	E	S	B	H	M	F	Z	Z	N	N	H
K	W	U	E	L	J	A	H	S	D	R	Z	N	N	I	Y	G	U	X	X	V	E	C
E	A	S	O	P	E	I	K	J	C	U	Q	D	G	M	O	I	N	S	Y	P	U	C
C	V	Y	Y	R	V	N	E	S	W	T	J	U	P	A	U	I	Y	X	E	A	R	K
R	I	P	R	O	G	E	R	I	A	D	V	M	Y	G	Y	D	A	N	B	L	O	Q
T	R	A	P	T	I	M	U	Z	D	S	Y	V	V	Y	I	Z	X	L	E	V	A	S	U
U	A	O	U	E	V	C	S	S	C	E	R	E	J	N	W	A	E	Z	X	T	I	L
U	L	N	Z	I	W	L	M	E	B	D	Z	N	I	G	V	F	G	L	R	E	S	F
K	U	D	I	N	F	O	E	Y	G	U	B	O	Y	C	H	L	A	M	Y	D	I	A
L	R	C	Y	S	Z	N	A	Z	T	A	N	M	F	K	M	I	Q	T	R	P	M	A
M	W	S	Z	E	M	E	R	G	B	Q	S	N	O	P	T	I	C	I	A	N	O	S

1. The roof of the mouth
2. The external genitals, usually referring to the female
3. A childhood disease in which bones lack calcium and are deformed because of vitamin d deficiency
4. The orange-yellow pigment in bile, causing jaundice if it builds up in the blood and skin
5. Tightness of the foreskin, which prevents it from being moved back over the head of the penis
6. The male sex cell produced in the testicles
7. An extremely rare condition in which the body ages prematurely
8. A cancerous tumor of the liver
9. A poisonous substance produced by certain animals
10. An exact copy of a gene, cell, or organism
11. The technique of creating pictures of structures inside of the body using x-rays, ultrasound waves, or magnetic fields
12. A term describing something related to or caused by a virus
13. Microorganisms that cause several human infections and can be transmitted sexually
14. The term used to refer to an unborn child from 8 weeks after fertilization to birth
15. A sample of cells spread across a glass slide to be examined through a microscope
16. A birth defect in which a normal body opening, or canal is absent
17. Large molecules made up of amino acids that play many major roles in the body, including forming the basis of body structures.
18. Muscle damage resulting from excessive stretching or forceful contraction
19. A person who specializes in the making and adjustment of eyeglasses and contact lenses
20. Relatively mild emotional disorders (such as mild depression and phobias)
21. Fluid released during ejaculation that contains sperm along with fluids produced by the prostate gland and the seminal vesicles

A. Hepatoma   B. Palate   C. Fetus   D. Proteins   E. Progeria   F. Rickets
G. Pudendum   H. Clone   I. Neurosis   J. Phimosis   K. Semen   L. Sperm
M. Atresia   N. Optician   O. Venom   P. Smear   Q. Bilirubin   R. Strain
S. Imaging   T. Chlamydia   U. Viral

218

F. Find the hidden words. The words have been placed horizontally, vertically, or diagonally. When you locate a word, draw an ellipse around it.

Y	A	N	E	M	I	A	Y	T	J	A	F	B	J	V	M	F	A	P	N	E	A	Y
M	U	X	L	M	O	N	I	T	U	O	O	B	S	R	X	L	S	Y	C	I	A	Q
R	O	J	X	K	T	H	R	U	S	H	R	R	O	D	F	A	Q	U	N	J	O	U
O	A	S	T	H	M	A	B	I	E	E	C	U	Y	J	P	U	L	S	E	W	A	V
R	C	P	Q	X	K	W	X	R	V	D	E	J	C	O	E	W	P	U	Q	P	O	E
K	Y	E	O	W	Y	J	A	I	D	V	P	B	W	T	E	N	A	X	S	O	Y	R
P	A	T	H	O	G	E	N	S	N	H	S	I	H	E	P	A	T	O	M	A	Q	N
U	W	R	F	I	B	R	O	I	D	G	E	L	M	S	A	M	I	W	I	K	D	I
J	V	L	T	C	P	L	A	S	M	A	M	E	Y	O	S	I	E	R	O	J	T	X
B	Y	B	E	O	R	G	A	N	I	S	M	D	A	K	F	T	N	O	R	M	H	V
D	H	L	T	Y	Q	B	N	H	S	G	J	U	L	D	U	O	T	L	T	J	I	C
U	F	A	A	A	G	V	T	G	A	U	S	C	G	W	Z	S	D	J	K	B	P	Z
C	X	D	N	U	B	P	L	A	Q	U	E	T	I	Z	G	I	A	L	E	F	Y	Q
F	A	D	U	X	L	W	G	G	O	I	O	R	A	Q	G	S	U	L	T	C	A	T
T	W	E	S	T	P	A	T	E	L	L	A	H	K	H	T	G	U	F	K	O	B	C
E	M	R	V	B	S	M	D	U	A	R	N	G	E	U	E	U	H	I	E	M	F	T

1. The medical term for muscle pain
2. Instruments resembling tweezers that are used to handle objects or tissue during surgery
3. An organ located in the pelvis whose function is to collect and store urine until it is expelled
4. A candidiasis infection
5. The process by which most cells divide to reproduce
6. Any substance capable of causing a disease
7. A disorder characterized by inflamed airways and difficulty breathing
8. An area of buildup of fat deposits in an artery, causing narrowing of the artery and possibly heart disease
9. The thick, greasy substance that covers the skin of a newborn baby
10. A tube that carries bile from the liver to the gallbladder and then to the small intestine
11. The expansion and contraction of a blood vessel due to the blood pumped through it
12. A possibly life-threatening condition in which breathing stops, for either a short or long period of time
13. Any single, functioning form of life
14. A condition in which the blood does not contain enough hemoglobin, the compound that carries oxygen from the lungs to other parts of the body
15. A noncancerous tumor of the uterus made up of smooth muscle and connective tissue
16. The colored part of the eye
17. Controlled analgesia- a system for administering pain - killing drugs in which the amount of drug delivered is controlled by the patient
18. A sometimes fatal disease affecting the brain and spinal cord
19. The liquid part of the blood, containing substances such as nutrients, salts, and proteins
20. The medical term for the kneecap
21. A cancerous tumor of the liver

A. Tetanus   B. Patella   C. Mitosis   D. Organism   E. Forceps   F. Asthma
G. Anemia   H. Myalgia   I. Bile duct   J. Bladder   K. Vernix   L. Fibroid
M. Pathogen   N. Apnea   O. Plaque   P. Pulse   Q. Iris   R. Patient
S. Plasma   T. Hepatoma   U. Thrush

G. Find the hidden words. The words have been placed horizontally, vertically, or diagonally. When you locate a word, draw an ellipse around it.

C	R	I	E	O	O	S	T	E	R	N	U	M	R	O	R	T	H	O	T	I	C	Z
O	R	B	I	T	A	O	P	L	A	C	E	N	T	A	P	Y	U	R	I	A	S	Y
R	D	A	N	C	C	P	P	O	R	V	V	A	R	T	E	R	I	T	I	S	X	F
J	C	I	M	M	N	N	S	A	O	I	L	F	Z	B	K	W	E	P	I	M	I	C
Y	A	R	T	E	E	E	F	T	S	R	F	R	E	L	A	P	S	E	V	E	L	Z
B	F	C	F	A	L	L	E	R	G	E	N	M	V	R	A	S	H	S	J	G	X	B
L	R	T	L	Y	H	I	J	O	C	M	L	C	R	S	P	H	C	O	I	T	U	S
J	N	G	V	G	E	J	U	P	L	I	U	Y	N	R	L	D	Z	M	K	O	U	M
T	S	T	N	M	P	I	U	W	M	A	P	I	O	U	E	Y	C	O	J	X	C	I
I	L	N	Z	O	A	G	V	F	Y	M	L	F	K	B	U	B	A	S	W	I	Y	G
A	O	W	A	Y	T	B	J	X	E	H	X	W	K	E	R	D	R	F	X	E	Z	R
A	U	F	L	X	I	V	A	S	C	U	L	A	R	L	I	H	O	O	V	J	R	A
C	N	Q	R	Q	C	P	J	J	G	H	M	M	Q	L	S	Q	T	C	O	H	C	I
C	H	Z	M	X	I	N	V	I	V	O	T	V	O	A	Y	T	E	P	Q	O	M	N
D	S	S	V	Q	Q	F	G	U	U	W	Q	X	M	O	E	O	N	I	J	Z	M	E
S	B	R	P	G	L	Y	C	O	G	E	N	Q	W	V	B	W	E	T	S	R	U	I

1. The presence of viruses in the blood
2. The socket in the skull that contains the eyeball, along with its blood vessels, nerves, and muscles
3. The return of a disease or symptom after it had disappeared
4. A skin condition characterized by inflamed, pus-filled areas that occur on the skin's surface, most commonly occurring during adolescence
5. A term used to describe something that is related to the liver
6. An orange pigment present in colored plants such as carrots that is converted by the body to the essential nutrient vitamin a
7. A mild viral infection (also known as German measles) that produces a rash and fever
8. A severe headache, usually accompanied by vision problems and
9. An organ formed in the uterus during pregnancy that links the blood of the mother to the blood of the fetus
10. Pertaining to blood vessels
11. "in the living body"; a biological process that occurs inside of the body
12. A substance that causes an allergic reaction
13. A device used to correct or control deformed bones, muscles, or joints
14. An area of inflammation or a group of spots on the skin
15. Inflammation of the walls of an artery that causes the passageway to become narrower
16. Inflammation of the lining of the lungs and chest cavity usually caused by a lung infection
17. The long, flat bone located at the center of the chest
18. Sexual intercourse
19. The main form that glucose, the body's energy source, takes when it is stored
20. The presence of white blood cells in the urine

A. Orthotic	B. Glycogen	C. Allergen	D. Viremia	E. Migraine	F. Arteritis	G. Pleurisy
H. Orbit	I. Rash	J. Vascular	K. Rubella	L. Coitus	M. Sternum	N. Carotene
O. Relapse	P. Acne	Q. Hepatic	R. Placenta	S. In vivo	T. Pyuria	

H. Find the hidden words. The words have been placed horizontally, vertically, or diagonally. When you locate a word, draw an ellipse around it.

T	Y	V	L	C	I	L	I	A	X	C	V	H	M	D	W	A	T	G	H	K	E	G
H	P	A	K	Q	A	G	Z	T	J	A	E	Y	A	D	V	Z	A	C	P	D	U	F
R	T	X	L	X	Q	L	O	O	S	U	Q	Q	O	A	A	R	R	R	U	N	L	C
A	T	Y	D	X	O	L	E	S	R	R	J	M	Z	S	C	W	T	X	S	C	M	E
B	L	J	V	R	K	Z	C	L	N	A	J	D	V	T	C	V	A	R	I	O	L	A
I	M	G	N	S	W	I	O	R	B	I	T	F	R	H	I	I	R	E	L	H	F	Y
E	B	B	C	P	W	T	N	B	N	G	E	P	L	M	N	J	Y	A	M	B	C	A
S	O	W	E	D	Y	G	A	N	G	L	I	O	N	A	E	H	G	O	U	T	Z	O
X	I	V	D	Y	S	P	N	E	A	P	U	D	E	N	D	U	M	W	G	X	O	L
M	L	X	Z	W	R	Q	P	U	Z	A	F	I	B	R	O	S	I	S	J	C	L	Z
H	Q	V	D	I	G	J	T	Y	D	H	W	E	Q	F	Q	Z	G	A	Z	W	A	B
Q	J	M	K	C	F	D	P	E	O	P	P	F	A	D	P	H	I	M	O	S	I	S
O	I	C	S	Z	V	O	V	M	Z	O	I	A	C	C	M	C	G	O	F	U	W	V
G	R	I	N	G	W	O	R	M	O	V	O	D	I	O	A	A	Q	W	R	S	W	E
B	G	B	N	A	L	N	W	C	M	C	B	M	J	Q	V	I	S	N	V	D	E	G
L	T	E	T	A	N	U	S	D	E	X	T	R	O	S	E	T	R	I	S	O	M	Y

1. A thick, yellowish or greenish fluid that contains dead white blood cells, tissues, and bacteria; occurs at the site of a bacterial infection
2. A fluid-filled cyst attached to a tendon sheath or joint
3. A "warning" signal that comes before a migraine headache or an epileptic seizure, which might include emotions or sensations of movement or discomfort
4. Tiny, hair like structures on the outside of some cells, providing mobility
5. A skin infection caused by a fungus that spreads out in an even circle, characterized by ring- like, scaly patches of red skin
6. Tightness of the foreskin, which prevents it from being moved back over the head of the penis
7. A disorder characterized by inflamed airways and difficulty breathing
8. A disorder marked by high levels of uric acid in the blood
9. The external genitals, usually referring to the female
10. An inflamed, raised area of skin that is pus-filled; usually an infected hair follicle
11. A preparation of weakened microorganisms given to create resistance to a certain disease
12. An infectious viral disease primarily affecting animals
13. Another term for smallpox
14. Difficulty breathing
15. A sometimes fatal disease affecting the brain and spinal cord
16. Abnormal formation of connective or scar tissue
17. The presence in the cells of three copies of a certain chromosome instead of the normal two copies
18. The socket in the skull that contains the eyeball, along with its blood vessels, nerves, and muscles
19. Another name for the sugar glucose
20. The hard deposit formed on teeth when mineral salts in saliva combine with plaque

A. Dyspnea	B. Rabies	C. Aura	D. Vaccine	E. Fibrosis	F. Variola
G. Gout	H. Ringworm	I. Orbit	J. Dextrose	K. Ganglion	L. Trisomy
M. Asthma	N. Tartar	O. Phimosis	P. Pudendum	Q. Boil	R. Pus
S. Tetanus	T. Cilia				

I. Find the hidden words. The words have been placed horizontally, vertically, or diagonally. When you locate a word, draw an ellipse around it.

N	F	X	Z	A	X	I	L	L	A	N	S	E	L	K	P	Y	E	I	D	G	W	J
S	I	R	S	C	A	G	C	C	A	L	C	I	U	M	M	C	H	A	N	C	R	E
Q	B	K	U	N	G	Y	F	A	V	A	L	V	E	A	Y	O	S	T	E	O	M	A
W	R	Z	Q	A	A	D	M	A	E	X	A	S	L	O	O	E	H	R	C	W	D	D
L	O	M	L	E	S	K	G	U	I	C	X	R	M	E	P	P	X	I	J	N	F	S
I	M	X	S	N	T	U	R	E	T	H	R	A	U	B	I	I	V	N	M	D	D	K
G	A	C	B	X	R	O	L	U	F	M	T	I	D	X	A	H	G	O	N	W	R	N
A	W	X	D	W	I	D	F	K	Y	U	R	D	T	A	P	E	W	O	R	M	D	O
T	P	C	L	H	N	W	Z	T	G	M	K	N	D	R	I	X	P	I	M	K	T	C
I	E	U	G	N	M	S	T	Y	E	P	U	A	Y	W	P	G	Z	O	Y	W	M	T
O	N	P	T	Q	C	H	B	H	Y	S	N	A	H	O	R	M	O	N	E	D	K	U
N	I	E	A	N	U	S	I	Z	C	H	V	K	T	L	Q	S	D	Q	H	N	K	R
G	S	S	U	S	L	G	E	S	E	D	Z	F	E	J	L	V	T	N	J	K	U	I
O	Q	Y	D	D	F	K	W	X	L	Q	Z	V	U	Q	B	F	S	I	S	E	Z	A
P	W	I	Q	F	J	Z	U	Z	L	P	A	L	K	A	L	O	S	I	S	H	X	T
V	Q	U	Q	O	G	V	I	V	M	Z	J	K	S	K	P	A	F	Q	G	U	Z	U

1. The opening through which feces are passed from the body
2. A noncancerous tumor of connective tissue
3. Medical term for the armpit
4. The medical term for nearsightedness
5. A structure that allows fluid flow in only one direction
6. A plentiful mineral in the body and the basic component of teeth and bones
7. The tiny structures that make up all the tissues of the body and carry out all its functions
8. A viral infection that causes inflammation of salivary glands
9. Urination or a sleep-disturbing need to urinate during the night
10. A hormone that stimulates the release of gastric acid in the stomach
11. A pus-filled abscess in the follicle of an eyelash
12. A chemical produced by a gland or tissue that is released into the bloodstream
13. Deoxyribonucleic acid; responsible for passing genetic information in nearly all organisms
14. A parasitic worm that lives in the intestines
15. A painless sore that has a thick, rubbery base and a defined edge
16. The process of closing a blood vessel or duct by tying it off
17. Dangerously decreased acidity of the blood, which can be caused by high altitudes, hyperventilation, and excessive vomiting
18. The external male reproductive organ, which passes urine and semen out of the body
19. The tube by which urine is released from the bladder
20. A noncancerous bone tumor

A. DNA	B. Calcium	C. Nocturia	D. Urethra	E. Alkalosis	F. Axilla
G. Ligation	H. Mumps	I. Stye	J. Cell	K. Penis	L. Tapeworm
M. Fibroma	N. Anus	O. Myopia	P. Gastrin	Q. Valve	R. Chancre
S. Hormone	T. Osteoma				

J. Find the hidden words. The words have been placed horizontally, vertically, or diagonally. When you locate a word, draw an ellipse around it.

P	M	Y	V	K	B	Y	B	R	X	B	U	L	L	B	T	L	I	E	R	T	J	J
G	V	Q	P	E	Y	K	Q	R	Y	W	V	E	D	C	P	R	L	P	K	U	G	X
L	H	M	M	J	Y	Y	E	Y	L	H	O	R	M	O	N	E	F	I	X	R	D	F
K	G	G	Y	D	G	A	N	G	R	E	N	E	E	R	V	L	X	L	Z	E	Q	B
P	G	C	O	X	P	G	X	E	A	X	K	W	Y	N	C	A	U	E	L	T	S	Q
E	A	A	S	Z	L	T	V	V	I	T	A	M	I	N	S	P	R	P	L	H	Y	X
P	T	M	I	G	P	G	L	A	U	C	O	M	A	J	R	S	X	S	U	R	G	F
S	O	G	T	A	J	X	A	H	F	A	S	I	L	E	E	E	L	Y	R	A	L	E
I	X	X	I	Z	R	P	M	G	G	D	H	Z	R	U	F	I	B	Z	E	V	O	F
N	I	S	S	H	C	Z	S	G	T	D	I	A	N	A	L	G	E	S	I	C	Z	U
M	C	V	S	T	O	O	L	U	K	M	Y	D	Q	T	E	Z	T	F	Q	A	P	K
S	I	P	R	U	R	I	T	U	S	R	J	H	I	X	X	M	T	X	U	Z	Z	J
T	T	D	Y	E	M	N	W	C	A	T	H	E	T	E	R	Z	H	E	R	N	I	A
X	Y	O	B	A	E	V	F	B	O	W	E	L	Y	B	M	Y	C	V	B	L	Z	S
M	O	I	B	N	R	Y	D	O	P	A	M	I	N	E	D	H	Z	W	V	B	D	M
T	L	U	C	I	G	D	C	H	U	V	I	B	X	N	A	N	U	S	S	S	Z	L

1. Complex substances that are necessary in small amounts to maintain health and ensure proper development and functioning of the body
2. A hollow, flexible tube inserted into the body to put in or take out fluid, or to open or close blood vessels
3. The bulging of an organ or tissue through a weakened area in the muscle wall
4. A drug that relieves pain, such as aspirin or acetaminophen
5. The enzyme found in gastric juice that helps digest protein
6. The opening through which feces are passed from the body
7. The tube by which urine is released from the bladder
8. A chemical that transmits messages in the brain and plays a role in movement
9. An automatic, involuntary response of the nervous system to a stimulus
10. A chemical produced by a gland or tissue that is released into the bloodstream
11. A thickened callus on the foot that is caused by an improperly fitting shoe
12. A disorder of the nervous system in which abnormal electrical activity in the brain causes seizures
13. Intestine
14. The medical term for itching
15. Death of a tissue because of a lack of blood supply
16. A disease in which eye damage is caused by an increase in the pressure of the fluid within the eye
17. The return of a disease or symptom after it had disappeared
18. Muscle inflammation, causing pain and weakness
19. The extent to which a substance is poisonous
20. Another term for feces

A. Glaucoma
B. Bowel
C. Reflex
D. Catheter
E. Vitamins
F. Epilepsy
G. Dopamine
H. Anus
I. Gangrene
J. Pruritus
K. Hormone
L. Urethra
M. Myositis
N. Stool
O. Pepsin
P. Toxicity
Q. Corn
R. Analgesic
S. Hernia
T. Relapse

K. Find the hidden words. The words have been placed horizontally, vertically, or diagonally. When you locate a word, draw an ellipse around it.

A	Z	N	Y	K	X	C	X	X	W	J	W	D	A	I	L	I	J	G	J	Q	L	I
M	B	G	R	I	W	G	T	G	D	A	H	V	P	C	N	F	N	K	E	F	J	G
F	Y	Q	C	A	L	L	U	S	U	N	I	A	P	O	E	M	I	I	A	S	M	R
S	A	F	E	S	E	X	M	R	S	T	P	O	G	Q	D	P	F	H	L	G	Y	E
B	D	W	V	E	L	B	C	G	D	I	W	P	X	I	T	G	S	P	U	V	N	C
U	T	R	A	C	H	E	A	O	K	B	O	A	T	V	R	S	P	Z	T	C	C	E
N	Q	T	J	J	U	N	R	L	H	O	R	Q	E	X	E	R	E	F	L	E	X	P
I	Z	P	G	J	C	E	V	G	Z	D	M	Y	O	V	M	J	U	W	V	R	X	T
O	J	B	D	O	M	U	I	Z	Q	Y	T	K	G	N	O	O	O	G	H	V	D	O
N	Q	Q	P	U	U	R	K	S	X	J	E	Z	U	N	R	U	J	O	M	I	Y	R
U	B	G	M	P	K	I	Q	Q	P	R	T	Y	C	A	L	C	I	U	M	X	V	V
H	S	K	R	G	R	T	T	S	E	A	A	H	A	C	Z	I	G	F	M	N	L	I
K	Y	P	H	O	S	I	S	H	V	D	N	A	S	A	B	R	U	X	I	S	M	L
P	U	E	B	R	A	S	F	O	Y	O	U	E	F	L	A	U	R	A	X	P	R	L
P	D	H	D	P	J	F	X	C	S	N	S	C	X	U	V	E	I	T	I	S	G	I
K	Y	D	E	U	Y	D	H	K	C	Q	M	F	A	S	Z	I	W	X	N	L	R	O

1. A small, parasitic worm that can live in the intestines of a human and may cause diarrhea, abdominal pain, and anemia
2. A hard, fluid-filled pad along the inside joint of the big toe
3. A reduced flow of blood throughout the body, usually caused by severe bleeding or a weak heart
4. Inflammation of a nerve, often characterized by pain, numbness, or tingling
5. A colorless, odorless, tasteless radioactive gas that is produced by materials in soil, rocks, and building materials; suspected of causing cancer
6. An unaware clenching or grinding of the teeth, usually during sleep
7. A sometimes fatal disease affecting the brain and spinal cord
8. A "warning" signal that comes before a migraine headache or an epileptic seizure, which might include emotions or sensations of movement or discomfort
9. An automatic, involuntary response of the nervous system to a stimulus
10. A plentiful mineral in the body and the basic component of teeth and bones
11. A thickened area of skin due to consistent pressure or friction, or the area around a bone break where new bone is formed
12. An involuntary, rhythmic, shaking movement caused by alternating contraction and relaxation of muscles
13. Excessive curvature of the spine, which usually affects the top part of the spine and causes a hump
14. A protein made by white blood cells that reacts with a specific foreign protein as part of the immune response
15. Measures taken to reduce the risk of acquiring a sexually transmitted disease, such as the use of a condom
16. A small, round organ making up the neck of the uterus and separating it from the vagina
17. The tube running from the larynx (the voice box) down the neck and into the upper part of the chest
18. A nerve cell that responds to a stimulus and produces a nerve impulse
19. Inflammation of the uvea
20. The millions of fingerlike projections on the lining of the small intestine that aid in the absorption of food

A. Antibody B. Callus C. Shock D. Calcium E. Uveitis F. Radon
G. Safe sex H. Neuritis I. Kyphosis J. Trachea K. Receptor L. Reflex
M. Bruxism N. Tetanus O. Whipworm P. Villi Q. Bunion R. Aura
S. Tremor T. Cervix

L. Find the hidden words. The words have been placed horizontally, vertically, or diagonally. When you locate a word, draw an ellipse around it.

X	K	E	N	E	C	R	O	S	I	S	R	L	I	N	U	S	B	M	U	M	P	S
C	D	L	P	G	V	Z	K	N	T	T	A	R	T	A	R	H	O	Y	Q	T	B	C
X	O	K	X	B	V	P	M	O	A	W	B	T	A	R	S	C	N	V	M	R	K	O
K	X	B	V	I	L	L	I	P	C	C	S	N	W	C	C	M	A	S	J	A	Z	Y
T	Y	C	O	N	X	U	V	E	I	T	I	S	X	O	A	Q	G	N	P	C	R	W
T	G	F	B	Z	I	A	X	V	D	E	K	G	A	T	B	N	U	R	U	T	J	E
I	E	M	I	N	E	R	A	L	O	O	U	F	X	I	I	C	Z	X	L	I	N	Z
X	N	P	A	N	A	L	G	E	S	I	C	T	H	C	E	X	J	T	S	O	J	M
L	W	E	A	P	U	O	U	N	I	N	B	B	T	G	S	O	L	X	E	N	Y	X
Q	V	D	C	R	C	U	A	A	S	G	O	C	U	L	A	R	O	Z	O	N	E	L
C	I	Q	U	O	K	E	Y	H	E	O	Z	F	R	D	M	I	T	O	S	I	S	O
M	V	M	F	X	R	A	H	J	Y	M	C	I	O	J	J	U	J	Z	U	H	J	L
E	L	H	J	I	B	Q	E	T	J	X	Z	B	A	C	Q	U	I	R	E	D	S	O
P	G	I	V	M	I	F	D	S	J	D	S	E	W	U	O	N	U	P	F	J	T	D
I	K	F	W	A	Q	K	D	Q	P	P	C	R	V	V	T	O	B	D	L	C	F	S
U	H	P	M	L	G	B	Q	Y	U	R	P	N	I	A	C	I	N	Y	K	H	W	D

1. The hard deposit formed on teeth when mineral salts in saliva combine with plaque
2. Describes something related to the eyes
3. Inflammation of the uvea
4. A condition marked by abnormally high acid levels in the blood, associated with some forms of diabetes, lung disease, and severe kidney disease
5. A word describing any condition that is not present at birth, but develops some time during life
6. A gas that is colorless, odorless, and tasteless
7. The process by which most cells divide to reproduce
8. A vitamin important in many chemical processes in the body; also known as vitamin b3
9. A drug that relieves pain, such as aspirin or acetaminophen
10. The use of tension to hold a body part in place or to correct or prevent an alignment problem
11. An addictive substance that blunts the senses
12. A highly contagious skin disorder caused by a mite that burrows into the skin and produces an intense, itchy rash
13. The medical term for the death of tissue cells
14. A viral infection that causes inflammation of salivary glands
15. A poisonous form of oxygen that is present in the earth's upper atmosphere, where it helps to screen the earth from damaging ultraviolet rays
16. Located nearer to a central point of reference on the body, such as the trunk
17. The millions of fingerlike projections on the lining of the small intestine that aid in the absorption of food
18. A substance that is a necessary part of a healthy diet (such as potassium, calcium, sodium, phosphorus, and magnesium)
19. A constituent of plants that cannot be digested, which helps maintain healthy functioning of the bowels
20. The expansion and contraction of a blood vessel due to the blood pumped through it

A. Narcotic   B. Scabies   C. Mumps   D. Acidosis   E. Necrosis   F. Mineral   G. Ocular
H. Niacin   I. Pulse   J. Villi   K. Acquired   L. Analgesic M. Proximal N. Oxygen
O. Tartar   P. Mitosis   Q. Ozone   R. Fiber   S. Uveitis   T. Traction

225

M. Find the hidden words. The words have been placed horizontally, vertically, or diagonally. When you locate a word, draw an ellipse around it.

Y	S	U	A	C	U	O	P	A	Z	V	Y	T	L	T	H	N	E	L	O	C	Q	J
K	J	S	M	S	U	F	I	S	T	U	L	A	X	M	X	L	N	I	M	S	X	F
T	I	T	F	N	E	U	R	O	N	P	Z	S	Z	M	H	G	Z	O	S	E	I	Y
I	L	E	Y	T	T	N	P	H	K	N	E	M	E	T	I	C	Y	D	K	Z	R	C
D	N	N	I	G	W	G	A	M	E	L	A	N	I	N	P	Y	M	I	I	W	O	J
Q	W	O	R	C	C	P	D	U	N	M	Z	N	E	L	H	M	E	N	S	Z	K	Q
L	X	S	A	O	R	E	F	Z	B	X	J	O	T	X	L	L	F	E	I	C	Y	K
D	C	I	L	C	E	N	J	B	L	A	D	D	E	R	E	X	I	S	F	H	T	W
N	S	S	E	C	Y	I	R	B	Q	H	L	U	Q	O	G	B	S	Q	Q	O	I	S
N	J	F	S	Y	I	S	F	J	B	T	I	L	J	N	M	P	S	M	X	G	P	Y
I	L	J	Z	X	S	R	H	E	W	M	J	E	I	M	M	P	U	A	E	C	F	V
A	P	P	E	N	D	I	X	B	N	U	C	L	E	U	S	K	R	R	E	A	R	E
I	R	C	R	Z	S	H	L	R	H	D	Z	S	U	R	Y	E	E	J	W	L	R	L
V	X	Y	O	H	S	K	O	N	R	H	S	V	K	Z	F	M	X	U	C	L	W	V
E	M	B	M	K	E	D	R	E	C	T	U	M	G	H	H	A	S	M	U	U	D	C
R	S	E	M	I	N	O	M	A	Z	B	U	N	I	O	N	W	X	D	P	S	V	H

1. Mucus and other material produced by the lining of the respiratory tract
2. The center or most important point of an object
3. A hard, fluid-filled pad along the inside joint of the big toe
4. A chemical, originating in a cell, that regulates reactions in the body
5. The pigment that gives skin, hair, and eyes their coloring
6. A groove or slit on the body or in an organ
7. Abnormal crackling or bubbling sounds heard in the lungs during breathing
8. An abnormal passageway from one organ to another or from an organ to the body surface
9. A substance that causes vomiting
10. The external male reproductive organ, which passes urine and semen out of the body
11. A small lump of tissue that is usually abnormal
12. A thickened area of skin due to consistent pressure or friction, or the area around a bone break where new bone is formed
13. Four fused bones that form a triangular shape at the base of the spine (also known as the tailbone)
14. A short tube located at the end of the large intestine, which connects the intestine to the anus
15. Narrowing of a body passageway
16. A short, tube-like structure that branches off the large intestine
17. Another term for a nerve cell
18. A type of testicular cancer that is made up of only a single type of cell
19. An element for the formation of thyroid hormones
20. An organ located in the pelvis whose function is to collect and store urine until it is expelled

A. Iodine B. Callus C. Emetic D. Rales E. Seminoma F. Enzyme
G. Fistula H. Nucleus I. Stenosis J. Rectum K. Coccyx L. Melanin
M. Fissure N. Phlegm O. Bunion P. Nodule Q. Penis R. Neuron
S. Bladder T. Appendix

N. Find the hidden words. The words have been placed horizontally, vertically, or diagonally. When you locate a word, draw an ellipse around it.

X	K	R	T	R	L	C	P	O	A	T	L	A	N	V	I	G	L	G	J	Z	S	C
Y	M	Y	O	S	I	T	I	S	F	B	O	D	P	R	K	G	U	F	Z	R	O	Q
U	O	A	M	K	P	V	E	K	E	L	O	E	U	A	B	S	P	V	R	Q	M	X
E	F	V	P	V	L	M	R	H	F	H	C	N	L	L	J	P	I	E	U	S	H	H
C	T	B	R	O	F	U	H	Y	M	D	Y	I	P	E	I	U	K	D	P	N	U	I
T	V	F	T	O	I	A	S	I	Q	X	T	T	B	S	P	C	W	Y	W	N	J	W
O	L	G	R	A	B	I	W	Z	I	J	E	I	M	Y	E	L	I	T	I	S	M	U
P	C	E	B	U	R	S	I	T	I	S	U	S	C	O	W	Z	N	O	T	V	T	I
I	H	I	V	M	O	X	X	G	J	T	P	A	R	A	N	O	I	A	J	U	H	K
C	R	Y	A	A	M	X	U	S	T	H	N	E	U	R	I	T	I	S	B	L	O	Q
U	O	X	S	L	A	W	O	S	I	A	J	V	R	V	T	G	M	O	A	V	Z	I
Z	N	Q	C	A	C	C	X	U	C	L	D	S	A	F	E	S	E	X	C	I	N	P
A	I	Y	U	R	O	X	K	B	A	A	Z	F	D	F	Q	R	E	A	Z	T	M	C
E	C	Z	L	I	W	A	U	R	A	M	V	G	O	L	P	X	D	Q	Z	I	Q	W
Q	U	I	A	A	Z	R	K	H	X	U	I	E	N	M	O	U	T	R	H	S	L	B
D	K	R	R	Y	C	R	U	U	N	S	Y	A	G	L	B	J	J	O	V	J	F	J

1. A structure in the brain that relays and processes incoming sensory information from the eyes and ears and from pressure and pain receptors
2. A disorder in which a person becomes overly suspicious and emotionally sensitive
3. Describes a disorder that continues for a long period of time
4. Occurring at an abnormal position or time
5. Inflammation of a bursa due to excessive pressure or friction, or from injury
6. An involuntary, repetitive movement such as a twitch
7. The soft tissue inside of a tooth that contains blood vessels and nerves
8. Inflammation of the vulva
9. Measures taken to reduce the risk of acquiring a sexually transmitted disease, such as the use of a condom
10. An egg cell that has not developed completely
11. A noncancerous tumor of connective tissue
12. Infection and inflammation of a gland, especially a lymph node
13. Muscle inflammation, causing pain and weakness
14. Inflammation of a nerve, often characterized by pain, numbness, or tingling
15. A colorless, odorless, tasteless radioactive gas that is produced by materials in soil, rocks, and building materials; suspected of causing cancer
16. A parasitic disease spread by mosquitos that causes chills and fever
17. Inflammation of the spinal cord, which can cause headaches, fever, muscle stiffness, pain, weakness, and eventually paralysis
18. Abnormal crackling or bubbling sounds heard in the lungs during breathing
19. A "warning" signal that comes before a migraine headache or an epileptic seizure, which might include emotions or sensations of movement or discomfort
20. Pertaining to blood vessels

A. Pulp
B. Myositis
C. Chronic
D. Adenitis
E. Thalamus
F. Vulvitis
G. Safe sex
H. Aura
I. Oocyte
J. Rales
K. Bursitis
L. Ectopic
M. Radon
N. Tic
O. Myelitis
P. Malaria
Q. Vascular
R. Paranoia
S. Neuritis
T. Fibroma

O. Find the hidden words. The words have been placed horizontally, vertically, or diagonally. When you locate a word, draw an ellipse around it.

O	F	E	V	U	J	G	L	R	X	P	R	O	V	G	E	S	S	R	E	W	X	I
B	X	C	T	L	F	L	F	W	O	Y	G	S	O	F	M	C	H	H	O	I	W	B
A	K	O	W	F	D	E	V	D	O	S	A	M	R	W	H	T	B	Y	S	B	A	M
C	B	B	U	N	I	O	N	Q	C	L	F	R	A	C	T	U	R	E	A	W	H	A
T	S	Q	V	E	R	N	I	X	Y	K	M	U	C	U	S	R	J	Q	R	O	A	H
E	M	A	T	R	O	P	H	Y	T	O	S	T	E	I	T	I	S	O	C	W	F	C
R	H	J	S	G	C	F	F	W	E	J	E	J	G	J	M	N	E	I	O	J	A	U
I	D	A	V	X	O	C	G	A	N	G	L	I	O	N	L	G	X	F	M	S	I	K
U	Y	Q	I	P	C	V	E	F	S	Y	S	C	I	J	F	W	C	M	A	Q	L	R
M	N	H	T	T	H	E	Z	D	F	R	H	S	L	V	I	O	I	I	Z	V	E	A
X	V	H	I	I	L	F	T	J	E	B	R	N	P	H	R	R	S	T	K	X	K	M
L	Y	Y	L	N	E	O	J	I	N	S	I	T	U	G	T	M	I	E	Z	I	C	T
J	K	Z	I	E	A	X	X	I	M	T	H	R	U	S	H	K	O	S	J	F	X	D
C	C	I	G	A	A	N	A	T	O	M	Y	P	P	J	P	H	N	N	L	V	O	W
G	L	O	O	O	F	L	G	K	R	H	O	R	K	J	Y	N	A	G	O	U	V
L	A	R	D	Q	S	V	F	X	O	K	N	O	D	U	L	E	A	R	W	X	V	V

1. A condition in which patches of skin on the body lose their color
2. A candidiasis infection
3. A tiny, single-celled microorganism, commonly known as a germ
4. "in place"; often describes a cancer that has not spread
5. The thick, greasy substance that covers the skin of a newborn baby
6. The structure of bodies
7. A cancer in connective tissue, fibrous tissue, or blood vessels
8. An egg cell that has not developed completely
9. A small lump of tissue that is usually abnormal
10. A skin infection caused by a fungus that spreads out in an even circle, characterized by ring-like, scaly patches of red skin
11. A slippery fluid produced by mucous membranes that lubricates and protects the internal surfaces of the body
12. The surgical removal of diseased tissue
13. The shrinkage or near disappearance of a tissue or organ
14. A fluid-filled cyst attached to a tendon sheath or joint
15. A group of common infections occurring on the skin, hair, and nails that are caused by a fungus
16. Inflammation of bone
17. A hard, fluid-filled pad along the inside joint of the big toe
18. A coiled organ in the inner ear that plays a large role in hearing by picking up sound vibrations and transmitting them as electrical signals
19. A bone break
20. Small eight-legged animals, many of which burrow and feed on blood

A. Bacterium   B. Mites   C. Fracture   D. Anatomy   E. Vitiligo   F. Bunion
G. Sarcoma   H. Excision   I. In situ   J. Tinea   K. Nodule   L. Oocyte
M. Osteitis   N. Thrush   O. Cochlea   P. Ringworm   Q. Ganglion   R. Mucus
S. Vernix   T. Atrophy

P. Find the hidden words. The words have been placed horizontally, vertically, or diagonally. When you locate a word, draw an ellipse around it.

D	A	Q	I	F	E	T	U	S	W	D	K	R	E	Z	V	A	L	V	E	U	P	U
B	C	K	N	M	X	Y	L	Y	J	O	S	V	U	L	V	I	T	I	S	M	B	W
G	V	Z	B	B	A	H	O	A	R	T	H	R	I	T	I	S	D	Z	I	F	S	K
L	G	F	E	M	U	R	A	H	R	N	F	L	O	A	T	E	R	S	I	M	D	H
O	P	T	I	C	I	A	N	Q	B	N	U	F	Q	B	P	J	C	N	Q	K	I	A
S	N	U	T	V	N	O	G	O	E	S	D	G	R	E	F	L	E	X	A	M	C	N
L	A	U	N	E	E	K	D	O	J	A	E	N	G	L	A	T	E	R	A	L	C	X
B	T	J	L	S	U	Y	D	E	A	D	X	G	I	T	X	U	Y	X	I	S	M	J
G	H	T	I	I	R	S	O	N	O	C	T	U	R	I	A	O	E	P	N	O	C	G
U	E	Q	G	C	O	R	A	O	Q	R	R	E	E	F	P	C	Z	J	H	S	V	F
R	R	X	A	L	S	T	M	G	V	X	O	I	R	G	M	K	I	N	A	P	F	J
O	O	B	M	E	I	U	J	P	Q	T	S	N	I	D	H	S	O	G	L	A	U	E
U	M	J	E	S	S	J	M	R	V	Q	E	V	Z	Y	T	A	T	C	E	S	G	I
Q	A	Z	N	H	O	O	K	W	O	R	M	I	W	A	A	F	Z	F	R	M	O	Y
O	Q	F	T	N	H	R	X	C	S	A	Q	V	E	T	R	T	K	U	K	W	P	Z
G	W	Y	B	P	J	T	E	O	J	M	U	O	A	S	P	E	R	M	I	A	N	C

1. Inflammation of the vulva
2. The bone located between the hip and the knee
3. Urination or a sleep-disturbing need to urinate during the night
4. Intelligence quotient; a measure of a person's intelligence as determined by specific tests
5. A structure that allows fluid flow in only one direction
6. An involuntary muscle contraction
7. A tough, elastic band of tissue that connects bones and supports organs
8. Small spots that float across the field of vision, caused by debris floating in the gel-like substance that fills the eye
9. The failure either to produce or to ejaculate sperm
10. "in the living body"; a biological process that occurs inside of the body
11. An automatic, involuntary response of the nervous system to a stimulus
12. Infestation by a small, round, blood-sucking parasite
13. Another name for the sugar glucose
14. A device used to introduce a powdered or misted drug into the lungs through the mouth, usually to treat respiratory disorders such as asthma
15. On one side
16. A person who specializes in the making and adjustment of eyeglasses and contact lenses
17. The term used to refer to an unborn child from 8 weeks after fertilization to birth
18. Relatively mild emotional disorders (such as mild depression and phobias)
19. Fatty deposits on the inner walls of blood vessels, which can cause narrowing and decrease blood flow
20. A disease of the joints characterized by inflammation, pain, stiffness, and redness
21. A small skin blister, or any sac in the body, that contains fluid

A. Reflex	B. Inhaler	C. Aspermia	D. Nocturia	E. Floaters	F. Spasm
G. IQ	H. Valve	I. Atheroma	J. Dextrose	K. Vulvitis	L. Neurosis
M. Fetus	N. Lateral	O. Ligament	P. Optician	Q. Vesicle	R. Arthritis
S. Femur	T. In vivo	U. Hookworm			

Q. Find the hidden words. The words have been placed horizontally, vertically, or diagonally. When you locate a word, draw an ellipse around it.

F	L	L	Q	C	D	R	J	G	S	M	F	F	H	P	K	P	J	Y	Y	I	T	G
U	M	S	H	D	X	D	Q	D	J	G	R	O	N	Z	I	T	T	M	M	I	W	P
T	A	G	O	J	E	M	P	D	U	F	A	M	I	L	I	A	L	A	C	J	W	O
E	D	U	L	F	K	I	D	N	E	Y	L	Z	Y	V	Z	T	G	L	Q	A	O	D
R	D	V	E	R	T	E	B	R	A	Z	E	Q	T	Q	B	V	Q	A	M	U	Q	L
U	I	D	A	X	J	D	R	I	Z	W	S	A	N	R	U	C	T	R	J	N	V	Y
S	C	M	P	Q	Z	R	L	J	O	S	Z	B	Y	M	K	Y	I	I	H	D	F	C
P	T	R	I	K	G	U	O	Q	H	V	R	W	S	A	S	Z	A	A	V	I	E	I
L	I	Z	P	Y	J	X	X	O	D	L	U	M	B	A	G	O	T	L	S	C	U	O
G	O	S	P	L	E	E	N	O	P	T	I	C	F	G	E	E	J	F	T	E	C	V
C	N	S	A	N	D	R	O	G	E	N	I	N	S	I	T	U	B	C	E	J	X	U
K	X	N	D	W	Q	P	U	S	T	U	L	E	Q	C	J	A	J	W	N	N	A	M
O	K	H	O	S	P	I	C	E	W	I	L	V	L	V	V	L	Y	F	T	E	Q	X
X	X	H	O	M	I	O	T	I	C	Z	T	S	V	L	A	R	Y	N	X	V	X	R
R	Q	P	E	U	E	A	I	C	I	N	H	F	U	X	C	I	O	B	B	U	E	Q
A	T	A	N	A	L	G	E	S	I	C	D	N	A	F	M	T	U	X	G	S	U	S

1. Any one of the 33 bones that make up the spine
2. Yellowing of the skin and whites of the eyes because of the presence of excess bilirubin in the blood; usually a sign of a disorder of the liver
3. A marking on the skin; can be present at birth (birthmark) or develop later (such as a mole)
4. A parasitic disease spread by mosquitos that causes chills and fever
5. A device used to hold tissues in place, such as to support a skin graft
6. A hormone (such as testosterone) that causes development of male characteristics and sex organs
7. Dependence on a substance (such as alcohol or other drugs) or an activity, to the point that stopping is very difficult and causes severe physical and mental reactions
8. Dull, aching pain in the lower back
9. The medical term for the voice box, the organ in the throat that produces voice and prevents food from entering the airway
10. A hospital or an area of a hospital dedicated to treating people who are dying, often of a specific cause
11. A term describing a disorder or characteristic (such as male pattern baldness) that occurs within a family more often than would be expected
12. Deoxyribonucleic acid; responsible for passing genetic information in nearly all organisms
13. Abnormal crackling or bubbling sounds heard in the lungs during breathing
14. A drug that causes the pupil to constrict
15. One of two organs that are part of the urinary tract
16. The hollow female reproductive organ in which a fertilized egg is implanted, and a fetus develops
17. A small blister containing pus
18. Pertaining to the eyes
19. "in place"; often describes a cancer that has not spread
20. A drug that relieves pain, such as aspirin or acetaminophen
21. An organ located in the upper left abdomen behind the ribs that removes and destroys old red blood cells and helps fight infection

A. Malaria B. Miotic C. Pustule D. Androgen E. Analgesic F. Stent
G. Vertebra H. Rales I. Nevus J. Uterus K. Lumbago L. Spleen
M. Kidney N. Optic O. Larynx P. Familial Q. Jaundice R. DNA
S. In situ T. Addiction U. Hospice

R. Find the hidden words. The words have been placed horizontally, vertically, or diagonally. When you locate a word, draw an ellipse around it.

M	E	Q	N	V	F	H	A	R	L	Q	D	H	J	P	R	M	O	R	W	K	D	T
V	N	B	E	P	W	S	E	I	Z	U	R	E	Y	I	K	F	V	L	W	O	U	V
B	E	B	R	X	B	O	I	M	M	U	N	I	T	Y	S	K	U	Q	N	N	T	J
Q	U	G	V	Z	O	O	N	O	S	I	S	D	A	V	M	C	M	L	Q	Y	Q	Q
P	O	G	E	J	I	S	H	G	E	G	S	O	T	Q	A	A	I	I	P	Z	J	P
R	J	V	F	Z	O	V	M	I	O	D	B	L	A	Y	L	N	V	P	E	K	P	V
O	O	O	S	E	L	E	N	I	U	M	T	V	D	K	L	C	J	O	G	A	V	W
G	D	L	N	E	C	R	O	S	I	S	Y	O	A	M	P	E	A	M	P	L	Q	A
E	K	V	W	L	Z	D	B	D	E	W	H	I	P	W	O	R	M	A	T	F	U	S
R	P	U	F	U	T	U	U	P	L	P	T	G	V	Q	X	H	V	R	M	L	F	N
I	K	L	O	N	X	G	R	R	T	U	O	K	R	U	S	Z	F	Q	A	F	C	H
A	X	U	E	G	U	C	S	E	P	X	G	I	P	A	S	M	E	D	U	L	L	A
O	F	S	N	S	S	R	I	P	Y	R	I	S	I	N	U	S	R	W	L	V	L	E
A	N	E	M	I	A	O	T	U	J	U	U	B	D	N	A	H	P	Z	H	P	O	E
N	A	S	V	R	R	U	I	C	X	E	T	W	V	L	H	Z	A	O	I	I	I	Q
M	L	A	K	U	C	P	S	E	F	B	Z	A	K	Y	R	I	E	Y	Y	M	Z	F

1. Sudden uncontrolled waves of electrical activity in the brain, causing involuntary movement or loss of consciousness
2. The medical term for the death of tissue cells
3. The center part of an organ or body structure
4. The foreskin
5. A condition in which the blood does not contain enough hemoglobin, the compound that carries oxygen from the lungs to other parts of the body
6. A parasite-caused or infectious disease in animals that can be transferred to humans
7. A noncancerous tumor of fatty tissue
8. A usually mild and temporary condition common in children under the age of 4 in which the walls of the airways become inflamed and narrow, resulting in wheezing and coughing
9. Another term for an egg cell
10. A bundle of fibers that transmit electrical messages between the brain and areas of the body
11. A group of diseases in which cells grow unrestrained in an organ or tissue in the body
12. An extremely rare condition in which the body ages prematurely
13. Deoxyribonucleic acid; responsible for passing genetic information in nearly all organisms
14. Resistance to a specific disease because of the responses of the immune system
15. Inflammation of a bursa due to excessive pressure or friction, or from injury
16. Two organs in the chest that take in oxygen from the air and release carbon dioxide
17. A small, parasitic worm that can live in the intestines of a human and may cause diarrhea, abdominal pain, and anemia
18. A cavity within bone or a channel that contains blood
19. A highly contagious and often fatal viral infection that has been completely eradicated by immunization
20. Twisting and obstruction of an area of intestine
21. An element needed by the body only in very small amounts that helps maintain tissue elasticity

A. Prepuce   B. Lungs   C. Lipoma   D. Whipworm   E. Bursitis   F. Zoonosis
G. Ovum   H. Anemia   I. Smallpox   J. Nerve   K. DNA   L. Medulla
M. Sinus   N. Cancer   O. Croup   P. Necrosis   Q. Immunity   R. Selenium
S. Progeria   T. Volvulus   U. Seizure

S. Find the hidden words. The words have been placed horizontally, vertically, or diagonally. When you locate a word, draw an ellipse around it.

O	P	R	S	I	N	I	N	B	G	B	R	Y	E	P	I	D	E	M	I	C	H	X
S	H	B	A	I	A	P	L	W	P	E	S	L	W	U	Y	U	C	P	W	J	D	C
U	O	T	R	X	M	O	D	V	L	Y	J	M	S	P	R	A	I	N	R	U	P	D
X	B	Q	L	M	U	T	A	G	E	N	K	T	R	N	Z	X	Q	O	P	G	D	L
V	I	P	D	U	X	I	I	K	U	O	B	I	B	F	J	V	A	R	I	C	E	S
Y	A	E	Z	J	R	E	Z	K	R	Y	J	L	H	T	T	G	X	Z	X	R	M	N
H	E	R	N	I	A	V	I	T	I	L	I	G	O	W	M	O	S	Z	R	U	O	A
F	W	J	L	Q	H	P	Y	L	S	O	G	O	Z	L	Y	K	T	Q	U	J	R	T
Q	O	P	E	Q	C	K	J	S	Y	V	C	Q	A	R	C	X	O	E	N	P	N	R
T	N	P	X	U	A	E	U	U	J	T	I	S	A	C	O	F	M	M	E	T	A	E
Q	B	F	Z	B	F	H	A	C	A	S	T	H	O	T	S	W	A	B	C	U	O	S
O	M	E	N	I	N	G	E	S	R	J	R	W	A	W	I	O	Q	O	R	K	U	I
J	H	I	C	A	N	E	U	R	Y	S	M	R	R	T	S	W	X	L	O	J	P	A
R	Q	S	H	I	X	N	L	K	Y	A	U	B	Y	P	A	S	S	I	S	E	R	I
J	G	E	W	B	L	V	F	E	B	R	I	L	E	F	S	Y	Y	S	I	Y	P	W
A	A	C	A	N	A	L	P	A	L	L	O	R	X	F	Z	Z	S	M	S	Z	O	S

1. A condition in which patches of skin on the body lose their color
2. A term used to describe something related to a fever, such as febrile seizures (seizures occurring in a child who has a fever)
3. A surgically formed opening on a body surface
4. A birth defect in which a normal body opening, or canal is absent
5. A surgical technique in which the flow of blood or another body fluid is redirected around a blockage
6. The three membranes that surround and protect the spinal cord and brain
7. The blockage of a blood vessel by an embolus—something previously circulating in the blood (such as a blood clot, gas bubble, tissue, bacteria, bone marrow, cholesterol, fat, etc.)
8. The tearing or stretching of the ligaments in a joint, characterized by pain, swelling, and an inability to move the joint
9. Abnormally pale skin
10. A tunnel-like passage
11. The bulging of an organ or tissue through a weakened area in the muscle wall
12. Any disease caused by a fungus
13. A hard plaster or fiberglass shell that molds to a body part such as an arm and holds it in place for proper healing
14. A term used to describe a disease that is rare then suddenly affects more people than usually expected
15. Inflammation of the lining of the lungs and chest cavity usually caused by a lung infection
16. Enlarged or twisted blood or lymph vessels
17. Anything that can increase the rate of abnormal change in cells, which can lead to cancer
18. The medical term for the death of tissue cells
19. Ribonucleic acid, which helps to decode and process the information contained in DNA
20. An abnormal swelling of the wall of an artery, caused by a weakening in the vessel wall
21. A persisting fear of and desire to avoid something

A. Pleurisy
B. Meninges
C. Mycosis
D. Mutagen
E. Hernia
F. Varices
G. Bypass
H. Embolism
I. Vitiligo
J. Epidemic
K. Stoma
L. Sprain
M. Phobia
N. Canal
O. Atresia
P. Necrosis
Q. Aneurysm
R. Pallor
S. Cast
T. Febrile
U. RNA

T. Find the hidden words. The words have been placed horizontally, vertically, or diagonally. When you locate a word, draw an ellipse around it.

Z	B	U	E	Z	W	J	M	C	A	L	L	U	S	F	I	B	R	O	M	A	E	U
K	I	T	I	M	R	A	H	E	V	R	E	L	A	P	S	E	V	I	R	A	L	L
L	A	E	J	T	H	Y	M	O	M	A	S	I	N	U	S	K	Y	X	O	K	X	C
D	P	R	F	T	I	N	N	I	T	U	S	R	Q	J	T	R	M	X	A	G	W	E
I	J	U	L	T	N	G	O	N	I	W	X	U	D	H	R	Y	F	H	B	D	P	R
P	Y	S	G	X	Z	P	T	S	Z	V	E	H	E	P	A	T	O	M	A	D	H	X
Z	C	R	X	R	K	H	R	E	T	I	N	O	I	D	C	R	A	W	O	G	S	K
N	I	L	O	R	D	O	S	I	S	K	L	F	W	R	T	W	B	Y	P	A	S	S
R	G	J	D	D	O	B	T	U	O	P	S	E	S	U	I	T	P	X	E	E	H	I
Q	Q	M	N	P	T	I	J	Z	E	P	F	K	A	B	O	O	K	Z	H	L	G	T
S	O	I	A	X	Q	A	D	L	E	K	M	C	R	E	N	N	J	D	D	D	O	G
P	H	A	R	Y	N	X	P	L	A	G	U	E	C	O	J	B	N	Z	D	J	E	P
D	A	H	E	M	E	Q	L	M	S	Z	S	A	O	L	J	D	P	Z	M	C	B	V
G	K	G	K	B	B	E	F	S	L	Y	S	A	M	A	Z	K	W	G	A	X	W	X
R	K	E	W	F	A	Y	Y	A	Q	H	C	T	A	W	M	A	S	T	I	T	I	S
Q	B	T	L	C	M	F	T	H	A	Z	Z	K	T	S	S	M	F	F	X	P	Z	C

1. The return of a disease or symptom after it had disappeared
2. A term describing something related to or caused by a virus
3. A serious infectious disease transmitted to humans through bites of rodent fleas
4. The use of tension to hold a body part in place or to correct or prevent an alignment problem
5. Another term for measles
6. A tumor of the thymus gland
7. The throat
8. A persisting fear of and desire to avoid something
9. The inward curvature of the spine at the lower back, which is normal to a certain degree
10. A cavity within bone or a channel that contains blood
11. A thickened area of skin due to consistent pressure or friction, or the area around a bone break where new bone is formed
12. Inflammation of the breast, which is usually caused by a bacterial infection
13. A substance resembling vitamin a that is used to treat skin conditions such as acne and has been reported to reduce skin wrinkling
14. A cancerous tumor of the liver
15. The hollow female reproductive organ in which a fertilized egg is implanted, and a fetus develops
16. An open sore that occurs on the skin or on a mucous membrane because of the destruction of surface tissue
17. A surgical technique in which the flow of blood or another body fluid is redirected around a blockage
18. A cancer in connective tissue, fibrous tissue, or blood vessels
19. A noncancerous tumor of connective tissue
20. Deoxyribonucleic acid; responsible for passing genetic information in nearly all organisms
21. A persistent ringing or buzzing sound in the ear

A. Hepatoma
B. Tinnitus
C. Bypass
D. DNA
E. Viral
F. Lordosis
G. Phobia
H. Sinus
I. Relapse
J. Ulcer
K. Uterus
L. Retinoid
M. Traction
N. Thymoma
O. Pharynx
P. Rubeola
Q. Fibroma
R. Callus
S. Plague
T. Mastitis
U. Sarcoma

A. Find the hidden words. The words have been placed horizontally, vertically, or diagonally. When you locate a word, draw an ellipse around it.

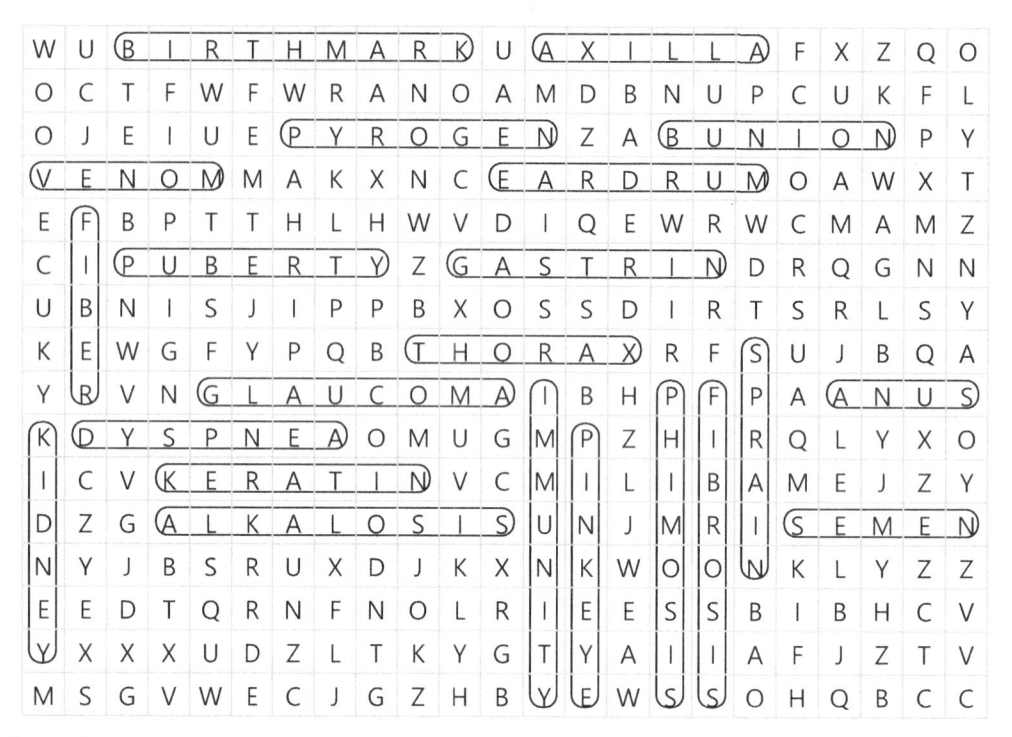

W	U	B	I	R	T	H	M	A	R	K	U	A	X	I	L	L	A	F	X	Z	Q	O
O	C	T	F	W	F	W	R	A	N	O	A	M	D	B	N	U	P	C	U	K	F	L
O	J	E	I	U	E	P	Y	R	O	G	E	N	Z	A	B	U	N	I	O	N	P	Y
V	E	N	O	M	M	A	K	X	N	C	E	A	R	D	R	U	M	O	A	W	X	T
E	F	B	P	T	T	H	L	H	W	V	D	I	Q	E	W	R	W	C	M	A	M	Z
C	I	P	U	B	E	R	T	Y	Z	G	A	S	T	R	I	N	D	R	Q	G	N	N
U	B	N	I	S	J	I	P	P	B	X	O	S	S	D	I	R	T	S	R	L	S	Y
K	E	W	G	F	Y	P	Q	B	T	H	O	R	A	X	R	F	S	U	J	B	Q	A
Y	R	V	N	G	L	A	U	C	O	M	A	I	B	H	P	F	P	A	A	N	U	S
K	D	Y	S	P	N	E	A	O	M	U	G	M	P	Z	H	I	R	Q	L	Y	X	O
I	C	V	K	E	R	A	T	I	N	V	C	M	I	L	I	B	A	M	E	J	Z	Y
D	Z	G	A	L	K	A	L	O	S	I	S	U	N	J	M	R	I	S	E	M	E	N
N	Y	J	B	S	R	U	X	D	J	K	X	N	K	W	O	O	N	K	L	Y	Z	Z
E	E	D	T	Q	R	N	F	N	O	L	R	I	E	E	S	S	B	I	B	H	C	V
Y	X	X	U	D	Z	L	T	K	Y	G	T	Y	A	I	I	A	F	J	Z	T	V	
M	S	G	V	W	E	C	J	G	Z	H	B	Y	E	W	S	S	O	H	Q	B	C	C

1. Medical term for the armpit
2. A thin, oval-shaped membrane that separates the inner ear from the outer ear and is responsible for transmitting sound waves
3. A poisonous substance produced by certain animals
4. Tightness of the foreskin, which prevents it from being moved back over the head of the penis
5. A constituent of plants that cannot be digested, which helps maintain healthy functioning of the bowels
6. A hard, fluid-filled pad along the inside joint of the big toe
7. A hormone that stimulates the release of gastric acid in the stomach
8. One of two organs that are part of the urinary tract
9. Abnormal formation of connective or scar tissue
10. A disease in which eye damage is caused by an increase in the pressure of the fluid within the eye
11. The tearing or stretching of the ligaments in a joint, characterized by pain, swelling, and an inability to move the joint
12. A tough protein found in skin, nails, and hair
13. The opening through which feces are passed from the body
14. Dangerously decreased acidity of the blood, which can be caused by high altitudes, hyperventilation, and excessive vomiting
15. The chest
16. Resistance to a specific disease because of the responses of the immune system
17. Any substance that causes a fever
18. Any area of discolored skin that is present when a baby is born
19. Difficulty breathing
20. Fluid released during ejaculation that contains sperm along with fluids produced by the prostate gland and the seminal vesicles
21. The period during which sexual development occurs
22. Inflammation of the membrane that covers the white of the eyes and lines the eyelids

A. Semen	B. Pinkeye	C. Glaucoma	D. Axilla
G. Eardrum	H. Anus	I. Sprain	J. Birthmark
M. Puberty	N. Bunion	O. Kidney	P. Immunity
S. Thorax	T. Phimosis	U. Pyrogen	V. Gastrin
E. Alkalosis	F. Fibrosis		
K. Fiber	L. Dyspnea		
Q. Keratin	R. Venom		

B. Find the hidden words. The words have been placed horizontally, vertically, or diagonally. When you locate a word, draw an ellipse around it.

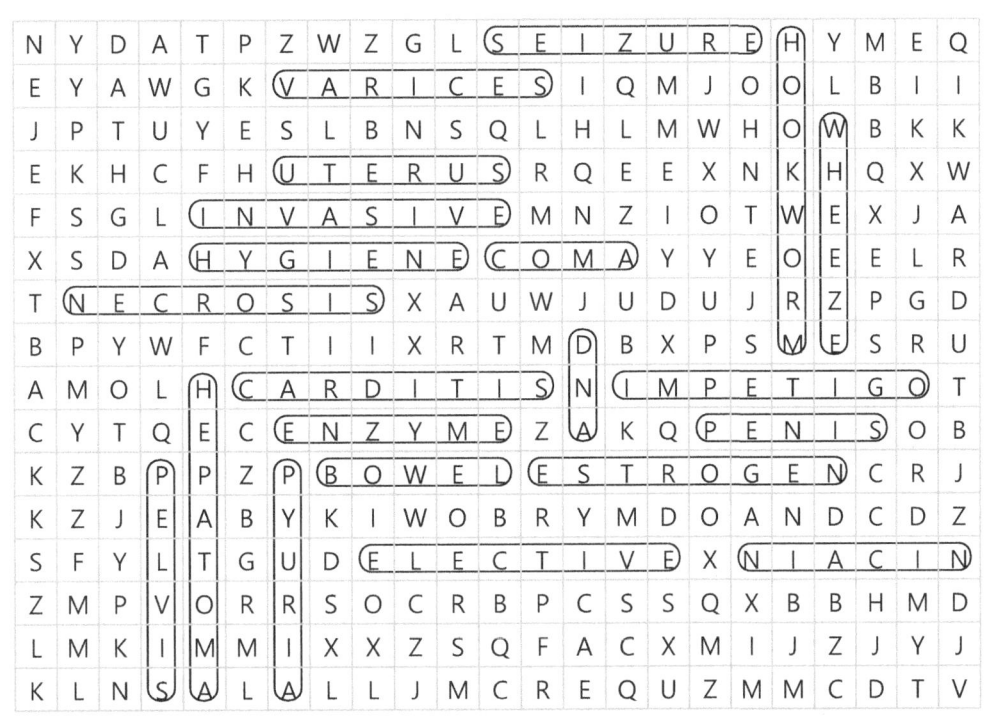

N	Y	D	A	T	P	Z	W	Z	G	L	S	E	I	Z	U	R	E	H	Y	M	E	Q
E	Y	A	W	G	K	V	A	R	I	C	E	S	I	Q	M	J	O	O	L	B	I	I
J	P	T	U	Y	E	S	L	B	N	S	Q	L	H	L	M	W	H	O	W	B	K	K
E	K	H	C	F	H	U	T	E	R	U	S	R	Q	E	E	X	N	K	H	Q	X	W
F	S	G	L	I	N	V	A	S	I	V	E	M	N	Z	I	O	T	W	E	X	J	A
X	S	D	A	H	Y	G	I	E	N	E	C	O	M	A	Y	Y	E	O	E	E	L	R
T	N	E	C	R	O	S	I	S	X	A	U	W	J	U	D	U	J	R	Z	P	G	D
B	P	Y	W	F	C	T	I	I	X	R	T	M	D	B	X	P	S	W	E	S	R	U
A	M	O	L	H	C	A	R	D	I	T	I	S	N	I	M	P	E	T	I	G	O	T
C	Y	T	Q	E	C	E	N	Z	Y	M	E	Z	A	K	Q	P	E	N	I	S	O	B
K	Z	B	P	P	Z	P	B	O	W	E	L	E	S	T	R	O	G	E	N	C	R	J
K	Z	J	E	A	B	Y	K	I	W	O	B	R	Y	M	D	O	A	N	D	C	D	Z
S	F	Y	L	T	G	U	D	E	L	E	C	T	I	V	E	X	N	I	A	C	I	N
Z	M	P	V	O	R	R	S	O	C	R	B	P	C	S	S	Q	X	B	B	H	M	D
L	M	K	I	M	M	I	X	X	Z	S	Q	F	A	C	X	M	I	J	Z	J	Y	J
K	L	N	S	A	L	A	L	L	J	M	C	R	E	Q	U	Z	M	M	C	D	T	V

1. Describes a treatment or procedure that is not urgent and can be arranged at the patient's convenience
2. The presence of white blood cells in the urine
3. A group of hormones (produced mainly in the ovaries) that are necessary for female sexual development and reproductive functioning
4. The hollow female reproductive organ in which a fertilized egg is implanted, and a fetus develops
5. Inflammation of the heart
6. Infestation by a small, round, blood-sucking parasite
7. Deoxyribonucleic acid; responsible for passing genetic information in nearly all organisms
8. The practice, maintenance, and study of health
9. A condition in which the area of the brain involved in maintaining consciousness is somehow affected, resulting in a state of unconsciousness in which the patient does not respond to stimulation
10. Sudden uncontrolled waves of electrical activity in the brain, causing involuntary movement or loss of consciousness
11. The group of bones in the lower part of the trunk that support the upper body and protect the abdominal organs
12. A highly contagious skin infection caused by bacteria, usually occurring around the nose and mouth
13. Intestine
14. Describes something that spreads throughout body tissues, such as a tumor or microorganism
15. Enlarged or twisted blood or lymph vessels
16. A chemical, originating in a cell, that regulates reactions in the body
17. A vitamin important in many chemical processes in the body; also known as vitamin b3
18. The external male reproductive organ, which passes urine and semen out of the body
19. A cancerous tumor of the liver
20. A high-pitched sound produced during breathing because of narrowing of the airways
21. The medical term for the death of tissue cells

A. Enzyme B. Seizure C. Hookworm D. DNA E. Elective F. Niacin
G. Impetigo H. Invasive I. Pyuria J. Hepatoma K. Pelvis L. Varices
M. Wheeze N. Coma O. Penis P. Uterus Q. Carditis R. Estrogen
S. Hygiene T. Bowel U. Necrosis

C. Find the hidden words. The words have been placed horizontally, vertically, or diagonally. When you locate a word, draw an ellipse around it.

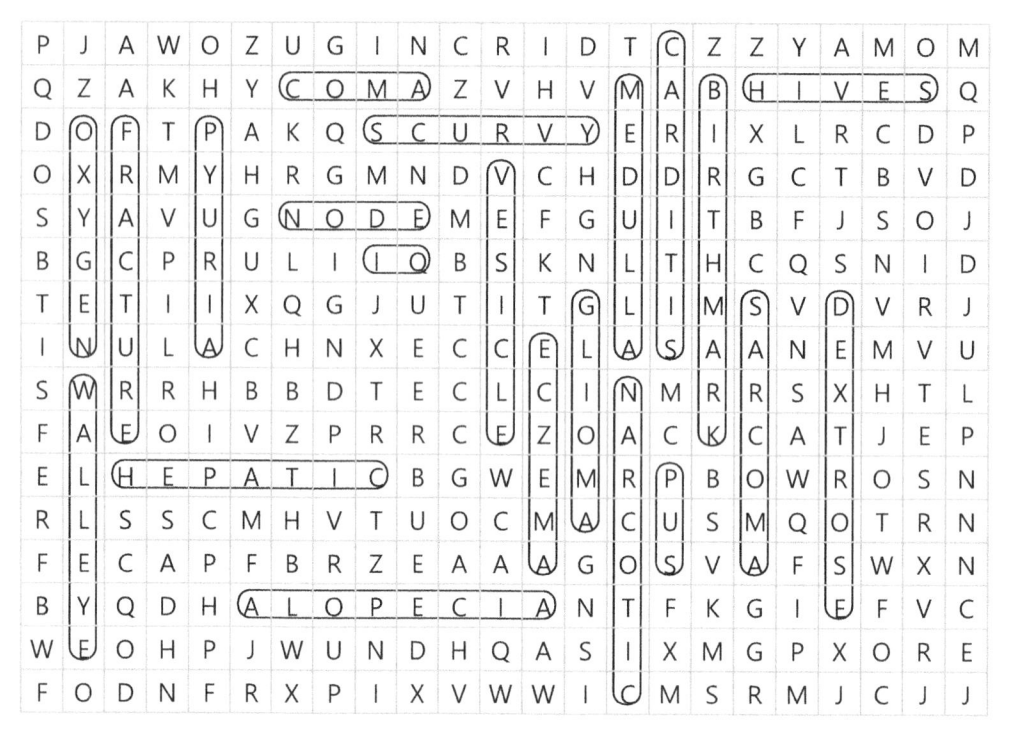

P	J	A	W	O	Z	U	G	I	N	C	R	I	D	T	C	Z	Z	Y	A	M	O	M
Q	Z	A	K	H	Y	C	O	M	A	Z	V	H	V	M	A	B	H	I	V	E	S	Q
D	O	F	T	P	A	K	Q	S	C	U	R	V	Y	E	R	I	X	L	R	C	D	P
O	X	R	M	Y	H	R	G	M	N	D	V	C	H	D	D	R	G	C	T	B	V	D
S	Y	A	V	U	G	N	O	D	E	M	E	F	G	U	I	T	B	F	J	S	O	J
B	G	C	P	R	U	L	I	I	Q	B	S	K	N	L	T	H	C	Q	S	N	I	D
T	E	T	I	I	X	Q	G	J	U	T	I	T	G	L	I	M	S	V	D	V	R	J
I	N	U	L	A	C	H	N	X	E	C	C	E	L	A	S	A	A	N	E	M	V	U
S	W	R	R	H	B	B	D	T	E	C	L	C	I	N	M	R	R	S	X	H	T	L
F	A	E	O	I	V	Z	P	R	R	C	E	Z	O	A	C	K	C	A	T	J	E	P
E	L	H	E	P	A	T	I	C	B	G	W	E	M	R	P	B	O	W	R	O	S	N
R	L	S	S	C	M	H	V	T	U	O	C	M	A	C	U	S	M	Q	O	T	R	N
F	E	C	A	P	F	B	R	Z	E	A	A	A	G	O	S	V	A	F	S	W	X	N
B	Y	Q	D	H	A	L	O	P	E	C	I	A	N	T	F	K	G	I	E	F	V	C
W	E	O	H	P	J	W	U	N	D	H	Q	A	S	I	X	M	G	P	X	O	R	E
F	O	D	N	F	R	X	P	I	X	V	W	W	I	C	M	S	R	M	J	C	J	J

1. A thick, yellowish or greenish fluid that contains dead white blood cells, tissues, and bacteria; occurs at the site of a bacterial infection
2. Inflammation of the heart
3. A gas that is colorless, odorless, and tasteless
4. A condition in which one eye turns outward
5. A term used to describe something that is related to the liver
6. Inflammation of the skin, usually causing itchiness and sometimes blisters and scaling
7. A bone break
8. The presence of white blood cells in the urine
9. A brain tumor arising from cells that support nerve cells
10. Intelligence quotient; a measure of a person's intelligence as determined by specific tests
11. Any area of discolored skin that is present when a baby is born
12. The common term for urticaria, an itchy, inflamed rash that results from an allergic reaction
13. A cancer in connective tissue, fibrous tissue, or blood vessels
14. Another name for the sugar glucose
15. A condition in which the area of the brain involved in maintaining consciousness is somehow affected, resulting in a state of unconsciousness in which the patient does not respond to stimulation
16. A small, rounded tissue mass
17. Baldness or loss of hair, mainly on the head, either in defined patches or completely
18. A disease caused by a lack of vitamin c, characterized by weakness, bleeding and pain in joints and muscles, bleeding gums, and abnormal bone and tooth growth
19. An addictive substance that blunts the senses
20. A small skin blister, or any sac in the body, that contains fluid
21. The center part of an organ or body structure

A. Alopecia
B. Hives
C. Node
D. Eczema
E. Birthmark
F. Glioma
G. Narcotic
H. Fracture
I. Hepatic
J. Pyuria
K. Pus
L. Dextrose
M. Carditis
N. Coma
O. Oxygen
P. Vesicle
Q. Walleye
R. Medulla
S. Scurvy
T. Sarcoma
U. IQ

D. Find the hidden words. The words have been placed horizontally, vertically, or diagonally. When you locate a word, draw an ellipse around it.

T	Z	D	O	Q	S	D	Q	L	Q	E	X	R	Z	E	B	D	N	E	W	X	U	K
U	D	W	P	A	B	U	L	I	M	I	A	O	Y	K	F	O	I	V	V	U	D	K
R	B	E	L	M	S	M	F	S	Z	Q	M	N	P	J	E	F	A	L	P	J	E	Z
S	A	G	U	S	P	M	U	C	O	C	E	L	E	S	A	L	C	P	B	W	E	B
R	L	E	M	C	R	L	C	H	Y	P	L	W	G	Y	N	A	I	I	B	A	H	I
K	F	N	B	K	Y	K	Z	O	B	M	W	A	L	L	U	D	N	X	M	U	I	I
M	Y	E	A	N	O	D	E	R	X	B	O	Z	U	A	C	U	T	E	E	N	V	L
P	N	V	G	B	E	O	T	M	J	Y	K	G	C	R	Q	T	C	G	L	L	E	B
F	P	C	O	M	V	I	I	O	Z	E	F	O	A	K	D	Z	U	K	A	S	S	Z
J	X	E	Z	H	I	Q	C	N	M	J	W	F	G	E	O	J	S	L	N	Z	E	I
K	G	L	I	O	M	A	L	E	Z	T	F	V	O	X	Z	Z	Z	V	O	L	C	L
G	X	U	T	M	Y	O	S	I	T	I	S	I	N	H	C	X	G	L	M	Z	T	L
L	T	Z	Q	F	R	R	Z	L	A	H	M	I	N	I	P	I	L	L	A	Z	O	P
R	I	B	I	I	R	R	Y	K	Y	G	U	Q	J	E	X	L	D	Z	R	A	P	H
T	B	I	N	V	A	S	I	V	E	X	Z	O	O	N	O	S	I	S	N	I	I	U
A	U	T	O	P	S	Y	H	E	L	Z	C	Y	S	T	G	Q	U	D	A	R	C	Y

1. A skin tumor composed of cells called melanocytes
2. Describes a condition or illness that begins suddenly and is usually short- lasting
3. A chemical produced by a gland or tissue that is released into the bloodstream
4. A brain tumor arising from cells that support nerve cells
5. An oral contraceptive containing only the synthetic hormone progesterone (birth control pills contain estrogen and progesterone)
6. A sac or body cavity that is swollen because of the production of mucus by the cells in its lining
7. Ribonucleic acid, which helps to decode and process the information contained in DNA
8. A hormone produced by the pancreas that converts stored carbohydrates (glycogen) into glucose, the body's energy source
9. Dull, aching pain in the lower back
10. A lump filled with either fluid or soft material, occurring in any organ or tissue
11. Describes something that spreads throughout body tissues, such as a tumor or microorganism
12. The common term for urticaria, an itchy, inflamed rash that results from an allergic reaction
13. Muscle inflammation, causing pain and weakness
14. The examination of a body following death, possibly to determine the cause of death or for research
15. Occurring at an abnormal position or time
16. The basic unit of DNA, which is responsible for passing genetic information
17. A vitamin important in many chemical processes in the body; also known as vitamin b3
18. A disorder in which a person eats large amounts of food then forces vomiting or uses laxatives to prevent weight gain (called binging and purging)
19. A small, rounded tissue mass
20. An involuntary, repetitive movement such as a twitch
21. A parasite- caused or infectious disease in animals that can be transferred to humans

A. Lumbago
B. Mucocele
C. Tic
D. Ectopic
E. Hives
F. Hormone
G. Bulimia
H. Node
I. Niacin
J. Cyst
K. Glucagon
L. RNA
M. Myositis
N. Acute
O. Melanoma
P. Minipill
Q. Glioma
R. Invasive
S. Gene
T. Autopsy
U. Zoonosis

E. Find the hidden words. The words have been placed horizontally, vertically, or diagonally. When you locate a word, draw an ellipse around it.

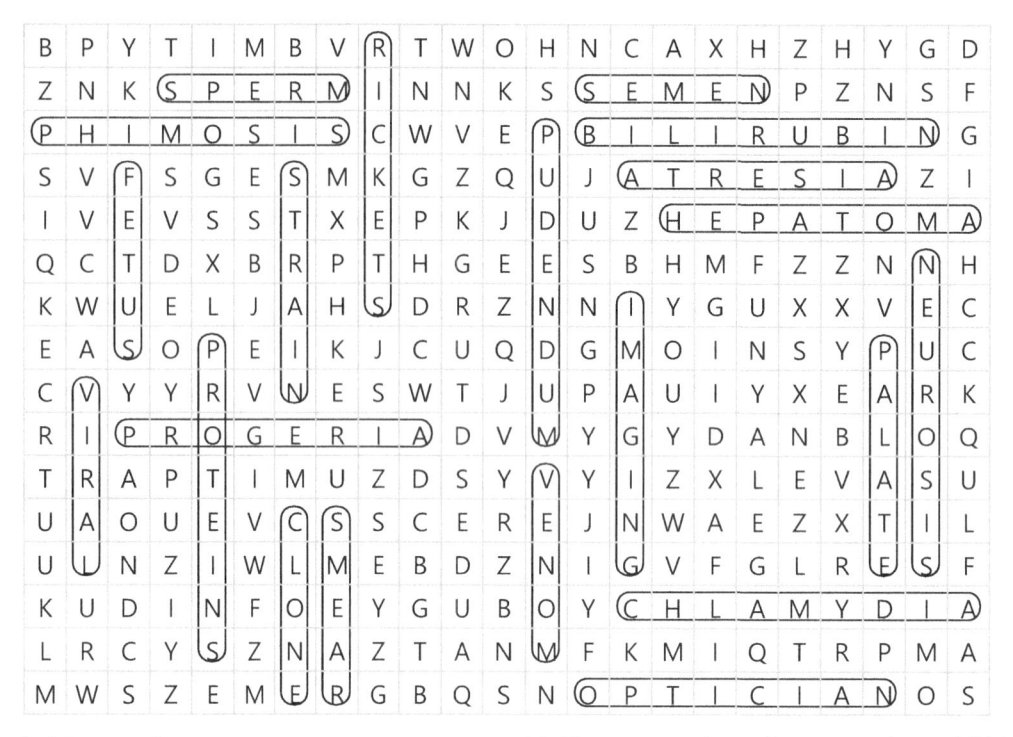

B	P	Y	T	I	M	B	V	R	T	W	O	H	N	C	A	X	H	Z	H	Y	G	D
Z	N	K	S	P	E	R	M	I	N	N	K	S	S	E	M	E	N	P	Z	N	S	F
P	H	I	M	O	S	I	S	C	W	V	E	P	B	I	L	I	R	U	B	I	N	G
S	V	F	S	G	E	S	M	K	G	Z	Q	U	J	A	T	R	E	S	I	A	Z	I
I	V	E	V	S	S	T	X	E	P	K	J	D	U	Z	H	E	P	A	T	O	M	A
Q	C	T	D	X	B	R	P	T	H	G	E	E	S	B	H	M	F	Z	Z	N	N	H
K	W	U	E	L	J	A	H	S	D	R	Z	N	N	I	Y	G	U	X	X	V	E	C
E	A	S	O	P	E	I	K	J	C	U	Q	D	G	M	O	I	N	S	Y	P	U	C
C	V	Y	Y	R	V	N	E	S	W	T	J	U	P	A	U	I	Y	X	E	A	R	K
R	I	P	R	O	G	E	R	I	A	D	V	W	Y	G	Y	D	A	N	B	L	O	Q
T	R	A	P	T	I	M	U	Z	D	S	Y	V	Y	I	Z	X	L	E	V	A	S	U
U	A	O	U	E	V	C	S	S	C	E	R	E	J	N	W	A	E	Z	X	T	I	L
U	W	N	Z	I	W	L	M	E	B	D	Z	N	I	G	V	F	G	L	R	E	S	F
K	U	D	I	N	F	O	E	Y	G	U	B	O	Y	C	H	L	A	M	Y	D	I	A
L	R	C	Y	S	Z	N	A	Z	T	A	N	W	F	K	M	I	Q	T	R	P	M	A
M	W	S	Z	E	M	E	R	G	B	Q	S	N	O	P	T	I	C	I	A	N	O	S

1. The roof of the mouth
2. The external genitals, usually referring to the female
3. A childhood disease in which bones lack calcium and are deformed because of vitamin d deficiency
4. The orange-yellow pigment in bile, causing jaundice if it builds up in the blood and skin
5. Tightness of the foreskin, which prevents it from being moved back over the head of the penis
6. The male sex cell produced in the testicles
7. An extremely rare condition in which the body ages prematurely
8. A cancerous tumor of the liver
9. A poisonous substance produced by certain animals
10. An exact copy of a gene, cell, or organism
11. The technique of creating pictures of structures inside of the body using x-rays, ultrasound waves, or magnetic fields
12. A term describing something related to or caused by a virus
13. Microorganisms that cause several human infections and can be transmitted sexually
14. The term used to refer to an unborn child from 8 weeks after fertilization to birth
15. A sample of cells spread across a glass slide to be examined through a microscope
16. A birth defect in which a normal body opening, or canal is absent
17. Large molecules made up of amino acids that play many major roles in the body, including forming the basis of body structures.
18. Muscle damage resulting from excessive stretching or forceful contraction
19. A person who specializes in the making and adjustment of eyeglasses and contact lenses
20. Relatively mild emotional disorders (such as mild depression and phobias)
21. Fluid released during ejaculation that contains sperm along with fluids produced by the prostate gland and the seminal vesicles

A. Hepatoma
B. Palate
C. Fetus
D. Proteins
E. Progeria
F. Rickets
G. Pudendum
H. Clone
I. Neurosis
J. Phimosis
K. Semen
L. Sperm
M. Atresia
N. Optician
O. Venom
P. Smear
Q. Bilirubin
R. Strain
S. Imaging
T. Chlamydia
U. Viral

238

F. Find the hidden words. The words have been placed horizontally, vertically, or diagonally. When you locate a word, draw an ellipse around it.

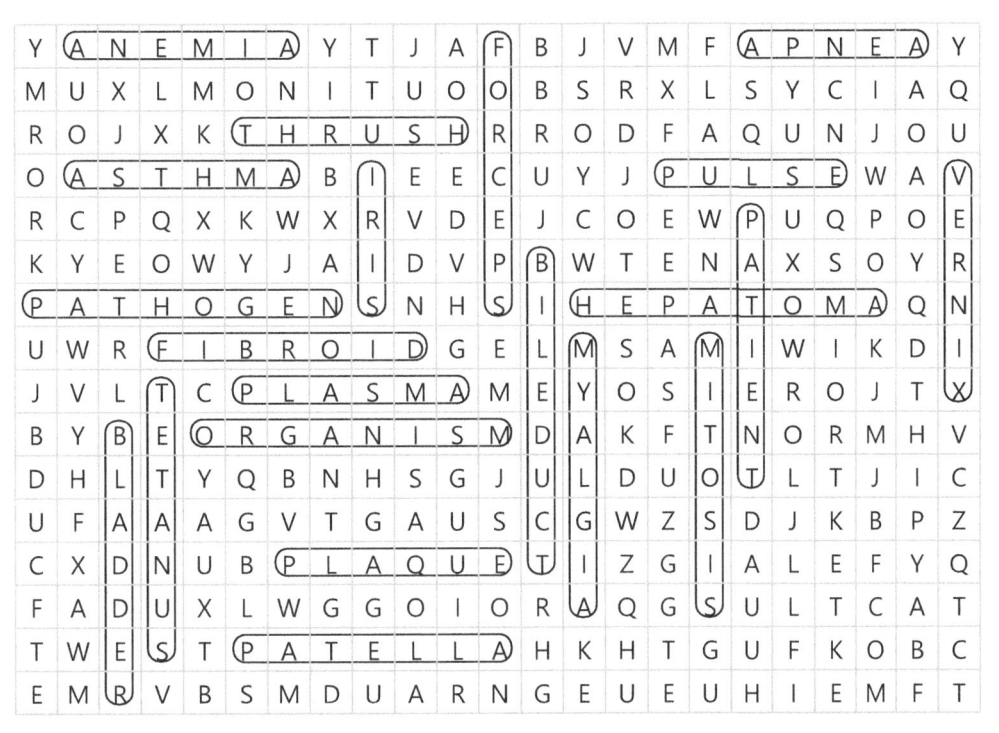

Y	A	N	E	M	I	A	Y	T	J	A	F	B	J	V	M	F	A	P	N	E	A	Y
M	U	X	L	M	O	N	I	T	U	O	O	B	S	R	X	L	S	Y	C	I	A	Q
R	O	J	X	K	T	H	R	U	S	H	R	R	O	D	F	A	Q	U	N	J	O	U
O	A	S	T	H	M	A	B	I	E	E	C	U	Y	J	P	U	L	S	E	W	A	V
R	C	P	Q	X	K	W	X	R	V	D	E	J	C	O	E	W	P	U	Q	P	O	E
K	Y	E	O	W	Y	J	A	I	D	V	P	B	W	T	E	N	A	X	S	O	Y	R
P	A	T	H	O	G	E	N	S	N	H	S	I	H	E	P	A	T	O	M	A	Q	N
U	W	R	F	I	B	R	O	I	D	G	E	L	M	S	A	M	I	W	I	K	D	I
J	V	L	T	C	P	L	A	S	M	A	M	E	Y	O	S	I	E	R	O	J	T	X
B	Y	B	E	O	R	G	A	N	I	S	M	D	A	K	F	T	N	O	R	M	H	V
D	H	L	T	Y	Q	B	N	H	S	G	J	U	L	D	U	O	T	L	T	J	I	C
U	F	A	A	G	V	T	G	A	U	S	C	G	W	Z	S	D	J	K	B	P	Z
C	X	D	N	U	B	P	L	A	Q	U	E	T	I	Z	G	I	A	L	E	F	Y	Q
F	A	D	U	X	L	W	G	G	O	I	O	R	A	Q	G	S	U	L	T	C	A	T
T	W	E	S	T	P	A	T	E	L	L	A	H	K	H	T	G	U	F	K	O	B	C
E	M	R	V	B	S	M	D	U	A	R	N	G	E	U	E	U	H	I	E	M	F	T

1. The medical term for muscle pain
2. Instruments resembling tweezers that are used to handle objects or tissue during surgery
3. An organ located in the pelvis whose function is to collect and store urine until it is expelled
4. A candidiasis infection
5. The process by which most cells divide to reproduce
6. Any substance capable of causing a disease
7. A disorder characterized by inflamed airways and difficulty breathing
8. An area of buildup of fat deposits in an artery, causing narrowing of the artery and possibly heart disease
9. The thick, greasy substance that covers the skin of a newborn baby
10. A tube that carries bile from the liver to the gallbladder and then to the small intestine
11. The expansion and contraction of a blood vessel due to the blood pumped through it
12. A possibly life-threatening condition in which breathing stops, for either a short or long period of time
13. Any single, functioning form of life
14. A condition in which the blood does not contain enough hemoglobin, the compound that carries oxygen from the lungs to other parts of the body
15. A noncancerous tumor of the uterus made up of smooth muscle and connective tissue
16. The colored part of the eye
17. Controlled analgesia- a system for administering pain - killing drugs in which the amount of drug delivered is controlled by the patient
18. A sometimes fatal disease affecting the brain and spinal cord
19. The liquid part of the blood, containing substances such as nutrients, salts, and proteins
20. The medical term for the kneecap
21. A cancerous tumor of the liver

A. Tetanus	B. Patella	C. Mitosis	D. Organism	E. Forceps	F. Asthma
G. Anemia	H. Myalgia	I. Bile duct	J. Bladder	K. Vernix	L. Fibroid
M. Pathogen	N. Apnea	O. Plaque	P. Pulse	Q. Iris	R. Patient
S. Plasma	T. Hepatoma	U. Thrush			

239

G. Find the hidden words. The words have been placed horizontally, vertically, or diagonally. When you locate a word, draw an ellipse around it.

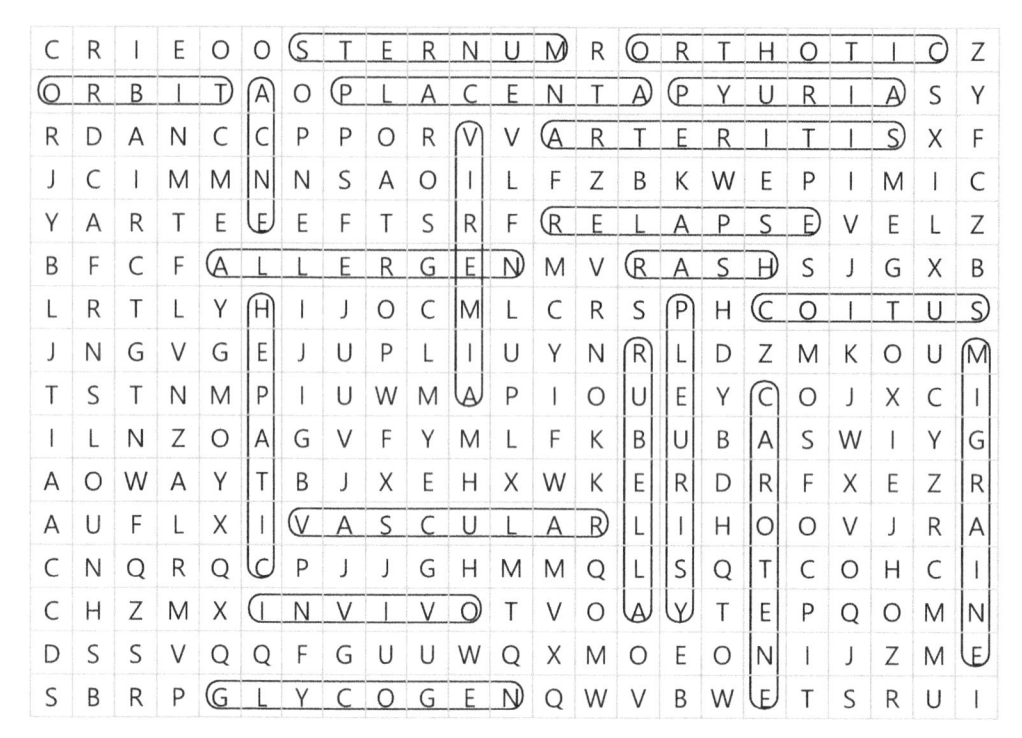

C	R	I	E	O	O	S	T	E	R	N	U	M	R	O	R	T	H	O	T	I	C	Z
O	R	B	I	T	A	O	P	L	A	C	E	N	T	A	P	Y	U	R	I	A	S	Y
R	D	A	N	C	C	P	P	O	R	V	V	A	R	T	E	R	I	T	I	S	X	F
J	C	I	M	M	N	N	S	A	O	I	L	F	Z	B	K	W	E	P	I	M	I	C
Y	A	R	T	E	E	E	F	T	S	R	F	R	E	L	A	P	S	E	V	E	L	Z
B	F	C	F	A	L	L	E	R	G	E	N	M	V	R	A	S	H	S	J	G	X	B
L	R	T	L	Y	H	I	J	O	C	M	L	C	R	S	P	H	C	O	I	T	U	S
J	N	G	V	G	E	J	U	P	L	I	U	Y	N	R	L	D	Z	M	K	O	U	M
T	S	T	N	M	P	I	U	W	M	A	P	I	O	U	E	Y	C	O	J	X	C	I
I	L	N	Z	O	A	G	V	F	Y	M	L	F	K	B	U	B	A	S	W	I	Y	G
A	O	W	A	Y	T	B	J	X	E	H	X	W	K	E	R	D	R	F	X	E	Z	R
A	U	F	L	X	I	V	A	S	C	U	L	A	R	L	I	H	O	O	V	J	R	A
C	N	Q	R	Q	C	P	J	J	G	H	M	M	Q	L	S	Q	T	C	O	H	C	I
C	H	Z	M	X	I	N	V	I	V	O	T	V	O	A	Y	T	E	P	Q	O	M	N
D	S	S	V	Q	Q	F	G	U	U	W	Q	X	M	O	E	O	N	I	J	Z	M	E
S	B	R	P	G	L	Y	C	O	G	E	N	Q	W	V	B	W	E	T	S	R	U	I

1. The presence of viruses in the blood
2. The socket in the skull that contains the eyeball, along with its blood vessels, nerves, and muscles
3. The return of a disease or symptom after it had disappeared
4. A skin condition characterized by inflamed, pus-filled areas that occur on the skin's surface, most commonly occurring during adolescence
5. A term used to describe something that is related to the liver
6. An orange pigment present in colored plants such as carrots that is converted by the body to the essential nutrient vitamin a
7. A mild viral infection (also known as German measles) that produces a rash and fever
8. A severe headache, usually accompanied by vision problems and
9. An organ formed in the uterus during pregnancy that links the blood of the mother to the blood of the fetus
10. Pertaining to blood vessels
11. "in the living body"; a biological process that occurs inside of the body
12. A substance that causes an allergic reaction
13. A device used to correct or control deformed bones, muscles, or joints
14. An area of inflammation or a group of spots on the skin
15. Inflammation of the walls of an artery that causes the passageway to become narrower
16. Inflammation of the lining of the lungs and chest cavity usually caused by a lung infection
17. The long, flat bone located at the center of the chest
18. Sexual intercourse
19. The main form that glucose, the body's energy source, takes when it is stored
20. The presence of white blood cells in the urine

A. Orthotic	B. Glycogen	C. Allergen	D. Viremia	E. Migraine	F. Arteritis	G. Pleurisy
H. Orbit	I. Rash	J. Vascular	K. Rubella	L. Coitus	M. Sternum	N. Carotene
O. Relapse	P. Acne	Q. Hepatic	R. Placenta	S. In vivo	T. Pyuria	

H. Find the hidden words. The words have been placed horizontally, vertically, or diagonally. When you locate a word, draw an ellipse around it.

T	Y	V	L	C	I	L	I	A	X	C	V	H	M	D	W	A	T	G	H	K	E	G
H	P	A	K	Q	A	G	Z	T	J	A	E	Y	A	D	V	Z	A	C	P	D	U	F
R	T	X	L	X	Q	L	O	O	S	U	Q	Q	O	A	A	R	R	R	U	N	L	C
A	T	Y	D	X	O	L	E	S	R	R	J	M	Z	S	C	W	T	X	S	C	M	E
B	L	J	V	R	K	Z	C	L	N	A	J	D	V	T	C	V	A	R	I	O	L	A
I	M	G	N	S	W	I	O	R	B	I	T	F	R	H	I	I	R	E	L	H	F	Y
E	B	B	C	P	W	T	N	B	N	G	E	P	L	M	N	J	Y	A	M	B	C	A
S	O	W	E	D	Y	G	A	N	G	L	I	O	N	A	E	H	G	O	U	T	Z	O
X	I	V	D	Y	S	P	N	E	A	P	U	D	E	N	D	U	M	W	G	X	O	L
M	U	X	Z	W	R	Q	P	U	Z	A	F	I	B	R	O	S	I	S	J	C	L	Z
H	Q	V	D	I	G	J	T	Y	D	H	W	E	Q	F	Q	Z	G	A	Z	W	A	B
Q	J	M	K	C	F	D	P	E	O	P	P	F	A	D	P	H	I	M	O	S	I	S
O	I	C	S	Z	V	O	V	M	Z	O	I	A	C	C	M	C	G	O	F	U	W	V
G	R	I	N	G	W	O	R	M	O	V	O	D	I	O	A	A	Q	W	R	S	W	E
B	G	B	N	A	L	N	W	C	M	C	B	M	J	Q	V	I	S	N	V	D	E	G
L	T	E	T	A	N	U	S	D	E	X	T	R	O	S	E	T	R	I	S	O	M	Y

1. A thick, yellowish or greenish fluid that contains dead white blood cells, tissues, and bacteria; occurs at the site of a bacterial infection
2. A fluid-filled cyst attached to a tendon sheath or joint
3. A "warning" signal that comes before a migraine headache or an epileptic seizure, which might include emotions or sensations of movement or discomfort
4. Tiny, hair like structures on the outside of some cells, providing mobility
5. A skin infection caused by a fungus that spreads out in an even circle, characterized by ring- like, scaly patches of red skin
6. Tightness of the foreskin, which prevents it from being moved back over the head of the penis
7. A disorder characterized by inflamed airways and difficulty breathing
8. A disorder marked by high levels of uric acid in the blood
9. The external genitals, usually referring to the female
10. An inflamed, raised area of skin that is pus-filled; usually an infected hair follicle
11. A preparation of weakened microorganisms given to create resistance to a certain disease
12. An infectious viral disease primarily affecting animals
13. Another term for smallpox
14. Difficulty breathing
15. A sometimes fatal disease affecting the brain and spinal cord
16. Abnormal formation of connective or scar tissue
17. The presence in the cells of three copies of a certain chromosome instead of the normal two copies
18. The socket in the skull that contains the eyeball, along with its blood vessels, nerves, and muscles
19. Another name for the sugar glucose
20. The hard deposit formed on teeth when mineral salts in saliva combine with plaque

A. Dyspnea	B. Rabies	C. Aura	D. Vaccine	E. Fibrosis	F. Variola
G. Gout	H. Ringworm	I. Orbit	J. Dextrose	K. Ganglion	L. Trisomy
M. Asthma	N. Tartar	O. Phimosis	P. Pudendum	Q. Boil	R. Pus
S. Tetanus	T. Cilia				

I. Find the hidden words. The words have been placed horizontally, vertically, or diagonally. When you locate a word, draw an ellipse around it.

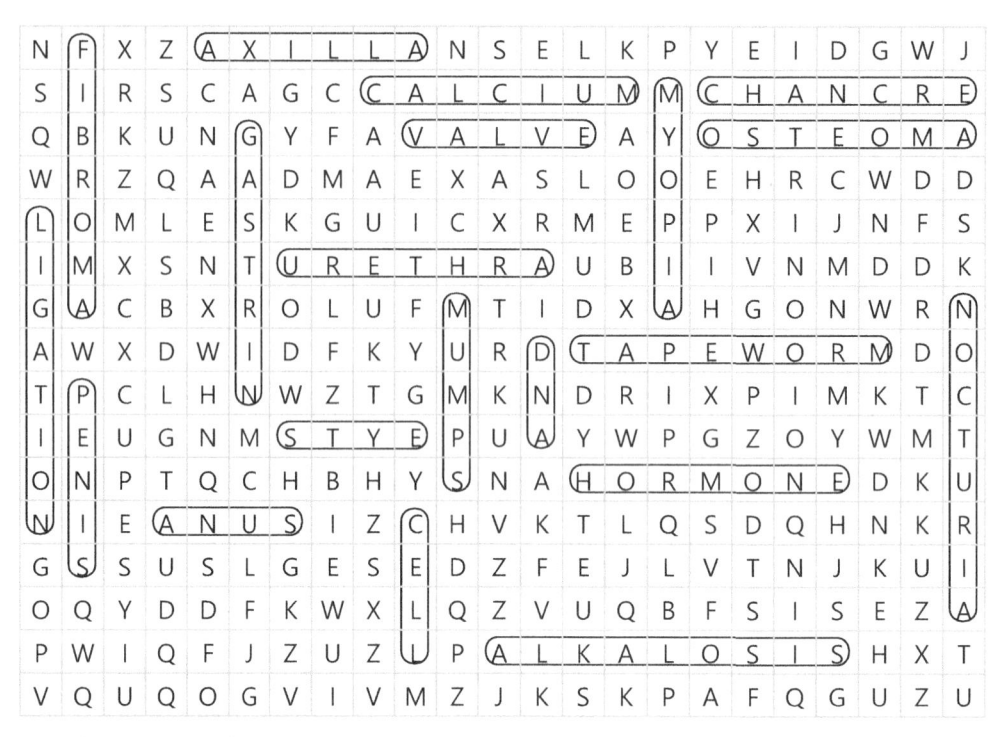

N	F	X	Z	A	X	I	L	L	A	N	S	E	L	K	P	Y	E	I	D	G	W	J
S	I	R	S	C	A	G	C	C	A	L	C	I	U	M	M	C	H	A	N	C	R	E
Q	B	K	U	N	G	Y	F	A	V	A	L	V	E	A	Y	O	S	T	E	O	M	A
W	R	Z	Q	A	A	D	M	A	E	X	A	S	L	O	O	E	H	R	C	W	D	D
L	O	M	L	E	S	K	G	U	I	C	X	R	M	E	P	P	X	I	J	N	F	S
I	M	X	S	N	T	U	R	E	T	H	R	A	U	B	I	I	V	N	M	D	D	K
G	A	C	B	X	R	O	L	U	F	M	T	I	D	X	A	H	G	O	N	W	R	N
A	W	X	D	W	I	D	F	K	Y	U	R	D	T	A	P	E	W	O	R	M	D	O
T	P	C	L	H	N	W	Z	T	G	M	K	N	D	R	I	X	P	I	M	K	T	C
I	E	U	G	N	M	S	T	Y	E	P	U	A	Y	W	P	G	Z	O	Y	W	M	T
O	N	P	T	Q	C	H	B	H	Y	S	N	A	H	O	R	M	O	N	E	D	K	U
N	I	E	A	N	U	S	I	Z	C	H	V	K	T	L	Q	S	D	Q	H	N	K	R
G	S	S	U	S	L	G	E	S	E	D	Z	F	E	J	L	V	T	N	J	K	U	I
O	Q	Y	D	D	F	K	W	X	L	Q	Z	V	U	Q	B	F	S	I	S	E	Z	A
P	W	I	Q	F	J	Z	U	Z	U	P	A	L	K	A	L	O	S	I	S	H	X	T
V	Q	U	Q	O	G	V	I	V	M	Z	J	K	S	K	P	A	F	Q	G	U	Z	U

1. The opening through which feces are passed from the body
2. A noncancerous tumor of connective tissue
3. Medical term for the armpit
4. The medical term for nearsightedness
5. A structure that allows fluid flow in only one direction
6. A plentiful mineral in the body and the basic component of teeth and bones
7. The tiny structures that make up all the tissues of the body and carry out all its functions
8. A viral infection that causes inflammation of salivary glands
9. Urination or a sleep-disturbing need to urinate during the night
10. A hormone that stimulates the release of gastric acid in the stomach
11. A pus-filled abscess in the follicle of an eyelash
12. A chemical produced by a gland or tissue that is released into the bloodstream
13. Deoxyribonucleic acid; responsible for passing genetic information in nearly all organisms
14. A parasitic worm that lives in the intestines
15. A painless sore that has a thick, rubbery base and a defined edge
16. The process of closing a blood vessel or duct by tying it off
17. Dangerously decreased acidity of the blood, which can be caused by high altitudes, hyperventilation, and excessive vomiting
18. The external male reproductive organ, which passes urine and semen out of the body
19. The tube by which urine is released from the bladder
20. A noncancerous bone tumor

A. DNA	B. Calcium	C. Nocturia	D. Urethra	E. Alkalosis	F. Axilla
G. Ligation	H. Mumps	I. Stye	J. Cell	K. Penis	L. Tapeworm
M. Fibroma	N. Anus	O. Myopia	P. Gastrin	Q. Valve	R. Chancre
S. Hormone	T. Osteoma				

J. Find the hidden words. The words have been placed horizontally, vertically, or diagonally. When you locate a word, draw an ellipse around it.

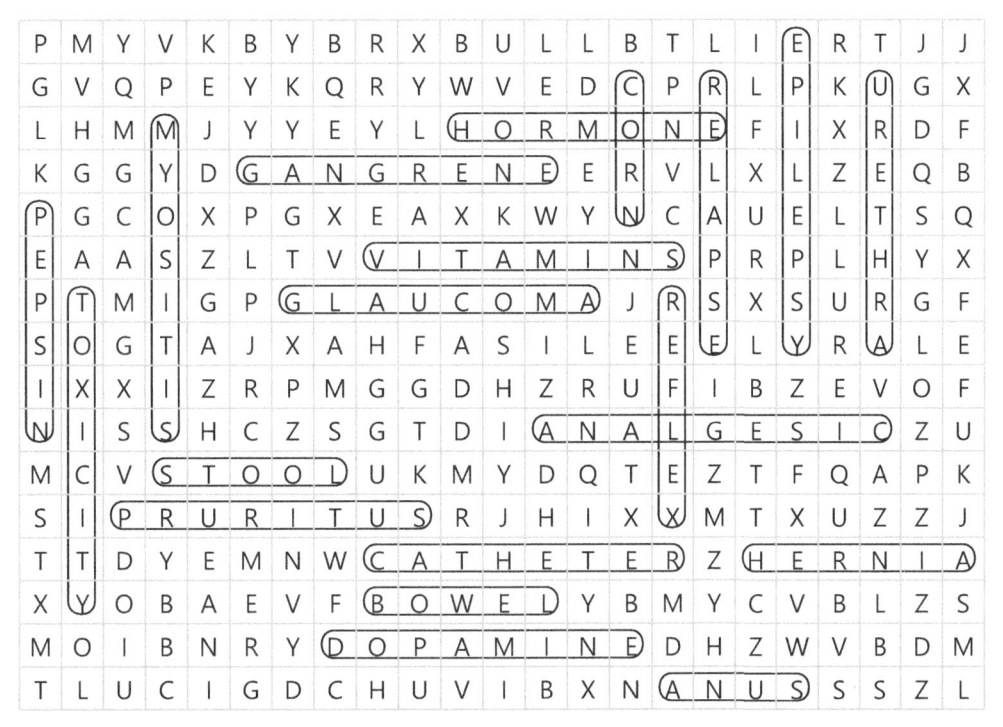

P	M	Y	V	K	B	Y	B	R	X	B	U	L	L	B	T	L	I	E	R	T	J	J
G	V	Q	P	E	Y	K	Q	R	Y	W	V	E	D	C	P	R	L	P	K	U	G	X
L	H	M	M	J	Y	Y	E	Y	L	H	O	R	M	O	N	E	F	I	X	R	D	F
K	G	G	Y	D	G	A	N	G	R	E	N	E	E	R	V	L	X	L	Z	E	Q	B
P	G	C	O	X	P	G	X	E	A	X	K	W	Y	N	C	A	U	E	L	T	S	Q
E	A	A	S	Z	L	T	V	V	I	T	A	M	I	N	S	P	R	P	L	H	Y	X
P	T	M	I	G	P	G	L	A	U	C	O	M	A	J	R	S	X	S	U	R	G	F
S	O	G	T	A	J	X	A	H	F	A	S	I	L	E	E	E	L	Y	R	A	L	E
I	X	X	I	Z	R	P	M	G	G	D	H	Z	R	U	F	I	B	Z	E	V	O	F
N	I	S	S	H	C	Z	S	G	T	D	I	A	N	A	L	G	E	S	I	C	Z	U
M	C	V	S	T	O	O	L	U	K	M	Y	D	Q	T	E	Z	T	F	Q	A	P	K
S	I	P	R	U	R	I	T	U	S	R	J	H	I	X	W	M	T	X	U	Z	Z	J
T	T	D	Y	E	M	N	W	C	A	T	H	E	T	E	R	Z	H	E	R	N	I	A
X	Y	O	B	A	E	V	F	B	O	W	E	L	Y	B	M	Y	C	V	B	L	Z	S
M	O	I	B	N	R	Y	D	O	P	A	M	I	N	E	D	H	Z	W	V	B	D	M
T	L	U	C	I	G	D	C	H	U	V	I	B	X	N	A	N	U	S	S	S	Z	L

1. Complex substances that are necessary in small amounts to maintain health and ensure proper development and functioning of the body
2. A hollow, flexible tube inserted into the body to put in or take out fluid, or to open or close blood vessels
3. The bulging of an organ or tissue through a weakened area in the muscle wall
4. A drug that relieves pain, such as aspirin or acetaminophen
5. The enzyme found in gastric juice that helps digest protein
6. The opening through which feces are passed from the body
7. The tube by which urine is released from the bladder
8. A chemical that transmits messages in the brain and plays a role in movement
9. An automatic, involuntary response of the nervous system to a stimulus
10. A chemical produced by a gland or tissue that is released into the bloodstream
11. A thickened callus on the foot that is caused by an improperly fitting shoe
12. A disorder of the nervous system in which abnormal electrical activity in the brain causes seizures
13. Intestine
14. The medical term for itching
15. Death of a tissue because of a lack of blood supply
16. A disease in which eye damage is caused by an increase in the pressure of the fluid within the eye
17. The return of a disease or symptom after it had disappeared
18. Muscle inflammation, causing pain and weakness
19. The extent to which a substance is poisonous
20. Another term for feces

A. Glaucoma
B. Bowel
C. Reflex
D. Catheter
E. Vitamins
F. Epilepsy
G. Dopamine
H. Anus
I. Gangrene
J. Pruritus
K. Hormone
L. Urethra
M. Myositis
N. Stool
O. Pepsin
P. Toxicity
Q. Corn
R. Analgesic
S. Hernia
T. Relapse

243

K. Find the hidden words. The words have been placed horizontally, vertically, or diagonally. When you locate a word, draw an ellipse around it.

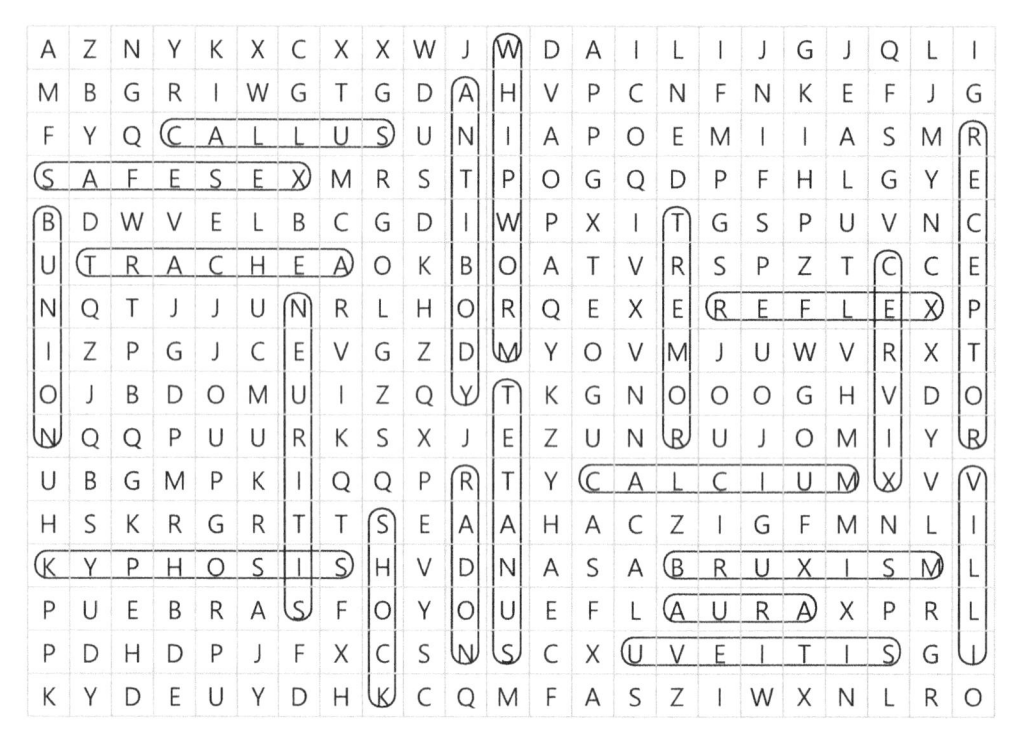

A	Z	N	Y	K	X	C	X	X	W	J	W	D	A	I	L	I	J	G	J	Q	L	I
M	B	G	R	I	W	G	T	G	D	A	H	V	P	C	N	F	N	K	E	F	J	G
F	Y	Q	C	A	L	L	U	S	U	N	I	A	P	O	E	M	I	I	A	S	M	R
S	A	F	E	S	E	X	M	R	S	T	P	O	G	Q	D	P	F	H	L	G	Y	E
B	D	W	V	E	L	B	C	G	D	I	W	P	X	I	T	G	S	P	U	V	N	C
U	T	R	A	C	H	E	A	O	K	B	O	A	T	V	R	S	P	Z	T	C	C	E
N	Q	T	J	J	U	N	R	L	H	O	R	Q	E	X	E	R	E	F	L	E	X	P
I	Z	P	G	J	C	E	V	G	Z	D	M	Y	O	V	M	J	U	W	V	R	X	T
O	J	B	D	O	M	U	I	Z	Q	Y	T	K	G	N	O	O	O	G	H	V	D	O
N	Q	Q	P	U	U	R	K	S	X	J	E	Z	U	N	R	U	J	O	M	I	Y	R
U	B	G	M	P	K	I	Q	Q	P	R	T	Y	C	A	L	C	I	U	M	X	V	V
H	S	K	R	G	R	T	T	S	E	A	A	H	A	C	Z	I	G	F	M	N	L	I
K	Y	P	H	O	S	I	S	H	V	D	N	A	S	A	B	R	U	X	I	S	M	L
P	U	E	B	R	A	S	F	O	Y	O	U	E	F	L	A	U	R	A	X	P	R	L
P	D	H	D	P	J	F	X	C	S	N	S	C	X	U	V	E	I	T	I	S	G	U
K	Y	D	E	U	Y	D	H	K	C	Q	M	F	A	S	Z	I	W	X	N	L	R	O

1. A small, parasitic worm that can live in the intestines of a human and may cause diarrhea, abdominal pain, and anemia
2. A hard, fluid-filled pad along the inside joint of the big toe
3. A reduced flow of blood throughout the body, usually caused by severe bleeding or a weak heart
4. Inflammation of a nerve, often characterized by pain, numbness, or tingling
5. A colorless, odorless, tasteless radioactive gas that is produced by materials in soil, rocks, and building materials; suspected of causing cancer
6. An unaware clenching or grinding of the teeth, usually during sleep
7. A sometimes fatal disease affecting the brain and spinal cord
8. A "warning" signal that comes before a migraine headache or an epileptic seizure, which might include emotions or sensations of movement or discomfort
9. An automatic, involuntary response of the nervous system to a stimulus
10. A plentiful mineral in the body and the basic component of teeth and bones
11. A thickened area of skin due to consistent pressure or friction, or the area around a bone break where new bone is formed
12. An involuntary, rhythmic, shaking movement caused by alternating contraction and relaxation of muscles
13. Excessive curvature of the spine, which usually affects the top part of the spine and causes a hump
14. A protein made by white blood cells that reacts with a specific foreign protein as part of the immune response
15. Measures taken to reduce the risk of acquiring a sexually transmitted disease, such as the use of a condom
16. A small, round organ making up the neck of the uterus and separating it from the vagina
17. The tube running from the larynx (the voice box) down the neck and into the upper part of the chest
18. A nerve cell that responds to a stimulus and produces a nerve impulse
19. Inflammation of the uvea
20. The millions of fingerlike projections on the lining of the small intestine that aid in the absorption of food

A. Antibody   B. Callus   C. Shock   D. Calcium   E. Uveitis   F. Radon
G. Safe sex   H. Neuritis   I. Kyphosis   J. Trachea   K. Receptor   L. Reflex
M. Bruxism   N. Tetanus   O. Whipworm   P. Villi   Q. Bunion   R. Aura
S. Tremor   T. Cervix

L. Find the hidden words. The words have been placed horizontally, vertically, or diagonally. When you locate a word, draw an ellipse around it.

X	K	E	N	E	C	R	O	S	I	S	R	L	I	N	U	S	B	M	U	M	P	S
C	D	L	P	G	V	Z	K	N	T	T	A	R	T	A	R	H	O	Y	Q	T	B	C
X	O	K	X	B	V	P	M	O	A	W	B	T	A	R	S	C	N	V	M	R	K	O
K	X	B	V	I	L	L	I	P	C	C	S	N	W	C	C	M	A	S	J	A	Z	Y
T	Y	C	O	N	X	U	V	E	I	T	I	S	X	O	A	Q	G	N	P	C	R	W
T	G	F	B	Z	I	A	X	V	D	E	K	G	A	T	B	N	U	R	U	T	J	E
I	E	M	I	N	E	R	A	L	O	O	U	F	X	I	I	C	Z	X	L	I	N	Z
X	N	P	A	N	A	L	G	E	S	I	C	T	H	C	E	X	J	T	S	O	J	M
L	W	E	A	P	U	O	U	N	I	N	B	B	T	G	S	O	L	X	E	N	Y	X
Q	V	D	C	R	C	U	A	A	S	G	O	C	U	L	A	R	O	Z	O	N	E	L
C	I	Q	U	O	K	E	Y	H	E	O	Z	F	R	D	M	I	T	O	S	I	S	O
M	V	M	F	X	R	A	H	J	Y	M	C	I	O	J	J	U	J	Z	U	H	J	L
E	L	H	J	I	B	Q	E	T	J	X	Z	B	A	C	Q	U	I	R	E	D	S	O
P	G	I	V	M	I	F	D	S	J	D	S	E	W	U	O	N	U	P	F	J	T	D
I	K	F	W	A	Q	K	D	Q	P	P	C	R	V	V	T	O	B	D	L	C	F	S
U	H	P	M	U	G	B	Q	Y	U	R	P	N	I	A	C	I	N	Y	K	H	W	D

1. The hard deposit formed on teeth when mineral salts in saliva combine with plaque
2. Describes something related to the eyes
3. Inflammation of the uvea
4. A condition marked by abnormally high acid levels in the blood, associated with some forms of diabetes, lung disease, and severe kidney disease
5. A word describing any condition that is not present at birth, but develops some time during life
6. A gas that is colorless, odorless, and tasteless
7. The process by which most cells divide to reproduce
8. A vitamin important in many chemical processes in the body; also known as vitamin b3
9. A drug that relieves pain, such as aspirin or acetaminophen
10. The use of tension to hold a body part in place or to correct or prevent an alignment problem
11. An addictive substance that blunts the senses
12. A highly contagious skin disorder caused by a mite that burrows into the skin and produces an intense, itchy rash
13. The medical term for the death of tissue cells
14. A viral infection that causes inflammation of salivary glands
15. A poisonous form of oxygen that is present in the earth's upper atmosphere, where it helps to screen the earth from damaging ultraviolet rays
16. Located nearer to a central point of reference on the body, such as the trunk
17. The millions of fingerlike projections on the lining of the small intestine that aid in the absorption of food
18. A substance that is a necessary part of a healthy diet (such as potassium, calcium, sodium, phosphorus, and magnesium)
19. A constituent of plants that cannot be digested, which helps maintain healthy functioning of the bowels
20. The expansion and contraction of a blood vessel due to the blood pumped through it

A. Narcotic	B. Scabies	C. Mumps	D. Acidosis	E. Necrosis	F. Mineral	G. Ocular
H. Niacin	I. Pulse	J. Villi	K. Acquired	L. Analgesic	M. Proximal	N. Oxygen
O. Tartar	P. Mitosis	Q. Ozone	R. Fiber	S. Uveitis	T. Traction	

M. Find the hidden words. The words have been placed horizontally, vertically, or diagonally. When you locate a word, draw an ellipse around it.

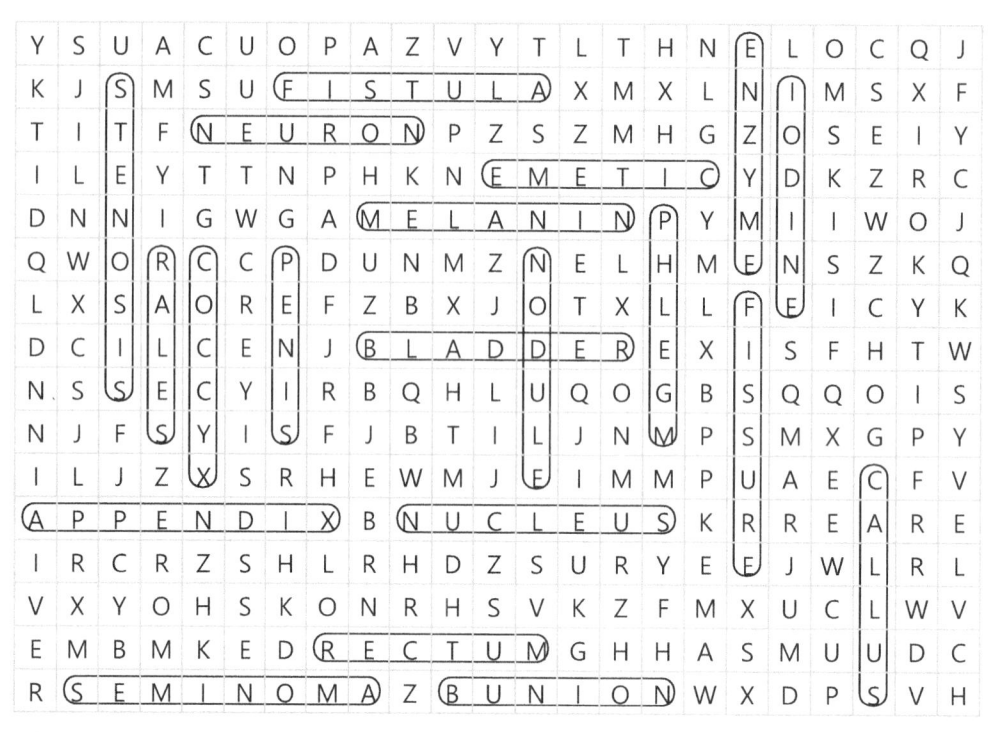

Y	S	U	A	C	U	O	P	A	Z	V	Y	T	L	T	H	N	E	L	O	C	Q	J
K	J	S	M	S	U	F	I	S	T	U	L	A	X	M	X	L	N	I	M	S	X	F
T	I	T	F	N	E	U	R	O	N	P	Z	S	Z	M	H	G	Z	O	S	E	I	Y
I	L	E	Y	T	T	N	P	H	K	N	E	M	E	T	I	C	Y	D	K	Z	R	C
D	N	N	I	G	W	G	A	M	E	L	A	N	I	N	P	Y	M	I	I	W	O	J
Q	W	O	R	C	C	P	D	U	N	M	Z	N	E	L	H	M	E	N	S	Z	K	Q
L	X	S	A	O	R	E	F	Z	B	X	J	O	T	X	L	L	F	E	I	C	Y	K
D	C	I	L	C	E	N	J	B	L	A	D	D	E	R	E	X	I	S	F	H	T	W
N	S	S	E	C	Y	I	R	B	Q	H	L	U	Q	O	G	B	S	Q	Q	O	I	S
N	J	F	S	Y	I	S	F	J	B	T	I	L	J	N	W	P	S	M	X	G	P	Y
I	L	J	Z	X	S	R	H	E	W	M	J	E	I	M	M	P	U	A	E	C	F	V
A	P	P	E	N	D	I	X	B	N	U	C	L	E	U	S	K	R	R	E	A	R	E
I	R	C	R	Z	S	H	L	R	H	D	Z	S	U	R	Y	E	E	J	W	L	R	L
V	X	Y	O	H	S	K	O	N	R	H	S	V	K	Z	F	M	X	U	C	L	W	V
E	M	B	M	K	E	D	R	E	C	T	U	M	G	H	H	A	S	M	U	U	D	C
R	S	E	M	I	N	O	M	A	Z	B	U	N	I	O	N	W	X	D	P	S	V	H

1. Mucus and other material produced by the lining of the respiratory tract
2. The center or most important point of an object
3. A hard, fluid-filled pad along the inside joint of the big toe
4. A chemical, originating in a cell, that regulates reactions in the body
5. The pigment that gives skin, hair, and eyes their coloring
6. A groove or slit on the body or in an organ
7. Abnormal crackling or bubbling sounds heard in the lungs during breathing
8. An abnormal passageway from one organ to another or from an organ to the body surface
9. A substance that causes vomiting
10. The external male reproductive organ, which passes urine and semen out of the body
11. A small lump of tissue that is usually abnormal
12. A thickened area of skin due to consistent pressure or friction, or the area around a bone break where new bone is formed
13. Four fused bones that form a triangular shape at the base of the spine (also known as the tailbone)
14. A short tube located at the end of the large intestine, which connects the intestine to the anus
15. Narrowing of a body passageway
16. A short, tube-like structure that branches off the large intestine
17. Another term for a nerve cell
18. A type of testicular cancer that is made up of only a single type of cell
19. An element for the formation of thyroid hormones
20. An organ located in the pelvis whose function is to collect and store urine until it is expelled

A. Iodine	B. Callus	C. Emetic	D. Rales	E. Seminoma	F. Enzyme
G. Fistula	H. Nucleus	I. Stenosis	J. Rectum	K. Coccyx	L. Melanin
M. Fissure	N. Phlegm	O. Bunion	P. Nodule	Q. Penis	R. Neuron
S. Bladder	T. Appendix				

N. Find the hidden words. The words have been placed horizontally, vertically, or diagonally. When you locate a word, draw an ellipse around it.

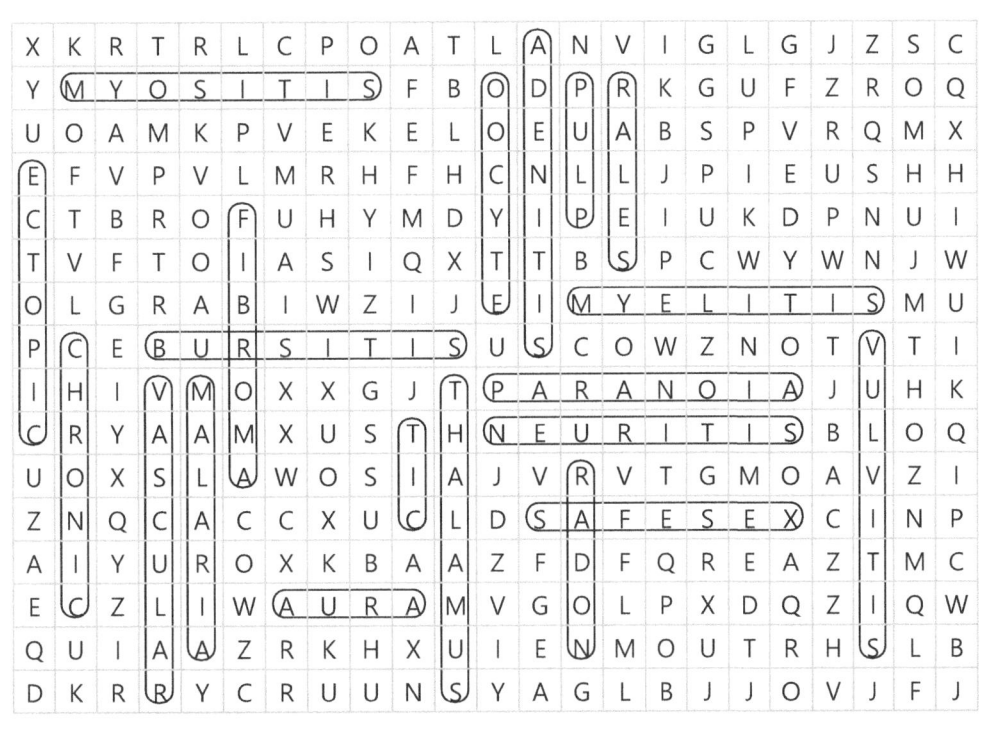

X	K	R	T	R	L	C	P	O	A	T	L	A	N	V	I	G	L	G	J	Z	S	C
Y	M	Y	O	S	I	T	I	S	F	B	O	D	P	R	K	G	U	F	Z	R	O	Q
U	O	A	M	K	P	V	E	K	E	L	O	E	U	A	B	S	P	V	R	Q	M	X
E	F	V	P	V	L	M	R	H	F	H	C	N	L	L	J	P	I	E	U	S	H	H
C	T	B	R	O	F	U	H	Y	M	D	Y	I	P	E	I	U	K	D	P	N	U	I
T	V	F	T	O	I	A	S	I	Q	X	T	T	B	S	P	C	W	Y	W	N	J	W
O	L	G	R	A	B	I	W	Z	I	J	E	I	M	Y	E	L	I	T	I	S	M	U
P	C	E	B	U	R	S	I	T	I	S	U	S	C	O	W	Z	N	O	T	V	T	I
I	H	I	V	M	O	X	X	G	J	T	P	A	R	A	N	O	I	A	J	U	H	K
C	R	Y	A	A	M	X	U	S	T	H	N	E	U	R	I	T	I	S	B	L	O	Q
U	O	X	S	L	A	W	O	S	I	A	J	V	R	V	T	G	M	O	A	V	Z	I
Z	N	Q	C	A	C	C	X	U	C	L	D	S	A	F	E	S	E	X	C	I	N	P
A	I	Y	U	R	O	X	K	B	A	Z	F	D	F	Q	R	E	A	Z	T	M	C	
E	C	Z	L	I	W	A	U	R	A	M	V	G	O	L	P	X	D	Q	Z	I	Q	W
Q	U	I	A	A	Z	R	K	H	X	U	I	E	N	M	O	U	T	R	H	S	L	B
D	K	R	R	Y	C	R	U	U	N	S	Y	A	G	L	B	J	J	O	V	J	F	J

1. A structure in the brain that relays and processes incoming sensory information from the eyes and ears and from pressure and pain receptors
2. A disorder in which a person becomes overly suspicious and emotionally sensitive
3. Describes a disorder that continues for a long period of time
4. Occurring at an abnormal position or time
5. Inflammation of a bursa due to excessive pressure or friction, or from injury
6. An involuntary, repetitive movement such as a twitch
7. The soft tissue inside of a tooth that contains blood vessels and nerves
8. Inflammation of the vulva
9. Measures taken to reduce the risk of acquiring a sexually transmitted disease, such as the use of a condom
10. An egg cell that has not developed completely
11. A noncancerous tumor of connective tissue
12. Infection and inflammation of a gland, especially a lymph node
13. Muscle inflammation, causing pain and weakness
14. Inflammation of a nerve, often characterized by pain, numbness, or tingling
15. A colorless, odorless, tasteless radioactive gas that is produced by materials in soil, rocks, and building materials; suspected of causing cancer
16. A parasitic disease spread by mosquitos that causes chills and fever
17. Inflammation of the spinal cord, which can cause headaches, fever, muscle stiffness, pain, weakness, and eventually paralysis
18. Abnormal crackling or bubbling sounds heard in the lungs during breathing
19. A "warning" signal that comes before a migraine headache or an epileptic seizure, which might include emotions or sensations of movement or discomfort
20. Pertaining to blood vessels

A. Pulp	B. Myositis	C. Chronic	D. Adenitis	E. Thalamus	F. Vulvitis	G. Safe sex
H. Aura	I. Oocyte	J. Rales	K. Bursitis	L. Ectopic	M. Radon	N. Tic
O. Myelitis	P. Malaria	Q. Vascular	R. Paranoia	S. Neuritis	T. Fibroma	

O. Find the hidden words. The words have been placed horizontally, vertically, or diagonally. When you locate a word, draw an ellipse around it.

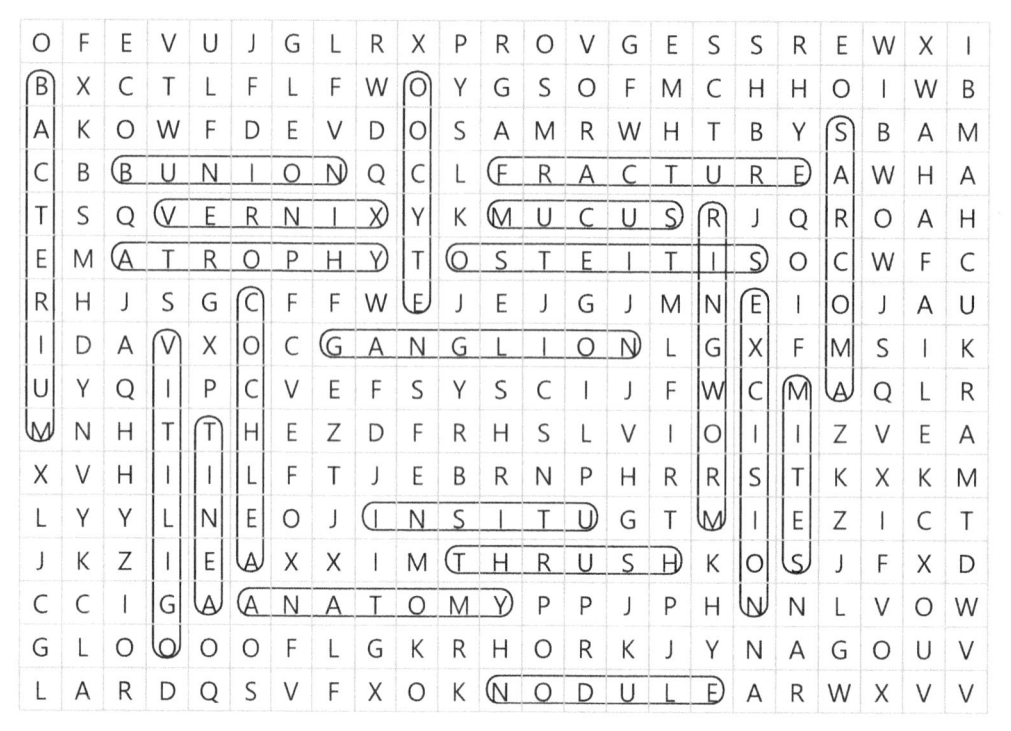

O	F	E	V	U	J	G	L	R	X	P	R	O	V	G	E	S	S	R	E	W	X	I
B	X	C	T	L	F	L	F	W	O	Y	G	S	O	F	M	C	H	H	O	I	W	B
A	K	O	W	F	D	E	V	D	O	S	A	M	R	W	H	T	B	Y	S	B	A	M
C	B	B	U	N	I	O	N	Q	C	L	F	R	A	C	T	U	R	E	A	W	H	A
T	S	Q	V	E	R	N	I	X	Y	K	M	U	C	U	S	R	J	Q	R	O	A	H
E	M	A	T	R	O	P	H	Y	T	O	S	T	E	I	T	I	S	O	C	W	F	C
R	H	J	S	G	C	F	F	W	E	J	E	J	G	J	M	N	E	I	O	J	A	U
I	D	A	V	X	O	C	G	A	N	G	L	I	O	N	L	G	X	F	M	S	I	K
U	Y	Q	I	P	C	V	E	F	S	Y	S	C	I	J	F	W	C	M	A	Q	L	R
M	N	H	T	T	H	E	Z	D	F	R	H	S	L	V	I	O	I	I	Z	V	E	A
X	V	H	I	I	L	F	T	J	E	B	R	N	P	H	R	R	S	T	K	X	K	M
L	Y	Y	L	N	E	O	J	I	N	S	I	T	U	G	T	W	I	E	Z	I	C	T
J	K	Z	I	E	A	X	X	I	M	T	H	R	U	S	H	K	O	S	J	F	X	D
C	C	I	G	A	A	N	A	T	O	M	Y	P	P	J	P	H	W	N	L	V	O	W
G	L	O	O	O	F	L	G	K	R	H	O	R	K	J	Y	N	A	G	O	U	V
L	A	R	D	Q	S	V	F	X	O	K	N	O	D	U	L	E	A	R	W	X	V	V

1. A condition in which patches of skin on the body lose their color
2. A candidiasis infection
3. A tiny, single-celled microorganism, commonly known as a germ
4. "in place"; often describes a cancer that has not spread
5. The thick, greasy substance that covers the skin of a newborn baby
6. The structure of bodies
7. A cancer in connective tissue, fibrous tissue, or blood vessels
8. An egg cell that has not developed completely
9. A small lump of tissue that is usually abnormal
10. A skin infection caused by a fungus that spreads out in an even circle, characterized by ring-like, scaly patches of red skin
11. A slippery fluid produced by mucous membranes that lubricates and protects the internal surfaces of the body
12. The surgical removal of diseased tissue
13. The shrinkage or near disappearance of a tissue or organ
14. A fluid-filled cyst attached to a tendon sheath or joint
15. A group of common infections occurring on the skin, hair, and nails that are caused by a fungus
16. Inflammation of bone
17. A hard, fluid-filled pad along the inside joint of the big toe
18. A coiled organ in the inner ear that plays a large role in hearing by picking up sound vibrations and transmitting them as electrical signals
19. A bone break
20. Small eight-legged animals, many of which burrow and feed on blood

A. Bacterium   B. Mites   C. Fracture   D. Anatomy   E. Vitiligo   F. Bunion
G. Sarcoma   H. Excision   I. In situ   J. Tinea   K. Nodule   L. Oocyte
M. Osteitis   N. Thrush   O. Cochlea   P. Ringworm   Q. Ganglion   R. Mucus
S. Vernix   T. Atrophy

P. Find the hidden words. The words have been placed horizontally, vertically, or diagonally. When you locate a word, draw an ellipse around it.

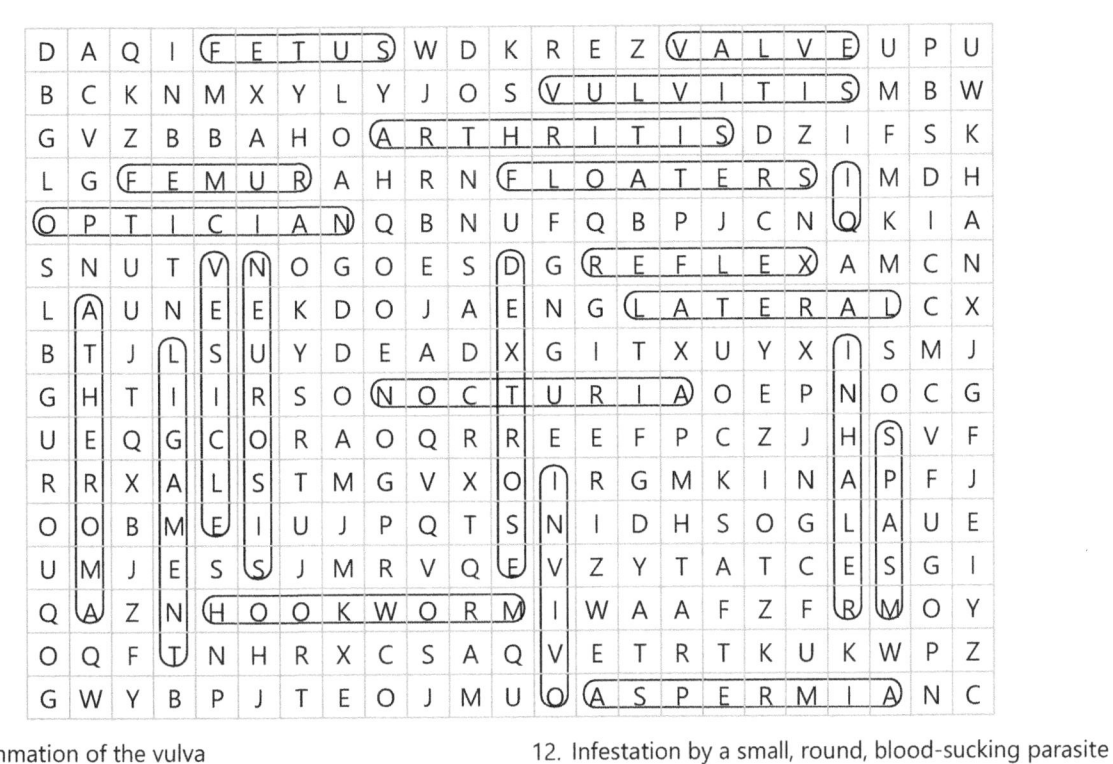

D	A	Q	I	F	E	T	U	S	W	D	K	R	E	Z	V	A	L	V	E	U	P	U
B	C	K	N	M	X	Y	L	Y	J	O	S	V	U	L	V	I	T	I	S	M	B	W
G	V	Z	B	B	A	H	O	A	R	T	H	R	I	T	I	S	D	Z	I	F	S	K
L	G	F	E	M	U	R	A	H	R	N	F	L	O	A	T	E	R	S	I	M	D	H
O	P	T	I	C	I	A	N	Q	B	N	U	F	Q	B	P	J	C	N	Q	K	I	A
S	N	U	T	V	N	O	G	O	E	S	D	G	R	E	F	L	E	X	A	M	C	N
L	A	U	N	E	E	K	D	O	J	A	E	N	G	L	A	T	E	R	A	L	C	X
B	T	J	L	S	U	Y	D	E	A	D	X	G	I	T	X	U	Y	X	I	S	M	J
G	H	T	I	I	R	S	O	N	O	C	T	U	R	I	A	O	E	P	N	O	C	G
U	E	Q	G	C	O	R	A	O	Q	R	R	E	E	F	P	C	Z	J	H	S	V	F
R	R	X	A	L	S	T	M	G	V	X	O	I	R	G	M	K	I	N	A	P	F	J
O	O	B	M	E	I	U	J	P	Q	T	S	N	I	D	H	S	O	G	L	A	U	E
U	M	J	E	S	S	J	M	R	V	Q	E	V	Z	Y	T	A	T	C	E	S	G	I
Q	A	Z	N	H	O	O	K	W	O	R	M	I	W	A	A	F	Z	F	R	M	O	Y
O	Q	F	T	N	H	R	X	C	S	A	Q	V	E	T	R	T	K	U	K	W	P	Z
G	W	Y	B	P	J	T	E	O	J	M	U	O	A	S	P	E	R	M	I	A	N	C

1. Inflammation of the vulva
2. The bone located between the hip and the knee
3. Urination or a sleep-disturbing need to urinate during the night
4. Intelligence quotient; a measure of a person's intelligence as determined by specific tests
5. A structure that allows fluid flow in only one direction
6. An involuntary muscle contraction
7. A tough, elastic band of tissue that connects bones and supports organs
8. Small spots that float across the field of vision, caused by debris floating in the gel-like substance that fills the eye
9. The failure either to produce or to ejaculate sperm
10. "in the living body"; a biological process that occurs inside of the body
11. An automatic, involuntary response of the nervous system to a stimulus
12. Infestation by a small, round, blood-sucking parasite
13. Another name for the sugar glucose
14. A device used to introduce a powdered or misted drug into the lungs through the mouth, usually to treat respiratory disorders such as asthma
15. On one side
16. A person who specializes in the making and adjustment of eyeglasses and contact lenses
17. The term used to refer to an unborn child from 8 weeks after fertilization to birth
18. Relatively mild emotional disorders (such as mild depression and phobias)
19. Fatty deposits on the inner walls of blood vessels, which can cause narrowing and decrease blood flow
20. A disease of the joints characterized by inflammation, pain, stiffness, and redness
21. A small skin blister, or any sac in the body, that contains fluid

A. Reflex	B. Inhaler	C. Aspermia	D. Nocturia	E. Floaters	F. Spasm
G. IQ	H. Valve	I. Atheroma	J. Dextrose	K. Vulvitis	L. Neurosis
M. Fetus	N. Lateral	O. Ligament	P. Optician	Q. Vesicle	R. Arthritis
S. Femur	T. In vivo	U. Hookworm			

Q. Find the hidden words. The words have been placed horizontally, vertically, or diagonally. When you locate a word, draw an ellipse around it.

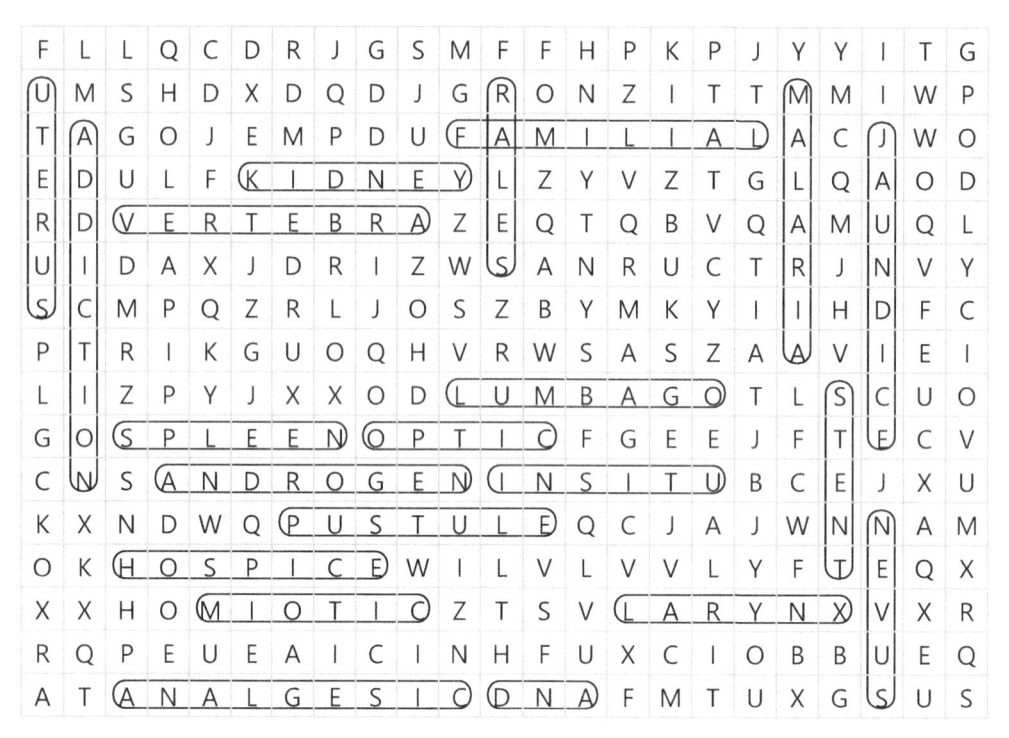

F	L	L	Q	C	D	R	J	G	S	M	F	F	H	P	K	P	J	Y	Y	I	T	G
U	M	S	H	D	X	D	Q	D	J	G	R	O	N	Z	I	T	T	M	M	I	W	P
T	A	G	O	J	E	M	P	D	U	F	A	M	I	L	I	A	L	A	C	J	W	O
E	D	U	L	F	K	I	D	N	E	Y	L	Z	Y	V	Z	T	G	L	Q	A	O	D
R	D	V	E	R	T	E	B	R	A	Z	E	Q	T	Q	B	V	Q	A	M	U	Q	L
U	I	D	A	X	J	D	R	I	Z	W	S	A	N	R	U	C	T	R	J	N	V	Y
S	C	M	P	Q	Z	R	L	J	O	S	Z	B	Y	M	K	Y	I	I	H	D	F	C
P	T	R	I	K	G	U	O	Q	H	V	R	W	S	A	S	Z	A	V	V	I	E	I
L	I	Z	P	Y	J	X	X	O	D	L	U	M	B	A	G	O	T	L	S	C	U	O
G	O	S	P	L	E	E	N	O	P	T	I	C	F	G	E	E	J	F	T	E	C	V
C	N	S	A	N	D	R	O	G	E	N	I	N	S	I	T	U	B	C	E	J	X	U
K	X	N	D	W	Q	P	U	S	T	U	L	E	Q	C	J	A	J	W	N	N	A	M
O	K	H	O	S	P	I	C	E	W	I	L	V	L	V	V	L	Y	F	T	E	Q	X
X	X	H	O	M	I	O	T	I	C	Z	T	S	V	L	A	R	Y	N	X	V	X	R
R	Q	P	E	U	E	A	I	C	I	N	H	F	U	X	C	I	O	B	B	U	E	Q
A	T	A	N	A	L	G	E	S	I	C	D	N	A	F	M	T	U	X	G	S	U	S

1. Any one of the 33 bones that make up the spine
2. Yellowing of the skin and whites of the eyes because of the presence of excess bilirubin in the blood; usually a sign of a disorder of the liver
3. A marking on the skin; can be present at birth (birthmark) or develop later (such as a mole)
4. A parasitic disease spread by mosquitos that causes chills and fever
5. A device used to hold tissues in place, such as to support a skin graft
6. A hormone (such as testosterone) that causes development of male characteristics and sex organs
7. Dependence on a substance (such as alcohol or other drugs) or an activity, to the point that stopping is very difficult and causes severe physical and mental reactions
8. Dull, aching pain in the lower back
9. The medical term for the voice box, the organ in the throat that produces voice and prevents food from entering the airway
10. A hospital or an area of a hospital dedicated to treating people who are dying, often of a specific cause
11. A term describing a disorder or characteristic (such as male pattern baldness) that occurs within a family more often than would be expected
12. Deoxyribonucleic acid; responsible for passing genetic information in nearly all organisms
13. Abnormal crackling or bubbling sounds heard in the lungs during breathing
14. A drug that causes the pupil to constrict
15. One of two organs that are part of the urinary tract
16. The hollow female reproductive organ in which a fertilized egg is implanted, and a fetus develops
17. A small blister containing pus
18. Pertaining to the eyes
19. "in place"; often describes a cancer that has not spread
20. A drug that relieves pain, such as aspirin or acetaminophen
21. An organ located in the upper left abdomen behind the ribs that removes and destroys old red blood cells and helps fight infection

A. Malaria B. Miotic C. Pustule D. Androgen E. Analgesic F. Stent
G. Vertebra H. Rales I. Nevus J. Uterus K. Lumbago L. Spleen
M. Kidney N. Optic O. Larynx P. Familial Q. Jaundice R. DNA
S. In situ T. Addiction U. Hospice

R. Find the hidden words. The words have been placed horizontally, vertically, or diagonally. When you locate a word, draw an ellipse around it.

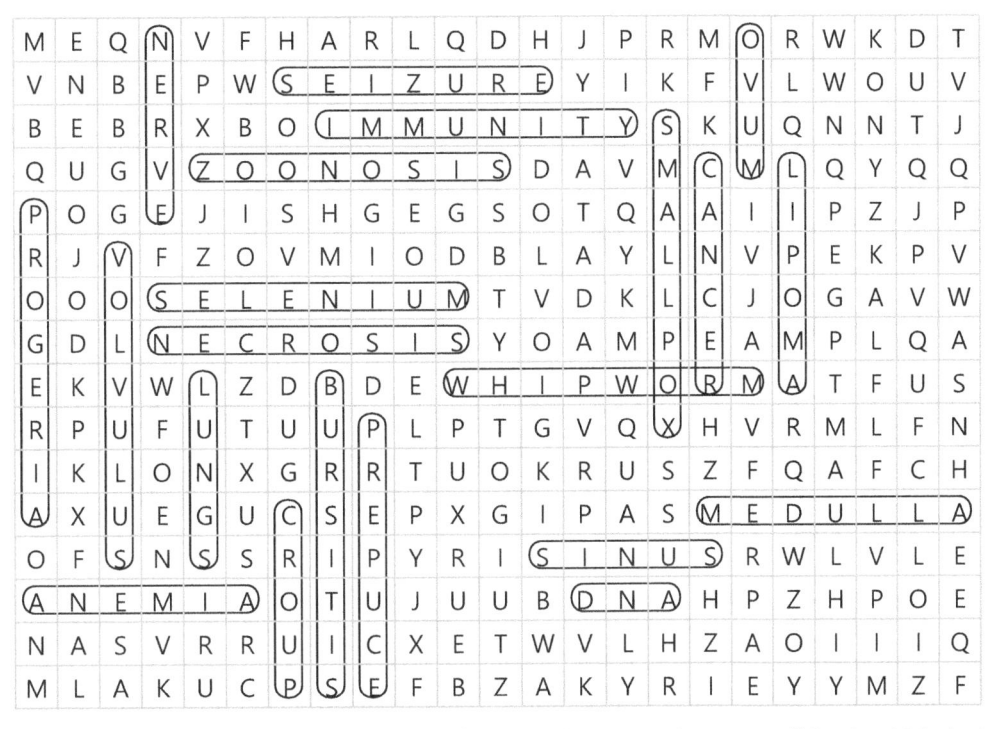

M	E	Q	N	V	F	H	A	R	L	Q	D	H	J	P	R	M	O	R	W	K	D	T
V	N	B	E	P	W	S	E	I	Z	U	R	E	Y	I	K	F	V	L	W	O	U	V
B	E	B	R	X	B	O	I	M	M	U	N	I	T	Y	S	K	U	Q	N	N	T	J
Q	U	G	V	Z	O	O	N	O	S	I	S	D	A	V	M	C	W	L	Q	Y	Q	Q
P	O	G	E	J	I	S	H	G	E	G	S	O	T	Q	A	A	I	I	P	Z	J	P
R	J	V	F	Z	O	V	M	I	O	D	B	L	A	Y	L	N	V	P	E	K	P	V
O	O	O	S	E	L	E	N	I	U	M	T	V	D	K	L	C	J	O	G	A	V	W
G	D	L	N	E	C	R	O	S	I	S	Y	O	A	M	P	E	A	M	P	L	Q	A
E	K	V	W	L	Z	D	B	D	E	W	H	I	P	W	O	R	M	A	T	F	U	S
R	P	U	F	U	T	U	U	P	L	P	T	G	V	Q	X	H	V	R	M	L	F	N
I	K	L	O	N	X	G	R	R	T	U	O	K	R	U	S	Z	F	Q	A	F	C	H
A	X	U	E	G	U	C	S	E	P	X	G	I	P	A	S	M	E	D	U	L	L	A
O	F	S	N	S	S	R	I	P	Y	R	I	S	I	N	U	S	R	W	L	V	L	E
A	N	E	M	I	A	O	T	U	J	U	U	B	D	N	A	H	P	Z	H	P	O	E
N	A	S	V	R	R	U	I	C	X	E	T	W	V	L	H	Z	A	O	I	I	I	Q
M	L	A	K	U	C	P	S	E	F	B	Z	A	K	Y	R	I	E	Y	Y	M	Z	F

1. Sudden uncontrolled waves of electrical activity in the brain, causing involuntary movement or loss of consciousness
2. The medical term for the death of tissue cells
3. The center part of an organ or body structure
4. The foreskin
5. A condition in which the blood does not contain enough hemoglobin, the compound that carries oxygen from the lungs to other parts of the body
6. A parasite- caused or infectious disease in animals that can be transferred to humans
7. A noncancerous tumor of fatty tissue
8. A usually mild and temporary condition common in children under the age of 4 in which the walls of the airways become inflamed and narrow, resulting in wheezing and coughing
9. Another term for an egg cell
10. A bundle of fibers that transmit electrical messages between the brain and areas of the body
11. A group of diseases in which cells grow unrestrained in an organ or tissue in the body
12. An extremely rare condition in which the body ages prematurely
13. Deoxyribonucleic acid; responsible for passing genetic information in nearly all organisms
14. Resistance to a specific disease because of the responses of the immune system
15. Inflammation of a bursa due to excessive pressure or friction, or from injury
16. Two organs in the chest that take in oxygen from the air and release carbon dioxide
17. A small, parasitic worm that can live in the intestines of a human and may cause diarrhea, abdominal pain, and anemia
18. A cavity within bone or a channel that contains blood
19. A highly contagious and often fatal viral infection that has been completely eradicated by immunization
20. Twisting and obstruction of an area of intestine
21. An element needed by the body only in very small amounts that helps maintain tissue elasticity

A. Prepuce
B. Lungs
C. Lipoma
D. Whipworm
E. Bursitis
F. Zoonosis
G. Ovum
H. Anemia
I. Smallpox
J. Nerve
K. DNA
L. Medulla
M. Sinus
N. Cancer
O. Croup
P. Necrosis
Q. Immunity
R. Selenium
S. Progeria
T. Volvulus
U. Seizure

251

S. Find the hidden words. The words have been placed horizontally, vertically, or diagonally. When you locate a word, draw an ellipse around it.

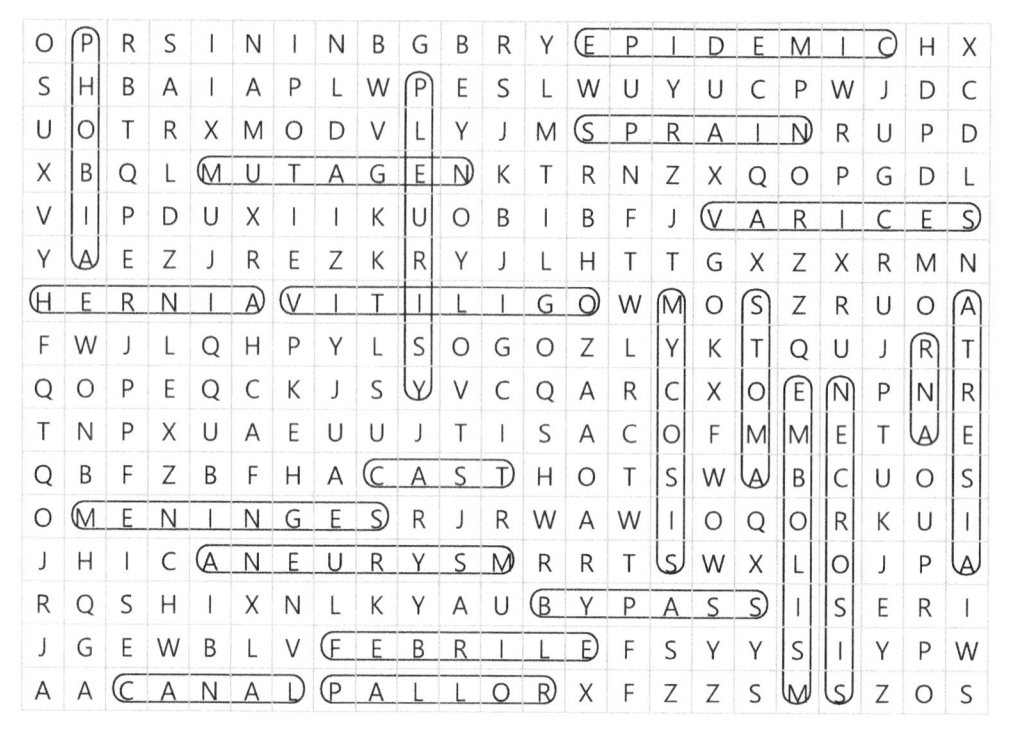

O	P	R	S	I	N	I	N	B	G	B	R	Y	E	P	I	D	E	M	I	C	H	X
S	H	B	A	I	A	P	L	W	P	E	S	L	W	U	Y	U	C	P	W	J	D	C
U	O	T	R	X	M	O	D	V	L	Y	J	M	S	P	R	A	I	N	R	U	P	D
X	B	Q	L	M	U	T	A	G	E	N	K	T	R	N	Z	X	Q	O	P	G	D	L
V	I	P	D	U	X	I	I	K	U	O	B	I	B	F	J	V	A	R	I	C	E	S
Y	A	E	Z	J	R	E	Z	K	R	Y	J	L	H	T	T	G	X	Z	X	R	M	N
H	E	R	N	I	A	V	I	T	I	L	I	G	O	W	M	O	S	Z	R	U	O	A
F	W	J	L	Q	H	P	Y	L	S	O	G	O	Z	L	Y	K	T	Q	U	J	R	T
Q	O	P	E	Q	C	K	J	S	Y	V	C	Q	A	R	C	X	O	E	N	P	N	R
T	N	P	X	U	A	E	U	U	J	T	I	S	A	C	O	F	M	M	E	T	A	E
Q	B	F	Z	B	F	H	A	C	A	S	T	H	O	T	S	W	A	B	C	U	O	S
O	M	E	N	I	N	G	E	S	R	J	R	W	A	W	I	O	Q	O	R	K	U	I
J	H	I	C	A	N	E	U	R	Y	S	M	R	R	T	S	W	X	L	O	J	P	A
R	Q	S	H	I	X	N	L	K	Y	A	U	B	Y	P	A	S	S	I	S	E	R	I
J	G	E	W	B	L	V	F	E	B	R	I	L	E	F	S	Y	Y	S	I	Y	P	W
A	A	C	A	N	A	L	P	A	L	L	O	R	X	F	Z	Z	S	M	S	Z	O	S

1. A condition in which patches of skin on the body lose their color
2. A term used to describe something related to a fever, such as febrile seizures (seizures occurring in a child who has a fever)
3. A surgically formed opening on a body surface
4. A birth defect in which a normal body opening, or canal is absent
5. A surgical technique in which the flow of blood or another body fluid is redirected around a blockage
6. The three membranes that surround and protect the spinal cord and brain
7. The blockage of a blood vessel by an embolus—something previously circulating in the blood (such as a blood clot, gas bubble, tissue, bacteria, bone marrow, cholesterol, fat, etc.)
8. The tearing or stretching of the ligaments in a joint, characterized by pain, swelling, and an inability to move the joint
9. Abnormally pale skin
10. A tunnel-like passage
11. The bulging of an organ or tissue through a weakened area in the muscle wall
12. Any disease caused by a fungus
13. A hard plaster or fiberglass shell that molds to a body part such as an arm and holds it in place for proper healing
14. A term used to describe a disease that is rare then suddenly affects more people than usually expected
15. Inflammation of the lining of the lungs and chest cavity usually caused by a lung infection
16. Enlarged or twisted blood or lymph vessels
17. Anything that can increase the rate of abnormal change in cells, which can lead to cancer
18. The medical term for the death of tissue cells
19. Ribonucleic acid, which helps to decode and process the information contained in DNA
20. An abnormal swelling of the wall of an artery, caused by a weakening in the vessel wall
21. A persisting fear of and desire to avoid something

A. Pleurisy
B. Meninges
C. Mycosis
D. Mutagen
E. Hernia
F. Varices
G. Bypass
H. Embolism
I. Vitiligo
J. Epidemic
K. Stoma
L. Sprain
M. Phobia
N. Canal
O. Atresia
P. Necrosis
Q. Aneurysm
R. Pallor
S. Cast
T. Febrile
U. RNA

252

T. Find the hidden words. The words have been placed horizontally, vertically, or diagonally. When you locate a word, draw an ellipse around it.

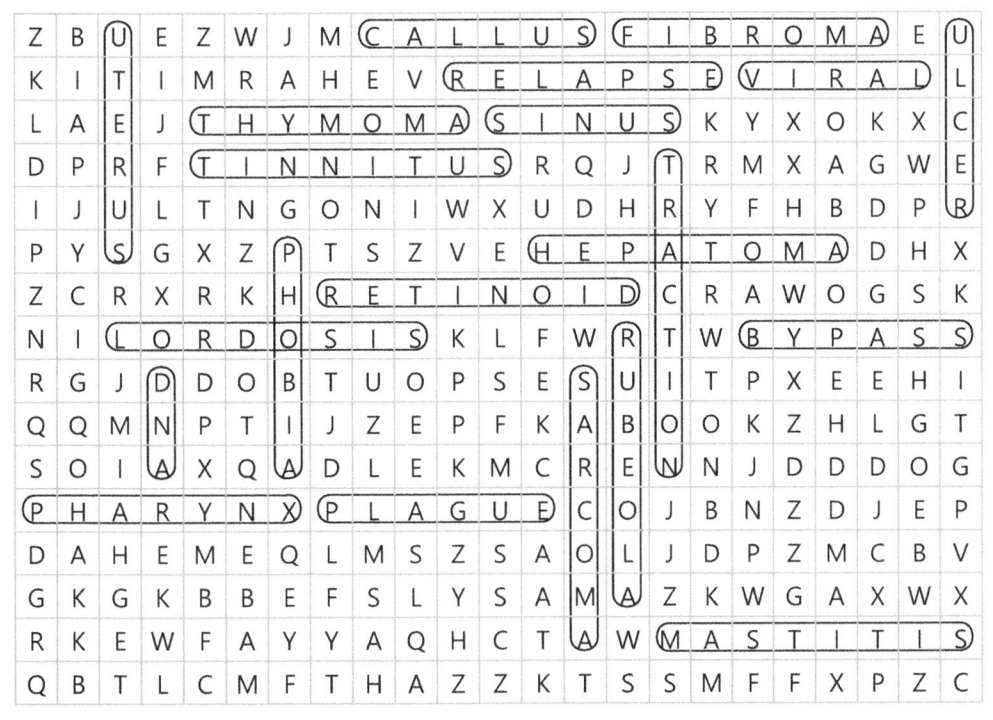

```
Z B U E Z W J M C A L L U S F I B R O M A E U
K I T I M R A H E V R E L A P S E V I R A L L
L A E J T H Y M O M A S I N U S K Y X O K X C
D P R F T I N N I T U S R Q J T R M X A G W E
I J U L T N G O N I W X U D H R Y F H B D P R
P Y S G X Z P T S Z V E H E P A T O M A D H X
Z C R X R K H R E T I N O I D C R A W O G S K
N I L O R D O S I S K L F W R T W B Y P A S S
R G J D D O B T U O P S E S U I T P X E E H I
Q Q M N P T I J Z E P F K A B O O K Z H L G T
S O I A X Q W D L E K M C R E W N J D D D O G
P H A R Y N X P L A G U E C O J B N Z D J E P
D A H E M E Q L M S Z S A O L J D P Z M C B V
G K G K B B E F S L Y S A M W Z K W G A X W X
R K E W F A Y Y A Q H C T U W M A S T I T I S
Q B T L C M F T H A Z Z K T S S M F F X P Z C
```

1. The return of a disease or symptom after it had disappeared
2. A term describing something related to or caused by a virus
3. A serious infectious disease transmitted to humans through bites of rodent fleas
4. The use of tension to hold a body part in place or to correct or prevent an alignment problem
5. Another term for measles
6. A tumor of the thymus gland
7. The throat
8. A persisting fear of and desire to avoid something
9. The inward curvature of the spine at the lower back, which is normal to a certain degree
10. A cavity within bone or a channel that contains blood
11. A thickened area of skin due to consistent pressure or friction, or the area around a bone break where new bone is formed
12. Inflammation of the breast, which is usually caused by a bacterial infection
13. A substance resembling vitamin a that is used to treat skin conditions such as acne and has been reported to reduce skin wrinkling
14. A cancerous tumor of the liver
15. The hollow female reproductive organ in which a fertilized egg is implanted, and a fetus develops
16. An open sore that occurs on the skin or on a mucous membrane because of the destruction of surface tissue
17. A surgical technique in which the flow of blood or another body fluid is redirected around a blockage
18. A cancer in connective tissue, fibrous tissue, or blood vessels
19. A noncancerous tumor of connective tissue
20. Deoxyribonucleic acid; responsible for passing genetic information in nearly all organisms
21. A persistent ringing or buzzing sound in the ear

A. Hepatoma
B. Tinnitus
C. Bypass
D. DNA
E. Viral
F. Lordosis
G. Phobia
H. Sinus
I. Relapse
J. Ulcer
K. Uterus
L. Retinoid
M. Traction
N. Thymoma
O. Pharynx
P. Rubeola
Q. Fibroma
R. Callus
S. Plague
T. Mastitis
U. Sarcoma

Made in the USA
Las Vegas, NV
15 March 2025